My Desire for History

D1528806

My Desire for History

Essays in Gay, Community, and Labor History

ALLAN BÉRUBÉ

Edited with an
Introduction by
John D'Emilio and
Estelle B. Freedman

The University of
North Carolina Press
Chapel Hill

Set in Scala
Manufactured in the United States of America.

The paper in this book meets the guidelines for permanence and
durability of the Committee on Production Guidelines for Book
Longevity of the Council on Library Resources.

The University of North Carolina Press has been a member
of the Green Press Initiative since 2003.

LIBRARY OF CONGRESS CATALOGING-IN-PUBLICATION DATA
Bérubé, Allan.
  My desire for history : essays in gay, community, and labor history /
by Allan Bérubé ; edited with an introduction by John D'Emilio and
Estelle B. Freedman.
    p. cm.
Includes bibliographical references and index.
  ISBN 978-0-8078-3479-4 (cloth: alk. paper)
  ISBN 978-0-8078-7195-9 (pbk.: alk. paper)
1. Gays—United States—History. 2. Lesbians—United States—
History. 3. Homosexuality—United States—History. 4. Bérubé,
Allan. I. D'Emilio, John.   II. Freedman, Estelle B., 1947–   III. Title.
HQ76.3.U5B466 2011
306.76'609730904—dc22
                        2010047550

cloth   15 14 13 12 11 5 4 3 2 1
paper   15 14 13 12 11 5 4 3 2 1

Dedicated to the memory
of Allan Bérubé (1946–2007)
and to all the pioneers of
lesbian and gay history

CONTENTS

. . . .

My Desire for History

Allan Bérubé and the Power of Community History

JOHN D'EMILIO AND ESTELLE B. FREEDMAN

Allan Bérubé was a community historian. He believed passionately in the power of history to change the way individuals and even whole groups of people understand themselves and their place in society. He projected a vision of history as a world-changing tool. The stories he told about the past—in public talks, in slide shows, and in writing—propelled people into varieties of activism. Allan Bérubé built community wherever he went.

In a 1992 keynote address delivered at a lesbian and gay studies conference in Quebec, Bérubé posed a question that captures the complexity of the life and the work represented in this collection. How, he asked, did "a Franco-American kid raised rural and working class in New England, whose earlier family history included no self-identified intellectuals or homosexuals—how did I learn how to become this new thing: a gay community-based historian?" (Chap. 10). How, indeed, did this 1960s conscientious objector and antiwar activist come to write the definitive history of lesbians and gay men in World War II? How did this college dropout become a self-taught, influential historian who in 1996 won a prestigious MacArthur Foundation "genius award"? In the process, how did he sustain his political activism, sharpen his own class and race consciousness, and continually inspire community building wherever he spoke or lived? Exploring these questions reveals not only the personal journey of an exceptional scholar-activist but also the broader phenomenon of the grassroots lesbian and gay history movement that emerged in the 1970s and laid the groundwork for the academic queer studies of the 1990s and beyond.

Best known for his Lambda Literary Award–winning book *Coming Out Under Fire: The History of Gay Men and Women in World War II* (1990), which was later adapted into a Peabody Award–winning documentary film, Bérubé also wrote extensively on the history of sexual politics in San Francisco and on the relationship between sexuality, class, and race.[1] In addition

Allan Bérubé in high school, Massachusetts, ca. 1964. Courtesy of the Allan Bérubé Collection at the GLBTHS, San Francisco.

to the essays he published in the gay press and the talks and classes he gave on college campuses, for two decades he crisscrossed the country presenting highly popular historical slide lectures to lesbian and gay community audiences as well as to gatherings of union members and organizers. At the time of his death, he was in the middle of drafting an innovative book about the radical, interracial, and queer-friendly Marine Cooks and Stewards Union (MCSU) from the 1930s through the 1950s.[2]

We had the good fortune to encounter Allan in the late 1970s, soon after he made the commitment to write lesbian and gay history. As academic historians and political progressives exploring the history of sexuality, we found much common ground with him. We also forged deep mutual friendships that shaped our lives and work for decades. Like all who knew Allan, we were devastated by his sudden death from ruptured stomach ulcers in December 2007, just after his sixty-first birthday.[3] As his friends and as trustees of his literary estate, we decided to make accessible his most influential published writings along with excerpts from his unfinished book project.[4]

The essays we have selected focus on four central concerns in Bérubé's work. The first section collects his early excavations of lesbian and gay community history, particularly for San Francisco; these essays reflect the sexual politics of the 1970s and 1980s. Part 2 explores the lives of lesbians and gay men during World War II, the project that culminated in *Coming Out Under Fire*; it includes pieces that illustrate Bérubé's skills as a practitioner of oral history. Part 3 includes the more self-reflective and theoretical writing that characterized Bérubé's work in the 1990s, as he turned his attention to the intersections of class, ethnicity, and sexuality and his own identity as a working-class and queer intellectual. In the final section, we have selected excerpts from his work-in-progress on the MCSU, in which he applies his insights into class and queerness to the history of a radical union. While there is some unavoidable overlap between a few of these essays, each one provides both a unique perspective and rich historical context.

In writing this introduction we have drawn from our personal knowledge; interviews with friends, family members, and associates of Bérubé; and some archival research. We each knew Allan too well, and were too deeply connected to him in personal and professional ways, to claim that we have written a detached critical biographical essay. Rather, we hope the introduction will frame these essays within the life and times that shaped him as a community historian. In addition to providing historical context, we hope to convey a sense of the intellectual, political, and personal life of the author who produced this compelling body of work.

. . . . . .

Allan Bérubé's development from a working-class, Franco-American youth growing up in a New Jersey trailer park to an influential historian and public intellectual began when he won a scholarship that enabled him to attend the Mount Hermon School for Boys, a private New England preparatory school. "I remember being terrified in high school that if I didn't get good grades and be in all kinds of extra-curricular activities, I would never get a scholarship to college, terrified that I would be stuck working in a factory like my uncles, since I had no skills," he later recalled. Long considered the "golden boy" in his family, as his sister Annette Bérubé remembered, he felt not only the pressure to succeed but also the embarrassment of having to work on campus, where wealthy boys "tended to look down on students like Allan." As a waiter in the school's dining room, he was not allowed to talk to the students he was serving, even though he attended classes with them. A Catholic in a Protestant setting, at Mount Hermon he listened to sermons by liberal ministers, including William Sloane Coffin, and found a small group of students who shared his concerns about civil rights and peace.[5]

Bérubé earned a scholarship to the University of Chicago and enrolled in 1964. He would come to label his journey there as one of "class displacement." Even as he studied English literature and delighted in poetry, he felt too intimidated to speak in class. During summers he returned to his parents' home in western Massachusetts, where he worked as a ward attendant at the nearby state mental hospital. The summer job, which was "filled with meaningful and disturbing experiences," contributed to his political consciousness. He realized "how little respect for human life and dignity exists in state mental hospitals" and recognized that "although I was doing no violence myself, I lacked the courage to speak out against the violence I was witnessing."[6] At Chicago his moral critiques of American society deepened. Inspired by those students who had been involved in Freedom Summer in Mississippi (1964), he began to tutor black high school students through the Woodlawn Project. At the time, Bérubé later explained, he distrusted politics and political groups, but he felt drawn to acts of conscience. A turning point occurred in 1966 when the university's compliance with the Selective Service System led him to join a sit-in at the administration building. At first uncomfortable with the prospect of breaking the law, he felt reassured when he determined that the protesters were "extremely responsible," that they were sincerely "trying to figure things out, and they were coming up with an analysis of power." He joined the sit-in, but he continued to value what he called "moral activism" rather than organized politics.[7]

Bérubé's senior year of college (1967–68) coincided with escalating protests and political upheavals. Mobilizations against the Vietnam War, the insurgent campaign of Senator Eugene McCarthy to unseat President Lyndon Johnson, and widespread rebellions after the assassination of Martin Luther King Jr. in April 1968 made places like the University of Chicago incubators for radical political activism. Faced with the dilemmas posed by the war and increasingly drawn to pacifism, Bérubé trained as a draft counselor and coedited an anthology of responses to the draft, titled *Living at War*. In the piece he contributed, "To Acknowledge Every Person as a Person," he explained the reasons behind his conviction that he could never serve in the military. "There is something holy about the life and person of every human being," he wrote. "The armed forces accept the killing of human beings as a legitimate means towards some end. . . . I do know that I have no authority to destroy any person's life." He and his close friend and college roommate Roy Guttman, another working-class scholarship student, met with Guttman's rabbi in nearby Skokie, Illinois, as they struggled to understand the moral basis for conscientious objection. Bérubé and Guttman also wrote and circulated a "Statement of Belief" based on principles of religious pacifism.[8]

Bérubé was not yet out as a gay man, but he was "totally in love with"

Guttman. Although comfortable with their intense friendship, the sexual component of his attraction preoccupied Bérubé, who feared at the time that he "might be mentally ill." In April 1968—the month of Martin Luther King's murder, the subsequent urban riots, and an escalating antiwar movement—Allan came out to Roy with the statement "I have a homosexual problem." Roy "listened," Allan recalled. "There was more to be said, and it never did get said," for just days later Guttman was killed in an apparently random race-related murder on the streets of Hyde Park near the university, a casualty of the violence that erupted after King's assassination. As Bérubé described it, "The world had turned completely dangerous. . . . Everything was falling apart." Deeply shaken, he stopped studying and attending classes, finally dropping out of school just weeks before he would have graduated.[9]

No longer a student, Bérubé faced the prospect of being drafted when he returned home to Massachusetts later in 1968. He applied successfully to have his Selective Service board reclassify him as a conscientious objector. For his two-year alternative service to military duty, he took a job in Boston with the American Friends Service Committee. Increasingly committed both to noncooperation with the war and to nonviolent civil disobedience, he risked arrest during the week of Memorial Day in 1969 by sitting in at his local draft board in Palmer, Massachusetts, and reading the names of all the soldiers killed in Vietnam, which at that time numbered over 30,000. When a police officer confronted him, Bérubé managed to avoid arrest by engaging him in a respectful discussion of Thoreau and Gandhi. The episode helped Bérubé clarify his motivation. "I was wondering whether my resistance [to the war] was based in my fear of being killed, of danger, or a lack of courage," he reflected years later. "I realized that week that I had the courage."[10]

Bérubé also realized that courage served him well "as someone who was about to come out at that time." Along with exposure to antimilitarist ideas by writers such as the pacifist Barbara Deming, Bérubé began rethinking issues of gender and sexuality. He first heard about gay liberation from a lesbian he met on one of the several Peace Walks he took across New England with other pacifists, stopping in small towns and engaging local people in conversation about the war.[11] From feminists in Boston he learned of the emerging critique of "sex roles," and he also began attending meetings of the Student Homophile League at MIT.

At the time Boston was overflowing not only with political radicals opposed to the Vietnam War but also with youths steeped in the growing counterculture. And, at the turn of the decade, it became one of the sites of an emerging gay liberation movement. Bérubé moved into a cooperative house in Roxbury where some former members of Students for a Democratic Society (SDS) were living. One visitor to the household in these months remembers "colorful vegetarian meals around the big table in the Victorian row house" and lively conversation punctuated by Allan's "gentle wit." Soon he became involved with a collective that was planning to start a gay liberation paper. One evening he mentioned this work to a friend, Allan Troxler. It was Bérubé's indirect way of coming out, and Troxler reciprocated by asking if he could work on the paper too. Before long, they were not only co-conspirators in the founding of what became *Fag Rag*, one of the main radical gay publications of the 1970s, but sexually intimate friends as well. Troxler, a North Carolina native, had dropped out of Swarthmore and, like Bérubé, had come to Boston where he, too, fulfilled his alternative service work as a conscientious objector. He remembers the time in Boston and, later, in Cambridge as "mighty heady days." The group households, the radical politics, and most of all, the new gay liberationist world they were building were thrilling. Their friendship, Troxler recalled, provided "a ticket to soar above our histories of fear and self-loathing."[12]

For many young adults who saw themselves as participants in the counterculture, these were years of geographic mobility. At some point in the early seventies, after they had finished their alternative service work, Bérubé and Troxler migrated to Vermont. They found a place near Montpelier, where some friends from Boston had already relocated. "We invented our rural selves," Troxler later wrote. For Bérubé, that meant, among other things, learning to play the dulcimer and to weave and crochet, as well as collecting leaves, berries, and flowers to use as natural dyes. At first, he just made clothes for himself. Soon he was making scarves, mittens, and other goods for sale, to help allay "his anxiety over paying the bills." With other gay men, he and Troxler planned Vermont's first public gay event, at the state's inaugural People's Fair in Burlington. But Bérubé also traveled back and forth to Boston, working in a hospital, selling his crafts, and maintaining his friendships there. His simultaneous longings for both urban and small-town worlds would recur throughout his life.[13]

One of the gay men who moved in and out of Bérubé's and Troxler's life in these years was Carl Wittman, a key figure in both the New Left and radical gay politics. As a student at Swarthmore, where he and Troxler first met, Wittman became a nationally prominent SDS activist in the early and mid-1960s. He achieved even greater notoriety as the author of "A Gay Manifesto" (1969), one of the most widely read and cited gay liberation essays of the era. By the early 1970s Wittman and his partner were living with other gay male radicals in Wolf Creek, Oregon. A visit to Vermont and

Massachusetts revived the friendship with Troxler and initiated a new one with Bérubé. By early 1973, the search for community led Troxler, and then Bérubé, to the San Francisco Bay Area. For a while they migrated back and forth to Oregon to visit Wittman, until Troxler decided to stay in Wolf Creek, where he and Wittman settled into a long-term relationship. Bérubé would make San Francisco his home for more than two decades.[14]

* * * * * *

Bérubé's identity as a gay community historian took root in the sexually and politically charged atmosphere of San Francisco in the 1970s. "I discovered a gay community when I visited San Francisco for the first time," he later explained. Soon he had joined a commune in the Haight-Ashbury district, a place described by a visitor as "full of fey bearded, long-haired gay hippies . . . a magical house full of looms, beautiful long rag runners on the stairs, everyone weaving all the time."[15] Troxler, who visited often, reflected that Bérubé's "belief in collective . . . came to full flower there on Ashbury Street. Someone was always busy at one of the looms in the loft on the fourth floor." Bérubé lived simply, supporting himself by selling mittens, hats, scarves, placemats, and rugs at curbside bazaars and later at The Soft Touch, a collectively run store on Haight Street, and at A Thousand Fingers, a cooperative gallery in the Castro district. In his free time, he explored the beaches, streets, and parks. "This is a city," he wrote in his journal, "for learning how to slow down and spend your days pleasantly."[16]

Long a magnet for bohemians, the Bay Area had a reputation as a sexually "wide open town." Well before the Stonewall riots catalyzed the modern gay liberation movement, San Franciscans had accumulated an impressive history of resistance. In 1951, in response to a suit by bar owner Sol Stoumen, the California Supreme Court ruled that the state could not revoke a liquor license simply because a tavern's patrons were homosexual. In the mid-1950s, Del Martin and Phyllis Lyon had formed the first national lesbian rights organization, the Daughters of Bilitis. In 1961, José Sarria, a waiter and drag performer at one of the city's bohemian bars, ran for a seat on the Board of Supervisors as an openly gay candidate. Five years later, transvestites in the Tenderloin neighborhood rioted against police harassment, and the next year, the hippie "summer of love" made San Francisco synonymous with the sexual revolution. It was a few years later, in the 1970s, that Bérubé gravitated to San Francisco, as did Harvey Milk and thousands of other gay men from around the country. Together they created a critical mass of sexually and politically conscious citizens. As the Castro district transformed into a middle-class gay enclave, Bérubé enjoyed visiting this nearby neighborhood where "gay could be ordinary." In San Francisco, pride replaced a once-stigmatized identity, community replaced isolation, and sexual revelry replaced sexual hiding.[17]

The process of transforming a once-tarnished identity into a positive base for community often involves the search for a usable past, whether for African Americans and Mexican Americans in the civil rights struggle or for women in the feminist movement. Indeed, the search for historical antecedents—whether racial, ethnic, or sexual—characterized large swaths of popular culture in the 1960s and 1970s. Alex Haley's best-selling book, *Roots* (1976), and the television adaptation of it were the most dramatic examples of this phenomenon, but grassroots versions of this impulse could be found in the Freedom Schools in Mississippi, in the local libraries and archives that the women's movement spawned, and in the pages of a newly established gay and lesbian press. In one of the earliest signs of a lesbian and gay history movement, in 1974 activists in New York City created the Lesbian Herstory Archives. Two years later, in 1976, New York self-trained historian Jonathan Ned Katz published *Gay American History*, a hefty collection of historical documents testifying to both gay oppression and gay resistance since the colonial era. The book inspired Bérubé to explore lesbian and gay history, especially San Francisco's, a task that he pursued with characteristic passion.[18]

Tumultuous political events in the late 1970s also fueled Bérubé's quest for historical insight into gay oppression. In 1977 Florida orange-juice spokeswoman Anita Bryant made headlines leading a voter-referendum campaign to repeal a gay rights antidiscrimination law enacted in Dade County, Florida. In early June, her "Save Our Children" crusade succeeded when a landslide vote rejected the ordinance. Bryant then traveled across the country, encouraging successful repeal campaigns in other cities. The next year, Californians faced a statewide ballot initiative, Proposition 6, that would have prohibited the employment of lesbians and gay men in the public schools. San Francisco activists played a key part in the successful mobilization against the measure. Just weeks after its rejection by voters, Harvey Milk, the first openly gay supervisor in San Francisco and a leader in the anti-Prop-6 campaign, was assassinated by Dan White, a conservative former supervisor. In May 1979, after a jury convicted White of manslaughter rather than murder, the gay community exploded with rage. Thousands of people marched on City Hall, where they smashed windows and set a row of police cars on fire. Police responded by storming the Castro; they invaded gay bars and assaulted pedestrians on the street.[19]

These events affected Bérubé deeply. His journal and his correspondence in this period recorded his participation in the meetings, vigils, and marches through which the San Francisco community mobilized. "We're not going away or back into the closet—we can't!" he wrote in his journal soon after the 1977 Dade County vote.[20] After attending a mass meeting in which candidates for elected office appealed for gay votes, Bérubé described the anger that spontaneously erupted. The crowd of 350 people, he reported, "booed [and] shouted 'Get out!'" at politicians perceived to be insensitive to the community.[21]

The politics of the era made Bérubé more determined to deepen his understanding of history. One night, after watching the extensive television coverage of Bryant's campaign, he made a list of things he now wanted to do: write about Nazi persecution of homosexuals, undertake a biographical study of the British writer Edward Lear, and "start a gay history study group." A week after the Dade County vote, he began to keep a "research log" that cataloged his efforts to explore these topics. At times during these years, feelings of urgency, even doom, coursed through him. "I'm feeling very powerless lately, powerless politically," he lamented in his journal. "Many of the gains we've made—gay rights laws, food stamps, abortion rights, etc.—can be reversed very easily." As his research progressed, historical analogies surfaced. "We talk often of the gay movement in Germany and how it was crushed by the Nazis," he mused. "Learning about the systematic crackdowns on gays in SF in the 50s in detail, following the openness of the war, is a little scary."[22]

All of this upheaval pushed Bérubé to learn the historian's craft. In the months after the Anita Bryant campaign, he began to visit libraries, spending hours in the Bancroft Library at the University of California at Berkeley looking through the papers of Noel Sullivan and, during a trip east, in the Houghton Library at Harvard, where he read the diaries of Edward Lear and materials about Horatio Alger. He contacted writers such as Jonathan Ned Katz, of *Gay American History* fame, and James Steakley, who had published an account of the early gay movement in pre-Nazi Germany. To Katz he wrote of his excitement that, at age thirty, he could now "use the skills I learned in college . . . in an unalienated way."[23] He purchased *The Modern Researcher*, by Jacques Barzun, which he found "very helpful." He immersed himself in the emerging literature of U.S. social and women's history. During this time, Bérubé gave himself the equivalent of a graduate education in research methods and historiography. Conscious of this redirection of his life, he compared his "growing devotion to discovering a gay history" to the desires of a close woman friend to have a child; in part, they agreed, having recently turned thirty contributed to their respective longings.[24]

Bérubé devoted much of the next three decades of his life to uncovering lesbian and gay history. The work brought him a delight and pleasure that anyone passionately committed to research will understand. Consider this description, written in the fall of 1979, of a day's work: "Today I got a grip on my work—my first step, which I'm really enjoying, is to do an index-card chronology of everything I know and have collected about early San Francisco gay history—organized by decade, so far. So I did this all day—listing municipal report statistics on sodomy arrests in SF, dates of newspaper articles, letters from gay people with gay content, publication of gay-related books, changes in laws, etc. I was in heaven."[25]

Bérubé also frequently expressed a yearning for "a small community/ circle of gay people who are writing/reading/researching about gay culture and history and can share their work in a non-competitive way." He wanted "people to talk out ideas with, learn from, criticize each other."[26] In a sense, he wanted to re-create for the study of gay history something of what he had experienced in the weavers' collective a few years before.

By early 1979, at least, Bérubé was no longer working alone. His irrepressible enthusiasm for history—anyone Allan met heard about his research—began to attract friends and acquaintances to the task of creating a new kind of community history. Eric Garber, a Colorado gay migrant, shared Allan's delight in research and often accompanied him to the newspaper room of San Francisco's main public library. Amber Hollibaugh, a member of the collective that operated Modern Times, an independent left-wing bookstore, engaged in spirited conversation about politics and history whenever Allan visited the store, and she pointed him toward books on women's and radical history. Others whose paths crossed his included Lynn Fonfa, a community activist who was working on a master's thesis on lesbian history; documentary film makers Frances Reid, Liz Stevens, and Rob Epstein; Jeffrey Escoffier, a transplanted activist from Philadelphia who later became editor of *Socialist Review* and a founder of the magazine *Out/Look*; Estelle Freedman, who taught women's history at Stanford; Gayle Rubin and John D'Emilio, who were each writing dissertations on gay topics; photographer Honey Lee Cottrell; and computer programmers Roberta Yusba and JoAnn Castillo, who wanted to learn more about lesbian and gay history.[27]

Early in 1979, several of them established the San Francisco Lesbian and Gay History Project. For the next several years, they met regularly for often intense conversations. They read books together, discussed the turbulent politics swirling around them, and shared their latest research findings in "show-and-tell" sessions. Remarkably, given the strong tendencies toward lesbian separatism in the 1970s, the project remained a mixed-sex group, al-

Allan and other members of the San Francisco Lesbian and Gay History Project, Gay Pride Parade, June 1980. From left: Honey Lee Cottrell, JoAnn Castillo, Roberta Yusba, Allan Bérubé, Estelle Freedman, Eric Garber, and Amber Hollibaugh. Courtesy of the Allan Bérubé Collection at the GLBTHS, San Francisco.

though lesbians met separately as well as with the male participants. While almost entirely white, it was also a mixed-class group and one that defined itself as politically activist.

From the beginning, the History Project believed that understanding history endowed individuals and communities with the power to act more effectively in their world. Bérubé especially wanted the history he was uncovering to be shared with the community. So, in addition to functioning as a reading group in sexual history and politics, the project began producing events in response to contemporary crises. In August 1979, in the face of continuing police harassment of the community after the City Hall rioting, the group convened a panel, "Spontaneous Combustion," at the feminist-run Women's Building. A packed hall listened to speakers Amber Hollibaugh, Jeff Escoffier, John D'Emilio, and Lois Helmbold, a historian who taught at San Jose State University, present episodes in the history of police-community relations, from raids on bars and bathhouses to street harassment of sex workers. One theme in particular kept surfacing: that the past was filled with examples of successful resistance, that a community need not remain passive targets of abuse.[28]

Even more successful was the premiere during June's Pride Month fes-
tivities of "Lesbian Masquerade," Bérubé's illustrated slide lecture based on
newspaper stories of women who had passed as men in nineteenth- and
early-twentieth-century San Francisco. The large auditorium was filled to
overflowing with an audience that seemed to cross every line of sexual and
gender identity that one could imagine. Bérubé's ability to project queer life
more than a hundred years back in time produced laughter, applause, tears,
and a thrill that rippled through the crowd. The excitement was palpable,
and it grew as he moved the audience through the lives of Jeanne Bonnet,
Milton/Luisa Matson, and Jack Garland/Babe Bean. After the presentation
was over, the crowd that pressed in upon Bérubé testified to the event's
power. This was no routine history lecture.

"Lesbian Masquerade" catapulted Bérubé from anonymity to a position
of great visibility in San Francisco and even beyond. He presented the slide
show to enthusiastic audiences throughout the Bay Area and, in the fall of
1979, traveled up and down the East Coast showing it in cities stretching
from Salem, Massachusetts, to Durham, North Carolina. But his growing
celebrity also provoked introspection and uncertainty. Bérubé took satisfaction in being part of a *community* project; indeed, other project members had
helped produce the premiere lecture. Now he confronted, in his own words,
"the old individual-in-relation-to-community issue." Where, he wondered,
does "my own work stand in relation to collective work and decisions?"[29] The
passionate identity politics and separatist climate of the times added fuel
to these concerns. Lesbians in the project debated the implications of a gay
man presenting lesbian history, as well as the title "Lesbian Masquerade,"
which implied a self-conscious but hidden lesbian identity in the past. With
Bérubé's cooperation, a group of lesbians in the project began to present the
slide lecture on their own. To facilitate its distribution, in 1983 Estelle Freedman and Liz Stevens produced an audiotape with slides, now titled "'She
Even Chewed Tobacco': Passing Women in Nineteenth-Century America."[30]
A videotape version of it continues to be shown in classrooms and to community groups. Bérubé meanwhile published a version of the script of "Lesbian Masquerade" in the national gay press (Chap. 1).

Fed by the interest in local history that his audiences displayed, Bérubé
continued his research into San Francisco's queer past. By 1980, he was
envisioning a book about gay history stretching from the Gold Rush days,
when San Francisco's reputation as "a wild and pleasure-loving city" solidi-
fied, through "the elements that led to the identifiable gay communities,
institutions, and consciousness of the '20s, '30s, and '40s," and culminating
finally in the flowering of a visible gay world during World War II and the

ensuing police crackdowns. The heightened visibility of Bérubé and the History Project enhanced the feasibility of such an ambitious venture, as new sources regularly kept surfacing. Bois Burk, an East Bay resident for half a century, contacted Bérubé and presented him with folders full of gay-related news articles that Burk had systematically clipped from the San Francisco press for decades. A gay doctor who learned about the History Project encouraged his older patients to volunteer their oral histories; Bérubé, as well as Garber, Epstein, and Escoffier, were only too happy to interview them. After one of his public presentations, a white lesbian in the audience made available her photo album from her years in the navy during World War II.[31]

As his research on San Francisco's past moved forward, Bérubé remained attuned to contemporary events, often seeing parallels between past and present. His attention turned particularly to the media demonization of gay male sexuality. The media had long expressed hostility to gay men, and in the Reagan era, a new conservatism that drew on Christian evangelicalism was making appeals to "traditional family values" a centerpiece of political mobilization. In April 1980, CBS-TV broadcast during prime-time hours an inflammatory documentary, *Gay Power, Gay Politics*, which raised the specter of a homosexual takeover of San Francisco. It led Bérubé to notice the ways that the demonizing of gays had played itself out in previous moments of the city's history. As he recorded in his journal: "My 50s work seems so crucial now that the New Right is becoming so powerful—crucial because it can delineate the patterns of sexual repression . . . we need to know about today in order to fight. Feels like this will become my 'political work' . . . that I will be doing in the next year."[32] He wrote an essay, "Behind the Specter of San Francisco," about the attacks on gays and lesbians during the mayoral campaign of 1959 and analogized with the present (Chap. 2). Significantly, it was published by *The Body Politic* in Toronto, a city experiencing a police crackdown of its own in the early 1980s.

The onset of the AIDS epidemic in the 1980s only heightened antigay rhetoric. References to the "gay plague," calls to quarantine gay men, and proposals to close gay male bathhouses all circulated widely. Once again, Bérubé's response was to turn to the past for analogies and enlightenment. He explored how medical scapegoating had a history in San Francisco, most notably in anti-Chinese measures at the turn of the century (Chap. 3). And he created another powerful application of the historical slide lecture, "Resorts for Sex Perverts," a pictorial history of gay bathhouses. In the face of AIDS, Bérubé took a strong public stance against the attacks on gay male sexual culture that emanated from without, as well as from within, the gay community. He argued against repression and prohibition, such as the closing of bathhouses, and insisted on the importance, historically, of sexual bonds as a basis for building community (Chap. 4). Lovemaking, he would later write, had long provided a "partial refuge" from an antigay social climate, but AIDS was taking "the safety out of our old shelters" (Chap. 9). Rather than demonize gay sex, he hoped to locate a new kind of shelter and build a new kind of community through the safer sex practices being pioneered and advocated by AIDS activists.

· · · · · ·

Even as he marshaled historical evidence from San Francisco's past to apply to contemporary issues, Bérubé found the focus of his research shifting. Of all his discoveries of new historical sources during these years, perhaps the most dramatic was the uncovering of a cache of several hundred letters written during World War II by a group of white gay male friends serving in the military. By a circuitous route, a friend of a friend told Allan of finding the letters packed away at the back of a closet in a vacant apartment that he was helping to clean out. They belonged to Harold Taylor (a pseudonym), one of the correspondents, who had died in 1975 and who had apparently meticulously preserved them for more than three decades. Don, the gay man who rescued them, had saved them for over four years, and now he passed them on to Bérubé. Reading through them for the first time aroused an almost spiritual response. "As I discover more and more of this story," he confided, "I can't help but think that it was all saved with the hope, an act of faith, that it could all be put together somehow."[33]

The Taylor correspondence so excited Bérubé that he used the material to construct a new slide lecture. Focused on World War II, it was designed initially to advance the San Francisco book project. San Francisco, after all, was a port of embarkation and return for millions of service members, while other young Americans had migrated to the Bay Area for employment in defense industries. During the war, many encountered city life for the first time on the streets of San Francisco; some likewise discovered their first gay and lesbian bars as well as the freedom to experience same-sex intimacy. Bérubé was able to recount the history of gays and lesbians in World War II in a way that also made the city's history come alive.

In picking so central and national a topic, Bérubé tapped into something more profound than he had initially anticipated. In the early 1980s, World War II was still vividly present in the memories of large numbers of Americans. Many of those who had fought in the war or worked in defense plants—"the greatest generation," as NBC news anchor Tom Brokaw later described them—were still alive. And the baby boomers, the men and women who helped create gay liberation in the 1970s, had grown up with movies about the "Good War." Here was Bérubé, in characteristic fashion, retelling this grand narrative. Yes, he recounted stories of oppression and injustice, as some gay men and lesbians faced courts-martial, imprisonment, and then discharge from the service. But he also told stories of heroism and selflessness, of camaraderie and solidarity, of fun and self-discovery. For his audiences who had experienced the silence, invisibility, isolation, and persecution of the 1950s, '60s, and '70s, Bérubé's lecture was a profound experience. He was documenting the presence of gays and lesbians in a pivotal event in U.S. history.

As with "Lesbian Masquerade," Bérubé took his show, which he titled "Marching to a Different Drummer," on the road. Everywhere he went, the reaction was the same. "People at my slide show are just entranced by the whole thing," he reported. "Everyone *loves* it." At one showing, at the Walt Whitman Bookshop in San Francisco, a black veteran whom he had previously interviewed was in the audience. After the presentation, he raised his hand to comment. "First time he spoke he started to cry, and stopped to compose himself," Bérubé wrote afterward. "Then he said I had 'worked magic.'"[34]

With these presentations Allan Bérubé powerfully drew community audiences to gay history. Though exceptionally gifted as a presenter, his effort was by no means a singular one. In the late 1970s and early 1980s, lesbian and gay history projects had emerged in a number of cities, and the slide talk had become something of a rage. Jim Steakley mesmerized audiences with his illustrated lecture on the German gay movement in the early twentieth century. Judith Schwarz, an independent researcher living in Washington, D.C., entertained and instructed with an account of a pre-Depression-era world of bohemian women in Greenwich Village. Gregory Sprague, a graduate student at Loyola University, began researching Chicago's queer past. He put together a slide show that helped bring some older Chicagoans out of the closet, and they in turn made themselves available to be interviewed by him. Sprague's work grew into a local history project that, a generation later, still lives on in the form of the Gerber/Hart Library, a rich repository of gay, lesbian, bisexual, and transgender (GLBT) books, newspapers, and archival collections.[35]

Sometimes Bérubé himself helped provoke these other ventures. Roberta Yusba, a friend of Jeff Escoffier, had joined the San Francisco History Project soon after the first showing of "Lesbian Masquerade." Inspired by it, she assembled her own presentation on the lesbian pulp novels of the 1950s and 1960s, filling it with images of cover art that not only were instructive but also often elicited gales of laughter. In November 1979, after Bérubé showed "Lesbian Masquerade" in the Boston area, a group of enthusiastic audience members formed a collective that evolved into the Boston Area Lesbian and Gay History Project. They developed a slide show, collected oral histories, and wrote pieces for the local press. Still in existence almost three decades later, the project in 1996 organized a massive exhibit at the Boston Public Library and then published *Improper Bostonians: Lesbian and Gay History from the Puritans to Playland*.[36]

Some of this local historical work preceded Bérubé's explorations. In Buffalo, New York, Elizabeth Kennedy and Madeline Davis created the Buffalo Women's Oral History Project in 1978. Motivated by a belief that it was their "political responsibility . . . to give this history back to the community," they not only gave talks around town but eventually produced *Boots of Leather, Slippers of Gold* (1993), which has become a revered work in the canon of lesbian history.[37] Members of the Lesbian Herstory Archives, including Joan Nestle and Deborah Edel, proselytized across the country, urging lesbians to see their lives and their communities as historically significant. Countless letters, photos, diaries, scrapbooks, and other memorabilia have been saved from the dump thanks to the zeal of the Herstory Archives.[38]

At the distance of a generation, this account of how Bérubé and others became pioneering founders of a movement to recover gay and lesbian history can sound like a wonderfully inspiring and romantic tale, filled with joyous discoveries and deep satisfaction. In terms of the thrill that the work brought to both the practitioners and the audiences, it *was* glorious. But it was also a story of immense and difficult struggle. Throughout these years, Bérubé labored with very few material resources to support his research. He enjoyed none of the benefits that a faculty position at a university provides: no salary or health insurance, no paychecks during the summer, no funded sabbaticals for writing. For a while, he went back to weaving scarves, which he could do in the evening, and sold them by word of mouth through friends and acquaintances. He worked as an usher and manager in local movie theaters and registered with an agency for temporary office workers. But the insecurity took a toll. "I am not cut out for 8–5 jobs," he wrote, after one long stretch of typing gigs. "I've been very frustrated lately, discouraged about ever getting the time I want and need to write. This business of squeezing it into lunch hour or Saturday nights is for shit. . . . This frustration from lack of money and time is just about driving me crazy." Fortunately, even in the hardest times he managed to retain a sense of humor that his friends knew well. After learning that an auto insurance company had agreed to pay him $4,500 in damages after he was hit by a reckless driver (this at a time when any money "left over after bills" made him feel "rich"), Bérubé drew on the popular culture of his childhood to express his delight: "This is like being 'Queen for a Day,' winning the washer *and* dryer, and a year's supply of Tide."[39]

In the summer of 1981, Bérubé took a major step. He decided to abandon his plan to write a book on San Francisco and instead to devote himself to the World War II story. Everything seemed to point him in that direction. "My showing of the slide show is scaring up all kinds of incredible new sources," he wrote. "The World War II stuff keeps pulling me toward it, from my own interest to other people's enthusiasm." Because its scope was national, he thought it would give him a better chance, as a first-time author, of attracting a publisher's interest. In the meantime, he reasoned, "the slide show could serve, for a year, as a means to supporting my work, scaring up sources, publicizing the book, and generally educating and raising people's spirits."[40]

Bérubé labored on the World War II book for the remainder of the 1980s. A key part of the work was the travel he did with the slide show, since he considered his tours a form of "public dialogue with the communities whose history I was documenting and to which I belonged."[41] The presentations, which he gave before local organizations, on college campuses, at academic conferences, and in the homes of veterans themselves, moved the book forward in a number of ways. Since there was so little published writing on gay and lesbian history, the talks in academic settings helped open a conversation about this new field of social history and evoked useful insights from other researchers and scholars. The community talks provided a different kind of assistance. Through them, new sources kept materializing. In Los Angeles, for instance, a man who had placed an ad in the *Advocate* in 1972, asking older gay men to write to him about their experiences in the era of World War II and before, volunteered to let Bérubé have all of the letters he had received.[42] The slide show also steadily provided new subjects to interview, especially when Bérubé did living-room showings in the home of someone, usually a veteran, whose network of friends was invited. With their memories brought to life by the talk and the images, they often began to narrate their own experiences to Bérubé, who was especially skilled at drawing out their stories. They frequently passed the hat as well, providing him with income to keep going.

The World War II project epitomized Bérubé's multipronged approach to community history. The countless showings of "Marching to a Different Drummer" helped not only to build community but also to create new networks of activists, especially among an older group of veterans who began to organize against antigay military policies that were as alive as ever in the 1980s. Through traditional methods of research in the National Archives, he uncovered a wealth of documents that had never before been used by historians. His many Freedom of Information Act requests, which provoked "battles with the Navy over secret documents they are withholding from me," eventually led to the release of thousands of pages of material, including detailed accounts of investigations designed to weed out women suspected of homosexual activity.[43] Bérubé saw all these efforts not only as aiding his book project but also as building an accessible public archive. Through the politically progressive Capp Street Foundation in San Francisco, he created a World War II Project that helped fund the oral history work, including transcriptions of his interviews. Meanwhile, he promised to donate all of his research materials to the Northern California Lesbian and Gay Historical Society, a spin-off of the San Francisco History Project that had been nurtured by Bill "Willie" Walker, who had joined the project in the 1980s.[44]

All along the way, Bérubé published pieces about the World War II story. He hoped these would build enthusiasm, change consciousness, uncover more sources and subjects to interview, and spark activism. Several of these essays appear in this volume: a 1981 article in the *Advocate*, a gay and lesbian newspaper with a national audience; a featured story in 1983 in *Mother Jones*, a monthly magazine devoted to the community-organizing impulses of the New Left; and a prominently placed piece in the 1984 Pride issue of the *Front Page*, a North Carolina lesbian and gay newspaper, in which Bérubé revealed the astounding story of the *Myrtle Beach Bitch*, a newsletter published during the war by gay GIs stationed at bases in the South (Chaps. 5–7).

The decision to write a book about lesbian and gay male soldiers during World War II had deep emotional implications for Bérubé's sense of himself. Taking himself seriously as a historian, despite his lack of undergraduate or graduate degrees, coincided with a conscious effort to challenge the constraints that he recognized as a product of his class and familial background. In soul-searching journal entries and letters, he described "how ashamed I was when I was growing up about living in a trailer, and how much of an outsider I was when we lived in a middle-class suburb for 3 years and when I went to prep school on a full scholarship."[45] Bérubé grappled with the obstacles to his becoming "a more powerful person," given his oppression "as a gay man, a working-class man, and as a radical." Yet, at the same time—with his characteristic moral seriousness—he acknowledged that "I also have other privileges—a good education, some middle-class skills, ambition, charm, being a white male, that I shouldn't ignore or take for granted, either." The critical role of support from others—including

Allan Bérubé and Brian Keith. Courtesy of the Allan Bérubé Collection at the GLBTHS, San Francisco.

members of the History Project in San Francisco as well as his youngest sister, Annette, who also lived in San Francisco and who held bake sales to raise money for Allan's research—enabled him to envision himself as a historian. In the process, he struggled against a self-acknowledged tendency to rely on others to take care of him, admitting to those closest to him that he feared taking advantage of them.[46]

A special and unique form of support came to Allan through his relationship with Brian Keith. They met in 1983, in a south-of-Market-Street leather bar, and quickly became intimate partners. In some ways, they could not have been more different. Keith was British and a biochemist at the University of California at Davis, where his research focused on plant growth. But he had also been an orphan, raised by an "auntie," while the death of Allan's mother when he was four had left him in the care of his grandparents on their farm until his father's remarriage. Allan and Brian bonded over these childhood experiences as well as over their class backgrounds. Brian was raised in an unmistakably working-class home, with the kind of sharp understanding of class that is so much a feature of British life. Among other things, Brian introduced Allan to the BBC television series *EastEnders*, about the working-class residents of a London neighborhood. The series provided endless opportunities for them to talk about "the hidden injuries of class," to borrow the title of a book that Allan often referenced.[47] Brian was a tremendous support to Allan in the face of the insecurities that class inequality bequeathed to him.

As was true for so many gay men in the 1980s, intimacy placed one at risk for profound and tragic loss. In 1986, just three years after they had met, Brian was diagnosed as having AIDS. In the era before protease inhibitors raised some hope of containing the effects of the infection, a rapid deterioration in health often quickly followed a diagnosis. Allan's sister Annette and a small circle of friends provided support for the couple as Allan cared for Brian through the last stages of the illness. Allan described some of that experience in "Caught in the Storm," one of his first autobiographical essays (Chap. 9). For his part, Brian extracted a promise that grief would not prevent Allan from finishing the book. He also made Allan the beneficiary of his life insurance policy, an act that provided Allan with the financial resources to complete the book and to buy an apartment in San Francisco.

. . . . . .

Coming Out Under Fire: The History of Gay Men and Women in World War II was published early in 1990. It was—and remains—an impressive achievement. At the time it was released, there were perhaps half a dozen books on U.S. lesbian and gay history. More than half of them were documentary collections or anthologies; none placed gay and lesbian history at the center of a national narrative.[48] Ten years earlier, it would have been almost impossible to imagine that a history such as the one Bérubé wrote was even there to be found. The fact that a story of such depth and consequence was produced outside the academy was a telling comment on the lack of receptivity of the university, in that generation, to such intellectual endeavors.

Reviewers at the time recognized the significance of the book and the labor that produced it. Writing in *Reviews in American History*, Elaine Tyler May described *Coming Out Under Fire* as "a masterpiece of social history" and "a triumph of individual initiative and scholarly community." Placing it within the broad themes of contemporary historical writing, she ranked it "among the best works of social history in which the most downtrodden emerge as agents of their own destiny in spite of powerful odds against them." In the *Journal of American History*, Clayton Koppes used the review to comment on what the book revealed about "the importance of who controls histories." Bérubé, he said, "found gay and lesbian GIs cooperative; excluded from history, they wanted him to tell their stories." By contrast, government records, both civilian and military, sometimes mysteriously disappeared or were arbitrarily withheld. "Such methods," Koppes argued, "help control a version of history that sustains a policy that, as the military's own studies conclude, is based on prejudice alone."[49]

Koppes's reference to military policy alerts us to one aspect of what made Bérubé's book especially compelling. He had written a history that spoke to a contemporary issue—the military's antigay policies—that was increasingly in the news. Reviewing *Coming Out Under Fire* in the Sunday *New York Times Book Review*, Doris Kearns Goodwin described it as "timely and valuable . . . particularly in the context of today's debate over who has the right to fight and die for his or her country." A review in the daily edition of the paper remarked on the nearly 100,000 men and women purged because of "the military's rigid anti-homosexual policies." Writers in papers ranging from the *Washington Post* to the *St. Louis Post-Dispatch* to the *San Francisco Chronicle* all commented on how the book's historical argument resonated with the present.[50]

As Bérubé pointed out in his book, military policy had shifted between the 1930s and 1950s from a prohibition against the commission of homosexual *acts* by military personnel to a more expansive policy that excluded from service all persons with homosexual *tendencies*. In other words, anyone who revealed that they felt attraction to members of the same sex, even if they never acted on those desires, was subject to discharge. Thus, Bérubé showed, a population was simultaneously created and threatened by governmental policies. In the 1970s, in the wake of the new visibility provoked by the gay liberation movement, a few service personnel came out of the closet and openly challenged the policy, among them air force sergeant Leonard Matlovich, who was on the cover of *Time* in 1975, and army sergeants Miriam Ben-Shalom and Perry Watkins. The cases of Ben-Shalom and Watkins dragged on for years, even producing some lower-court victories. But the challenges only led the armed services to tighten their policies. By 1981, one could be dishonorably discharged for the "intent to commit" a homosexual act.[51]

By the late 1980s, with the upsurge in militancy provoked by the AIDS crisis, lesbian and gay activists were tackling the military exclusion issue head-on. After news surfaced of antilesbian purges at the Parris Island Marine Corps Training Depot, Sue Hyde of the National Gay and Lesbian Task Force formed the Military Freedom Project (MFP). Drawing in organizations such as the American Civil Liberties Union, the National Organization for Women, and Lambda Legal Defense and Education Fund, the MFP was the driving force bringing media attention to the plight of lesbian, gay, and bisexual military personnel. Making use of Bérubé's historical knowledge, activists invited him to Washington, D.C., to reprise his "Marching to a Different Drummer" slide show as a fundraiser to benefit their efforts to combat the military exclusion policy.[52]

A pacifist and former draft counselor, Bérubé had come to see the economic and political importance of access to the military for many gay men and lesbians. As History Project member and anthropologist Gayle Rubin recalled, Bérubé "saw that the ban on gays in the armed forces fell most heavily on working class and poor queer youth for whom the military was a mechanism for social mobility. He saw the loss of benefits resulting from homosexual discharges in terms of economic hardship. And he understood that for modern nation states, military service was intimately connected to full citizenship."[53]

The effort to repeal the ban became a front-page national news story in 1992–93. During the presidential campaign, the Democratic candidate, former Arkansas governor Bill Clinton, on a number of occasions promised an immediate lifting of the ban. But soon after he won the election, Clinton found himself facing a determined opposition from the Joint Chiefs of Staff and congressional leaders in both parties. As it became obvious that this would be a key political battle in Washington, a small group of wealthy gay men, including Hollywood figures such as David Geffen and Barry Diller, funded a new professional lobbying effort, the Campaign for Military Service (CMS), that bypassed grassroots mobilizations like the MFP and took over the work in Washington to end the military's antigay policies.

Considered an expert on the issue of gays in the military by virtue of his book, Bérubé found himself drawn into this political controversy. Journalists sought out this community-oriented public historian to obtain historical background for their articles. The CMS wanted him to help craft messages that might resonate with the public and with congressional leaders. When Senator Sam Nunn, a Democrat from Georgia who chaired the Armed Services Committee and was vocally opposed to lifting the ban, announced that he was scheduling hearings on the policy, the CMS included Bérubé on its list of potential witnesses. They brought him to Washington, where he stayed for several weeks consulting and preparing his testimony. He worked not only with the CMS but also with Senator Ted Kennedy's staff, who sought his advice on the type of questions Kennedy should raise.

For Bérubé, the gays-in-the-military debate was sobering. Senator Nunn, who kept tight control over the hearings, had little interest in a full and open airing of all sides in the debate, and Bérubé was never called as a witness. The twenty-two-page statement he wrote did get used in preparing the minority reports of both the House and Senate armed services committees.[54]

Allan outside the Castro Theater in San Francisco during the opening of the documentary film based on *Coming Out Under Fire* (1994). Courtesy of the Allan Bérubé Collection at the GLBTHS, San Francisco.

But overall, he wrote afterward, "what was frustrating was experiencing the enormous power of Nunn and the military to define, run, erase and implement whatever they wanted, with us hardly present at all." It was, he observed, an example of "total unchecked power." Although President Clinton and some other Democratic Party liberals touted the "Don't Ask, Don't Tell" policy that became law in the summer of 1993 as an important step forward, to Bérubé it was a disaster: "not 'half a loaf' as both the gay and mainstream press is calling it, not even a crumb, not even the faint aroma of a baked good in the vicinity."[55]

The experience also sharpened his skepticism toward the tactics and strategy used by "the mainstream movement," as represented in this instance by the CMS. "It highlighted," he wrote that summer, "the 'gay rights' dead-ends we've gotten trapped in. . . . Of course, we were outnumbered," he continued, "much less powerful, inexperienced, and not ready for this fight. But," he added, "there are disruptive strategies that the powerless can use . . . that have the potential of putting the big guys on the defensive by our changing the rules."[56]

Film provided one mechanism for changing hearts and minds about gays in the military. After director Arthur Dong approached Bérubé about making a documentary based on *Coming Out Under Fire*, the two collaborated on the script, and in 1994 the film premiered at the Castro Theater in San Francisco. Funded in part by the Corporation for Public Broadcasting and the National Endowment for the Humanities, it was filled with on-camera interviews with some of the gay and lesbian veterans Bérubé had talked with for his book. The film brought Bérubé's historical research to a broader popular audience. It also made explicit the connection between history and contemporary events by ending with footage from the 1993 Senate hearings.

· · · · · ·

The "disruptive strategies that the powerless can use": Underneath Bérubé's use of the word "disruptive" lie some far-reaching changes that had occurred since the days when he and others first formed the History Project. The AIDS epidemic of the 1980s brought huge numbers of gay men, lesbians, bisexuals, and transgender people out of the closet, far more than had responded to the radical gay and lesbian liberation message of the early 1970s. This massive outpouring of energy and resources enabled the building of stronger organizations and institutions as well as the creation of much wider networks of activists and intellectuals. Some of these, as Bérubé suggested, were very "mainstream" in their orientation. They lobbied legislatures, worked within the electoral system, and built nonprofit organizations that provided useful services. But others, especially toward the end of the 1980s and into the early 1990s, deliberately employed militant disruptive tactics and consciously embraced points of view that challenged conventional norms. Chapters of ACT UP (the AIDS Coalition to Unleash Power) blocked traffic on the Golden Gate Bridge, invaded the New York Stock Exchange on Wall Street, and staged a major demonstration outside the offices of the Food and Drug Administration. In October 1987, with his civil disobedience affinity group, the Forget-Me-Nots (all of whom were surviving partners of men who had died of AIDS), Bérubé participated in a massive nonviolent sit-in on the steps of the Supreme Court building in Washington, D.C., to protest the Court's *Hardwick* decision, which upheld state sodomy statutes.

The rise of "queer" in this era—from "queer nation" as an umbrella term meant to unite a range of sexual and gender identities to "queer studies" as a disruptive intellectual endeavor—was one important manifestation of this change. It meant that someone like Bérubé, without mainstream institutional ties, nonetheless found himself increasingly embedded in a dense world where the lines dividing activists, organizers, intellectuals, writers,

Police arresting Allan in Washington, D.C., in 1987 during demonstrations at the Supreme Court protesting the *Hardwick* decision. Courtesy of the Allan Bérubé Collection at the GLBTHS, San Francisco.

and scholars grew blurred. In the 1990s, he had the opportunity to teach a course called "Queer Life and Social Change" in the Community Studies Program, which had been founded to bring together scholarship and community organizing, at the University of California at Santa Cruz. He was also able to participate in events like the annual Out/Write conference for GLBT writers, conceived in part by Jeff Escoffier, whom he knew from his History Project days; Creating Change, the yearly gathering of grassroots activists sponsored by the National Gay and Lesbian Task Force, where John D'Emilio served first on the board and later on the staff; and conferences and colloquia such as the inaugural Quebec Lesbian and Gay Studies Conference in Montreal in 1992.

With the opportunity that these venues provided, and the push that came from his own recent experiences—Brian's death, the success of his book, and the frustrating outcome of the military policy debate—Bérubé intentionally began to reflect on and mine his personal experience. These autobiographical explorations, the most important of which are contained in Part 3 of this collection, served many purposes. They allowed him to understand his work not just as a product of individual achievement but rooted as well in the ethnic, racial, class, and sexual politics of U.S. history. As this activist historian became the analyst of his own biography, he was able both to reclaim his roots and to look at their complicated legacies. He experienced class constraints as well as racial privilege. Sexual desire had provided one kind of escape route, yet it also contained him within a new set of boundaries. At a time when a range of academic writers were insisting on intersectional theoretical frameworks and forms of political organizing, Bérubé was mining his own history to arrive at a personally usable past, and in the process, he developed a more vibrant and powerful style of writing.

In "Intellectual Desire," his keynote address at the Quebec Lesbian and Gay Studies Conference (Chap. 10), Bérubé wrote, "It was only a matter of time before I'd see and feel these connections between class, ethnicity, and sexuality, then use my intellect to make sense of them." The phrasing implies that there was something preordained about the meanings he imparted to his life experience or the decisions he reached about his work priorities. Yet there was nothing inevitable about it. He was choosing to pursue certain paths rather than others, in his work and in his life. In particular, he tells us, he "made the decision to put race and class at the center of my gay writing and activism" (Chap. 12).

In practice this meant that Bérubé chose as his next major research endeavor a history of the Marine Cooks and Stewards Union. A relatively small union whose members were especially concentrated on the West Coast, the MCSU experienced its heyday between the 1930s, an era of intense labor militancy, and the early 1950s, when government crackdowns on radical unions largely eviscerated it. In many ways the project grew organically from his previous work on World War II and San Francisco. The navy and the merchant marine figured importantly in the story about gays and the military during the war, while the San Francisco Bay Area was a major center for shipping and for the navy. A number of Bérubé's informants for the World War II project also had prior histories at sea and knew of or were involved in the maritime labor radicalism of the 1930s. One interview subject in particular, Stephen "Mickey" Blair, appealed powerfully to the "sentimental nostalgia" that, Bérubé acknowledged, often "infused my writing" (Chap. 10). Blair shared Bérubé's French Canadian ethnic heritage; he remained throughout his life firmly anchored in the working class; he developed a radical, left-wing analysis of American capitalism and society; and finally, like Bérubé, he was gay. As was so often the case in his oral history work over the years, Bérubé's subjects became not merely sources of information but dear friends and comrades as well.

Bérubé worked on the MCSU book for the rest of his life. He brought to it skills and styles of work that had characterized his earlier endeavors. He relentlessly tracked down subjects to interview, a task that proved more onerous than it had been for his World War II project. By the early 1990s, survivors of the labor strife of the 1930s were well into their seventies, if not older, and there had been far fewer maritime workers to begin with than there were veterans of World War II. He meticulously pored through labor periodicals of the era, the radical press that might have covered sympathetically the strikes and organizing drives, and the mainstream press that typically did not. He also immersed himself in the trade publications and business records of the shipping industry, particularly those connected with the luxury cruise liners that employed many of his working-class subjects. Bérubé began as well to collect material objects related to his subject—postcards, pulp fiction, model ships, and the like—so that he might root his story firmly in the culture of the era. In part because his subject was not as expansive as World War II, the search for material was daunting. "He never stopped doing research," Bert Hansen, a historian friend of his from this period, remembered.[57] Another friend, Peter Nardi, recalled the day Bérubé and he explored the Queen Mary when it was docked in Long Beach, California. Looking closely at a mural in the ship's bar, Allan erupted with delight when he detected two men holding hands. "He was so excited," Nardi recalled.[58]

In settling on the MCSU as his next project, Bérubé once again found himself in a pioneering role. Just as he was among the first to engage in local gay and lesbian history with his San Francisco research, and among the first to implant gay and lesbian history in mainstream historical narratives with his World War II book, so his study of the MCSU was breaking new ground. It wasn't so much that the subject matter addressed working-class queer life. For instance, Elizabeth Kennedy and Madeline Davis in their 1993 study of Buffalo had focused sharply on working-class lesbians, while George Chauncey's 1994 study of New York City addressed class differences in male sexual expression.[59] Bérubé, however, was venturing into labor history. He was locating queerness in an occupation and workplace. He was examining, in a generation before the formation of an identity-based social movement that addressed sexuality, whether some workingmen were able to embrace their sexual or gender-crossing selves on the job and how those dynamics played out in the maritime world. The project impelled him to begin thinking more broadly about the connections between work and sexuality, an effort reflected in the essay "'Queer Work' and Labor History" (Chap. 14).

As he had done before, Bérubé prepared a slide lecture on his topic that served both to educate and to facilitate further research. He presented it around the United States many times, including to trade unionists in their union halls, before organizations of GLBT labor activists, at labor history meetings, on college campuses, and at academic conferences. "No Race-Baiting, Red-Baiting, or Queer-Baiting!," a title he used in one of its iterations, hints at what he was learning through his research (Chap. 16). With his promise to himself to put race and class at the center of his writing and activism, and with a determination to scrutinize the unconscious "whitening practices" that tend to erase the presence of people of color, Bérubé reconstructed a surprising tale of a multiracial, multiethnic, politically radical, and queer-inflected union. The story was unlike anything that appeared in the annals of either labor history or the history of sexuality. After hearing the lecture, one prominent labor historian responded, "This is truth stranger than fiction."[60] The MCSU story as excavated by Bérubé promised to upend assumptions about the field.

In support of his work, Bérubé received a yearlong fellowship in 1994 at the Center for Lesbian and Gay Studies (CLAGS) at the City University of New York. Established in the late 1980s by historian Martin Duberman, with support from anthropologist Esther Newton and other progressive academics, CLAGS had won funding from the Rockefeller Foundation to support innovative work in the emerging field. CLAGS prided itself on maintaining porous boundaries between the university and the community. It drew to its many events an audience not only of academics but of activists and community members as well.[61] CLAGS provided Bérubé with immediate connections with a large number of activist writers and intellectuals. And his living situation proved ideal. Jonathan Ned Katz, whose work had originally inspired him to do historical research, rented Bérubé a room in his Greenwich Village brownstone. "It was like a commune," Katz recalled. Katz worked on his book manuscript on nineteenth-century male relationships, Bérubé began drafting his on the MCSU, and they shared their progress each day over lunch. The year was so stimulating and intellectually satisfying that when his fellowship ended, Bérubé decided to leave San Francisco after two decades and move permanently to New York City.[62]

Not surprisingly, Bérubé quickly embedded himself in a wide network of relationships, much as was true of his life in San Francisco. Friends from his San Francisco History Project days, like Amber Hollibaugh and Jeff Escoffier, were now living in New York. With them and Katz, along with feminist intellectuals Carole Vance and Judith Levine, Bérubé participated in a writer's support group that met for years. He made contact with union activists in the city, found additional subjects to interview, and began exploring the maritime history and politics of New York, as part of his MCSU story. With Bert Hansen, he scoured Manhattan's flea markets on weekends, looking for things related to his own Franco-American heritage as well as objects related to ocean liners, maritime life, and the trailer parks of his youth. "He had a really good eye," Hansen recalled, and his early years of living in a trailer as a child had taught him how to organize objects efficiently in the relatively tiny living spaces that Manhattan provided.[63]

In New York during this period, Bérubé was also able to put old research to new purposes. In the mid-1990s, fears about a potential spike in HIV infections provoked a new round of efforts among city officials and some gay activists to regulate the sexuality of gay men. In order to make Times Square and midtown Manhattan more attractive to tourists, New York's new mayor, Rudolph Giuliani, proposed the use of zoning laws to close down bathhouses and other commercial venues where men had sex with men. While some gay community members helped drive the effort to shut down sex venues, many others protested as well. Wayne Hoffman, a community activist and journalist in New York City, remembers "a town hall meeting about the bathhouse closures, an extremely contentious meeting, and Allan gave the opening speech about the history of the baths."[64] Over the next couple of years, other such opportunities presented themselves. A revised version of Bérubé's piece on the historical role of the baths was included in an anthology edited by Dangerous Bedfellows, an activist collective in New York of which Hoffman was a member.[65]

In the midst of all this activity, Bérubé received a phone call in the summer of 1996 that many writers, artists, and academics dream about. Jonathan Ned Katz, in whose house he was living at the time, described the moment. "I was sitting in the kitchen one morning and he said 'I got it, I got it!' And I said 'What did you get?'" Katz recounted. "He'd gotten a call from Catherine Stimpson." The director of the prestigious fellowship program at the John D. and Catherine T. MacArthur Foundation, Stimpson told Bérubé that he was a recipient of one of the foundation's fellowships. Colloquially known as the "genius award," it carried a total stipend of $300,000 paid out over five years.[66]

The announcement set off a round of celebrations. Nan Boyd, a younger historian whom Bérubé had mentored while she wrote her dissertation on San Francisco queer history, attended "an impromptu pizza party" at Katz's house. Over the next few weeks, she recalled, Bérubé "endlessly discussed what it meant, what money and recognition meant, and how he could now stop worrying about basic living expenses and finish the project on the

Marine Cooks and Stewards Union." Wayne Hoffman, who had become close to Bérubé during the bathhouse debates, said of the fellowship that it "changed everything for him." Beyond the money and notoriety, it put an establishment stamp of approval on the kind of history that he produced. No one working on specifically gay or lesbian scholarship had ever received a MacArthur grant before.[67]

As sometimes happens, the fellowship proved a complicated blessing. On one hand, it allowed Bérubé to buy his own place in Manhattan and live independently. For the first time in his life, immediate concerns about money faded into the background. He was able to indulge the bane and blessing of every historian, the urge to search for every last document. He also had the freedom to engage in activist work, and he participated in these years in many of the key conferences on queer sexual politics. But on the other hand, the award also seemed to raise the stakes. At MacArthur Foundation gatherings, where he mingled with the other "geniuses," Bérubé found himself again in a setting where class privilege was taken for granted. The events left him feeling like a pretender among intellectual royalty. Suddenly, the topic of the book wasn't original enough. Instead, as Bert Hansen recalled, he now thought he had to do "something new and different." He began buying books on writing. He created story boards in his apartment, as if he were writing a screenplay. He experimented with first-person narratives, injecting himself into the story as the interviewer of the historical characters, as can be seen in "Trying to Remember" (Chap. 15).[68] He wrote and rewrote drafts, never producing a complete one. The start of a new draft produced new titles, as his computer files indicate: "Dream Ships Sail Away," "The Power of Legendary Queens," "Red, Black, and Queer," "Shipping Out," "Sailing to Paradise." Work on the manuscript was no doubt emotionally complicated by the fact that there was no happy ending to the story he wanted to tell. The radical union created by his working-class heroes during the turbulent era of the Great Depression was almost completely destroyed by the Cold War witch hunts of the early 1950s.

· · · · · ·

As the new century began, Bérubé found himself without a complete draft and, once again, without money. The MacArthur grant had finally run out. Upheavals in the publishing industry had left him with a new editor for his MCSU book, someone less attuned to his work. His publisher demanded either a completed manuscript or a return of the advance he had received when he signed the book contract. And a serious romantic relationship, with

San Francisco celebration of Allan's MacArthur Foundation fellowship, 1996. Annette
Bérubé is third from the right in the front row; Allan is in the center of the second row;
above him to the right is Bill "Willie" Walker, a found of the GLBT Archives. Photograph
by Rosa Maria Pegueros. Courtesy of the Allan Bérubé Collection at the GLBTHS, San
Francisco.

a working-class man of French Canadian origins, had ended unexpectedly
and painfully.

In a dramatic shift in direction, Bérubé moved out of New York City and
resettled in Liberty, New York, a small town in Sullivan County at the edge
of the Catskill Mountains. In the middle decades of the twentieth century,
the area had enjoyed a tourist-induced prosperity. The center of what was
affectionately called "the Borscht Belt," Sullivan County was peppered with
resorts, camps, and entertainment venues that served summer vacationers,
especially from Jewish families living in New York City and other northeast-
ern cities. But by the 1990s, that era of prosperity had long passed, and Liberty had become one of many upstate New York towns experiencing serious
economic decline.

At first he stayed with Jonathan Ned Katz and his partner, David Gibson,
who owned an old farmhouse where they spent weekends. Bérubé took regular trips to Liberty with them as a respite from both city life and his book
manuscript. Allan, Jonathan, and David formed relationships with many
of the local people. When the three of them learned that a landmark building in the town center was slated for demolition, they worked with other
residents to save it and succeeded in having it placed on a historic register.
Together they began imagining other projects to restore Liberty to its glory
days. Gibson bought an old movie theater in downtown Liberty, and Bérubé

managed it, hiring local high school students to sell tickets and work the concession stands. "We wanted to help revive the town," Katz recalled, but "there were huge obstacles. . . . The economy defeated us, and irrational exuberance. None of us really knew how to do it."[69]

For Bérubé, the initial experiences in Liberty made him want to live there full time. Throughout his adult life he had helped to create communities, whether in rural Vermont or in Boston and San Francisco communes. Despite his love of urban living, small-town life and the sense of belonging it promised attracted him. Having built friendships with a number of Liberty's residents, in 2002 Bérubé sold his apartment in Manhattan, bought a place in Liberty, and settled in the town. He threw himself into the life of the community. Bérubé became a member of the Liberty Volunteer Fire Department. Twice he was elected to public office as a trustee of the Village of Liberty, its governing body. With others, he launched an effort that led to the listing of over 100 downtown buildings on the New York and the National Register of Historic Places. He converted his property into a bed-and-breakfast inn that he ran himself. He won awards from the Chamber of Commerce of Liberty and Sullivan County. Strengthening his ties to the area even more, he formed an intimate partnership with John Nelson, a nurse-practitioner who commuted to Manhattan for a job working with HIV-positive young people. Together they opened a business in downtown Liberty that specialized in 1930s, 1940s, and 1950s collectibles. They playfully named it Intelligent Design Antiques.[70]

Through these changes, the MCSU book remained largely on hold. Bérubé's various Liberty projects cannot be reduced to a nostalgic effort to reproduce a romanticized version of the small-town working-class life that he knew as a boy. He had to make a living, and he had found a community of good friends and loved ones. Bérubé would go back to the manuscript from time to time, fiddling with his latest draft but not making substantial progress. For a while he dropped it completely. Friends tried to prod him along, but without much success. Katz remembers an effort that he made. "I very gingerly sat down with him. You have a block on this," Katz told him. "You keep restarting it."[71]

Sometime in 2007, Bérubé went back to the manuscript in a serious way. The draft he was working on in the months before his death is qualitatively different from the earlier versions saved on his computer. He seemed at last to have found a structure for the narrative and a voice with which to tell it. The first eighty or so pages have the grace and flow of a novel, and another eighty pages simply need the pencil of a good editor. He also had outline notes for some of the remaining half of the story. As we write this intro-

John D'Emilio, Estelle Freedman, and Allan Bérubé, ca. 1980. Courtesy of the Allan Bérubé Collection at the GLBTHS, San Francisco.

duction, it remains undetermined whether a complete manuscript can be constructed through a process of borrowing from earlier drafts in an effort to realize the vision of the last one. In the meantime, in order to preview the history of the MCSU, we have included in Part 4 two selections based on this research. "Trying to Remember" comes from a 2003 draft of the manuscript. "No Red-Baiting, Race-Baiting, or Queer-Baiting!" is the text of the illustrated lecture he gave in many settings around the country; it offers an overview of the project (Chaps. 15–16).

Allan's sudden death in December 2007 was a loss for the community he was part of in Liberty as well as for his family, his friends and loved ones, and the historical profession. For us, compiling this book has been a painful reminder of our own personal loss, but it has also been a labor of love. Allan was an intimate friend at crucial periods of each of our lives, and he remained dear to us over the years. He was the glue that held together members of the History Project in San Francisco; he moved between the academy and the community, enriching both realms for his efforts; he mobilized World War II veterans to meet one another and helped them gain the recognition they so long deserved. At the end of his life he was engaged in further acts of historical recovery, through his local activism in Liberty and his original research on the MCSU.

Whether or not a completed book on the MCSU appears, we think this collection of Allan Bérubé's published and unpublished work provides a compelling picture of the history he produced and the politics he espoused in his lifetime. We hope as well that it keeps alive his vision of a community-oriented public history and his conviction that historical research and knowledge has the power not only to captivate individual readers but also to motivate them to organize for change in their world.

NOTES

1. The 1994 film, also titled *Coming Out Under Fire*, was cowritten by Bérubé and director Arthur Dong.

2. For a bibliography of Bérubé's writings, see the posting on the website of OutHistory: <http://outhistory.org/wiki/Allan_B%C3%A9rub%C3%A9:_December_3%2C_1946-December_11%2C_2007>.

3. For an obituary, see *New York Times*, December 16, 2007, 12.

4. Bérubé's papers have been deposited at the Gay, Lesbian, Bisexual, Transgender Historical Society (GLBTHS) in San Francisco.

5. Allan Bérubé to John D'Emilio, April 2, 1981, letters in possession of John D'Emilio (hereafter cited as AB to JD); Annette Bérubé to Estelle Freedman, email communication, November 21, 2009; Ian Lekus interview with Allan Bérubé, December 17, 1999, 4, original transcript in possession of Lekus (hereafter cited as Lekus interview). Bérubé had two other siblings in addition to Annette: Diane and Florence.

6. CO Statement, box 12, Bérubé Papers.

7. Lekus interview, 6–7.

8. Allan Bérubé and David Worstell, eds., *Living at War: A Collection of Contemporary Responses to the Draft* (Chicago: n.p., 1968); Lekus interview, 7.

9. Lekus interview, 9.

10. Ibid., 18.

11. Ibid., 25, 28–29.

12. Untitled essay by Allan Troxler, November 2009, in possession of authors (hereafter cited as Troxler essay).

13. Ibid.

14. Ibid. For Wittman's essay, "A Gay Manifesto," see Karla Jay and Allen Young, *Out of the Closets: Voices of Gay Liberation* (New York: Douglas/Links, 1972), 330–41.

15. "Intellectual Desire" (paper presented at La Ville en Rose: Le premier colloque Québécois d'études lesbiennes et gaies [First Quebec Lesbian and Gay Studies Conference], Concordia University and the University of Quebec at Montreal, November 12, 1992, published in *GLQ: A Journal of Lesbian and Gay Studies* 3, no. 1 [February 1996]: 139–57, reprinted in *Queerly Classed: Gay Men and Lesbians Write about Class*, edited by Susan Raffo, 43–66 [Boston: South End Press, 1997]); Rob Dobson to John D'Emilio, email communications, August 30, 31, 2010.

16. Troxler essay; Allan Bérubé Journals, June 1, 1974, box 19, Bérubé Papers (hereafter cited as Bérubé Journals).

17. For discussions of San Francisco in the 1960s and 1970s, see Elizabeth Armstrong, *Forging Gay Identities: Organizing Sexuality in San Francisco, 1950–1994* (Chicago: University of Chicago Press, 2002); Nan Boyd, *Wide Open Town: A History*

of Queer San Francisco to 1965 (Berkeley: University of California Press, 2003); John D'Emilio, "Gay Politics, Gay Community: San Francisco's Experience," in *Making Trouble: Essays on Gay History, Politics, and the University*, 74–95 (New York: Routledge, 1992); and Marcia Gallo, *Different Daughters: A History of the Daughters of Bilitis and the Rise of the Lesbian Rights Movement* (New York: Carroll and Graf, 2006).

18. See Alex Haley, *Roots: The Saga of an American Family* (New York: Doubleday, 1976), and Jonathan Ned Katz, *Gay American History: Lesbians and Gay Men in the U.S.A.* (New York: Crowell, 1976). *Roots* was also an immensely popular twelve-part miniseries that aired on ABC-TV in 1977.

19. See Randy Shilts, *The Mayor of Castro Street* (New York: St. Martin's Press, 1982), and the documentary film *The Times of Harvey Milk*, produced by Rob Epstein and Richard Schmiechen (1984).

20. Bérubé Journals, July 9, 1977.

21. AB to JD, November 23, 1979.

22. Bérubé Journals, July 11, 16, 1977; AB to JD, May 19, 1980.

23. Draft of letter to Katz, Bérubé Journals, August 19, 1977.

24. Bérubé Journals, May 14, 1979, November 1, 1977.

25. AB to JD, November 21, 1979.

26. Bérubé Journals, August 10, 1977.

27. The group of individuals who came together in the History Project in these years proved extraordinarily productive and influential. They brought long activist resumes with a variety of organizations. The individuals and the work they produced include Rob Epstein, director of the documentary films *The Times of Harvey Milk* (1984) and *Common Threads: Stories from the Quilt* (1989), each of which won an Oscar for best documentary film; Jeffrey Escoffier, *American Homo: Community and Perversity* (Berkeley: University of California Press, 1998); Eric Garber, *Uranian Worlds: A Guide to Alternative Sexuality in Science Fiction, Fantasy, and Horror* (Boston: GK Hall, 1990), coauthored with Lyn Paleo; Amber L. Hollibaugh, *My Dangerous Desires: A Queer Girl Dreaming Her Way Home* (Durham: Duke University Press, 2000); and Gayle Rubin, "Thinking Sex: Notes for a Radical Theory of the Politics of Sexuality," in *Pleasure and Danger: Exploring Female Sexuality*, edited by Carole Vance, 267–319 (New York: Routledge, 1984). Frances Reid and Elizabeth Stevens produced *In the Best Interests of the Children* (1977), an award-winning documentary film on lesbian mothers and child custody. John D'Emilio and Estelle Freedman coauthored *Intimate Matters: A History of Sexuality in America* (New York: Harper & Row, 1988).

28. John D'Emilio, personal recollection.

29. AB to JD, November 23, 1979.

30. *She Even Chewed Tobacco*, video produced by Elizabeth Stevens and Estelle Freedman, 1983, distributed by Women Make Movies (<http://www.wmm.com/filmCatalog/pages/c216.shtml>); San Francisco Lesbian and Gay History Project, "'She Even Chewed Tobacco': A Pictorial Narrative of Passing Women in America," in *Hidden from History: Reclaiming the Gay and Lesbian Past*, edited by Martin Duberman, Martha Vicinus, and George Chauncey Jr., 183–94 (New York: New American Library, 1989).

31. Quotation is from AB to JD, January 8, 1980; other examples come from AB to JD, June 17, 1980, and February 8 and March 10, 1981.

32. Bérubé Journals, November 4, 1981.

33. AB to JD, December 5, 1979.

34. AB to JD, April 2 and February 22, 8, 1981.

35. James Steakley, "Homosexuals and the Third Reich," *Body Politic* 11 (January/February 1974); Judith Schwarz, Kathy Peiss, and Christina Simmons, "'We Were a Little Band of Willful Women': The Heterodoxy Club of Greenwich Village," in *Passion and Power: Sexuality in History*, edited by Kathy Peiss and Christina Simmons, with Robert A. Padgug, 118–37 (Philadelphia: Temple University Press, 1989); for Gerber/Hart Library, see <http://www.gerberhart.org/>.

36. The History Project, *Improper Bostonians: Lesbian and Gay History from the Puritans to Playland* (Boston: Beacon Press, 1999).

37. Elizabeth Lapovsky Kennedy and Madeline Davis, *Boots of Leather, Slippers of Gold: The History of a Lesbian Community* (New York: Routledge, 1993), xvi.

38. See the Lesbian Herstory Archives website at <www.lesbianherstoryarchives.org>.

39. AB to JD, January 28, August 4, 1980, December 16, 1979, February 8, 1981.

40. AB to JD, July 9, 1981.

41. Allan Bérubé, *Coming Out Under Fire: The History of Gay Men and Women in World War II* (New York: Free Press, 1990), x.

42. AB to JD, June 1, 1981.

43. AB to JD, June 6, 1982.

44. The society later renamed itself the GLBT Historical Society; see <www.glbthistory.org>. Walker's papers are deposited at the historical society.

45. AB to JD, April 2, 1981.

46. "Talk with Amber," July 24, 1981, box 19, Bérubé Papers.

47. Richard Sennett and Jonathan Cobb, *The Hidden Injuries of Class* (New York: Knopf, 1972).

48. Works already published in 1990 include Katz, *Gay American History*; Jonathan Ned Katz, *Gay/Lesbian Almanac: A New Documentary* (New York: Carroll and Graf, 1983); John D'Emilio, *Sexual Politics, Sexual Communities: The Making of a Homosexual Minority in the United States, 1940–1970* (Chicago: University of Chicago Press, 1983); Martin Duberman, *About Time: Exploring the Gay Past* (New York: Meridian, 1986); Duberman, Vicinus, and Chauncey, *Hidden from History*; and Lillian Faderman, *Surpassing the Love of Men: Romantic Friendship and Love between Women from the Renaissance to the Present* (New York: Morrow, 1981).

49. Elaine Tyler May, "History without Victims: Gays in World War II," *Reviews in American History* 19, no. 2 (June 1991): 255–59, and Clayton R. Koppes, review of *Coming Out Under Fire* in *Journal of American History* 78, no. 1 (June 1991): 377–78.

50. *New York Times Book Review*, April 8, 1990, 9; *New York Times*, May 2, 1990, C20; *Washington Post*, April 22, 1990, D3; *St. Louis Post-Dispatch*, July 3, 1990, 4D; *San Francisco Chronicle*, May 13, 1990, 5.

51. Matlovich appeared on the cover of the September 8, 1975, issue of *Time*. For a detailed account of the history of the military's policy and the challenges to it in the 1970s, see Randy Shilts, *Conduct Unbecoming: Gays and Lesbians in the U.S. Military* (New York: St. Martin's Press, 1993).

52. These events are discussed in Urvashi Vaid, *Virtual Equality: The Mainstreaming of Gay and Lesbian Liberation* (New York: Anchor, 1995).

53. Gayle Rubin, "Remembering Allan," memorial at GLBTHS, May 17, 2008, in possession of authors.

54. See Senator Edward Kennedy's comments in the *Congressional Record*, September 9, 1993, retrievable at <http://dont.stanford.edu/regulations/KennedyViews.html>.

55. AB to JD, August 3, 1993.

56. Ibid.

57. Bert Hansen, telephone interview with John D'Emilio, October 2, 2009 (hereafter cited as Hansen interview).

58. Nardi to D'Emilio, email communication, February 17, 2010.

59. See Kennedy and Davis, *Boots of Leather, Slippers of Gold*, and George Chauncey, *Gay New York: Gender, Urban Culture, and the Making of the Gay Male World, 1890–1940* (New York: Basic Books, 1994).

60. John D'Emilio, personal recollection.

61. For information about CLAGS and its history, see <http://web.gc.cuny.edu/clags/index.html>.

62. Jonathan Ned Katz, telephone interview with John D'Emilio, September 28, 2009 (hereafter cited as Katz interview).

63. Hansen interview.

64. Wayne Hoffman to Bert Hansen, email communication, October 2, 2009.

65. Dangerous Bedfellows, ed., *Policing Public Sex* (Boston: South End Press, 1996).

66. Katz interview.

67. Nan Alamilla Boyd, "Remembering Allan Bérubé," CGLH Newsletter 22, no 1 (Spring 2008), 4; Hoffman to Hansen, October 2, 2009.

68. Hansen Interview.

69. Katz Interview.

70. For information on Bérubé's years in Liberty, see the biographical data on the website of OutHistory: <http://outhistory.org/wiki/Allan_B%C3%A9rub%C3%A9:_December_3%2C_1946-December_11%2C_2007>.

71. Katz Interview.

PART I

A Community Historian
Exploring Queer San Francisco

Lesbian Masquerade

This essay is a revised version of an illustrated lecture that Bérubé first presented in San Francisco in June 1979. Inspired by the section in Jonathan Ned Katz's Gay American History *(1976) titled "Passing Women"—which revealed a long tradition of women who dressed, lived, and worked as men—Bérubé searched through San Francisco newspapers for local evidence of the phenomenon. He places his stories in the context of the newly emerging field of U.S. women's history and sets them as well in the local setting of San Francisco. Although very much constructed as a discovery of hidden lesbian lives, the showings of "Lesbian Masquerade" also inspired some of the first explorations of transgender history. The essay was originally published in* Gay Community News, *a Boston-based politically progressive newspaper with a national circulation. Like much of the community press in the post-Stonewall era, it not only reported news but served as an outlet for early writing in gay and lesbian history.*

In the last few years lesbian and gay historians have begun piecing together a history of the varied experiences of lesbians in America. They have discovered, for example, large collections of love letters between middle-class women who attended nineteenth-century women's colleges or who were active in the early feminist, labor, and settlement house movements. They have also found evidence of lesbian relationships among women who worked in nineteenth-century factories and department stores and who lived in residence and boardinghouses.

Perhaps the most visible lesbians of nineteenth-century America were women who passed as men and married other women. American newspaper headlines such as "Poses, Undetected, 60 Years as a Man," "A Gay Deceiver of the Feminine Gender," and "Death Proves 'Married Man' a Woman" announced the shocked discoveries of these women's deceptions. These reports appear to become more frequent beginning in the mid-1800s and represent, I suspect, only the tip of an iceberg. They are possibly the most visible

Originally published in *Gay Community News*, November 17, 1979, 8–9.

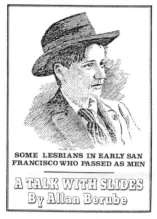

LESBIAN MASQUERADE

SOME LESBIANS IN EARLY SAN
FRANCISCO WHO PASSED AS MEN

A TALK WITH SLIDES
By Allan Berube

8:00 PM Thursday
JUNE 21, 1979
WOMEN'S BUILDING
3543 18th Street
SAN FRANCISCO

$2 DONATION $2

!ALL ARE WELCOME!

A BENEFIT FOR THE
S. F. GAY HISTORY PROJECT
Wheelchair accessible
Free child care: 431-7184
Signed for the hearing impaired

Flyer for Bérubé's first slide lecture, with an image of "Babe Bean" (Elvira Virginia Mugarietta), one of the women who passed as men featured in the talk. Courtesy of the San Francisco Lesbian and Gay History Project Papers at the GLBTHS, San Francisco.

evidence of a larger social phenomenon in which many American women chose to abandon their feminine roles and successfully pass as men.

A brief historical background might help explain why these women chose to pass as men in mid-nineteenth-century America. Before the nineteenth century, most Americans lived in villages or on farms where work, while thought of as women's work or men's work, was integrated with home life. In this young country everyone's labor was valuable, and women were known to work as innkeepers, farmers, shopkeepers, and merchants in villages and towns.

As cities grew and industrial capitalism expanded, men left their households to enter a world of paid labor from which women were excluded: a world of business, politics, and civil service where men socialized with each other in taverns, beer halls, and saloons. Women found few opportunities in this all-male world and were hired only as the lowest-paid workers in factories, a place reserved mostly for immigrant women. While men worked for wages outside the home, the work inside the home—housework, rearing children, providing for the family's domestic needs—became the unpaid work of women.

At the same time that men were separating their world from women's, the differences between the sexes were artificially exaggerated so that, according to historian Mary Ryan, "by 1860 sex had cut a bold gash across all of society and culture, bluntly dividing American life and character into two inviolable spheres labelled male and female." Not only was the home feminized and the workplace masculinized, but extreme masculine and feminine values were assigned to articles of clothing, emotions, language, skills, and mannerisms.

Many women began measuring their lives against a new ideal of womanhood based on this exaggerated femininity. The ideal middle-class woman in mid-nineteenth-century America did not work for wages; instead, she was supported by her husband or father. She was supposed to be maternal and sentimental and remain at home taking care of her children. Seldom in the company of men, she lived in a nearly all-female world. She didn't drink, smoke, swear, or travel alone. She was soft spoken, wore corsets and petticoats—never shirts or pants—and bore the responsibility of keeping the men in her life properly moral and religious. She was assumed to be sexually passive and pure and did not discuss sexual matters, which belonged only in the world of men.

Not all women, of course, lived according to this middle-class ideal of womanhood. Most black women and men, for example, labored under the same oppressive system of slavery, a system that treated both men and women as property. Immigrant and working-class women did work for wages, but these wages were so low that it was nearly impossible for a working woman to support herself. Middle-class women who were unmarried had few options and faced poverty and social disapproval as "spinsters" and "old maids."

. . . . . .

In the future centuries it is probable that woman will be the owner
of her body and the custodian of her soul. . . . [But now] the well cared
for woman is a parasite and the woman who must work is a slave. . . .
Do you blame me for hating to again resume a woman's clothes

and just belong? Is it any wonder that I determined to become
a member of the privileged sex, if possible?
— *Cora Anderson/Ralph Kerwinieo*, 1914

Women in mid-nineteenth-century America began to find it increasingly difficult to escape these economic and social restrictions. Some women resisted these restrictions on their lives in imaginative and often extreme ways. Married women, for example, sometimes formed passionate and devoted relationships with other married women that lasted for decades. Other women entered the all-male public world and, despite public scorn, began movements for abolition of slavery, labor unions, moral reform, birth control, and women's suffrage.

Still other women entered the privileged world of men by successfully "passing" as men. For many women, passing as a man was one way to live an economically independent life. "I made up my mind," wrote Lucy Ann Lobdell in 1855, "to dress in men's attire to seek labor, as I was used to men's work. And as I might work harder at housework, and only get a dollar per week, and I was capable of doing men's work, and getting men's wages, I resolved to try to get work away among strangers." Lucy Ann Lobdell lived with a woman as "husband" and "wife" for over a decade. A woman named Charles Warner recalled that in the 1860s, "when I was about 20 I decided that I was almost at the end of my rope. I had no money and a woman's wages were not enough to keep me alive. I looked around and saw men getting more money and more work, and more money for the same kind of work. I decided to become a man. It was simple. I just put on men's clothing and applied for a man's job. I got it and got good money for those times, so I stuck to it." Charles Warner passed as a man in Saratoga Springs, New York, for over sixty years.

A woman who passed not only earned more money for the same work; she could also open a bank account and write checks, own a house and property, travel alone, even vote in local and national elections. In 1876, for example, a woman living as Albert B. Clifton told a Long Island judge that she "prefers men's clothing because she can see more and learn more as a man than as a woman." And Murray Hall, who passed for over twenty-five years and twice married women, became a prominent New York politician in the 1880s and 1890s and voted for years in both primary and general elections.

How did these women successfully pass as men? In addition to wearing men's clothes, often borrowed from a brother or cousin, these women had to perfect men's language and tone of voice, as well as gestures, walk, and habits, including smoking and drinking. They had to be physically strong, confident on the street, and be able to flirt with women. For some women, this behavior came naturally. Others, like "Mr. L. Z.," a lesbian in Boston, "took great pains to observe carefully the ways of masculinity in general and even has taken lessons in manly deportment from an actor under the pretext of turning to the stage." Descriptions of these women included much more than clothing. "She drank," went a typical account, "she swore, she courted girls, she worked as hard as her fellows, she fished and camped, she even chewed tobacco."

Passing involved great risks, especially discovery, which meant a loss of freedom and independence, and could create a scandal and bring on arrest or even a court order to wear women's clothes. Some women risked their lives rather than be discovered. Murray Hall suffered from breast cancer for years, and only when she was near death did she risk seeing a doctor, who neither cured her nor kept her secret. Physicians were most to be feared. Many of the passing women we know about today were exposed to the press by doctors in hospitals, prisons, and the military.

Many passing women, but not all, courted, lived with, or married other women. Mid-nineteenth-century reports sometimes explained these marriages as expressions of women's rights. An 1867 San Francisco newspaper story, for example, about Mary Walker, a passing woman from Richmond, Virginia, and her female fiancée noted that "they are not to be married at present, as women's rights have not attained to that degree of development." We may not know for sure if all of these relationships were sexual, but it is important to affirm that these women were capable of fulfilling each other sexually, even if they had to keep their sexuality a secret.

Women who passed as men not only gained economic independence; they also could become sexually assertive and attractive to other women without raising eyebrows. This was an unusual experience for many nineteenth-century women, who were raised to be sexually passive. All passing women had to decide how they would relate to other women. These relationships ranged from bachelorhood to publicly marrying another woman and living as husband and wife. Some women may have passed in order to justify their sexual love for women. Others may have passed as husbands to gain social acceptance for a love that would otherwise have been condemned. For still other women, passing may have come first, providing a woman with a series of experiences, such as being able to live independent of men, that allowed two women to live together in a lesbian relationship without a man's support. In any case, the connections between passing and sexuality are complex, and the motives of passing women need to be explored further.

· · · · · ·

It is an odd thing, but everyone who disappears is said to have been seen at San Francisco. It must be a delightful city, and possess all the attractions of the next world.

— *Oscar Wilde*, 1891

In 1854, thirty-five-year-old Lydia Ann Puyfer was arrested in New York City for wearing men's clothes. When asked why she was thus attired, she explained to the judge that she was "from Gowanus, Long Island, that she had stolen her cousin's clothing with the intention of shipping as a seaman, and that she was bound for California."

Lydia Ann Puyfer was not alone on her journey to California. From the days of the 1849 Gold Rush, San Francisco's reputation as a wild and pleasure-loving city that tolerated all types of "eccentrics" attracted people considered social misfits "back East." Its reputation as a "gay mecca" is not a sudden product of the 1970s but has roots that go far back into the nineteenth century.

While accounts of lesbians who passed as men appeared in nineteenth-century newspapers from all over the United States, an examination of the accounts from a single city such as San Francisco can ground these women's lives in local history. From a preliminary search through scrapbooks of early San Francisco newspaper clippings for lesbian- and gay-related materials, I have found many detailed accounts of lesbians who passed as men. I suspect that a search through newspapers of most American cities, together with oral histories of older lesbians, would uncover similar stories. The San Francisco accounts are already beginning to reveal a lost local tradition of passing women, many of whom were well known during their lifetimes in San Francisco and throughout California.

Jeanne Bonnet, for example, grew up in San Francisco as a tomboy and in the 1870s, in her early twenties, was arrested dozens of times for wearing male attire. She visited local brothels as a male customer and eventually organized French prostitutes in San Francisco into an all-woman gang whose members swore off prostitution, had nothing to do with men, and supported themselves by shoplifting. She traveled with a special friend, Blanche Buneau, whom the newspapers described as "strangely and powerfully attached" to Jeanne. Her success at separating prostitutes from their pimps led to her murder in 1876.

Another San Francisco woman, "Babe" Bean, passed for forty years as a male Red Cross nurse, soldier, and charity worker. She was discovered in 1897 when she briefly became a reporter for a Stockton, California, daily newspaper, where she described her experiences passing in hobo camps, prisons, gambling halls, and saloons, and on the city streets.

The following narrative of Luisa Matson's life in San Francisco from 1895 to 1907 is one kind of detailed account of a lesbian passing as a man that can be compiled from local newspaper articles. The reporters who wrote these articles, of course, expressed a male bias that saw passing women as "imitation men" and ignored these women's "wives" and lovers. This bias distorts nearly every nineteenth-century account of passing women and reflects an attitude that the "masqueraders" were curiosities, while their lovers were ordinary women. In the following story of Luisa Matson's life I have included as much about her lover, Helen Fairweather, as the newspapers revealed.

A SECRET FOR YEARS
LUISA WATSON MASQUERADED AS A MAN
Her Sex Revealed in Jail
Once Engaged to a Young Lady

In late January 1895, police arrested Milton B. Matson in Los Gatos, California, twenty-five miles south of San Francisco, for passing bad checks. Matson had been running a summer resort in nearby Ben Lomond and had run up a series of debts which he was unable to pay. Police booked him at the county jail in San Jose and threw him into the tank with "the rabble and tramps and petty larcenists." Four days later police hurriedly removed Matson from the all-male cell and took him upstairs to the sheriff's private office for questioning.

The district attorney had discovered that Matson had received bank orders made out to Luisa Elisabeth Blaxland Matson. When asked who this woman was, Matson replied, "My half sister."

"'Matson,' the D.A. said impassively, 'those orders are either forged or you and Luisa Elizabeth Blaxland Matson are one and the same person, and you are a female.'

"'Then the question is easily solved,' exclaimed Matson, 'for I am a male.'"

The officers were not convinced, however, and before long Milton B. Matson admitted that she was a woman. "She seemed very much embarrassed that her deception had been discovered. She tried hard to make the officers promise not to disclose her secret to anyone. She was particularly anxious that the story be kept from the prisoners." Reporters, of course, were close at hand, and Luisa Matson's story began to unfold.

Forty-year-old Luisa Matson had passed as a man all her adult life, supporting herself by working in the hotel and real estate business in Australia and California. She supplemented her income with small monthly remittances from her disapproving family in England. "In my early youth," she explained, "I was sort of a nondescript. I was fond of outdoor sports, and before I was 17 years of age I was attired in garments about half-masculine. When I became two or four or six and twenty, somewhere around there, I put on the entire male garb. I did not find it at all inconvenient; in fact, it seemed natural to me from the first."

The next day a full interview with Matson appeared in the *San Francisco Call*, beginning with the following curious headline:

LOS GATOS FOLKS SAY SHE WAS GAY
BUT THE PRISONER SAYS SHE HAS BEEN
STRAIGHT ALL HER LIFE
A DENIAL OF HER LOVE AFFAIR

The word "straight," incidentally, was not used on the West Coast to mean "heterosexual" until the mid-twentieth century. In this headline, "gay" probably meant "living a wild life," and "straight" may have meant "moral and law-abiding." Yet it is curious that these words were used as opposites in 1895, especially in reference to a love affair between two women.

Upon entering the sheriff's office for the interview, Matson "was seated at a desk which [had] been provided for her." Her light-colored trousers were turned up at the bottom in true English style. A black cutaway coat and eyeglasses contributed to make a very natty appearance. As the reporter and artist entered, she rose to the full majesty of her five feet and seven inches and gazed sternly at the intruders.

"'It seems outrageous,' she declared, 'that a man cannot have any peace, but must be badgered to death by reporters.'" There was a moment of stunned silence in the room, then she smiled. As the interview progressed she showed her sense of humor in spite of her nervousness.

Luisa Matson, as Milton B., while running her summer resort, had apparently met a grammar school teacher named Helen Fairweather from San Francisco. Helen Fairweather, noted a reporter, "became enamored with the proprietor, who truly makes a fine-looking man. Milton B. apparently reciprocated her affection, and when vacation was over the twain were engaged to be wed." Matson, or the "alleged man," as the reporter called her, denied that she passed as a man in order to marry a woman. "She says her relations with the young lady were purely platonic. 'I have no reason whatever for wearing this garb,'" she said, "'except monetary matters. . . . I have no other reason in the world.'"

An enterprising reporter, recognizing a good story, set off for Los Gatos to interview residents about Matson. She had succeeded in fooling all of Los Gatos, they admitted, adding that she "showed her ability to drink the best brands of whiskey, let loose at times the artillery of profanity and could tell a racy story, with the best of the boys." The proprietor of a boardinghouse where both women had stayed confirmed that Fairweather had told him about her engagement to Matson. Another reporter in San Francisco tried to interview Helen Fairweather, but she was not at her apartment. Her stepmother, however, was home and willing to talk. The report that her stepdaughter had fallen in love with a man who was really a woman came as strange news to her. "'You see,' she said, 'in the first place my daughter is not a young girl, and then she is an invalid, and has been for months. She never told me anything . . . about being in love or being engaged. . . . She left home for the benefit of her health and that, I believe, occupied her attention more than would an affection of the heart.' She also said that no ill-feeling exists between her step-daughter and herself."

In spite of her "good nature which even the prison walls would not banish," Luisa Matson was fed up with the whole affair. "I would have been straight all my life," she said, "and this is the first time I have ever been in trouble. When I get out of here I intend to leave America as soon as possible. I shall assume feminine apparel. There will not be further developments in the matter."

When Matson was released from jail the next day, she celebrated by going on a "big drunk" in Los Gatos. While she was drunk, she told a reporter that she had received several offers from men to exhibit her in dime museum sideshows, where they wanted to bill her as "Mr. Matson Miss." (Three months later, Matson made newspapers again when Alex Plunkett, a sixteen-year-old effeminate young man, was mistaken for a woman passing as a man, and the *San Francisco Chronicle* called him "another case of a Mr. Matson Miss." The newspapers, however, were eager to cover the scandal of the Oscar Wilde trials in London and quickly forgot Luisa Matson.)

Eleven years later, on April 18, 1906, two strong earthquake tremors shook San Francisco for forty-eight seconds. Few people died from the earthquake itself, but within hours uncontrollable fires swept through the city. When the fire was finally extinguished three days later, nearly 500 square blocks had been destroyed, hundreds were dead, and most San Franciscans were left homeless.

The army set up canvas tents in the parks throughout the city to house the homeless. San Franciscans from all walks of life were thrown together in these refugee camps. Sometimes, recalled one survivor, "it was difficult to distinguish men from women. The supply of women's clothing had been exhausted, and many women could be seen dressed in ordinary soft shirts and overalls. In that garb they walked about their tents unconcernedly."

Luisa Matson was among the refugees. She had neither resumed female attire nor left America, as she had threatened eleven years earlier. Instead, she had remained in San Francisco working as a man, S. B. Matson, in the cataloging department of the San Francisco Public Library. Losing her job and home in the Great Fire, she moved to a permanent refugee settlement called Point Lobos, where she occupied a small cottage, half of which she rented to a tailor who didn't know "he had a landlady instead of a landlord." She was "not inclined to mingle much with her neighbors" but was well liked in the camp and fondly known as the kindly "old gentleman." On the morning of July 2, 1907, Matson did not appear at the door to her cottage. Concerned neighbors broke open the locked door to find her in bed and unconscious, suffering from a stroke. They rushed her to Park Emergency Hospital, but she died later that night and was discovered to be a woman.

Among Matson's belongings were some letters from "Helen," "which told of schoolwork and impending vacation and a postcard dated [two weeks earlier] wishing the masquerader 'many happy returns' on his birthday, and adding, 'May see you Monday at trysting place.' This card was signed 'H' and was in the handwriting of the letter from the schoolteacher." A neighbor in the camp told a reporter that a schoolteacher from a nearby grammar school frequently visited Matson at her cottage.

The press again interviewed Helen Fairweather's stepmother. She confirmed that the postcard message was in her stepdaughter's handwriting. "My stepdaughter fell in love with this person before it [sic] was a woman," she explained. "This circumstance caused a breach in the family and from that time until the fire my daughter did not live at home. The matter of which I have just spoken has always been a tabooed subject in this house and I had not heard that Miss Fairweather ever saw this person now."

This time a reporter managed to interview Helen Fairweather herself. She denied continuing a friendship with Luisa Matson or visiting her at her cottage. "It could not be said that I was in love with her under the misapprehension that she was a man; there was simply a regard which was passed naturally away. I have seen nothing of the person for some time. It could not be said, even, that I have felt an interest in the matter." She added that she had a double in San Francisco and that people frequently wrote letters in her handwriting and signed her name to them.

"The woman who died yesterday," concluded the *San Francisco Call*, under the name S. B. Matson and who lived and dressed as a man was Luisa Elizabeth Matson, who a decade ago figured in the most peculiar case of sex-deception ever practiced in California. For she, who had forfeited femininity and followed the fortunes that trousers might bring, had while masquerading won the affection of Miss Helen Fairweather, a teacher in the San Francisco department.

. . . It is said that Miss Fairweather continued to be a friend of the mysterious woman to the time of her death. . . . Miss Fairweather's stepmother . . . told the tale of the strangest romance of California's annals.

While Luisa Matson, Jeanne Bonnet, Babe Bean, and other nineteenth-century passing women lived as "eccentric" loners isolated from other women like themselves, evidence suggests that some passing women formed social networks with each other as early as the turn of the century. A report from 1903, for example, revealed a group of at least ten women who passed as men and worked for the New York Central Railway in Buffalo, New York, "some of these being porters [most likely black women], train agents, switchmen," and cooks. "They often met together and made themselves not a little merry over the success of their transference from one class of humanity to another."

By the turn of the century the male-dominated psychiatric profession in America had "discovered" passing women and added them to their growing list of sexual perverts. Some doctors described passing women as typical of all lesbians. "The female invert," wrote an American doctor in 1915, "likes to . . . dress herself entirely in men's attire and disguise her identity. She further prefers the occupations of men." The early newspaper accounts had seen the masculine behavior of these women as a "peculiar" desire for women's rights and equality with men. Psychiatrists by the turn of the century, however, interpreted the same masculine behavior as symptoms of sexual perversion. They invented new names for the growing numbers of women they diagnosed as suffering from this perversion, such as female inverts, tribadists, sapphists, men-women, gyanders, feminosexuals, uraniads, and women who suffered from "viraginous disorders" and "delusional masculinity." Twentieth-century newspapers began to associate "passing" with "sexual perversion," and in the late 1920s, for example, the *San Francisco Chronicle* used the term "woman invert" to describe these women.

By the 1920s and '30s, women who passed as men, as well as women who wore men's clothes to identify themselves as lesbians, began socializing in cafes and nightclubs in some American cities. These were possibly the beginnings of what we know today as women's and lesbian bars. Some of these clubs were operated by women and were frequently raided by the police. In the early 1930s, for example, two Chicago nightclubs, the Roselle Club, operated by Eleanor Shelly, and the Twelve-thirty Club, operated by Becky Blumfield, were shut down by the mayor and police. Investigators reported that "women in male attire were nightly patrons of the places." Many of the couples were married to each other, and one woman revealed the name of a black minister on Chicago's South Side who performed marriage ceremonies for these women. It is not yet known how many passing women chose these early women's clubs as more comfortable alternatives to all-male taverns and saloons.

The opening of these clubs gave some lesbians a new visibility in American cities. By this time, too, the words "dike," "bull-dyke," and "bull-dagger" had become common slang for these women. J. R. Roberts has discovered that in the 1870s the word "dike" meant "a man who was all dressed up," or "diked out," perhaps for a night out on the town. By 1900 the word "bull-dyker" was used in the red-light district of Philadelphia to mean "lesbian lovers." In the 1920s and '30s a number of black artists recorded songs about these women, including "Prove It on Me Blues," by Gertrude "Ma" Rainey in 1928, and "Mannish Women," by Rev. J. M. Gates in 1929. In 1935 blues singer Bessie Jackson recorded a song entitled "B-D Women," meaning "Bulldagger Women." Her song is typical of 1930s black music about these urban lesbians in men's clothes as it describes the oppression and celebrates the economic independence and rebellious spirit shared by a generation of lesbians who passed as men:

> Comin' a time, B-D women ain't gonna need no men.
> The way they treat us is a low down and dirty shame.
>
> B-D women, they all done the way they plan,
> They can lay their jive just like a natural man.
>
> B-D women, you know they sure is rough,
> They all drink up plenty whiskey and they sure can strut their stuff.
>
> B-D women, you know they work and make their dough,
> And when they get ready to spend it they know just where to go.*

*AC/DC Blues: Gay Jazz Re-issues, vol. 1, Stash Records, 1977, ST-106

SELECTED BIBLIOGRAPHY

Books

Foster, Jeannette. *Sex Variant Women in Literature*. Oakland, Calif.: Diana Press, 1976.

Katz, Jonathan Ned. *Gay American History*. New York: Crowell, 1976.

Articles

Bullough, Vern, and Bonnie Bullough. "Lesbianism in the 1920s and 1930s: A New-found Study." *Signs: Journal of Women in Culture and Society* 2, no. 4 (1977).

Cook, Blanche Wiesen. "Female Support Networks and Political Activism: Lillian Wald, Crystal Eastman, Emma Goldman." *Chrysalis*, no. 3 (1977), 43.

Cooper, Janet. "Female Crushes, Affections, and Friendships in Children's Literature." *Gai Saber* 1, no. 2 (Summer 1977).

Faderman, Lillian. "Lesbian Magazine Fiction in the Early 20th Century." *Journal of Popular Culture* 11, no. 4 (Spring 1978).

Roberts, J. R. "Dyke Re-Search." *Sinister Wisdom* 9 (Spring 1979).

———. "Lesbian Hoboes." *DYKE*, no. 5 (Fall 1977).

Sahli, Nancy. "Smashing: Women's Relationships before the Fall." *Chrysalis*, no. 8 (Summer 1979).

Schwarz, Judith. "Directory of American Lesbians in History." *Lesbian Connection* 4, no. 3 (August 1978).

———. "Old Maids, Spinsters & Maiden Ladies." *Lesbian Voices* 2, no. 1 (Winter 1975–76) and no. 2 (March 1976).

———. "Researching Lesbian History." *Sinister Wisdom* 5 (Winter 1978).

———. "Yellow Clover: Katharine Lee Bates and Katharine Coman." *Frontiers* 4, no. 1 (1979).

Smith-Rosenberg, Carroll. "The Female World of Love and Ritual." *Signs* 1, no. 1 (1975).

Behind the Specter of San Francisco

This discussion of the 1959 mayoral campaign in San Francisco is a good example of how Bérubé employed history to illuminate contemporary events. In April 1980, CBS television aired nationally a news special, Gay Power, Gay Politics, *that raised the prospect of homosexuals dominating San Francisco politics and transforming the city into a sexual playground. Bérubé's response was to tell the story of an earlier era in the city when the specter of homosexual power was used by politicians to inflame public opinion. The historical lesson he hoped to communicate was that efforts at repression might also breed resistance and organization. Bérubé's piece was published in* The Body Politic, *based in Toronto, a city that was experiencing its own wave of antigay political repression in the early 1980s.*

The year 1954 marked, perhaps for the first time, official recognition of the large post–World War II gay migration to San Francisco. Early in the year the daily newspaper, the *Examiner,* began the weeklong front-page exposé on the local "sex-deviate" problem, exploiting a routine drive against "scores" of gay men whom police rounded up, questioned, and ordered to leave town. An *Examiner* editorial called for police and the courts to "stop the influx of homosexuals" before "San Francisco finds itself as the complete haven for undesirables." As a result of this exposé, the grand jury met to investigate "why San Francisco has become the magnet for homosexuals from all parts of the Pacific Coast" and heard a "sex-detail" inspector testify that his department could not control the "alarming increase of perverts here since the end of World War II." By the end of the year, city and county officials had begun mapping their strategy to try to reverse this homosexual immigration.

Several months later the California legislature, following suit, legalized the state liquor board's attempts to close gay bars. In January 1956, newly elected San Francisco mayor George Christopher appointed a police chief who stepped up local enforcement of antihomosexual laws. The next four years witnessed a continuing campaign by both government authorities and

Originally published in *The Body Politic,* April 1981, 25–27.

San Francisco Examiner headline announcing crackdown on gays, June 27, 1954. Courtesy of the Allan Bérubé Collection at the GLBTHS, San Francisco.

the press against the steadily growing San Francisco gay population and its bars and meeting places.

It was in this repressive atmosphere that Mayor Christopher began his 1959 reelection campaign. He had earned a reputation as a hotheaded, pro-big-business mayor who was tough on vice and organized crime. His challenger, city tax assessor Russell Wolden, found backing from labor, veterans, tax-cut advocates, and Democratic Clubs. The first few months of their campaign remained quiet and uneventful.

On October 7, however, Wolden made a political move that shook the city like an earthquake. As gay and straight San Franciscans sat down to their evening meals, their radios announced an important message from candidate Wolden. At 6:45 his broadcast began.

This was "not a political speech," he cautioned, "but a heart-to-heart talk with the people of San Francisco, especially mothers and fathers." Mayor Christopher, he charged, had allowed their city to become "the national head-quarters of the organized homosexuals in the United States. . . . The number of sex deviates in this city has soared by the thousands. . . . The number of establishments which cater exclusively to homosexuals also has increased enormously. . . . All of the places are 'pick up joints' where homosexuals are on the prowl for 'dates' and new contacts. . . . Inside can be seen crowds of young men, carrying on homosexual flirtations. This unsavory wicked situation is allowed to fester and spread like a cancerous growth on the body of San Francisco."

"Pick up your telephone book," he continued to his stunned radio audience.

You'll see the Mattachine Society—spelled M-A-T-T-A-C-H-I-N-E—
listed in it. The Mattachine publish and sell sex literature of the most
lurid, distasteful and disgusting variety. The Mattachine Society is
the national voice of organized sex deviates. . . . The Daughters of
Bilitis are a sort of women's auxiliary to Mattachine. . . . From these
thousands (of subscribers) come the sex gangs whose abnormal ap-
petites are catered to by these bars and other joints whose operations
I have just described. . . . Last month at a convention of sex deviates
in Denver, Colorado, a resolution passed by the Mattachine Society
praised Mayor Christopher by name for creating a favorable climate
in San Francisco for their activities.

"This is a matter of grave concern for every parent," Wolden concluded.
"It exposes teenagers to possible contact and contamination in a city admit-
tedly overrun by deviates. . . . Every San Francisco neighborhood is threatened by the bold shadow they cast over the entire community."

Wolden's charges also appeared, with a supportive editorial, in the same
evening's issue of the *Progress* newspaper.

By the next day City Hall, newsrooms, gay bars, and even schoolyards
buzzed with word of Wolden's political bombshell. On the one hand, he had
clearly stepped beyond the bounds of common decency. His broadcast had
"invaded San Francisco homes," objected one letter writer to the *News-Call
Bulletin*, "at the very time the family is assembled—the dinner hour. . . .
The tactic of directing this sordid message to children, is as morally disgusting as distributing illustrated copies of the Kinsey Report on the steps of
every school." As a result, the city's families found themselves in a difficult
position. "San Francisco parents," recalled a reporter two years later, "were
uncomfortably alone among the fathers and mothers of America that fall in
having to field such questions from eleven- and twelve-year olds as 'Daddy,
what is a homosexual?'" Overnight, Russell Wolden had made "sex deviate"
into a household word.

Wolden's charges, on the other hand, also insulted other San Franciscans
who were proud of the city's traditional tolerance of nonconformists. "Sex
deviates," as long as they kept to themselves, posed no more a threat than
the city's well-known population of eccentrics, bohemians, and currently,
beatniks. "How discouraging to read," observed a letter from a "mother of
four children," that "a tolerant attitude toward homosexuality is considered

. . . to be a diabolical insult." One frustrated moral crusader, inspired by Wolden's broadcast, wrote to nearly every newspaper attacking her city's too-tolerant sensibility. "Everyone," she complained, "except the most moronic slug knows that . . . San Francisco is the deliriously delightful paradise of the degenerate and deviate . . . but all you get if you so much as imply it is a blank, negative or disapproving stare."

"The 'homosexual issue,'" quipped local columnist Herb Caen, well aware of the city's large gay population, "is no issue at all. It could also cost (Wolden) a lot of votes. As somebody once observed, there are enough of 'em in town to elect (female impersonator) Walter Hart as mayor." It would still be years, however, before many gay San Franciscans risked writing letters to the press in their own defense.

Wolden's broadcast had provoked the most widespread public discussion of homosexuality the city had witnessed thus far. Was there really a sex-deviate problem? What was this Mattachine Society, anyway? How would Mayor Christopher counter Wolden's charges?

Christopher's quick reaction was to exploit the scandal to the benefit of his own campaign. Refusing to dirty his hands by addressing the gay issue directly, the mayor praised his police department, attacked Wolden's "smear" tactics, and defended the good name of San Francisco. "This accusation," he pontificated, "is the dying gasp of a desperate politician. . . . My opponent has degraded our city. Furthermore, I am deeply regretful that his sordid campaign material has been thrown on the doorstep of every home." Wanting "no formal arrangements with Mr. Wolden of any kind," Christopher canceled all scheduled debates with his opponent. His strategy was to remain pure and aloof, letting Wolden dig his own grave.

The charge that San Francisco police were soft on homosexuals provoked a vehement response from the city's finest. Under Christopher's administration they had conducted a vigorous antigay campaign, including such tactics as dragnet sweeps of Polk Street, arresting every man for blocks and releasing at the station only those men who appeared to be heterosexual.

The Wolden issue, in fact, forced into the open the full extent of San Francisco police activity against gays in the late 1950s. "The San Francisco Police Department," boasted Deputy Police Chief Al Nedler, "has always had a special squad to check on sex deviates. They are doing a good job. Since the first of January they have made over 150 arrests. San Francisco is *not* the headquarters for sex deviates." "If anything," chimed in Police Chief Thomas Cahill, "they know from our sustained drive they're not wanted here, and most take the hint," adding that police had cracked down on seventeen bars identified as "gay hangouts" in the last two years. "A special unit of the vice squad," reassured *News-Call Bulletin* in a special seven-part series defending the police, "is detailed to keep tabs on possible deviate colonies, and is augmented from time to time by special squads of plainclothesmen from districts—notably North Beach and South of Market—where homosexual invasions may begin."

Such military metaphors as "squads," "deviate colonies," and "homosexual invasion" were typical of how San Francisco officials perceived gay migration in the late 1950s. Front-page banner headlines such as "City Opens War On Homosexuals—Officials to Map Strategy" appeared all too often in Bay Area newspapers during those years.

If San Francisco's police had not been soft on homosexuals, why had the Mattachine Society passed a resolution praising them for their "enlightened" policy? Reporters found the answer to this question in the activities of ex–police informer William Brandhove, a supporter of Wolden's campaign. Brandhove, according to a second wave of front-page exposés, began a single-handed crusade against the city's "sex deviates" in order to stigmatize Christopher's administration and thus ensure Wolden's election. This former infiltrator of the Communist Party joined the Mattachine Society and showed up as one of fifty delegates to their national convention in Denver. Brandishing an "unlimited expense account," he paid for a stenotypist to record the Mattachine proceedings, then, according to Mattachine officials, introduced the pro-Christopher resolution for discussion. "He said it would be a wonderful goodwill gesture," Mattachine secretary Don Lucas reportedly explained to the *Examiner*, "that would accomplish a great deal public relations-wise in San Francisco."

Returning to the Bay Area, Brandhove obtained a notarized copy of the resolution from his stenotypist, then, he admitted, "turned it over to my attorney, who, by coincidence, is treasurer of Wolden's campaign." Recently uncovered U.S. Justice Department memos, though heavily censored, suggest FBI involvement in the Brandhove affair. Following Wolden's broadcast, the FBI monitored Brandhove's activities in Denver and San Francisco and stepped up their ongoing surveillance of both the Mattachine Society and the Daughters of Bilitis (DOB).

The tiny Mattachine Society responded to Wolden's charges by initiating a David-and-Goliath slander suit to the tune of $1,100,000. This aggressive legal action, as well as its unholy alliance with the mayor, the police, and the press against Wolden, gave the struggling organization unprecedented publicity, much of it favorable or at least neutral. The *News-Call Bulletin*, for example, calling the society a "small group dedicated to the problem of homosexuality," ran an article entitled "Mattachine Society—How It Got Its

Name." The article quoted paragraphs from the *Mattachine Review*, printed their address, and noted that the society "performs educational, research and social service functions in helping the community better understand sex problems." This kind of publicity for a gay organization was exceptional in the 1950s. The press, however, portrayed Mattachine as the "good" homosexuals, different from the deviates on the streets. Mattachine Society officials reported suffering no reprisals as a result of this sudden public exposure.

While newspapers gave favorable publicity to the predominantly male Mattachine Society, they altogether ignored the Daughters of Bilitis. Wolden, however, not only referred in his speeches to this independent lesbian organization as the "women's auxiliary of Mattachine"; his campaign literature went even further. "You parents of daughters," warned one leaflet, "do not sit back complacently feeling that because you have no boys in your family, everything is all right. . . . To enlighten you as to the existence of a Lesbian organization composed of homosexual women . . . make yourselves acquainted with the name 'Daughters of Bilitis.'" This leaflet, distributed door-to-door, concluded with DOB's San Francisco address and telephone number.

Such hostile publicity, while certainly bringing DOB to the attention of many lesbians for the first time, also made DOB more vulnerable to attack. The organization responded by calling an emergency meeting to prevent a panicked exodus from their ranks. But instead of an exodus, the crisis brought together an unexpectedly large number of DOB members, who voted to put out a special issue of *The Ladder*, their national magazine, and to remove mailing and membership lists from their office. For the duration of the mayoral race, DOB operated out of the back of a station wagon, with boxes of their papers hidden under a blanket. DOB founders Del Martin and Phyllis Lyon later discovered that San Francisco police had in fact attempted to search their empty office as a result of Wolden's exposé.

Needless to say, Russell Wolden's mudslinging backfired on him, drawing criticism from every quarter and splitting his own backers. Except for the *Progress*, the traditionally divided local press ran a united front of editorials defending the mayor and police and calling for Wolden's withdrawal from the mayoral race. Ben Swig, owner of the Fairmont Hotel and Wolden's finance chairman, complained, "I don't want any mudslinging. I don't want any part of it." Adolph Schuman, millionaire and Wolden fundraiser, while remaining a Wolden supporter, explained, "If I'd known we were going to go around saying how many homosexuals were running around San Francisco, I would have stopped it." The San Francisco Labor Council, in a heated debate, recommended censoring its candidate for "using the homosexuality issue as a political football." Jack Morrison, an officer of the Democratic Club, reported receiving "countless" calls from Democrats "sickened and disappointed" at Wolden's tactics and angrily withdrew his own support. Other top Democrats followed suit.

These defections, however, had little effect on Wolden's campaign strategy. Another pro-Wolden exposé appeared in the *Progress*, including the names of gay bars and homosexual arrest statistics. Wolden accused the press of conspiring against him, initiating another round of editorial retaliations. To add insult to injury, his headquarters mailed reprints of his radio speech to PTAS, religious groups and civic leaders throughout the city. The *Examiner*, seeking a political lynching, reversed its earlier position and called for Wolden to stay in the race. "The public," it proclaimed, "should not be denied its right to pass judgment on a man . . . who would openly defame his city by calling it a haven for sex-deviates on the basis of 'evidence' planted by one of his own supporters." Overcome with heated self-righteousness, the *Examiner* seemed to have forgotten that just five years earlier its own editorial had also called San Francisco a "complete haven" for homosexuals.

Wolden, originally favored to win the race, lost the election with only 39 percent of the vote. His "sex-deviate issue" destroyed him. Attempting to heal a wounded and insulted city, Mayor Christopher's victory speech reassured San Franciscans that "it is time to forget the unpleasantness that has occurred the past few months. San Francisco is on the move in the eyes of California, the Nation and the World."

San Francisco was indeed on the move. The following four years, under Christopher's second term in office, saw perhaps the most repressive and highly publicized antigay police campaign in San Francisco's history. Arrests and convictions skyrocketed, nearly every gay bar had its license revoked, and police arrested more than 100 men and women in the city's biggest gay bar raid ever. In response, gay bar owners banded together to form the Tavern Guild, several new gay civil rights groups were organized, and a local gay press emerged, taking a strong antipolice stand. In addition, an openly gay man, José Sarria, ran for city supervisor, columnists began referring to the "limp-wrist vote," and political candidates sought the endorsement of gay organizations.

By 1965 police actions against gays had become so blatant and well publicized that church leaders joined together in public protest and the press even began to criticize the police. Lesbian and gay activists formed a "Citizen's Alert" hotline to report antigay police activity and pressured the police department into appointing a liaison to the gay community. Gay and lesbian organizations continued to multiply and won both an uneasy truce with police and the respect of city officials.

In the wake of the Wolden-Christopher crisis, the gay community came of age in San Francisco. It emerged as a visible and politically maturing minority attempting to have its fair say in city government. It is this vital part of our history that CBS, Briggs and Bryant, and Toronto's New Right would deny us, preferring their own distorted "spectres" of gay takeovers and sex in the streets. They have not yet learned what our own historians are beginning to discover: that once we have come out, the most repressive times have often shown us our greatest strengths.

SOURCES

Contemporary issues of San Francisco's *Chronicle, Progress, News-Call Bulletin,* and *Examiner;* "The Campaign That Deviated," by Jim Kepner in *ONE Magazine* (November 1959); *Lesbian/Woman,* by Phyllis Lyon and Del Martin (Bantam, 1972); *Christopher of San Francisco,* by George Dorsey (Macmillan, 1962); copies of antigay literature from last year's Toronto election supplied by Bert Hansen and the Canadian Gay Archives; FBI documents obtained by William Hartman through the Freedom of Information Act; and many discussions with John D'Emilio and Jeffrey Escoffier and the San Francisco Lesbian and Gay History Project. For further information on the early Mattachine Society, see "Dreams Deferred," a three-part series by John D'Emilio in *The Body Politic* (November 1978, December 1978–January 1979, and February 1979). For other analyses of San Francisco gay history, see "Gay Power, Gay Community: San Francisco's Experience," by John D'Emilio, *Socialist Review* (January–February 1981), and "Heterosexual Culture and the Gay Movement," by Jeffrey Escoffier, forthcoming in *Socialist Review* [published as "Sexual Revolution and the Politics of Gay Identity," *Socialist Review* (July–October 1985)—Eds.].

Don't Save Us from Our Sexuality

By 1984, when this essay first appeared, AIDS was coming to dominate gay male life in the United States. The situation was particularly acute in San Francisco, which had the heaviest concentration of diagnosed cases of any city in the nation. AIDS exacerbated the tendency, discussed in the previous essay, to demonize gay male sexuality, a situation complicated by the fact that the epidemic provoked some within the gay community to call for government regulation of sexual expression. When proposals calling for the closure of gay bathhouses began to circulate, Bérubé wrote this short piece in response. He used an earlier epidemic of bubonic plague in San Francisco to reveal how, in the past, other unpopular minorities—in this case, the Chinese immigrant community—were targets of censure by public health authorities and became scapegoats for a disease.

Once called the "Gay Plague," the AIDS epidemic continues to take its deadly toll in the gay community. The mysterious disease exhausts doctors, baffles researchers, challenges public health officials, divides the gay community, panics the public, and tantalizes the Moral Majority. It triggers everyone's anxieties about the nitty-gritty of gay sex.

Such a climate breeds desperate attempts to find simple solutions. Stop AB-I [a gay rights bill in the California legislature], blame the victims, become monogamous or celibate, close gay restaurants, pass new antisodomy laws. This week, with the closing of all gay bathhouses and sex clubs imminent, this process of AIDS scapegoating seems to have gotten out of control. We are about to throw out the baby with the bathwater.

Gay bathhouses and sex clubs aren't the first institutions to be scapegoated for the city's inability to stop an epidemic. At the turn of the century, the San Francisco Board of Health took extreme measures against the residents and buildings of Chinatown during an outbreak of the bubonic plague.

By the late nineteenth century, one quarter of California's nearly all-male Chinese population, without work after building the railroads, had moved

Originally published in *Coming Up!*, April 1984, 11.

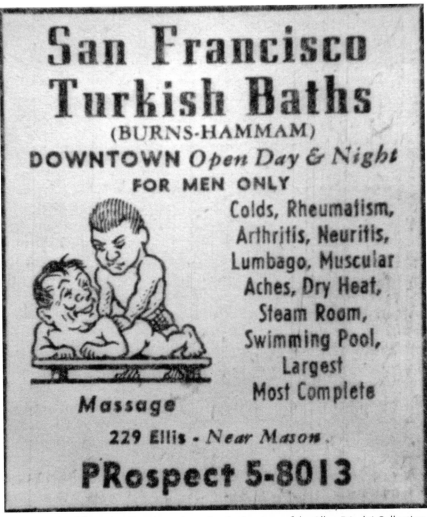

San Francisco Turkish Baths

(BURNS-HAMMAM)

DOWNTOWN *Open Day & Night*

FOR MEN ONLY

Colds, Rheumatism, Arthritis, Neuritis, Lumbago, Muscular Aches, Dry Heat, Steam Room, Swimming Pool, Largest Most Complete

Massage

229 Ellis - *Near Mason*.

PRospect 5-8013

Turkish Bath ad from San Francisco phone book. Courtesy of the Allan Bérubé Collection at the GLBTHS, San Francisco.

to San Francisco's Chinatown. There they re-created their unique culture despite poverty and overcrowded living conditions. But racial discrimination, street attacks, anti-Chinese riots, and a movement for immigration restrictions and deportations threatened their existence as a people and a community.

From the time it was first established in 1870, the San Francisco Board of Health considered Chinatown the main source of disease in San Francisco, citing current medical theories to blame Chinatown's "unwholesome odors" for spreading sickness through the air, instead of ending the overcrowding and poverty forced on the residents by racial prejudice. This medical scape-goating left the Chinese extremely vulnerable to a local health panic. On May 6, 1900, the panic hit when the city's first case of bubonic plague was officially diagnosed in a Chinese male. The next day a rope and police guard were placed around Chinatown to quarantine its residents. During the next few months, health officials ordered every house in Chinatown disinfected, and both Chinese and Japanese Californians were forbidden to leave the state without federally issued medical certificates. Federal health officials began plans to set up detention camps for San Francisco's 14,000 Chinese people at Angel Island, China Cove, and in a Mission Rock warehouse.

Under attack while its own people were dying, the Chinese community fought for its survival. Faced with inadequate health care from the city, the Chinese community opened and financed its own Tung Wah Dispensary. Their lawyers took legal action against the quarantine measures and de-tention camps and won in federal courts, angering public health officials. When health inspectors began door-to-door searches, panicked residents locked their doors, hid their sick in basements, and rioted in the streets.

Despite this resistance, health officials continued to scapegoat the Chi-nese people in an effort to stop the epidemic. In the spring of 1903, the state Board of Health recommended that Chinatown be razed to the ground and saturated with chloride of lime and carbolic acid. Some buildings were condemned and destroyed, but before the plan could be completed, the 1906 earthquake and fire had destroyed downtown San Francisco, including Chi-natown. Of the 121 cases of plague recorded in the city during the epidemic, 118 died, almost all of them Chinese. As a result, bubonic plague became known as "an Oriental disease, peculiar to rice-eaters."

In 1907, a second outbreak of bubonic plague hit San Francisco; but this time few victims were Chinese, and the Board of Health had scientific evi-dence that rats and fleas, not the people and buildings of Chinatown, spread the disease. A citywide campaign to rat-proof basements and alleys quickly stopped the epidemic.

The gay community in 1984 is as vulnerable to health panics and scape-goating as was the Chinese community in 1900. Both communities have been forced into urban undergrounds and stigmatized as sources of disease. Because most of its victims in the United States have so far been gay men, AIDS, like the "Oriental disease, peculiar to rice-eaters," has become stereo-typed as a homosexual disease, peculiar to promiscuous bathhouse patrons.

Gay bathhouses have populated sexual landscapes of American cities since at least the turn of the century. San Francisco's first gay bathhouse opened downtown fifty years ago near Third and Market. These institutions have been remarkably resilient despite decades of harassment, entrapment, arrests, raids, license challenges, arson, and physical attacks on patrons. Recent attacks on bathhouses—like the mass arrests in Toronto in 1981—have been met with legal actions, angry demonstrations, and riots. Despite their problems, gay bathhouses have been so strongly defended because they have evolved into liberated zones where gay men—and more recently lesbians—can go for a few hours and escape the sex fears of society. They are unique, ever-changing erotic territories with their own rituals, folklore, language, and traditions. It is their mere presence as erotic territory that triggers the sex fears of gay and straight people alike and has made them one of the most vulnerable and defended gay institutions.

Today gay men need our bathhouses more than ever, but as radically changed institutions. Although there is no known cure for AIDS, it can be prevented if gay men limit their sexual activities to what is now being called "safe sex." AIDS prevention thus requires a massive effort to change gay men's sexual behavior—not an easy task—through sex education, peer support, and use of prophylactics (sailors used navy-issued condoms to fuck each other on destroyers during World War II) and by creating places to go for safe sex. Bathhouses are ideally suited for conversion to safe sex education and play areas. Large numbers of gay men still go to the baths, and many have sex nowhere else. Bathhouses provide showers, sex videos, fantasy rooms, mirrors, expensive bondage equipment, flower arrangements, lounges for talking, music—all the romantic and kinky elements that enhance safe sex practices with erotic fantasy but which many men cannot afford—or dare to have put—in their own homes.

Bathhouse owners have been living in a never-never land, pretending that AIDS and safe sex don't exist. A few are to be praised for recently offering free condoms, surgical scrub soap, individual lubricant packets, jack-off nights, and safe sex literature and forums. These are important steps in the right direction. Community groups and the health department should suggest more changes, and a community watchdog committee should monitor the baths to make sure these changes are put into effect immediately. Patrons have the responsibility to learn what is safe, practice it with a vengeance, teach each other, and come up with new ideas (like installing jack-off phone booths at the baths to call from the comfort of your home). The conversion of the bathhouses to safe sex play areas can become a model in AIDS prevention for other cities and can serve as yet another example of how adaptive we can be when we are fighting for our lives.

The closing of all gay bathhouses, on the other hand, will force casual sex underground, may help spread AIDS, and will invite a wave of political repression. When in 1956 state and local authorities put the heat on all lesbian and gay bars, gay bathhouses, and cruising areas in San Francisco, patrons took over straight bars, went to bars in San Mateo, Oakland, and San Jose, and had huge parties in their homes. A prohibition on bathhouses and sex clubs would similarly drive gay men into nearby cities, the parks, bathrooms, and "sexual speakeasies"—illegal clubs subject to pay-offs, raids, arrests, poor sanitary conditions, and underworld control. Gay men and women in their fifties and older can describe to you in excruciating detail the nightmare of fear, suspicion, health risks, and even suicide that is created in a sexual underworld forced underground.

Closing the baths is dangerous in other ways, too. By focusing on the sites of sexual activity instead of on actual sexual practices, it promotes the illusion that romantic sex with one person in private is safe. In addition, each time we beg the city to close one of our institutions, we place our whole community in jeopardy, especially the vulnerable people and places on our "sexual fringe." We in San Francisco have achieved respect as a social and political minority, but in much of the country gay men and women are still called sex deviates, sex perverts, sex degenerates, and queers. Gay bars and political groups in Mississippi and Oklahoma, for example, are considered sexually and morally dangerous by public officials who would love to have new reasons for making them illegal. If we in San Francisco ask the city to close our baths and sex clubs, then a dangerous message will be heard across the country: Gay men and women want to be saved from their own sexuality.

Bathhouses have to change and change fast. But symbolic actions such as closing the baths before we have even tried to transform them are dangerous and set the stage for a frightening scenario similar to that of Chinatown eighty years ago. Scapegoating didn't stop the plague then and it's not likely to stop AIDS now. But it will *invite* a wave of attacks on our communities. Instead of wasting time defending our very right to exist, as Chinatown was forced to do, we need to devote all our energy and resources, including bathhouses and sex clubs, to the task of making the sexual changes that will save our lives.

SOURCE

The source for the history of the San Francisco plague epidemic is Joan Traumer, "The Chinese as Medical Scapegoats in San Francisco, 1870–1905," *California History*, Spring 1978.

Resorts for Sex Perverts
A History of Gay Bathhouses

As the AIDS epidemic worsened and the sexual politics it provoked intensified, Bérubé de-
voted himself to historical research that was specifically sexual in its focus. The result was
this intervention in the public policy debates about how to respond to the epidemic. Based
on another innovative slide lecture and first published in a San Francisco gay newspaper
in the immediate wake of the city's closure of gay bathhouses, the article builds on and
extends the thematic concerns of the previous two essays. In it, Bérubé describes gay male
sexuality and the places where it could be expressed as forms and sites of resistance. Sex-
ual expression became a route to the creation of community, and the bathhouses proved
to be key locations where this happened over time. Arguing that, in the past, attempts at
repression have failed, he calls instead for more creative solutions that make use of gay
male spaces like bathhouses to educate the community about safer sex practices. One of
his more popular pieces, it has been reprinted and revised a number of times, as debates
about gay male sexuality and AIDS continued into the 1990s and beyond.

For centuries, society has stigmatized homosexual men and women as sin-
ners, criminals, and diseased because of their sexuality. Baths and bars were
the first institutions in the United States that contradicted these stigmas
and gave gay Americans a sense of pride in themselves and their sexuality.
As such, gay bars and baths are an integral part of gay political history.

Before there were any openly gay or lesbian leaders, political clubs, books,
films, newspapers, businesses, neighborhoods, churches, or legally recognized gay rights, several generations of pioneers spontaneously created gay
bathhouses and lesbian and gay bars. These men and women risked arrest,
jail sentences, loss of families, loss of jobs, beatings, murders, and the humiliation that could lead to suicide in order to transform public bars and
bathhouses into zones where it was safe to be gay. In a nation which has for

Originally published as "The History of Gay Bathhouses," *Coming Up!*, December 1984,
15–19. This version comes from the *Journal of Homosexuality* 44, no. 3/4 (2003): 33–53.

Title slide for Bérubé's lecture "Resorts for Sex Perverts." Courtesy of the Allan Bérubé Collection at the GLBTHS, San Francisco.

generations mobilized its institutions toward making gay people invisible, illegal, isolated, ignorant, and silent, gay baths and bars became the first stages of a movement of civil rights for gay people in the United States.

For the gay community, gay bathhouses represent a major success in a century-long political struggle to overcome isolation and develop a sense of community and pride in their sexuality, to gain their right to sexual privacy, to win their right to associate with each other in public, and to create "safety zones" where gay men could be sexual and affectionate with each other with a minimal threat of violence, blackmail, loss of employment, arrest, imprisonment, and humiliation.

Early History of Gay Bathhouses in the United States

The transformation of Turkish baths, Russian baths, public baths, health resorts, and spas into gay institutions began in the late nineteenth and early twentieth centuries in the United States. In California as in other states, all sex acts between men were illegal as "crimes against nature." Thus, men having sex with each other had no legal right to privacy. Records of California state appeals court cases around the turn of the century contain many cases of men who were arrested after landlords, housekeepers, neighbors, policemen, and YMCA janitors drilled tiny holes in walls; peeped through keyholes, transoms, and windows; or broke down doors to discover men having sex with each other. Because all sex acts between men were considered public and illegal, gay men were forced to become sexual outlaws. They became experts at stealing moments of privacy and at finding the cracks in society where they could meet and not get caught.

These "cracks in society" expanded as the rapidly growing cities of the late nineteenth and early twentieth centuries created more and more public places where men could be anonymous and intimate with each other. These included public parks at night; certain streets and alleys; empty boxcars in train yards; remote areas of beaches; YMCA rooms, steam rooms, and shower stalls; public restrooms in department stores, train stations, bus depots, parks, subway stations, and public libraries; balconies of silent movie theaters; cheap hotel rooms; parked automobiles; and bathhouses. These locations were attractive because they offered the protection of anonymity, a degree of privacy, and the possibility of meeting men interested in sex. They were dangerous because men who went there could be arrested, blackmailed, beaten, robbed, or killed.

Despite these dangers, a growing number of men risked having sex in these semipublic places. In San Francisco, early popular spots included the Ferry Building, Union Square, Market Street from the Embarcadero to Fifth Street, the corner of Powell and Market, the Embarcadero, the YMCA, the men's rooms in Macy's and the Emporium, the streets in the Tenderloin, the balconies of the Unique Theater and other movie houses on Market Street, the all-night cafeterias and their toilets on Market Street between Fifth and Third Streets, the Harman Baths, Sutro Turkish Baths, and the changing booths at Sutro Baths near the Cliff House.

Bathhouses evolved into gay institutions not by themselves, but in the context of the slowly developing sexual landscape in the nation's cities. Men—both heterosexual and homosexual—chose to meet each other in the bathhouses as alternatives to other places, usually for reasons of safety and privacy.

Historical records beginning in the 1890s document the four major stages in which bathhouses evolved into homosexual institutions.

1. *Ordinary Bathhouses*: Places where men would occasionally have sex but where it was unusual.
2. *Favorite Spots*: These bathhouses—and YMCAS—developed reputations as "favorite spots" for men to have sex with each other. Word got out that a certain manager, masseur, employee, or police officer

would look the other way when they were on duty, or that homo-sexuals were known to gather there at certain hours, usually in the afternoon or late at night. Some private bathhouse owners tried to prevent their places from becoming popular homosexual spots and called in the police or hired thugs and private guards. Others did not discourage their specialized clientele, paid off the cop on the neighborhood beat, told the managers and employees to keep things discreet, and increased their profits.

3. *Early Gay Bathhouses*: Mostly evolved in the 1920s and 1930s. Physically, they were no different than other Turkish or Russian baths, except that sex was permitted in closed and locked cubicles. These places were subject to raids by vice squads, in which the employees, managers, and owners could be arrested with their patrons. The owners sometimes tried to protect their patrons from arrest, blackmail, and violence if at all possible without hurting their businesses.

4. *Modern Gay Bathhouses*: In the 1950s and 1960s, the first of these began to open. These places were meant to be exclusively gay and catered to the sexual and social needs of gay men. With the be-ginning of the gay liberation movement in the 1970s, these bath-houses went through dramatic changes. Today there are approxi-mately 200 gay bathhouses in the United States, from Great Falls, Minnesota, and Toledo, Ohio, to New York City, Los Angeles, and San Francisco.

Many of the advantages of modern gay bathhouses were already recog-nized in the newspaper, medical, and legal reports describing the earliest "favorite spots."

1. *Safety*: Patrons felt they were more protected from blackmail at the baths than in other public places; the baths seemed to offer an alternative to sex in the public parks; and there was additional safety in numbers and in their identification as homosexual baths, because those who would be offended by the behavior there would not go there or would leave.

2. *Democracy and Camaraderie*: Some accounts describe "the early gay bathhouses" as refuges from society's prejudice against homo-sexuals, as oases of freedom and homosexual camaraderie. The clientele was primarily homosexual and from a variety of occupa-tions and classes, temporarily "democratic" in their nakedness. Members of the staff, too, were sometimes homosexual, making

these early baths one of the first identifiably gay social and sexual institutions.

3. *Privacy*: Sex took place in an establishment separated from the general citizenry. This created the first urban zone of privacy, as well as safety, for gay men.

4. *Erotic Facilities*: Cabins, steam rooms, dressing rooms, pools, and hot air rooms were all available for meeting other patrons. At primarily homosexual establishments, patrons could feel secure that other patrons would not be offended by physical intimacy between men.

5. *A Social Environment*: Old friendships could be renewed; "new intimacies" were "ever in the air." Patrons socialized with each other in the common areas.

6. *Protection*: The management and employees often tried to protect the patrons from violence and blackmail: The police generally allowed the bathhouses to stay open because they were discreet "outlets for the vast homosexual life of the city" and because some of the "best citizens" went there.

The Early History of Gay Bathhouses in San Francisco

In San Francisco, the first references to sex between men in the city's Turkish baths began in the 1890s. By the late 1920s and early '30s, a few of these "favorite spots" began to turn into predominantly gay bathhouses. These are the earliest gay bathhouses in San Francisco that anyone alive today remembers. One was known as the Palace Baths near the Palace Hotel; another was known as Jack's Baths on Third near Mission Street.

When these gay bathhouses emerged in the 1920s and 1930s, they offered homosexual men a new option: They could meet and have sex in a gay bathhouse, in addition to having sex with heterosexual men in a public bathhouse. Many men who came out before there were any gay baths looked down on having sex with other gay men. They had learned to prefer "servicing" straight men in semipublic places.

It was a later generation of gay men who, partly by using the gay bathhouses, learned to enjoy having sex with and loving other gay men. At a time when no one was saying "gay is good," the creation of an institution in which gay men were encouraged to appreciate each other was a major step toward gay pride. Since then, several generations of gay men—partly because of the opportunities provided them by gay bathhouses and, later, gay bars—have learned to prefer sexual partners who are also gay. The bathhouses, thus, are partly responsible for this major change in the sexual behavior and self-acceptance of gay men.

These first gay baths in San Francisco went through dramatic changes during World War II. Thousands of servicemen went to the baths in San Francisco before shipping overseas.

Many were afraid they would never return from the Pacific and felt they deserved one last chance to enjoy other men in the freedom of the baths. The baths were an important alternative to picking someone up in Union Square, the main gay cruising park in the city, because they offered a safe and private place at a time when hotel rooms downtown were impossible to find. They were also a useful alternative to the gay bars that began to open in San Francisco during the war, because many of the bars were declared "off-limits to military personnel."

During the 1950s, two major changes took place that affected the baths in San Francisco. For the first time, baths like the Club Turkish Baths in the Tenderloin had opened with the intent of catering to a homosexual clientele. These were the city's first modern gay bathhouses. But this happened at a time when an antihomosexual panic was sweeping the country, inspired by McCarthyism, and bathhouses as well as bars became the primary targets of antigay crackdowns and panics. The protective anonymity at the baths helped many gay men survive the crackdowns of the 1950s.

Despite the stepped-up attacks on gay baths and bars during the 1950s, which one local newspaper called a "war on homosexuals," more baths—and bars—slowly opened as explicitly gay institutions. In May of 1954, possibly the first guide to San Francisco's gay bars and baths was printed. It was a mimeographed sheet handed out at a Mattachine Society meeting—San Francisco's first gay organization. Warning that it was "Confidential and Unofficial," it listed Jack's Baths, the Club Baths on Turk, the Palace Baths on Third Street, and the San Francisco Baths on Ellis. In the 1960s, a second generation of modern gay baths opened, including Dave's Baths on Broadway (which moved from Sansome and Washington and claimed to be the first gay-owned bathhouse in San Francisco), the Baths on Twenty-first Street, and the Ritch Street Baths.

By the late 1960s and throughout the 1970s, gay bathhouses went through dramatic changes. They established themselves as a major gay institution that could both shape and respond to the rapid social, sexual, and political changes that were taking place. These important changes included

- San Francisco's Embarcadero YMCA, along with many YMCAs in other cities, had earned reputations as "favorite spots" for sexual activity at least as early as World War II. By the 1960s, according to men who were early frequenters of the Y, sexual activity there began to decline. Many of these men attribute this decline to the opening of gay baths during the same period.

- In March 1966, as gay bathhouses continued to open in San Francisco, the assistant police chief announced a "'crackdown' . . . on public baths . . . suspected of tolerating . . . homosexual problems." Undercover police arrested a Methodist minister at the Twenty-first Street Baths for "making sexual advances to a policeman," as well as a clerk who refused to call the police after the arrest of his patron. The crackdown was short lived, and the minister's trial ended in a hung jury.

- When the "Summer of Love" in 1967 created a new communal ethic among the hippie generation, "orgy rooms" were installed in some bathhouses where group sex became more popular.

- In January 1976, Representative Willie Brown's "consenting adult sex bill" went into effect in California. As a result, gay bathhouses and the sex that went on in them became legal for the first time.

- In January 1978, to test whether this new law applied to bathhouses, officers from Northern Station raided the Liberty Baths on Post Street and arrested three patrons for "lewd conduct" in a public place. This was the first bathhouse raid since the 1966 crackdown, but Police Chief Charles Gain denied that the police were beginning a new crackdown. The district attorney's office dropped the charges against the three men. "There's no question this was a private place," the DA's office said.

- In the late '70s, with the new technology that allowed the projection of videotapes onto large screens, bathhouses began installing video rooms where patrons could masturbate alone or with each other while watching gay sex videos that many could not afford to have at home. In fact, masturbation became a more acceptable practice in the bathhouses partly as a result of these videos.

- In the 1960s, '70s, and '80s, several bathhouses, including Dave's, the Barracks, Liberty Baths, and the Bulldog Baths, encouraged gay artists who were their employees or patrons to decorate the walls with erotic murals. For some artists, these murals were the first opportunity to create and display their art for an exclusively gay audience.

- In the 1970s, fantasy environments were installed that re-created the erotic situations that still were illegal, public, and dangerous outside the walls of the baths. Glory holes re-created the toilets. Mazes re-created park bushes and undergrowth. Steam rooms and gyms re-created the YMCA, and video rooms re-created the balconies and back rows of movie theaters. Cells re-created and transformed the environment of prisons and jails, where generations of gay men have ended up for risking sex in toilets, parks, and the YMCA.

- In the 1970s, some bathhouses featured entertainers that appealed to a gay male audience. The best-known was Bette Midler, who began her career performing to gay men at the Continental Baths in New York City. In San Francisco, one bathhouse opened a "Starlite Cabaret," which featured local singers and bands. Country-western bands also began playing on Western Night at the baths.

- Several bathhouses began to feature weekly "Movie Nights," when they presented current Hollywood films. At the same time, Hollywood produced two major films situated in gay bathhouses: "The Ritz" and "Saturday Night at the Baths."

- Many gay bathhouses threw parties for their members on major holidays: Lesbian and Gay Pride Day, Halloween, New Year's Eve, Christmas, Valentine's Day. These parties were a tremendous service to the gay men whose families had rejected them and for whom holidays represented a particularly depressing time of year. Holiday parties at the baths, especially for the men who frequented them regularly, could become a social event with familiar people that affirmed their sexuality. They offered a welcome alternative to loneliness and isolation.

- Also in the '70s, the City Clinic began to conduct free VD testing, usually by gay health workers, in many of the baths on a regular basis.

- In the 1970s, as the gay press in San Francisco began to come of age, newspapers like *Kalendar, Bay Area Reporter,* the *Sentinel,* the *Crusader, Databoy,* the *Voice, Coming Up!* and others were distributed for free in the bathhouses as well as the bars.

- Throughout the 1970s and 1980s, gay bathhouses offered their patrons a variety of new services: snack bars and cafes, dance floors for disco and country-western dancing, and theme nights such as Buddy Night and Western Night. They also served the gay community by sponsoring benefits for community organizations.

The 1980s witnessed even more dramatic changes at the baths. With the increased popularity of exercise and bodybuilding, gyms and workout rooms were installed. In the last year, safe sex posters, brochures, cards, and condoms have been displayed and given out, and safe sex forums have been held on the premises. In the last few months, orgy rooms, mazes, and glory holes have been boarded up. Several bathhouses introduced "jack-off" nights, and some made their facilities available to private gay male jack-off clubs.

The Urban Politics of Gay Bathhouse Raids, Closures, and Surveillance in Historical Perspective

Since they were first discovered by city officials in the United States, gay bathhouses and bars have been kept under surveillance by undercover police officers. Yet police departments have also tolerated gay baths and bars as practical solutions to the difficult law enforcement problems of controlling sex in public places. During periodic "anti-vice drives," "clean-up campaigns," and "morals drives," bars and bathhouses have been harassed, raided, and shut down by police, state liquor agents, district attorneys, military police, and arsonists. During these drives, plainclothes police officers have compiled secret reports on the sexual behavior inside bars and baths—"sexual behavior" that has included dancing, caressing, kissing, and invitations to one's home. Plainclothes officers have used entrapment techniques to entice gay men and women into illegal sexual activities. The city and state used this sexual "evidence" to close gay bars and baths in an attempt to deny homosexuals any legal places to congregate.

Since the nineteenth century, these campaigns against gay bars and baths have developed in urban politics as a strategy for attaining specific political goals, new laws, election to office, larger police budgets, and moral crusades. Their success at preventing homosexuals from gathering in public or in stopping gay sexual acts has at best been short lived.

On the surface, the goals of the early antibath and antibar campaigns in San Francisco were to protect the public morals, health, and safety by

- rounding up all homosexuals and driving them out of the city once and for all;
- eliminating all sex between men in public, semipublic, and even private places; and
- preventing homosexual men and women from meeting or socializing in public.

No campaign against San Francisco's gay bars or gay bathhouses has succeeded in attaining these three goals. Bars and baths remained open; homosexuals always stayed one step ahead of the police in finding new places to meet or have sex; gay men and lesbians were forced to become more politically aware and organized. These campaigns have always failed to achieve their stated goals because the social costs became too high or the real goals were eventually achieved: a new antigay law, a larger budget, or election to public office.

While the general public may quickly forget them, the stories of how gay men and women survived or were destroyed in these bathhouse and bar raids have passed down from one generation to another, told and retold as part of the unique history and culture of the lesbian and gay communities. As a result, gay men and women carry with them a lingering mistrust of government and its attempts to intervene in their lives. Any government attempt to once again eliminate all bars or all bathhouses, no matter how well motivated, cannot help but take its place in the long history of government attacks on homosexuals and their meeting places that has created this mistrust and kept it alive.

In addition, such a drastic measure as the closure of all gay bathhouses cannot avoid the unexpected social costs that have plagued city governments, the gay community, and the general public during similar campaigns in the past.

A Historical Perspective on the Bathhouse Closure, San Francisco, 1984

San Francisco has never attempted to close every gay bathhouse and sex club in San Francisco before. But from 1954 to 1965, the SFPD, the DA's office, state ABC agents, the *Examiner*, and the grand jury all joined forces in an attempt to shut down all gay bars. By 1955, these agencies succeeded in pressuring the California legislature to pass a law allowing the revocation of a bar's liquor license if it had the reputation as a "resort for sexual perverts." The anti–gay bar drive began in 1954 because, according to Police Chief Michael Gaffey, "a small army of homosexuals had invaded the city, many of them apparently driven here after other cities had been closed to them by similar raids." During these years, massive drives against gay and lesbian bars swept most large American cities as the bars developed into the major gay institution in the United States. These national antihomosexual campaigns created a growing population of gay refugees moving from city to city looking for safe places to live.

During a major crackdown in San Francisco following the passage of the "resorts for sex perverts" law, gay men and women were driven to Oakland, San Mateo, and San Jose. Police chiefs in these neighboring communities complained of a "huge influx" of "undesirables" and began conducting surveillance and raids of local bars whose weekend crowds had suddenly swelled with gay San Franciscans.

By 1958, fifteen of San Francisco's twenty gay bars had had their licenses challenged, and hundreds of bar patrons had been arrested. In 1959, one bar owner's appeal reached the California State Supreme Court, which ruled that homosexuals had a right to gather in public and that gay bars could remain licensed. But arrests and bar raids continued in the early 1960s, with police sending in undercover agents looking for "lewd acts" on the premises. By 1965, after hundreds of bar patrons had been arrested, public opinion began to turn against the police and in support of leaving gay bars alone. While many public officials still wanted to eliminate gay bars, the new pragmatic approach was summed up by the assistant district attorney: "It's better to have homosexuals in one resort rather than spread throughout the city."

An unexpected consequence of this ten-year attempt to close all gay bars was to transform the gay community into a politically aware minority in local politics. During the gay community's campaign to defend the bars, the Tavern Guild was formed, a gay press emerged and was distributed through the bars and baths, defense committees were set up, those arrested learned to plead not guilty in court, and the Council on Religion and the Homosexual was formed. By 1965, city officials finally realized that gay bars were a permanent part of the city and could not be eliminated without tremendous social, financial, and human costs. More than 120 lesbian and gay bars now operate in San Francisco.

It is impossible to predict exactly what social, financial, and health costs will result from the current bathhouse closure in San Francisco. However, in the two weeks since the closure of the baths, a pattern is already taking shape, which indicates that, as in past campaigns against the bars, the unexpected social and financial costs to the city threaten to become extremely high.

Goals: To stop the spread of AIDS by preventing gay men from
  engaging in "high risk" sexual contact with each other.
Targets: Gay bathhouses, sex clubs, and adult bookstores.
Agents: San Francisco Health Department, mayor's office, private
  undercover detectives, San Francisco Police Department,
  the courts.

Social/Financial Costs

(1) DISPERSION OF GAY BATHHOUSE PATRONS

Outside San Francisco: A bathhouse owner in Oakland reports that the weekend after the bathhouse closure, his business increased 142 percent, indicating that, as in the 1956 crackdown on gay bars, some bathhouse patrons prefer to relocate their sexual activity to other bathhouses remaining open. This places the burden of changing the sexual behavior of San Francisco residents onto our neighboring city governments.

To Old Sexual Territories: Historically the development of gay bathhouses has offered gay men and the police a practical solution to the danger and the law enforcement problems associated with sex in public places. Elimination of gay bathhouses should therefore re-create the pre-bathhouse sexual landscape. Reports have already appeared in the gay press, and stories are spreading through the gay community, that street arrests have stepped up on Polk Street and south of Market, and that mounted police have increased surveillance of Buena Vista Park. This suggests that sexual activity that had occurred in the baths is now occurring with more frequency in the parks and streets, and that the burden of controlling this behavior is now placed on the police department. If this is the case, then men who were previously law-abiding in their sexual activity are now being driven to criminal behavior. Bathhouse closure removes the legal alternative to "outlaw" sex and encourages the practice of sex outside the law.

Another "old territory" for sexual activity is the YMCA. Since the degree of sex activity in the YMCAs declined as gay bathhouses opened, it might be expected that sexual activity in the YMCAs would increase as bathhouses are closed. This predictable consequence has already taken place. On November 1, signs went up at the Central YMCA in response to increased sexual activity in the steam room and dry room following the bathhouse closure. "The Central YMCA is not a bathhouse," the signs read. "We will not function as one." The next day the steam room and dry room were closed. On November 3, they were reopened, but with the introduction of continual surveillance of the facilities.

(2) FINANCIAL COSTS

According to the health department's supplemental budget request, the initial expense of hiring detectives to conduct the surveillance that led to closure was $35,000, and an additional $25,000 has been requested for continued surveillance. To this must be added the costs of sending undercover

San Francisco police officers into the baths to compile the mayor's secret bathhouse sex report in March. Additional immediate costs include court costs following sex arrests, filing the city's suit against the bathhouses, and processing the bathhouse and sex club closures through the state appeals courts, with the possibility that, as in the past, the bathhouses will ultimately remain open.

(3) POLITICAL CONSEQUENCES

As might be expected, bathhouse closure has already forced portions of the gay community to organize themselves around defending the baths, as the gay community has done in the past to defend the bars in San Francisco and the baths in Toronto. New gay organizations already include the Northern California Bathhouse Owners' Association, the Adult Entertainment Association, the Community Partnership (a coalition of gay community groups), and the Committee to Preserve Our Sexual and Civil Liberties. In addition, antigay organizations, including the Moral Majority, the Cops for Christ, and a group in San Antonio, Texas, have begun to use the bathhouse closure to fuel their antigay campaigns.

Conclusions

As a historian whose research has focused on the social effects of attacks against gay institutions in the past, it is clear to me that the attempted closure of the baths will only relocate the sexual activity that has taken place in the baths. In addition, the unexpected social, financial, and health costs to the gay community, the city, and the general public will be high. Bathhouse closure will create more problems than it will solve.

To avoid unexpected social problems and still take strong measures to halt the spread of AIDS, I suggest that

1. *Bathhouses should be used as a community resource to promote safe sex and safe sex education.* Bathhouses have undergone dramatic changes over the last 100 years, changes that gay men have sometimes risked and lost their lives to bring about. They have become an integral part of the gay community. In the last year they have changed even more dramatically by taking measures to encourage safe sex practices and education. The baths should be allowed to continue these rapid changes in order to serve the community's needs during the present health crisis. They should entice gay men into them, especially if they now engage in high-risk sex, so they

can be exposed to more safe sex education. They should function as erotic environments where safe sex activity can be encouraged and where men can enjoy sexual intimacy and affection in an environment that is safe, clean and pro-gay.

2. *Bathhouses should be preserved as zones of safety, privacy, and peer support as long as gay men are attacked for their sexuality.* Harvey Milk once called our society "fiercely heterosexual," a dangerous place to be gay. Since his murder six years ago last month, things have not changed. Gay men and lesbians are still assaulted and attacked every day for their sexuality. A national survey recently discovered that over 90 percent of gay men and lesbians have been physically attacked or otherwise victimized because they were gay. Gay bathhouses still represent one of the very few places where gay men can escape the antigay hostility that still is out of control in our city and our nation.

3. *A working relationship of cooperation and trust between the city and the gay community is critical in the fight against AIDS.* Bathhouse closure, together with the sex arrests and political backlash that are likely to follow, will make city agencies and the gay community adversaries once again. This will increase mistrust and lack of compliance with government health programs. Until recently, a remarkable aspect of the fight against AIDS has been the cooperative relationship between the government and the gay community that is unprecedented. The breakdown of that relationship will endanger lives and obstruct the health measures necessary to halt the spread of AIDS.

To defend its case for closure, the health department has already begun to stigmatize segments of the gay community. It has called bathhouse owners "merchants of death" and bathhouse patrons "Evel Knievels of medicine." It has also revived the old rhetoric of crime and disease that was used to attack the bars. Part of the old antigay rhetoric was that "sick" people went to the bars to spread the "disease" of homosexuality. In its press statement announcing closure of the baths, the health department similarly portrayed the bathhouse as "not fostering gay liberation" but instead "fostering disease and death." This inflammatory rhetoric and scapegoating only adds to the gay community's fears that it is once again under attack.

Recently, reports that the Centers for Disease Control considered establishing an HTLV-3 [an earlier name for what is now called HIV] name registry have also increased gay men's fears of government persecution. As a result of these fears, a UC Berkeley epidemiological study that the gay community desperately needs may now be doomed for lack of volunteers. The bathhouse closure further increases the mistrust of health authorities. Fears have even been expressed that confidential bathhouse membership lists might be used to discriminate against these men.

My research over the past five years has revealed that the gay community's fears that the government will compile massive lists of names, enforce quarantines, and establish detention camps for homosexuals are justified. Both the army and navy after World War II compiled lists of over 10,000 men suspected of being homosexual. In 1956, the FBI compiled a fifty-three-page list of homosexuals in San Francisco and their friends. The federal government still has these lists. Several times during World War II, the Navy Department considered a plan to set up detention camps where homosexuals identified by the military would be interned for the duration of the war, not to punish them, but allegedly to protect the nation.

As a historian, it is clear to me that yet another government campaign to dismantle gay institutions, even in the well-motivated attempt to stop the spread of AIDS, will only backfire. Instead, the city should join the gay community in using these institutions creatively. The city's goals should include positive steps toward (1) dispelling fears that the city is attacking the gay community, (2) rebuilding a working relationship of trust and cooperation with the gay community, and (3) decreasing scapegoating and restoring morale. Bathhouse closure, surveillance of sexual activity, sex arrests, the compiling of lists of names, and scapegoating will only undermine these goals.

Instead of wasting its time defending its bathhouses, its bars, and its very right to exist, the gay community must be allowed to devote all of its resources, including the bathhouses, toward promoting the research, health programs, and safe sex educational measures that will save lives.

PART II

A National Historian

Reexamining World War II

Marching to a Different Drummer
Lesbian and Gay GIs in World War II

This is the first essay that Bérubé published based on the research that culminated in his award-winning book, Coming Out Under Fire: The History of Gay Men and Women in World War II *(1990). In it, he draws on oral histories, correspondence, and other documentary evidence to reconstruct the experience of gay men and lesbians during World War II. Written in the tradition of the New Social History of the 1960s and 1970s, it relates the experience of ordinary Americans rather than the rich, famous, and powerful. Bérubé makes the argument that World War II was "a turning point" in gay and lesbian history and that it "lay the groundwork for gay life as we know it" by helping to build the urban communities of the postwar decades. In that sense, the war years were to Bérubé "as crucial . . . as the 1969 Stonewall Rebellion." Written while he was still in the early stages of research for the book, it was published in the* Advocate, *the national gay newspaper with the largest circulation at the time. It spread the word about his project and helped him find other men and women to interview.*

The U.S. military has a long tradition of purging homosexuals from its ranks. In January 1982, the Pentagon released a directive that may be its strongest antigay policy to date. "Homosexuality is incompatible with military service," the directive explained, because it undermines military discipline, creates security risks, and gives the military a bad reputation. Even a member of the armed forces who "has stated that he or she is a homosexual" or "desires" to "engage in homosexual conduct" is considered a threat to the military under these rules.[1]

The massive mobilization of all Americans for World War II allowed the U.S. military to adopt its first explicit antihomosexual policy, which included provisions for temporarily utilizing homosexual men and women

Originally published in the *Advocate*, October 15, 1981, 20–25. Revised for *Hidden from History: Reclaiming the Gay and Lesbian Past*, edited by Martin Duberman, Martha Vicinus, and George Chauncey Jr., 383–94 (New York: New American Library, 1989).

Jumping with Jodie, World War II all-male musical produced by black soldiers stationed in Germany. Army Signal Corps photograph SC-208040 (National Archives). Courtesy of the World War II Project Papers at the GLBTHS, San Francisco.

in situations that served the war effort. As one Women's Army Corps (WAC) officer testified early in 1944, during a secret investigation into lesbian activity in the WAC, "The Surgeon General's Office in the latest circular letter, particularly for soldiers overseas, [stressed] that homosexual relationships should be tolerated" as long as they were private, consensual, and did not disrupt the unit.[2] The military, in spite of its contempt for homosexuals, was not above using lesbian and gay GIs when it needed them to win a war.

The implementation of this secret policy was just one of the radical social changes that made World War II a turning point in the lives of lesbian and gay Americans. The massive war mobilization forced many American women and men to discover their homosexuality for the first time, to end their isolation in small towns and find other people like themselves, and to strengthen their identity as a minority in American society. Their experiences in the military and on the assembly line, their discovery of gay nightlife in the cities, and their struggle to survive the postwar antigay crackdowns all helped to lay the groundwork for gay life as we know it today. World War II was as crucial to these women and men as the 1969 Stonewall Rebellion would be to a later generation, but its impact was lost in the tragedy of a world war, with no gay movement or gay press to record its history.

Most Americans, when they talk about World War II, begin by telling what they were doing on December 7, 1941, the day Pearl Harbor was attacked. Stuart Loomis, a gay man who was twenty-one and still living in a Nebraska town, remembers "sitting upstairs in the balcony of Walgreen's drugstore late in the afternoon, listening to a rebroadcast of President Roosevelt's announcement to Congress and talking with my friends—my gay set—over malted milks and peanut butter sandwiches, about what we were going to do. What was going to happen to us?"[3]

Stuart Loomis's generation soon discovered that the war mobilization made them part of a massive migration of Americans. More than 15 million civilians—mostly women—moved across state lines during the war, lured by the millions of new defense jobs, while nearly as many men were drafted into the military. Black workers moved to northern and West Coast cities where they found new jobs; servicemen and their families flocked to port cities; Japanese Americans were "relocated" to internment camps while the government shipped Mexican farm workers into California to replace the evacuated Japanese workers. This massive mobilization radically changed the character of American life during the war. Women, for example, found a new opportunity to leave male-run households and live in all-female worlds. As wage earners working in well-paying defense jobs, wearing men's clothes to do "men's work," and living, working, and relaxing with each other, many women for the first time fell in love with other women, socialized with lesbians, and explored the gay nightlife that flourished in the crowded cities.

Lisa Ben left a small northern California town and moved to Los Angeles to find secretarial work. "I got my own room," she recalled,

> with kitchen privileges, and from there I met some gay girls. They lived on the floor above me, and one day we were all sunbathing on the garage roof, and they got to talking and I got to listening. . . .
> So when I heard these girls talk, I started talking, and finally they asked me, "Do you like boys, or do you go out strictly with girls?"
> And I said, "If I had my rathers, I'd go out strictly with girls," and they said, "Have you always felt this way?" and I said, "Yes," and they said, "Well, then you're like we are" and I said, "You mean, you're like that?" Then they took me to a girls Softball game. . . . Then we went to the If Club, dancing, and ah!, that was where I met lots of girls.[4]

Lisa Ben's coming-out experience so radically changed her life that immediately after the war, she began the first lesbian newsletter in the United States, which she called *Vice-Versa*.

Perhaps the most unusual experience for American women in World War

II was the chance to enlist in the military, the largest women's branch being the Women's Army Corps, with nearly 150,000 women in the ranks. Unlike male branches of the military, however, which consisted primarily of draftees, the WAC was an all-volunteer corps. A nationwide campaign encouraged women to sign up with the WACs as well as with the Women Marines, the Women's Army Air Corps, the WAVEs, and the Coast Guard SPARs. The official rationale for recruiting women was that they were "releasing men to fight," but authorities later admitted that women also enlisted to overcome the restrictions of conventional women's roles, to learn new skills, and, for "a certain number of women," to "be with other women."[5] These women who chose to "be with other women" enlisted in great numbers, and lesbians seem to have made up a large percentage of the corps.

WAC officers faced a difficult dilemma when it came to formulating a policy on lesbian relationships within the corps. On the one hand, since the public had stigmatized the WAC as an army of lesbians and prostitutes, officers tried to prevent any disruptive witch hunts that might further discredit the corps and its recruiting program. On the other hand, while encouraging intimacy because it helped the corps, officers tried to discourage any overt homosexual behavior. The official WAC policy on homosexuality was made clear in a secret lecture to officer candidates in 1943, which warned against "indulging in witch hunting or speculation." It was explained that, without men, women naturally formed "relationships in companionship and working together." The lecture even acknowledged the experience of coming out in the WAC: "Sometimes [a relationship] can become an intimacy that may eventually take some form of sexual expression. It may appear that, almost spontaneously, such a relationship has sprung up between two women, neither of whom is a confirmed active homosexual."[6]

The lecturer was right. Life in the military provided many opportunities for women to form lesbian relationships. "Sami," a lesbian veteran, described how she came out in the navy during the war:

> I was sitting in the barracks in Florida, and this one woman that I
> admired greatly—she was a little older than I, very articulate, very up,
> and a lot of fun—I just adored her. We were sitting next to each other
> on the couch with our feet propped up on the table and she started
> stroking my leg, and I thought, "Wow! What's all this!" And I just
> got terribly excited about it. I just was instantly enchanted with this
> woman and had a lot of sexual attraction toward her. Eventually we
> got in bed together. We never talked about it but we had a mad, mad
> love affair. . . . She had said that she had never related to a woman

before. We didn't talk about what we were doing, we just did it and felt good about it. I just thought, well, this is the way it's going to be forever.[7]

Women in every branch of the military had similar experiences during the war. WAC officers were instructed by their superiors that only women whom they could prove to be "addicted to the practice" were to be discharged. "Any officer," warned the lecturer, "bringing an unjust or unprovable charge against a woman in this regard will be severely reprimanded."[8]

Early in 1944 the policy against witch hunting was put to a test. The mother of a WAC recruit wrote to Washington, complaining that Fort Oglethorpe, a WAC basic training camp in Georgia, was "full of homosexuals and sex maniacs." The inspector general's office sent an emergency team to investigate. Witnesses testified that

> women having the appearance of perverts have been observed at Fort Oglethorpe; . . . these women affect mannish appearance by haircut, by the manner of wearing the clothing, by posture, by stride, by seeking "to date" other girls such as a man would, and when with other girls pay all the bills. . . . These addicts have certain signals by which they recognize each other. . . . The signal is said to be a whistle of the "Hawaiian War Chant." . . . Expressions common between them are said to include, "We're going to have a gay time tonight"; "Are you in the mood?" and "Messing around."

In spite of this testimony, the investigative team concluded that they could not find any real homosexual "addicts" and concerned themselves rather with how to keep as many of these women in the WAC as possible. Clearly Washington needed lesbian WACs to do their part in winning the war. The report recommended that there be no further investigations for the duration of the war.[9]

Gay men, as well as women, discovered that the war mobilization also gave them new opportunities to come out, but for different reasons. The tension of living in the all-male world of the military, the comradeship that came with fighting a common enemy, and the loneliness of being away from home in strange cities looking for companionship all helped to create a kind of "gay ambiance," as one veteran put it. Servicemen openly cruised each other in the anonymity of crowded bus and train stations, city parks, restrooms, YMCAS, beaches, and streets. They doubled up in hotel beds, slept on the floor in movie theaters, and went home with strangers when there was no other place to sleep.

While this gay ambiance was attractive to many gay men, foremost in their minds after Pearl Harbor was an eagerness to participate in the war effort. Their patriotism was sometimes dampened, however, by rumors that the military was mistreating gay servicemen. Shortly before Pearl Harbor, both the army and navy made it their policy to keep all homosexuals out of the service. While men in World War I had been court-martialed for committing homosexual acts, never before had the U.S. military set out to identify and reject all homosexual recruits.

This impossible task created a dilemma for military authorities. How could they eliminate homosexuals from their ranks when they needed every warm body they could get? And how were they going to tell exactly who was genuinely homosexual? The military assigned the task of identifying homosexuals to draft board members and military doctors, who were supposed to become experts on homosexuality overnight. Standardized psychiatric testing, developed after World War I, made their job a little easier. Millions of men were asked at induction physicals if they had ever had homosexual feelings or experiences. For many, this was the first time that they had had to think of their lives in homosexual terms. This mass sexual questioning was just one of the ways that homosexuality became an issue during the war.

Gay men who wanted to serve in the military could easily get past this screening, however. "I walked into this office," recalls Bob Ruffing, who enlisted in the navy, "and here was this man who was a screaming belle—lots of gold braid but he was a queen if I ever saw one. And he asked me the standard questions, ending up with, 'Did you ever have any homosexual experiences?' Well, I looked at him right in the eye and said, 'No.' And he looked right back and said, 'That's good.' Both of us lying through our teeth."[10]

Most of these interviews lasted no more than three minutes. How could you identify a homosexual in three minutes? Easy, reported *Newsweek*. You could tell homosexuals by "their effeminate looks and behavior and by repeating certain words from their homosexual vocabulary and watching for signs of recognition." This screening, needless to say, identified only obviously effeminate men, many of whom were not gay. "Scores of these inverts," *Newsweek* complained, "managed to slip through induction centers." The military, in fact, accepted possibly a million or more gay men into the ranks during the war.[11]

Many gay soldiers, however, did not even know they were homosexual until they were in the armed forces, where life in the barracks was especially charged with homosexual tension. A wartime psychiatric study of barracks life described what it called "homosexual buffoonery," a game that straight men played with each other. "In the barracks," the study observed, usually when the men are getting undressed . . . various persons will "kiddingly" assume the role of the overt homosexual. One soldier, returning from the shower in the nude, will be greeted with catcalls, salacious whistling, comments like "Hey Joe! You shouldn't go around like that—you don't know what that does to me!" Joe will respond by wriggling his hips in a feminine fashion after coyly draping a towel around himself. . . . Others act the part of active solicitors for sexual favors. "How much do you want for sleeping with me tonight?"; "Come into my bed and I'll give you the time of your life."[12]

Young gay draftees had to grow up fast to survive being surrounded by all this joking about queers. While some gay men found safety in keeping to themselves, others sought out each other for support. "When I first got in the navy," recalled one man, "in the recreation hall, for instance, there'd be eye contact, and pretty soon you'd get to know one or two people and kept branching out. All of a sudden you had a vast network of friends, usually through this eye contact thing, sometimes through outright cruising. You could get away with it in that atmosphere."[13] These circles of gay friends were well known in military life. "You kind of migrated to other gays in the barracks," explained an army man, "and sometimes it would be referred to as the 'fruit corner' or the 'fruit salad.' But not with much violent intent. You were thought to be queer, but nobody could prove anything, unless you were caught."[14]

While the military generally tolerated gay men because of the manpower shortage, getting caught having sex with a man could be a serious crime. The brigs were notorious for guards who enjoyed beating up gay prisoners as well as prisoners of color. If a gay man was thrown in the brig, he found himself in a no-man's-land, where even his gay friends avoided him to protect themselves.

Some gay men could not take the harassment or isolation of life in the military and tried to get out. Army regulations clearly stated that homosexuality was an "undesirable habit or trait of character" and sufficient grounds for discharge. The catch-22 procedure for discharge, however, involved special board hearings, hospitalization in the psychiatric ward, the risk of a court-martial, and even a prison sentence. Discharges for homosexuality, often printed on blue paper, were sometimes called "blue discharges"; neither honorable nor dishonorable, they labeled a gay man or lesbian as an "undesirable." Blue discharges could have "HS" or other codes for homosexual stamped on them, disqualifying a veteran from all GI rights and benefits and often preventing women as well as men from getting a civilian job. The thousands of men and women who received these discharges formed the first wave of gay veterans to seek refuge in New York, San Francisco, Los Angeles, and other cities during the war.

As a result of these discharge procedures, military psychiatric wards were often filled with gay patients, some trying to get out of the military, others being kicked out. Psychiatrists took advantage of these captive patients to develop new techniques for identifying homosexuals. One study of over 200 gay patients in an army hospital in 1944 observed, "Homosexuals tend to group together and it is interesting to observe the speed and certainty with which they are able to recognize one another. Within a few hours after admission to the ward, the homosexual will have located others of his type and becomes one of the group. They tend to stay grouped together and rarely include heterosexuals in their activities. . . . It is wise to insist that these cases be hospitalized for observation."[15]

A study of 1,400 patients in another hospital made its purpose even clearer. Homosexuals, the study observed, did not show a "gag reflex" when a tongue depressor was put down their throat. This "Gag Reflex Test," the study concluded, "is a definite aid in screening candidates not only for the military services, but for positions where the sexual deviate must be eliminated."[16] This military identification of homosexuals set a precedent for the massive screenings and purges of homosexual women and men and their acquaintances from federal agencies following the war.

While the military discharged thousands of men for being homosexual during the war, few were sent to prison. Those who were, however, were segregated, often received brutal treatment, and were set up as examples for the rest of the troops. A black serviceman stationed at the racially segregated Tuskegee Army Air Field in Alabama describes how officers treated black soldiers charged with homosexuality:

> The way they dealt with the black troops was that if you were identi-
> fied as a "punk" or you were caught or confessed, you were removed
> from your position and you were given a pair of blue fatigues. You
> were made to know that if you got in trouble there was nobody going
> to help you. "Even Mrs. Roosevelt ain't gonna come down here." They
> even pointed out a tree where several people had been lynched. And
> you learned that very early. They put them in the blue outfits, put
> them in a barracks by themselves, where the sissies, the punks, were.
> Each was assigned eight men to march them three times a day from
> the barracks to the mess hall, taking the catcalls and stuff. It was hor-
> rible. I remember one man—I went up to him one morning and I put

my hand on him and said, "It's terrible what's going on," and he said, "Stay away from me, or you'll be called one too."[17]

Most gay men stayed in the military and ultimately received honorable discharges. For these men, being gay in the military could have its special advantages, particularly for young draftees who had never left home. "You see," a twenty-year-old draftee wrote to a gay friend in 1945, "the army is an utterly simplified existence for me—I have no one to answer to as long as I behave during the week and stay out of the way of the MP on weekends. If I go home, how can I stay out all night or promote any serious affair? My parents would simply consider me something perverted and keep me in the house."[18]

With weekend passes and furloughs, the military gave its personnel the freedom to explore the gay nightlife that flourished during the war. In large cities, servicemen and women found gay bars like Bradley's in Hollywood, the Black Cat in San Francisco, Mary's Tavern in Denver, and a small number of lesbian bars, such as the If Club in Los Angeles and Mona's in San Francisco. These were among the first exclusively gay or lesbian bars in America. They branched out from, and sometimes replaced, the bohemian cafes, hotel bars, skid row taverns, nightclubs, and cafeterias of the 1930s where "queers," "fairies," and "dykes" could blend in with other social outcasts. These few meeting places of the Depression could not handle the large number of homosexuals uprooted by the war. As a result, lesbians and gay customers moved from bar to bar looking for a place that would accept their business. Bar owners sometimes discovered that catering to a gay crowd could improve their business, at least until the police or military put the heat on. Lesbians and gay men took advantage of a more tolerant social climate during the war to stake out a new public turf in these bars. Later, in the 1950s and 1960s, the successors to these wartime bars, which lawmakers called "homosexual hangouts," became a major battleground in the fight for public meeting places free from harassment.[19]

While lesbians and gay men could meet each other in these bars, or military bases, and even in defense plants, it was difficult for anyone to maintain a lasting relationship during the war. Lovers were transferred to other bases; couples and circles of friends split up as troops, including women's units, were sent overseas. Sometimes lovers never came back. Countless lesbians and gay men during the war faced the deaths of their lovers silently and alone.

A black aircorpsman who was stationed in the South remembers how he faced the death of his boyfriend.

In those days we couldn't tell anybody who we were. But we liked to be together. I used to send him books, and I had lunch with him. We played the game of "circling," which is all you could do in those days. He came up to my office one morning and he said, "I'd like to have lunch with you. Can you meet me at 12:00 at the PX?" I said that would be good. And at 11:45 I looked out the window and I could see this burst. His plane blew up in front of my face. He was killed. You never really get over something like that. And you know, something happened. I stopped living for a while. And I couldn't grieve, because I'd be a punk if I grieved, and be treated like those men in the blue outfits.[20]

Because of these separations, letters and photographs became absolute necessities of life. But lesbians and gay men writing letters to their lovers and friends faced the special problem of wartime censorship. Military censors, of course, cut out all information that might aid the enemy, but this surveillance made it necessary for gay and lesbian correspondents to be careful not to expose their homosexuality. To get around this, gay men befriended sympathetic censors or tricked others by using campy phrases, signing a woman's name (like Dixie or Daisy), or changing the gender of their friends. Sailors became WAVES, boyfriends became WACS, Robert became Roberta. There must exist, hidden in closets and attics all over America, a huge literature of these World War II letters between lesbians and between gay men that would tell us even more about this important part of American history.

By the end of the war, in August 1945, most Americans were exhausted from years of casualties, rationing, long work hours, and separations from loved ones and were anxious to settle down to a normal life again. Unfortunately, "normal life" meant different things to different people. For black Americans, it meant losing wartime jobs and stepping up their fight against segregation and discrimination. For women, it meant a return to the home as wives and mothers. And for lesbians and gay men, it meant witch hunts, bar raids, arrests, and a retreat to the closet.

The tolerance that some homosexual men and women experienced during the war proved to be all too temporary. Many patriotic lesbians and gay men saw their wartime freedom disappear as the country they fought for began to turn against them with the advent of peace. Churches, the media, schools, and government agencies conducted a heavy-handed campaign to reconstruct the nuclear family, to force women back into their traditional roles, and to promote a conservative sexual morality. A tactic of this campaign was to isolate homosexual men and women and identify them, like Communists, as dangerous and invisible enemies. These attacks on non-conformists of all kinds soon replaced the live-and-let-live climate of the war years.

Throughout the war, to prepare for peacetime, the government, industry, and the media had carefully controlled the radical social changes that were necessary to win the war. Advertisements reminded women that even though their labor was desperately needed in heavy industry, their jobs were only temporary and ultimately belonged to men. America was supposed to come first both in war and in peace, and their return as head of the household was one of the goals that men and women were both supposed to be fighting for. By early 1945, as soon as the end of the war was in sight, the media began to prepare the nation's women and men for their reentry into "normal" life. "Rosie the Riveter," the media's symbol for women working in heavy industry during the war, disappeared from the magazine covers, replaced by the traditional symbol of American womanhood: the young mother and wife, whose fantasies were of babies, whose only joy was to please her husband and children and to buy new appliances for her kitchen. The media took the reality of postwar families struggling to reestablish their lives and transformed it into hard-hitting propaganda for the nuclear family. Lesbians and gay men, many of them unable or unwilling to conform to this narrow family ideal, stood out more and more as "queers" and "sex deviates" who endangered the fragile security of the postwar American family.

While the media tried to lure women back into the home, the government drove women out of industry and the military. Thousands of women working in shipyards, for example, were fired shortly after V-J Day. Antilesbian witch hunts in the military, generally avoided during the war, spread like an epidemic after the war. The extent of these witch hunts is still unknown, but we are beginning to realize that they affected hundreds of women. Many lesbian veterans remember them with horror and pain. "I was trained as an aviation machinist mate," remembers a woman stationed at a Florida naval base in 1945, "which is not a usual women's task. [My] first important love relationships with women were in the navy. And then—this was near the end of the war—the interrogation came about and I was terrified. I remember I was interrogated and was scared to death and just lied through my teeth. I stopped running around with the women I was running around with and felt very isolated. The other people that I had been really friendly with—the relationships just were cut off completely."[21] In the film *Word Is Out*, Pat Bond recalled what happened to her WAC unit stationed in occupied Japan after the war: "They started an incredible witch hunt in Tokyo. Unbelievable, sending five hundred women home for dishonorable discharges. Every day there were courts-martial and trials—you were there testifying against your friends, or they were testifying against you . . . until you got afraid to look your neighbor in the eye. Afraid of everything."[22] These women had nowhere to turn. Gay and lesbian organizations did not yet exist, and liberal and radical organizations refused to help homosexuals who pleaded with them for support.[23]

According to some veterans, similar military purges affected gay men after the war at U.S. bases in Europe, Asia, and stateside. Thousands of men were put in detention barracks and shipped home with dishonorable discharges on special "queer" ships. On some bases, gay office workers were able to sabotage these purges by warning their friends just before the investigation teams arrived. Many of these discharged personnel could not return to their hometowns, so they remained in port cities, where they became a part of the rapidly growing urban gay population in the early 1950s.

The civilian world had its counterpart to the military witch hunts. The U.S. Senate and many state legislatures held unprecedented antihomosexual hearings, causing the firing of thousands of men and women from government jobs merely for being suspected of "homosexual perversion." The FBI began nationwide surveillance of gay and lesbian bars, compiling enormous lists of homosexuals and "associates of homosexuals." In addition, local antigay crusades swept through many American towns and cities, particularly where gay bars had become most visible and were continuing to multiply. Refugees from these crackdowns moved from city to city, looking for more tolerant surroundings. A San Francisco grand jury even held special hearings to curb what it called a postwar "invasion of sex deviates." States began to pass laws to close down the growing number of bars that catered to "sex perverts," both male and female. Massive bar raids and street arrests received prominent coverage in the press. Pulp magazines, exploiting the national paranoia, ran antigay articles in nearly every issue, with titles such as "Hidden Homos and How to Spot Them."

How did the postwar years affect the new generation of lesbians and gay men? Many returning veterans based their decisions for civilian life on their newly discovered homosexuality. "I can't change," wrote a gay GI in a letter shortly before his discharge in 1946. "I have no desire to change, because it took me a long, long time to figure out how to enjoy life. For you'll agree, I'm not going back to what I left."[24] Many veterans left their parents, abandoned small towns, and migrated to large cities they had seen for the first time during the war. There they created lesbian and gay neighborhoods, risked going to the growing number of lesbian and gay bars, and looked for work that would allow them to lead relatively open lives. Others, who had found lovers after the war, tried to settle down into quiet, private lives and even joined the exodus to the suburbs. Reuniting with wartime friends, they socialized with other gay couples in their homes and avoided the bars. With the heat on in public gay life, private homes were often the safest places to be gay.

While this backlash pushed many into the closet, it also forced others to realize the extent of their oppression, their identity as a minority, and the power of their numbers. Like the GI facing his discharge, many could not go back to what they left. Some even came out with a vengeance. It was thus no accident that the postwar years witnessed the birth of a small gay and lesbian movement in America, beginning with veterans' social groups, the Mattachine Society, and the Daughters of Bilitis. The taste of freedom during the war, the magnitude of the postwar crackdown, and the example of the growing black civil rights movement caused more and more lesbians and gay men to think of themselves as an unjustly persecuted minority. They increasingly realized that when they defended their new bars from attacks by queer bashers, when lesbians kicked straight men out of their bars, when bar owners challenged the cops and liquor control boards, and when lesbian and gay defendants began to plead "not guilty" in court, they were actually fighting to establish a public turf of their own, defending their right to gather in public places. After they returned home, the generation of World War II veterans began to lay the groundwork that made the Stonewall Rebellion and gay liberation possible.

Acknowledgments

This article was originally published in the *Advocate*, October 15, 1981, and is based on the script of the author's slide lecture "Marching to a Different Drummer." The author wishes to thank the following people for their assistance and support in developing the script for this slide/lecture: Jonathan Katz, John D'Emilio, JoAnn Castillo, and others doing lesbian and gay history research; the members of the San Francisco Lesbian and Gay History Project; the women and men who agreed to be interviewed about their World War II experiences; the women and men who sponsored showings of the presentation in their homes to raise funds for initial research expenses; and many others whose names cannot be included here.

1. Department of Defense Directive 1332.14 (encl. 3), Enlisted Administrative Separations, January 28, 1982, Section H, pp. 1-9 to 1-13.

2. Report, "Investigations of Conditions in the 3d WAC Training Center, Fort Oglethorpe, Georgia," July 19, 1944, p. 25, file 333.9, Record Group 159, National Archives.

3. Author's interview with Stuart Loomis, March 25, 1980, San Francisco.

4. Leland Moss, "An Interview with Lisa Ben," *Gaysweek*, January 23, 1978, 14–16.

5. William C. Menninger, *Psychiatry in a Troubled World* (New York: Macmillan, 1948), 106.

6. "Sex Hygiene Course, Officers and Officer Candidates, Women's Army Auxiliary Corps," May 27, 1943, War Department Pamphlet no. 35-1 (Washington, D.C.: Government Printing Office, 1943), "Lecture I: Introduction," 3–4, and "Lecture V: Homosexuality," 24–29.

7. Interview with "Sami" (pseud.) by JoAnn Castillo, San Francisco Lesbian and Gay History Project.

8. "Sex Hygiene Course," 28–29.

9. Report, "Investigations," 1, 29–30. For a comparison between World War II and postwar military policies toward lesbians, see Allan Bérubé and John D'Emilio, "The Military and Lesbians during the McCarthy Years," *Signs: Journal of Women in Culture and Society* 9, no 4 (Summer 1984): 759–75, reprinted in *The Lesbian Issue: Essays from Signs*, edited by Estelle B. Freedman, Barbara C. Gelpi, Susan L. Johnson, and Kathleen M. Weston, 279–95 (Chicago: University of Chicago Press, 1985).

10. Author's interview with Bob Ruffing, May 14, 1980, San Francisco.

11. "Homosexuals in Uniform," *Newsweek*, June 9, 1947, 54. The estimate of 1 million gay servicemen equals 6.25 percent of the 16 million men who served in World War II. Alfred Kinsey's study, which was in part conducted during the war, concluded that 4 percent of white males in the United States were exclusively homosexual after adolescence and that 8 percent were exclusively homosexual for at least three years between the ages of sixteen and fifty-five. See Alfred C. Kinsey, Wardell B. Pomeroy, and Clyde E. Martin, *Sexual Behavior in the Human Male* (Philadelphia: W. B. Saunders, 1948), 650–51.

12. Irving L. Janis, "Psychodynamic Aspects of Adjustment to Army Life," *Psychiatry* 8 (May 1945): 170–71.

13. Author's interview with Bob Ruffing.

14. Author's interview with Ben Small, July 22, 1980, San Francisco.

15. Lewis H. Loeser, "The Sexual Psychopath in the Military Service," *American Journal of Psychiatry* 102 (July 1945): 92–101.

16. Nicolai Gioscia, "The Gag Reflex and Fellatio," *American Journal of Psychiatry* 107 (November 1950): 380.

17. Author's interview with [anonymous], May 28, 1980, San Francisco.

18. Letters from "Marty" to "Howard" (pseuds.), January 30, 31, 1945, in collection of the author.

19. On the local and state campaigns against lesbian and gay bars in the San Francisco Bay Area during the 1950s and 1960s, see "'Resorts for Sex Perverts,'" a slide lecture by Allan Bérubé.

20. Author's interview with [anonymous].

21. Interview with "Sami."

22. Nancy Adair and Casey Adair, eds., *Word Is Out: Stories of Some of Our Lives* (San Francisco: New Glide Publications/A Delta Special, 1978), 60–61.

23. See, for example, 1951 correspondence between lesbian WAAFs and the American Civil Liberties Union in Bérubé and D'Emilio, "The Military and Lesbians during the McCarthy Years."

24. Letter from "Dan" to "Howard" (pseuds.), December 17, 1945, in collection of author.

Coming Out Under Fire

In this essay, Bérubé shifts his gaze toward military policy and the Selective Service System, which he describes as "a stigmatizing machine." He recounts the ways that lesbian and gay military personnel were "fighting two wars," one against the external enemy and the other against a set of policies that led to courts-martial, witch hunts, imprisonment, and dishonorable discharges. As with his historical accounts of police repression and arrests in San Francisco, Bérubé is at pains to argue that repression also breeds resistance. "The current spirit of resistance," he writes, "was born under fire." The essay can be seen as an attempt to create cross-generational links between those who fought back against the military policies of the war years and those who gave birth to gay liberation in the 1970s.

January 1943: After more than a year of war, U.S. forces have begun bombing German cities and are recapturing Guadalcanal, and the Selective Service System has drafted nearly 4 million men. In Sioux Falls, South Dakota, nineteen-year-old Burt Gerrits, after a year of indecision, finally enlists in the navy. Like many teenage recruits, he doesn't know yet that he is homosexual; but at the Treasure Island Naval Base Hospital in San Francisco, where he becomes an aide on the psychiatric ward, his journey toward self-discovery begins.

"Most of the people on the ward were just very pleasant patients," a silver-haired Gerrits recalls now, four decades later. "They weren't sick. They'd sit around in the day room playing cards and chatting. I just loved talking with them.

"Then I discovered on the diagnosis charts of many of the men that their 'illness' was homosexuality. They were being discharged from the navy because they were gay. And things began to make sense to me."

During World War II, "things began to make sense" to millions of Americans who had never thought about homosexuality before, particularly to

Originally published in *Mother Jones*, February/March 1983, 23–29, 45.

African American press coverage of Blue Discharges, *Pittsburgh Courier*, October 20, 1945. Courtesy of the World War II Project Papers at the GLBTHS, San Francisco.

isolated lesbians and gay men who, as a result of the war effort, found themselves in situations in which they could discover who they were and meet others like themselves. Our war mobilization, in fact, was the catalyst for a gay awakening in the United States that continues today.

The postwar years, however, saw the worst wave of antigay hysteria in U.S. history, a panic so terrifying that few Americans, gay or straight, will talk about it even now. Yet this all-out war on homosexuals could not halt the gay awakening begun by World War II and, instead, only hastened the emergence of a self-aware minority ready to fight for its survival. Today, after the uncertain safety of more than a decade of gay liberation, gay veterans of World War II are just beginning to talk about those difficult years, allowing a suppressed chapter of U.S. history to "come out" at last.

Fighting Two Wars

The homosexual patients Burt Gerrits met in his psych ward were there because during World War II, the U.S. military had begun to "manage" its homosexual personnel for the first time. "There was no explicit homosexual policy, as such, prior to 1943," explained a confidential report prepared for the U.S. Navy some years after the war. "Homosexual conduct normally was handled . . . as a general court-martial offense," punishable by a prison sentence and a dishonorable discharge. But in January 1943, upon recommendations from psychiatrists and due to a "probable large wartime influx of homosexuals," the navy established its first policy regarding homosexuality, and by early 1944, both the army and navy had added a layer of less-stringent regulations concerning personnel who merely had "tendencies." Thus, that period became the time in U.S. history when the military—then controlling the lives of more than 16 million Americans—began to build the machinery to define, identify, classify, treat, "salvage," and discharge homosexual personnel.

Part of this new machinery was the screening of homosexuals at draft boards and induction centers, where psychiatric examiners were instructed to watch for "effeminacy in dress or manner" or even "a patulous rectum" as telltale signs of homosexuality. Yet identifying and rejecting every gay recruit came second to building a vast army, and by the end of the war even the War Department was bending its own rules, directing induction centers to relax psychiatric standards when major troop buildups were needed. Still, according to estimates in the 1948 Kinsey report, *Sexual Behavior in the Human Male*, tens of thousands of homosexuals were identified and rejected from wartime service. The Selective Service System had in fact become a stigmatizing machine, labeling many of the nation's young men as sex perverts and forcing them to flee their own hometowns.

Despite military screening procedures, "scores of these inverts," reported *Newsweek* shortly after the war, "managed to slip through induction centers." In fact the government's policy forced perhaps 1 million or more patriotic gay men and women to lie at recruiting stations so that they could "illegally" defend their country, becoming, as military officials called them, "reverse malingerers."

The lesbians and gay men who slipped through psychiatric screening faced a more troubling situation once they were in the service. Army and navy regulations, under which homosexual personnel could be discharged or court-martialed, created a climate of fear, while in many units the practice of tolerating "well-behaved" homosexuals encouraged a degree of freedom and experimentation. These mixed messages came about because the primary goal, in spite of the military's contempt for homosexuals, was to win the war. Sometimes this meant mass purges before a major campaign; other times it meant keeping known homosexuals on active duty because they were indispensable to their units. As a result, lesbian and gay GIs found themselves fighting two wars: one to defend their country, the other to survive a military policy that could turn around and brand them "undesirable" at any moment.

Blue Angels

While Selective Service screening could stigmatize homosexual draftees with a 4-F classification, the new army procedures could do the same with an undesirable or "blue" discharge, so called because it was printed on blue paper. Neither honorable nor dishonorable, these discharges bypassed a costly and time-consuming court-martial and sacrificed GI rights. Created largely for homosexuals and other personnel with "undesirable habits or traits of character," a blue discharge could take away GI benefits and prevent a veteran from getting a civilian job. Both army and navy psychiatric wards were filled with gay patients being processed out for these discharges.

Early in 1944, Howard Taylor (a pseudonym)—a twenty-one-year-old army corpsman stationed at Camp Crowder in Missouri—wrote a letter to his base psychiatrist that led to his receiving a blue discharge. "I have been in the army just a few days over a year," his letter began, "and in this year my whole life has taken a turn which at the time of induction I would have thought impossible. . . . I was immediately sized up as a 'fairy.' The men can make life one miserable hell with their jibes and taunts and petty persecutions." This abuse interfered with Taylor's ability to do his job, so he wanted an honorable discharge because he felt the army was at fault.

In response to Taylor's letter the psychiatrist merely stamped the words "self-confessed homosexual" on his file and took no further action. Only after Taylor suffered an emotional breakdown six months later and was hospitalized did officers seriously consider him for discharge. His mother—a Chicago housewife whose husband ran a neighborhood hardware store—began calling army officials to see how she could help her son. Fearful that army officials would shock his mother with the truth, Taylor wrote to her himself. His troubled letter from the psychiatric ward reveals his inner war between a deepening sense of injustice and his shame at being labeled sick and undesirable.

"My dear, the only thing wrong with me," he wrote to his mother,

> is that I am a confirmed homosexual and for that reason find army life a strain and a torture beyond my powers of endurance. . . .
>
> Everything that I feared would happen if I stayed here in the service *has* happened. And I *am* sick, sick to death of it all. I cannot prevent myself from feeling outraged at the injustice of the government's returning me to a society with whose contempt I shall be in constant struggle, and further burdening me with the stigma which is automatically attached to the person receiving a [blue discharge].

And now you know it all. The last terrible barrier between us is down and I am revealed shamefaced and defiant, in all my abnormality and cowardice. That I should be forced to write such a letter and to endure the pain such a confession inflicts is only one more cause for me to hate the army, the government and my fellow man. What *your* reaction will be, I refuse to contemplate.

Don't be too severe with me. Please understand how heartbreaking it is for me to write such a letter. I feel that I have disgraced you, betrayed you in the worst possible way.

Taylor's mother responded immediately to her son's painful letter. "My own bewildered, harassed, sweet dear," she began,

I sent you a night letter to settle the worry as to "how I would react" to your desperately brave letter. . . .

I think you have done yourself immeasurable harm by not coming to us sooner with your problem. We shall treat it as a sickness, and either you will fight to overcome it or adjust yourself and your life to it. But, I do think it is important that you should put up a fight for your full rights and privileges.

Please, dear, don't think that this is going to make any difference to anyone. All of your present friends are loyal to you for *you*, as is, so don't assume a cringing attitude. We shall never discuss it except at your desire, but I hope that you have opened up the way to a more honest relationship with Pa and me. We have always tried to be so very honest with you.

The army denied Taylor's request for an honorable discharge and sent him home just before Christmas with a blue discharge. For years after the war he wrote to the gay friends he had met at Camp Crowder, nearly all of whom also received blue discharges. Hundreds of their wartime letters were discovered in Taylor's empty house in San Francisco a year after his death in 1975. In their letters these men ironically nicknamed themselves the "blue angels."

WAC Crackdown

Not all parents of homosexual GIs reacted with as much warmth as Howard Taylor's mother. In 1944, the mother of a twenty-year-old private stationed at a Women's Army Corps (WAC) basic training camp discovered some love letters that had been sent by a WAC sergeant to her daughter. Shocked, she immediately wrote to Washington, charging that the WAC was "full of homosexuals and sex maniacs" and threatening that "unless this vice is cleaned out I am going to reveal that scandal to the world."

A year earlier, in 1943, when the Women's Army Corps officially became a branch of the army, WAC officials had established a policy for dealing with lesbian personnel. They understood that intimacy among enlisted women helped to unite the corps—even that a significant number of women in the corps were lesbians—but they were also under pressure to prevent any scandals that might fuel rumors that all WACs were "dykes" and thus damage recruiting efforts. As a result, while stressing the need to keep women's overt homosexual as well as heterosexual behavior in check, WAC officials instructed officers to avoid antilesbian witch hunts and to discharge only women they could prove to be "addicted to the practice."

The War Department responded to charges that the WAC was "full of homosexuals and sex maniacs" by dispatching an emergency investigative team to the WAC private's basic training camp, where secret hearings were conducted for nearly a month. Declassified documents obtained through the Freedom of Information Act reveal that this investigation was as much a sex education course for the two male and two female investigators as it was an inquisition for the WACs themselves. The team questioned officers and enlisted women, seized letters between lovers, and even visited the mother of the WAC private, who said she was sorry she had started the whole thing.

During the hearings the team heard the word "lesbian" for the first time and learned about rumors that WAC recruiters encouraged lesbians to enlist. The investigators questioned a second lieutenant who freely admitted she was gay and wanted to take the rap for her lover by accepting a discharge; they interrogated another woman until they broke her, forcing her to describe her specific sexual practices and threatening to tell her family unless she named names.

As a result of this testimony the investigators concluded that "homosexual addicts have gained admittance to the WAC," but that the camp was "not 'full of homosexuals and sex maniacs.'" They recommended that the second lieutenant who wanted a discharge resign and that the women involved in lesbian relationships be transferred to separate bases. They recommended that no further investigations be made during the war but observed that after the war the problem might require more specific action. The War Department knew the nation needed these "women behind the men behind the guns" if the United States was going to win the war.

Witch Hunts

Although the WAC cautioned against antilesbian witch hunts during the war, the army and navy conducted periodic witch hunts of gay servicemen almost as a matter of policy. Commanding officers sometimes purged their units of homosexuals during their general cleanup of "ineffective" soldiers before major troop shipments, and military intelligence—which spied on both gay civilians and military personnel throughout the war—ordered roundups of homosexuals as security risks. Arrests of GIs in gay bar raids could also spark witch hunts, with suspects ordered to turn in their friends or face prison sentences.

Stan Carlow, an army mess sergeant and officers' steward, was caught up in one of these purges in Australia, after having served twenty-three months overseas. One February morning in 1944, he read an army intelligence bulletin instructing enlisted men with homosexual tendencies to report to their medical officers, who would ship them home with no loss of benefits, for their own good and for the sake of the army. Carlow felt he had such "tendencies," and so, following orders, he and some friends reported to their medical officer the next morning.

"A nightmare resulted from all of this," Carlow wrote in an affidavit to an army discharge review board in 1979. "We were treated as insane people." The men were transferred from one hospital to another, finally arriving at the Sixth Army Hospital in Brisbane, where they were joined by other GIs who had also followed the same instructions. Half of them were committed to psychiatric wards. The other half were thrown into a stockade behind barbed wire.

After several months, Carlow and his fellow inmates were taken to intelligence headquarters and told to sign confessions. "A week later we were put onto a merchant marine ship which had been rammed in the Brisbane harbor and listed as unseaworthy by the Coast Guard." This "queer ship" took the men to Seattle, where they were given blue discharges. An officer told Carlow that if he ever tried to wear his country's uniform again, he'd be thrown into federal prison. On the morning of July 27, 1944, the army stripped him of his Coral Sea badge and other medals and handed him a one-way ticket home.

"I felt that I had been betrayed," Carlow recalls with bitterness. "The army had lied to us. It wasn't right what they did to me. I'd just gone along with an army order. I felt they shouldn't be allowed to get away with things like that." In January 1981, after four decades of rejecting his appeals, an army board finally upgraded his undesirable discharge to honorable and apologized for the army's "acts of injustice" against him during World War II.

The stories of most blue angel appeals, despite the men's persistence, did not have such "happy" endings. The undesirable discharge for homosexuality, concluded one top naval psychiatrist years after the war, is "a punishment that lasts forever."

Camp Life

While military purges and discharge procedures brought some homosexuals together in "queer stockades" and psychiatric wards, military life also provided gays with more genial opportunities to discover one another. Pat Bond, who today is a writer and performer living in San Rafael, California, remembers her reception at a WAC basic training camp: "As I walked in with my suitcase, I heard a woman from one of the barracks windows saying, 'Good God, Elizabeth, here comes another one!' Everybody was going with someone or had a crush on someone. Always the straight women I ran into tended to ignore us, tended to say, 'Who cares? It leaves all the men for us.'"

On many bases gay men, too, found it easy to meet one another. Some of these gay men used their campy sense of humor to entertain other GIs as well as themselves. Drag shows—an army tradition as old as peeling potatoes—were so popular that *Life* magazine ran two pictorial features on them during the war. Of course, not all GIs in drag were gay, but many of these shows reflected a gay "campiness." Straight and gay GIs alike remember them as a welcome relief from, as one GI put it, the "drab, horrible rut" of military routine.

In 1943, Norman Sansom—who served in the Army Air Corps' Special Services in Georgia—and two of his buddies put together a comedy drag routine as part of a musical show on their base. Wearing gowns donated by a women's dress shop in Savannah, they sang, "We've got glamour and no lie / Can't you tell when we [swish] by? / Isn't it campy? Isn't it campy?" This "female" trio ended their act by lifting their dresses and roller-skating offstage Bea Lillie–style. They brought the house down and received rave reviews in the *Savannah Morning News*.

Weekend passes and leaves also gave men and women in the service the freedom to enjoy the gay nightlife that began to flourish in some cities during the war. They gathered in gay bars such as Bradley's in Hollywood, Lucky's Rendezvous in Harlem, the Black Cat and Techau in San Francisco, and Mary's Tavern in Denver, and in the few lesbian bars such as the If

Club in Los Angeles and Mona's in San Francisco. Bars in Chicago's Palmer House, New York's Astor Hotel, and San Francisco's Mark Hopkins, among others, were also well-known meeting places for gay officers, enlisted men, and civilians.

In the fall of 1944, Burt Miller, a twenty-one-year-old naval officer from Seattle, was stationed just outside Los Angeles. "I hadn't learned about the bars yet, but frequently I'd eat dinner at the Biltmore Hotel," recalls Miller, who is now a college instructor in San Francisco.

> One night, after dinner, I walked through the bar—about 75 percent of the men were in uniform—and I asked myself, "Can what I think is going on here *be* going on?" I stopped to find out and sure enough it was! I was in that bar every night.
>
> It was there I learned that there could be a camaraderie, that people who initially had nothing but their homosexuality in common could get together and like one another and talk. That just utterly astonished me! I'd never seen it before. I don't think the outside world knew it, and I don't think most gay people knew it. I'm sure that thousands of men had the same experience I did—discovering that there is a gay society.

Sometimes this enthusiasm spilled out of the bars. A letter to Howard Taylor from an army buddy captured the madcap urgency of a Saturday night date with his favorite boyfriend on a weekend pass.

> Andy wanted to go to Hollywood so we took a cab. What a ride! There in the back seat we renewed all the old fires. In Hollywood we wound up at notorious Bradley's. . . . His friends came and Andy and I rode in a broken rumble seat down Hollywood Boulevard. . . . Everyone on the street stared after us, and Andy launched into the thunderous strains of "Meet Me in St. Louis, Louie." We went to another bar and drank and drank . . . promised to write one another and said sweet nothings. As it approached midnight Andy had to catch the train back to San Diego. We went to the station and both of us got into the middle of the train line—millions of sailors—I hung all over Andy, and the whole thing was like that scene in *Since You Went Away*. God only knows what the Shore Patrol thought!

Unknown Soldiers

Lesbians and gay men could meet each other in bars, in barracks, and even in defense plants, but it was hard for anyone to maintain a lasting relationship during the war. Lovers were transferred to other bases, and groups of friends split up, as troops—including women's units—were shipped overseas. Sometimes lovers never came back. Even today, it is difficult for gay veterans to remember the pain of having to face the deaths of their lovers silently and alone.

"Jack was killed March 4, 1945," remembers Burt Miller,

just inside Germany. He had volunteered to go on an advance scouting party to try to pin down German machine gunners and he got hit. He died in horrible pain that lasted for hours.

The day I heard about it, our ship had just come back to Saipan from the invasion of Okinawa. We'd been circling around off Japan for weeks. I had my glasses out to see what ships were there and found my brother's ship; so I got up on the light, flashed the ship and said I wanted to talk to my brother. After a couple of messages back and forth, a message began to come over: DID—YOU—KNOW— THAT—JACK—WAS—KILLED? That's how I heard.

I couldn't talk to anybody for the rest of the day. I couldn't cry and I couldn't tell anybody. I was alone. It was the most terrible day I've spent in my life.

In spite of the general contempt for homosexuals in the military, some straight servicemen relied on their gay friends, especially on the battlefield. "I was a combat medic," say George Dohmann, a disabled vet now living in Connecticut, who enlisted in the army at eighteen. "No one asked me if I was gay when they called out 'Medic!' and you went out under fire and did what you were trained and expected to do. Buddies from medical training days were dying like flies and it became lonely. I was wounded at Cherbourg during the Normandy invasion and in the Battle of the Bulge. There were many gays in the medics and so many of them gave their lives. I think the Jerry Fallwells should know that!"

Sometimes the compassion of other soldiers broke through the isolation of the gay GIs. Ben Small, who also served in the army, remembers what happened when his lover was killed in the Philippines:

I went into a three-day period of hysterics. I was treated with such kindness by the guys I worked with, who all were totally aware of why I was hysterical. It wasn't at all because we were being bombed; it was because my "boyfriend" had been killed. One guy in the tent came up to me and said, "Why didn't you tell me you were gay? You could have talked to me." This big, straight, macho guy. There *was* a sort of compassion then.

A lieutenant and an enlisted man in my unit also were lovers. In this raid where my lover was killed, the lieutenant was injured; so he was being shipped back to the States. We all went to the plane to see him off. It was an amazingly touching moment when he and his lover said goodbye, because they embraced and kissed in front of all these straight guys, and everyone dealt with it so well. I think it was just this basic thing about the separation from someone you cared for, regardless of sex. It was a little distilled moment out of time when your prejudices were suspended and you could be part of what that meant. After the war, it was all over.

Postwar Panic

"Where do I go from here?" asked a vet in a 1944 magazine ad—a question many lesbian and gay veterans were asking themselves. How *would* a peacetime America react to the gay awakening created by World War II?

Throughout the late 1940s, gay social life continued to grow more visible: More gay bars opened, providing, for many gays, the first public meeting places they had ever had. Talk of a "homosexual minority" surfaced, and articles and letters about this new minority began to appear in major magazines. In 1948, the first Kinsey report focused even more public attention on homosexuality. Its findings—that one-third of American white males had had adult homosexual experiences and that as much as 10 percent of the white male population was homosexual for three years of their lives or more—reassured isolated gay men that they were not alone. Still, despite increasing talk of a homosexual minority, many lesbian and gay veterans feared that their growing visibility might make them easier targets.

By 1950 the question of whether the postwar years would turn into the best of times or the worst of times for gay Americans was finally answered. The climate for the powerless in the United States had worsened steadily since the war's end. Women, racial minorities, and the disabled lost defense jobs. Unions were attacked. The media began idealizing the nuclear family and defending it by attacking "sex deviates." Liberal and conservative politicians stirred up anti-Communist hysteria to fuel the Cold War. Fed by these reactionary political winds, a virtual war on gays spread like wildfire. The worst fears of many veterans who had witnessed antigay witch hunts in wartime were coming true. The peacetime panic had begun.

Senator Joseph McCarthy threw the first firebomb in February 1950 when he accused the State Department of firing and then rehiring a "flagrant" homosexual in 1946. Leaders of both major political parties then jumped on the bandwagon, with Republicans accusing the Truman administration of harboring homosexuals, and Democrats responding that they were making every effort to rid the government of homosexual security risks. When Republican National Chairman Guy Gabrielson warned that "sexual perverts" were "perhaps as dangerous as the actual Communists," he elevated the "homosexual angle," according to the *New York Times*, "to the national political level."

The Senate appointed a bipartisan investigative subcommittee that concluded that homosexuals should be fired from government jobs and that the government should work with police and the FBI to identify homosexual government employees. As a result, hundreds of workers lost their jobs. The FBI also stepped up its surveillance of gays. By the time Eisenhower took office, establishing one's moral purity as well as one's loyalty was a prerequisite for getting and keeping a government job.

Antigay crackdowns at the local level also swept the country, and how greatly widespread they were is still the best-kept secret of the McCarthy era. Universities expelled students and fired teachers on rumors that they were queer. Wichita, Kansas, police began an "inquisition" of sexual deviates, calling on several public school teachers to testify, and Boise, Idaho, police interrogated 1,400 citizens in efforts to break a homosexual ring that never existed. On the East Coast, Miami began what newspapers called a "lasting war on perverts," and in New York City, seventy-one civic and trade groups joined a *Journal-American* campaign to rid the city of "sex fiends and degenerates," with gay and lesbian bars as prime targets. Local newspapers routinely printed the names and addresses of homosexuals arrested in police dragnets. With gay refugees fleeing these nightmares, city after city—including Portland, Tacoma, and San Francisco on the West Coast—imagined it was undergoing a "homosexual invasion" and was in danger of becoming the "sex pervert capital" of the United States.

In the 1950s, gay men and women did not come out voluntarily as they do today. They were dragged out, victims of a nation peculiarly obsessed with exposing homosexuals. The consequences of this exposure were severe: life as refugees, jail terms, broken homes, ruined careers, extortion, hopelessness, and suicide.

Nevertheless, each attempt to punish, "manage," or isolate gay Americans—from the queer stockades, psych wards, and blue discharges of World War II to the all-out war on homosexuals in the 1950s—only reinforced gay identity as an emerging minority. The new gay networks and social institutions created during the war persisted, despite pervasive efforts to destroy them in the postwar years. Thus, it was no accident that in the 1950s a gay and lesbian political movement surfaced in the United States, beginning with veterans' social groups, the Mattachine Society, and the Daughters of Bilitis.

A later generation of gays would point to the famous 1969 bar fight at Greenwich Village's Stonewall Inn as the beginning of gay liberation. But the current spirit of resistance and solidarity predates the 1960s. It was born under fire during World War II and the Cold War.

Rediscovering Our Forgotten Past

A recurring characteristic of Bérubé's research and writing is the uncovering of stories that defied common assumptions about the past. As with "Lesbian Masquerade" and its accounts of women who successfully passed as men and loved other women, "Rediscovering Our Forgotten Past" recounts the incredible story of a few gay men—"queens" in the language of the time—who performed in drag and even published a few issues of a "campy" newsletter while in the service during World War II. Bérubé inserts himself into the essay in ways that allow one to see the relationships he built with his oral history subjects, so that past and present interact in these efforts to recover lost histories. The essay also helped to bring together aspects of Bérubé's own past. It was published in the 1984 Pride Issue of the Front Page, *a gay community newspaper produced in the Triangle area of North Carolina, where Allan Troxler and Carl Wittman, two close friends from Bérubé's gay liberation years, were then living.*

Most histories of the gay movement and gay life in America focus only on San Francisco, New York, Los Angeles, and other northern and West Coast cities. The South has an equally rich gay past, but it is often locked in the memories of men and women who are only now feeling safe enough to talk about the years before "gay liberation."

World War II may have transformed gay life in the South more than any other event before the 1970s. The massive war mobilization threw millions of young men and women from all over the country onto the military bases that sprung up almost overnight in every southern state. The army and navy used these southern bases to train recruits before shipping them overseas. Many young men crowded onto these bases soon discovered they were homosexual and began to meet other soldiers and sailors like themselves.

In 1943, two of these GIs stationed at a South Carolina air base had met so many gay servicemen on other southern bases that they decided to start a newsletter for their new friends. Because they were stationed at the Myrtle

Originally published in the *Front Page*, June 26–July 9, 1984, 1, 9–11.

The Bitches' Camouflage

"A BI-MONTHLY TINKLE"

VOLUME 69   SECT VIII

FOUNDED 1969

LOST IN A DREAM...Comes to life and is most ardanently HAPPY in the South Pacific islands where Natue-Boo and Mother Nature haunts

That well recalled REPUBLIC PICTURE star, "Larry De Ruiz" has contacted us and tells us girls to save our money and not to buy so much jewlery, as she is busy bribbing the natives and stringing shells and nuts for our "Duration Party" at the Waldorf in 1944. Miss Carolota (The Red Empress) tells that Esther Carbine Griffin is still with her and rattles about making more pocket money there on the ISLANDS....prehops, she's DOING big things with BIG people....such was the case at "CHATUM and HUNTER FIELDS" (respectively)

MINNIE HA HA LON-DACTIOUS CAMPBELLE RE-ITTERATES FROM MIAMI B

Those who loved and honored the cherished memory of one Lonnie Campbell will be happy to read that that mad-iferous bAG is still existing in the lower right hand corner of our map, where the beaches are long and the females scarce. She's trainin there for 6 weeks, but "at what" -- we haven't been able to uncover. Probably that new course: "How To Man-euver your MAN in the wilds of thee georgous Brener Pass"   Keep swishing, JhL!

PUBLISHED AS A MATTER OF COMMAND:

Addresses of the girls:

HONEY Henieke: 27th Airdrome Sqdn
Kearney, Nebraska

THELMA BISHOP: 278 West 11th St
New York (14), N.Y.

LAURA BEE SPENCER: % Billbred Magazine
New York Office,
New York, N.Y.

P.S. THELMA BISHOP, the wizard of the lino-type in New York...suggests a buzz to her will prove most intriging entertainment while fer- lowing in or around the New Yorik locale.....
P.P.S. Junior WEE WILLIE WOODESIA, wishes to tell Miss Thelma B that she was sorry not to have looked her up in N.Y., but what her train accident en route to N.Y., it was a bad trip & he was only able to see OKLAHA and do a few pressing jobs....here and there. Be sure and read her story of her far-low in this edition.

LEONA BEE-THE-ONE ANDERSON OF SHEPPARD ON THE LAD GOES FOR A BRIGHTIE SCARLET RED HEAD OF THE SERVICE

It was amazing and delightful to hear of that brilliant triumph which Miss ???????? (Blank) Anderson made there at Sheppard Fld not so long ago. We do hope that CUNT is settled now and really going down on more ex otic things. Even a red houded Service Club hostess.........Jesus--! She's also informed us that she is to see such notables as Mme Neuhauser and Mildred Voigt on her next trip to the Eastern Coast. All we ask is that a complete snub is given that Poison-faced NIN BUTARI, who no-doubt is still waiting tables in some low celes dive in New York. E-gods, that one "bothers" mey ass.

A LA REINE' CREATION

Before I heard the doctor tell
   The danger of a kiss,
I had considered kissing you
   the nearest thing to bless.

But now I know Bilology (mistake)
   And sit, and sigh and moan,
Six million mad bacteria,
   And I thought we'd be alone.

"The Bitches," a Myrtle Beach, S.C., GI newsletter, 1940s. Courtesy of the World War II Project Papers at the GLBTHS, San Francisco.

Beach Bombing Range, they named their newsletter the *Myrtle Beach Bitch*. Campy, patriotic, and naive, these young pioneers had no idea they had put together one of the first gay papers in the United States. They also weren't prepared for the high price they'd have to pay for their innocent project.

Last Christmas in San Francisco, two of the men associated with the *Myrtle Beach Bitch*—Woodie Wilson, one of the editors, and his war buddy

Norman Sansom, a "subscriber"—had their first reunion since the end of World War II. Norman had told me about the *Myrtle Beach Bitch* and his good friend Woodie when I had interviewed him in 1981 for my book on gay Americans during World War II. So when Woodie arrived from Pennsylvania, Norman invited me to take my tape recorder over to his house to preserve Woodie's story about how he started the *Myrtle Beach Bitch*.

I arrived early in the afternoon. Norman fixed us drinks, and all three of us gathered around the dining room table. As Woodie started talking, I began to realize that his story not only captured the spirit of gay life in the wartime South but also revealed some of the hidden origins of the gay press in America.

Woodie's story began like the stories of millions of other young Americans who served in World War II. He enlisted in the Army Air Corps just before his twenty-first birthday in June 1942. By the end of the summer he was stationed at Keesler Field in Biloxi, Mississippi, where he was trained as an airplane engine mechanic to service the new B-24 bombers. At Keesler Field, Woodie met a "gang" of gay GIS, especially the "tall MP."

Woodie remembers well the day he first met the tall MP. During his free time after classes, he told me, he would walk over to the War Department Theater to catch the first-run Hollywood movies that were the only entertainment on the base. On one of these hot Mississippi summer evenings, Woodie was standing in the long line of men waiting to get into the theater. He passed the time by watching the MPs keep the men in line. "And this very tall—over six-foot-four I'm sure—absolutely blonde young MP came up and he would swing his club and he'd say, 'Get up, girls! Get up, girls! Get up, girls!' And obviously he was a gay fellow! He kept saying 'girls' to whoever was standing in line. And there would be lots of giggling in the line and a lot of horseplay like 'Oh what do you want, you fairy!' But they kept him part of the MP division on that base.

"So very carefully I started to talk to him one night at the service club on the base," Woodie continued. "And he introduced me to two or three other people. We all played cards together at the service club when we had time off. And suddenly I realized I had a fast friendship with these guys who hung out in the service club and particularly this MP. It wasn't sex—nobody wanted to go to bed with anybody. They were just guys who were giddy, swishy, and gay. They didn't all like one another, but they all knew one another. We were from all over the United States. And I began learning about places I had never been."

"The Female Trio"

In the spring of 1943, Woodie had to leave his new gay "gang" and his "tall MP." The army transferred him first to Shepherd Field, Texas, then to Hunter Field near Savannah, Georgia, where he was assigned as a glider mechanic to a squadron preparing to ship off to Europe.

But Woodie wasn't without friends for long. "Oddly enough," he told me, "guess who appeared again? The tall MP, still in the Military Police, still swinging her little club around and as gay as pink ink!" And Hunter Field was where Woodie met Norman.

Woodie first saw Norman at an audition for a musical variety show that Special Services was putting on called *Private Maxie Reporting*. "What we actually auditioned for was the men's chorus," Norman explained. "But they found out that the show needed some humor." So the three gay GIs—Woodie, the tall MP, and their new friend Norman—decided to put together a "specialty act," a comedy routine in drag. "Let's put on a show in the barn!!" Woodie laughed, quoting Judy Garland from the Andy Hardy movies. "Only we put it on in the Municipal Auditorium in downtown Savannah, Georgia!"

Norman described how they got their act together. First they came up with a little skit, Norman explained, and "did a dry run for the cast and crew and it broke them up—they thought it was just fantastic. So they said, 'OK, go ahead and embellish on it and we'll fit it somewhere in the show if we find that it's dragging.'"

Next the three corpsmen

went into town, into downtown Savannah, and we walked into this dress shop. We told the shop owner that we were doing this show and could she contribute some dresses that might not be selling. Well, she was absolutely blown out of her mind to see three soldiers walk in and ask for dresses! But at that time everybody was so anxious to do something for the war effort. So when we told her what we needed them for, she felt she was doing a very patriotic thing by donating them to us. She was very cooperative and took us into the dressing room. We tried on a lot of gowns! Let me tell you, there was a show going on in that shop with all the customers milling around because, if you can imagine, here was a six-foot-six MP and the two of us, trying on dresses. And she didn't just loan them to us, she gave them to us. We in turn told her that we would give her complimentary tickets to the show.

For the next few weeks, the trio and the rest of the show's cast "rehearsed like hell."

Their comedy drag routine wasn't the only "gay" part of the GI review. Norman played a lieutenant on the Officer Candidate School (OCS) application board, and Woodie played Pfc. Bloomingslip, an OCS applicant who, according to the program, "Wears a Green Carnation." "That was something that was written into the show," Woodie explained. "Whoever wrote it wanted it to show a homosexual and I certainly volunteered to be Private Bloomingslip! And of course he wore a green carnation. So here is Norman being one of the OCS board. I skip in with this little cap and the green carnation and say to the OCS board, 'My name is Private Bloomingslip. I was told to report in here. I think to be an officer would just be too, too queer.' I remember that was my line!"

Besides the men's chorus, or "Chorus of Boys," that Norm and Woodie auditioned for, the show also had a "Chorus of Girls" made up of "women who were all local girls from Savannah." Ironically, it was the presence of these women in the cast that introduced the trio to gay life in Savannah. Since the cast had to "rehearse into the night," Norman told me, the women were not permitted to come onto the base. "So it was arranged to put the soldiers up at the De Soto Hotel in town. The Municipal Auditorium was across the street from the De Soto Hotel, which meant we could rehearse in the auditorium, and then, in order not to be arrested for being out after hours, we could cross the street and go right back to the De Soto Hotel and stay there and sleep. That's how we found out that the bar at the De Soto Hotel was really the 'closeted' gay bar of Savannah. That's where we did our drinking and had our fun."

But on opening night, it was the trio's drag number that brought the house down. "This was the thing that really saved the show," Norman remembers. "The drag that we did wasn't the glamorous-type drag. We didn't have fancy wigs and perfect makeup or anything like that. I think our wigs were mops, actual mops that you use to mop the floor." They wore GI shoes under their long dresses because they wanted to end their skit by lifting their skirts and roller-skating offstage, Bea Lillie–style. Roller skates didn't clamp well onto high heels.

For their comedy routine, the three GIs in drag sang a song they wrote for the show:

Here you see three lovely "girls"
With their plastic shapes and curls.
Isn't it campy? Isn't it campy?

We've got glamour and that's no lie.
Can't you tell when we swish by?
Isn't it campy? Isn't it campy?

Those GIs all stop and stare,
And we don't even bat an eye.
You'd think that we were shy.
Now isn't that campy? Isn't that campy?

So now drink a toast to these lovely "girls,"
Doing their utmost to upset you most.
Now who do you think is campy?
Now who do you think is campy?

"We were the three drag queens of the world," Woodie said with pride. "I wish somebody had a picture of us. But we do have the review of our second night from the *Savannah Morning News*." Woodie read the headlines from the yellowed newsclippings: "AIR BASE SHOW DRAWS BIG CROWD. 'PVT. MAXIE REPORTING' PROVES SUCCESSFUL." Then he found the paragraph about their drag act: "The 'female trio,' who almost stopped the show on the opening night, were again received by a roar of ovation. Clad in clinging evening dresses, the three drew howls from the audience, which mounted when they returned on roller skates for an encore. Lyrics sung by the three were composed by themselves. Private Sansom was also make-up man for the men's chorus." "You certainly were!" Woodie teased Norman and began his good-natured, campy laugh.

"It's fun to think back on that," Woodie told me, his laughter subsiding. "It comes back much better now that I'm here with Norman after all these years."

The *Myrtle Beach Bitch*

Woodie had to leave his friends again when the army sent him to Myrtle Beach Bombing Range in South Carolina.

> They had me as a glider mechanic assigned to an aircraft squadron and we were all under camouflage trees right down to the ocean. The bombers went out and bombed on the ocean. That was where they tested. This new unit was forming to go overseas. I was assigned to be the officers' clerk—taking care of all the officers' records that were connected with my squadron.
>
> Well, who comes along who's the chief clerk of the orderly room

where we were working? The tall MP! We called him Sister Kate by now because we had been the three sisters in the show. So from then on "she" was Sister Kate.

Of course, we kept in touch with Norman from the moment we found ourselves on the same base again. And that's when we formed the famous *Myrtle Beach Bitch*.

From Hunter Field, Norman was transferred to Walterboro, South Carolina. Right after his arrival, he got a letter from his two friends in Myrtle Beach. "They told me they were going to publish a newsletter to come out every month because there were a lot of us gays in the Air Corps."

Woodie explained how he and the tall MP came up with the idea to put out the *Myrtle Beach Bitch*.

Sister Kate and I were two people who had lots of time on our hands. I had met gays in how many fields by this time, like Norman, that we knew had gone off to other places but we kept in touch. So we just started having a ball in the orderly room typing up these things, and then running them off on the mimeograph machine. Of course we were busy all day long, and sometimes into the evening, doing the rosters and all the damned things you had to do to prepare to go overseas. We could come in at night if we wanted to do extra work. So it was perfectly all right.

"The *Myrtle Beach Bitch* might have been issued five times in its life," Woodie went on.

I would say that the first one might have had three or four pages to it. I think we even did little crazy drawings. The second one might have been four pages. Another one I can remember was just one page. It was just a mimeographed standard size piece of paper that was stapled together.

We wrote in it that Norman had gone to Walterboro, South Carolina. And we mentioned "Ray" that we'd met in Mississippi, and we wrote "Miss Ray," or "Martha Ray," or whatever we called her, "That bitch is out doing Clovis, New Mexico." And this one went there, and doesn't everybody remember Woodie's Brad that he used to get under the mess hall with, we think he's at OCS in Florida. It was things like that.

"It was a gossip column," Norman added. "Who was going with whom. Who was sleeping with whom. Who 'divorced' each other and were going with someone else. Who had graduated from a Pfc. lover to a captain or a lieutenant. So all of this kept everybody up on who they knew had 'bettered' themselves, so to speak, by 'marrying into' the officers' club. And the names were mentioned, either the first name or the last name, or their feminine name that we gave them—Carol or whatever."

"And don't forget," Woodie added, "Kate was in charge of all service records of everybody in that unit, and I was in charge of all the officers' service records. We could have been the biggest busy-bodies of the world and written about those people. But those people didn't mean shit to us. All our fun was other than Myrtle Beach. Because we'd just come from this mad show in Savannah, we'd been together in Keesler where it was gay, and there wasn't anything exciting in Myrtle Beach."

"One thing I do remember," Norman said to Woodie, "that I thought was so clever was when you did the parody of 'The Night before Christmas.' It went something like, ''Twas the night before Christmas and all through the field, not a single queen was stirring, not a single high heel.'"

Norman's excitement about the newsletter turned a little more serious. "It was almost like receiving a newsletter from home," he said, "because it was the only communication we had about people we had met in other bases. It let us know who was overseas and where they were."

"We were saying," added Woodie,

"Guess who's still alive! The two that you know at Keesler, Shepherd, and Hunter Field at Savannah! We're still around, and we haven't jumped off yet. And this is what's happening to us, what's happening to you?"

We didn't get that much mail back. We wondered, "Were they off in the Aleutians? Had they gone out to the Pacific yet?" Some of them *did* write and say, "Oh, I'm at Scott Field going to radio school," so we would mention that in the *Myrtle Beach Bitch*. Or somebody would say, "I'm at Indio, California, at the Desert Training Center and I'm going into town every night to the canteen where the Hollywood stars are." And they might send us a little scribble about what stars threw a party for them. Those things got into our paper.

I remember us getting it together and having a wonderful time. By the way, with the help of a poor fellow who knew we were both gay but just got laughs and belly laughs from us. He worked with us in the same orderly room. I think we even gave him a campy name, but never disclosed who he was. I don't think he typed. He was in charge of the mimeograph machines in the orderly room. He inked our mimeograph for us. So we wrote in the *Myrtle Beach Bitch*, "Guess what Sister Kate and Miss Woodie are doing now. They have somebody in this orderly room that you girls should see! You wouldn't believe it!!" He was not gay. He just enjoyed the fact that we were.

We couldn't have had a big mailing list. Only the people that we had met, Kate and I. We sent out ten, twelve copies at most.

"But you can't go by those numbers," Norman was quick to explain. "I know when I got mine I passed it on to somebody else whose name might have been on it and maybe he mailed it to somebody else. So it was recirculated. It reached more than just ten or fifteen people."

"You never saved the *Myrtle Beach Bitch*?" Woodie asked Norman. "Nobody saved anything," Norman answered, then turned to me. "You see, people didn't save things in those days because we were all so afraid, not only of the service but of our families." "I'd love to have a copy of it," Woodie said. "There were copies up until 1964 that I knew of. And by the way, Kate and I always kept a copy. That was the worst thing we ever did.

"Because that's when the shit hit the fan."

Woodie paused for a moment, trying to remember precisely what happened on that day forty years ago.

The first I knew about it, I was called in to the office by my adjutant, and he said, "Have you ever heard of the *Myrtle Beach Bitch*?" And I stood at attention and I said, "Yes, sir, I have." He said, "Do you have any ideas about who has written the *Myrtle Beach Bitch*?" And I said, "Yes, sir, I do. It's me." And he said, "Go over to your barracks right now." And he sent for Kate too and told her to report to her barracks. The provost marshal was there, with two MPs apiece at our bunks. And right in front of us, they picked up our foot lockers, took them away and put us into the stockade. Surrounded by barbed wire.

The stockade was full of both black and white prisoners who had done all sorts of things: AWOL, stealing, manslaughter. We all had blue uniforms with a "P" on our backs for "prisoners." We were in that stockade over three and a half months awaiting trial. We were taken out every morning with guards to clean up the beach. We picked up trash, raked leaves and pine needles, and were always under the eye of a guard. The Myrtle Beach Bombing Range never looked better!

The investigation went on slowly. We would be interviewed one day, then we'd work for two weeks. Then we'd be interviewed three times in three days. We never gave them the names of anybody. We refused. We said we didn't know. But we must have had names and addresses in a book in the footlockers that they searched. Or maybe we kept it in the orderly room. Kate and I always wondered, did they ever find anything in the orderly room? And we'll never know.

Eventually it got around what we were in for. We were *gay*. But we still didn't know what the charges were. Then I began to realize we might be tried for homosexual acts committed in the service—that just blew my mind. I was getting madder and madder and gayer and gayer! I didn't give a shit. I was just giving hell to everybody. When we showered, I carried on, "screaming" like a queen. The guards kept saying, "That Wilson, watch him. He's our problem." I was called in to the provost marshal several times. He said, "Will you quiet it down? Quit screaming like a sissy."

And would you believe it, they came into the stockade barracks and built two special cells, *two special cells*, out of two-by-fours around our beds! That gave us just enough space to turn around and pass cigarettes through the bars. We would come out of our little cells in the morning and go to work. We were all marched to eat over at the mess hall and marched back to go to the bathroom but we were kept there at night because they wouldn't trust us with the rest of the prisoners. Real caged pigeons, only I guess we were called the peacocks. We were not allowed to go around from bunk to bunk, like all the other prisoners and visit and talk. But we could talk to them through the bars and they'd talk to us. We were treated rather good by the inmates themselves. They didn't ostracize us. But that was the nearest thing to segregation I have ever in my life known as a white man.

The trial—a general court-martial—was quick. We went in and sat at a table. I can remember being nervous. Of course, we were admitted homosexuals. I think from the moment we got the first interrogation, we both said we were gay. But that was the one thing at the general court-martial we were not sentenced for. Because we and our lawyers had stipulated everything. We had them cross out everything that said "homosexual." So our charges were "misuse of government property"—which would have been the mimeograph machine, the paper we printed it on, the typewriters—and "misusing our franking privileges." When you mailed a letter in the service, you had to write "free" in the corner of the envelope where the stamp usually was. Imagine using our franking privileges and putting your return address on the envelope to send out the *Myrtle Beach Bitch*! I mean, my

God! It's silly—right there, in ink! We were also charged with "sending vulgar and obscene letters." They called the *Myrtle Beach Bitch* vulgar and obscene.

And I can remember when it was read to me that I would be dishonorably discharged from the service without pay and rights, I realized that our lark had been really a bad thing to do. I was very upset. I thought the world was awful. I hated being locked up in a cage in that stockade. I felt very humiliated. Yet I don't think I was ever gayer! I must have made more wisecracks in that stockade and had more fun. Kate would scream out, "Oh, shut up, Woodesia!" She called me Woodesia and I called her Kate. You see, we kept it up! Fuck 'em! Fuck 'em! We were going to hang, that's all there was to it. We were going to be discharged.

Then I was really worried because there had been a case or two ahead of ours during the three months we were awaiting trial and we knew that he was sent to Fort Leavenworth before being dishonorably discharged. And sure enough, within three days we were put on a train, sent to Columbia, South Carolina, and then straight to Greenhaven Federal Prison in Stormville, New York. And we were sent there for one year.

· · · · · ·

Woodie, Norman, and I kept talking all afternoon and into the early evening. About Woodie and Kate's year in the federal prison. About gay bar life in Biloxi, Wichita, and New York City during the war. About how Woodie met his lover of twenty-five years in 1957. And about all his jobs in the hotel business until he retired. The three of us filled the room with memories, campy laughter, and silent tears.

I asked Norman and Woodie how it felt to be together again after not seeing each other for over thirty years. Norman said, "Fabulous. I can't get enough of him." Woodie said, "Seeing each other is marvelous. It was so nice of Norman to say, 'You've got to come to San Francisco some day!' 'All right,' I said, 'Christmas in San Francisco!'"

Woodie's lover died of cancer in 1982. Woodie is now fighting cancer himself. "Last Christmas was very dull. I'd lost my lover in September and here it was the first Christmas without him. That was pretty rough. So I thought, 'This Christmas I'm not going to sit home again and think about this.' You go through shock, grief, and then you recover. I think I'm on recovery. It was a long time. He was the love of my life."

When it was time for me to go, the sky was completely dark, and the

Christmas lights Norman had strung on his balcony shined brightly through the sliding glass doors. I gave them both a hug and kiss goodbye. I wasn't sure anyone had ever said it to him in so many words, so I told Woodie two things: that I and my generation were forever indebted to him for trying to start a gay press that we all now take for granted, and that he had done nothing to deserve going to prison. Until our afternoon together, Woodie had never told the whole story of the *Myrtle Beach Bitch* to anyone, not even his lover. When I asked him why, he answered, "I guess I was a little ashamed." I thanked him for deciding to finally let go of his secret.

Three weeks later, Woodie sent me a letter. He wrote that on his way home to Pennsylvania, he had stopped in Alabama for another reunion: this time with Sister Kate, the tall MP. They had "dug up large quantities of great memories" together, and Kate had agreed to tell me *his* story of the *Myrtle Beach Bitch* and to try again to locate copies. In a P.S. at the end of his letter, Woodie asked me to check on Norman for him every once in a while to see how he's doing. And he added, "He's a one in a trillion friend to me."

. . . . . .

(As this issue of the *Front Page* was going to press, word came that Woodie Wilson had died of a heart attack on June 14, 1984, while vacationing in Atlantic City.)

The Military and Lesbians during the McCarthy Years

Coauthored with John D'Emilio, this piece extends the history of lesbians in the military from the war years of the 1940s into the McCarthy era of the 1950s. Combining an in-terpretive introduction with documents, it provides a look at military policy as well as at the impact on and response of women in the service. Whereas the war years seemed to open up opportunities for self-discovery, community, and freedom of expression, the anticommunist crusades of the Cold War created a climate that favored crackdowns on any departures from the normative, whether involving political views or sexual and gender expression. Composed during the first Reagan administration and the early years of AIDS, it seems to carry the warning that progress can be reversed, that good times can turn to bad. The first work of Bérubé directed at a scholarly audience, it was published in a special lesbian issue of Signs, *a feminist academic journal.*

The following documents shed light on a little-known area of women's history: the policy of the U.S. military toward lesbian personnel during the Mc-Carthy era and its impact on women serving in the armed forces. The first three documents—indoctrination lectures on homosexuality designed for WAVE (navy) recruits in 1952—both articulate the military's implicit ideol-ogy concerning lesbians and demonstrate the means by which the military implemented its policy. The second set of documents—1951 correspondence between the American Civil Liberties Union (ACLU) and lesbians being purged from the WAF (air force)—records the effects of military policy on individual women in the air force.

These letters and lectures are evidence of the "homosexual scare" of the 1950s, which was a side effect of Cold War tensions and American fears about national security. Early in 1950, a State Department official testified before the Senate that several dozen employees had been dismissed on charges of homosexuality. The revelation provoked an uproar, and for the remainder of the year Republican leaders exploited the homosexual issue

Originally published in *Signs* 9, no. 4 (Summer 1984): 759–75.

U.S. Army recruitment poster, World War II. Courtesy of the World War II Project Papers at the GLBTHS, San Francisco.

as a means of discrediting the Truman administration's national security policy. A Senate investigation into the employment of "homosexuals and other sex perverts" painted a menacing picture of the infiltration of the federal government by "sexual deviates" whose presence allegedly threatened the moral welfare of the nation.[1] The popular press kept the homosexual issue alive with reports of dismissals from government service and exposés of alleged homosexual "rings." Scandal writers in stories with such titles as "Lesbians Prey on Weak Women" charged that there were cells of lesbians in the schools and in the military bent on seducing the innocent.[2]

Rhetoric portraying sexual deviance as a threat to national security had its analogue in more repressive policies. During the early 1950s the government explicitly excluded homosexuals and lesbians from all federal jobs; many private employers, particularly those under government contract, followed suit.[3] The military's response to the "homosexual menace" was especially severe. By the end of the 1940s, the military was discharging about a thousand men and women per year on charges of homosexuality. But as the campaign against sexual deviance intensified in the 1950s, the number discharged rose to over 2,000 per year.[4]

Women in the military were particularly vulnerable to these antihomosexual policies. A secret investigative board noted in 1957 that the rate of detection for homosexual activity in the navy had been "much higher for the female than the male" even though "homosexual activity in the female is difficult to detect."[5] As unmarried female volunteers in an intensely masculine institution, women in the military constituted a socially deviant group that too easily fit the popular stereotype of lesbians. Their deviation from the norms of female behavior was especially highlighted by the reassertion of traditional gender roles in the postwar years. By contrast, during World War II, the demands of massive mobilization had allowed large numbers of American women to step temporarily outside their usual roles not only to enlist in the military but also to work in heavy industry, to live away from husbands and other kin, and to look to each other for companionship. After the war, these options faded rapidly.[6]

The contrast between wartime and postwar attitudes toward women is revealed by comparing military policy toward lesbian personnel during and after the war. In 1943, the Women's Army Auxiliary Corps (WAAC), the largest women's branch of the military with nearly 150,000 women in its ranks, prepared a series of sex hygiene lectures aimed at officer candidates.[7] The lecture on homosexuality detailed wartime policy toward lesbian personnel, explaining that "more consciousness of sex and more difficulties concerning it are to be expected in times of war than in times of peace. Whenever individuals are removed from their homes, their communities, and their social groups, they may be thrown into different and often exacting situations." The lectures recognized the value of friendship between women who had left home to serve in the corps: "This can be one of the finest relationships in companionship and working together. Sometimes it can become an intimacy that may eventually take some form of sexual expression." The lectures minimized the differences between women who participated in homosexual expression and "normal" women, stating that the former "are exactly as you and I, except that they participate in sexual gratification with members of their own sex."

The wartime lectures explicitly warned against antilesbian witch hunts. "You, as officers, will find it necessary to keep the problem at the back of your mind, not indulging in witch hunting or speculating. . . . Above all, you must approach the problem with an attitude of fairness and tolerance to assure that no one is accused unjustly." The unusual circumstances of military life could encourage women to have their first homosexual experiences, the lecture continued. "It may appear that, almost spontaneously, such a relationship has sprung up between two women, neither of whom is a confirmed, active homosexual." In the event that an officer discovered a woman in her outfit had "gravitated toward homosexual practices," the lecture advised one of four possible solutions: guidance, using a "reasonable and unscornful approach"; supervision, "such as the shifting of rooms"; transfer, "when it seems likely that a change of environment might help to eliminate the cause"; or, as a last resort, discharge. Only the most overt, disruptive, and intransigent lesbian "addicts" who jeopardized the efficiency and morale of the unit were to be discharged. But "any officer," warned the lecture, "bringing an unjust or unprovable charge against a woman in this regard will be severely reprimanded."[8]

These guidelines were not always followed. Branches of the military did at times search for and harass lesbian personnel, and some women were discharged from the service. But the demands of war placed constraints on the military, and instances of harassment coexisted with the relatively tolerant approach suggested by these lectures. This wartime policy gave way to a more repressive policy toward lesbian personnel in the 1950s, as the navy lectures reprinted below illustrate.[9] In 1952, teams of naval officers were told to implement a "program for the indoctrination of naval personnel at Naval Training Centers on the subject of homosexuality."[10] Guidelines instructed the indoctrination teams to characterize homosexuality as "one of the very bad things in life." "In training of personnel," program guidelines explained, "emphasis upon homosexuality becomes necessary because there are few other means for obtaining information about it. Information about narcotics, stealing, lying and other crimes flows continuously to people through the press, radio, and institutions of learning. . . . During this period emphasis is going to be placed on another very bad thing that exists in life but about which the majority of people know little or nothing." Naval officers were not to "dress up" the subject in "high flown technical language. Homosexuality is wrong, it is evil, and it is to be branded as such," the guidelines insisted. "No pulling of punches or inferences that the matter is not serious. . . . Homosexuality . . . is an offense to all decent and law-abiding people, and it is not to be condoned on grounds of 'mental illness' any more than other crime such as theft, homicide, or criminal assault."[11]

The 1952 program included three lectures on homosexuality, specifically designed for WAVE recruits, that reflect the era's tightening strictures against homosexuality as well as against women who deviated from social norms. The lectures explicitly reject the guidance and counseling suggested to army officer candidates during World War II. Instead, the postwar policy considered "first-timers" as guilty as the "practicing homosexual" and subject to immediate discharge. No penalties for false accusations were mentioned. Rather, this Cold War policy instituted a system of sexual surveillance that encouraged WAVES to inform on each other. Although each lecture advised WAVES to talk over their personal problems with an officer, the primary duty of chaplains and psychiatrists, as naval officers, was to protect the navy by detecting and discharging homosexual personnel. Thus, a WAVE who confided in her officer could unknowingly initiate an antilesbian purge. The 1952 lectures did recognize the value of female friendship in the navy but warned that friendships that became too involved might lead to sexual activity. Antihomosexual rhetoric is used throughout the lectures to warn women recruits that sex must take place only within the institution of marriage, to bolster the traditional role as wife and mother, and to ensure that women in the military, despite their socially deviant status, adhere to the norms of feminine behavior. The lectures project a stereotype of lesbians as sexual vampires: manipulative, dominant perverts who greedily seduce young and innocent women into experimenting with homosexual practices that, like narcotics, inevitably lead to a downward spiral of addiction, degeneracy, loneliness, and even murder and suicide.

The experiences detailed in the set of correspondence below document how this more repressive Cold War policy affected individual women who enlisted in the air force.[12] According to one of the letter writers, the implementation of this policy amounted to "psychological warfare" in the relentless search for lesbians. Investigating officers extracted confessions with promises of speedy discharge and then used the self-incriminating statements to pressure women into naming names. The air force had the option of discharging an accused woman administratively rather than acceding to her demand for a trial by court-martial. Thus, women lacked the power to meet their accusers, to examine and to refute the evidence, and to cross-examine witnesses.[13] When a female officer intervened to inform women under her command of their rights in an investigation, she was relieved of her command. The authors of the letters express a sense of helplessness in the face of orders that emanated from a remote and powerful Washington.

The targeting of women who stepped beyond the boundaries of heterosexuality had devastating effects. In the purge detailed here, at least two of the accused women committed suicide. But, even for the survivors, a military discharge on grounds of homosexuality represented a lifelong stigma. Besides the trauma of the experience, such a discharge during the 1950s precluded civilian employment with the government as well as in a wide range of other jobs. Many women enlisted in the military for the mobility it promised—the opportunity to leave home and travel, to gain job skills, and to enter nontraditional occupations. The disgrace attached to expulsion for lesbianism dashed these expectations.

Despite the grim picture that the letters paint, they are also portents of the future. The authors are, after all, writing to the ACLU for help, and both women display a clearly articulated sense of outrage and injustice. In this instance their request for help was denied because at the time the ACLU held that homosexuality was relevant to an individual's military service.[14] But the letter writers were not alone in their search for recourse. Heightened concern about homosexuality during the 1950s and the intensification of penalties against lesbians and gay men propelled some of them to take action on their own behalf. By the mid-1950s, a lesbian rights organization, the Daughters of Bilitis (DOB), formed in San Francisco, with branches opening later in other cities. In the succeeding years, DOB, along with male homosexual organizations, targeted the antihomosexual policies of the military and civilian agencies of the federal government that had intensified during the 1950s.[15]

Indoctrination of WAVE Recruits on Subject of Homosexuality [1952]

LINE OFFICER'S PRESENTATION

Good morning/afternoon! I am _____ . The officer on my right/left is Dr. _____ . The officer on my left/right is Chaplain _____ . We would like to speak to you today about a subject with which, very likely, many of you have never been confronted and on which most of you, perhaps, have never heard a formal discussion. The subject is homosexuality. . . . I shall speak to you as a woman officer because there are some things about homosexuality that concern us as women in the service. This presentation is to tell you the facts concerning homosexuality and most important of all, how to avoid becoming involved with homosexuals. . . . My purpose today is to: (1) warn you that there are homosexuals, (2) inform you why the Navy doesn't tolerate homosexuals in the Naval service, (3) tell you what can happen if you are foolish enough to commit a homosexual act, (4) and most important of all, to show how any one of you may become involved in a homosexual act unless you understand the circumstances under which the homosexual may make an approach to you.

Let us first review the definition of homosexuality. It is sexual gratification of an individual through physical contact with another person of the same sex. A homosexual, then, is one who gratifies her sex desires by being sexually intimate with another woman.

You may ask, how can a young woman who has always led a wholesome life become involved? There are several techniques which may be used by the practicing homosexual to lure you into involvement in a homosexual act.

One of the most commonly used techniques is for the practicing homosexual to use friendship as a means to secure for herself a partner in her homosexual acts. . . . The practicing homosexual may begin her approach to you as a sympathetic, understanding and motherly person. At first she will present the same appearance as many of your friends. She will have many interests in common with you, but as time progresses you will be aware that she is developing this friendship as much as possible along emotional lines. This person may begin to demand all of your time, and to shower you with expensive gifts, and to pay all the expenses when you are out together. Even though you may never have indulged in alcohol, she may initiate you into the "art of social drinking." She may plan activities that will end in parties where heavy drinking is being done. She may plan more and more time for the two of you to be alone . . . late rides in her car, intimate conversations between the two of you, and physical advances such as embraces. As time goes by, she may propose that you take a week-end trip with her to a near-by city, to sightsee or take in a show. This trip will involve sharing a hotel or motel room. When you are alone . . . she orders drinks . . . , and more and more alcohol is consumed. Then follow the improper physical advances and a homosexual act is committed. . . .

A woman homosexual may use a technique that is opposite to the one of kindliness, protective sympathy, and understanding. Her approach may be signalled by domineering, severely bossy, mentally cruel or bossy conduct toward the individual approached. This technique is to secure the domination of the sought individual, and to gain mastery and control over her. Just how this dominance is secured, whether through timidity or fear does not matter; it may lead to seduction.

The "Come-on-and-no-risk" approach is still another technique that may be used, and it fits into the battle against boredom. Navy women may be propositioned to indulge, just a little bit, in homosexuality, "because you can have a lot of fun with no after effects." Frankly, what is being said is that you can experience sexual stimulation and sexual satisfaction in a homosexual act without risk of pregnancy. . . .

It is important that you understand the Navy's policy toward homosexuality. The policy of the Navy is quite positive in that all persons found guilty of so much as one single homosexual act while in the Naval service must be eliminated from the service. The "first timer" or experimenter is just as liable to separation as the confirmed homosexual. A woman is not tried for being a homosexual, she is tried for committing a homosexual act. One thing is certain, she is going out of the Navy and fast. Under certain circumstances she will be given an undesirable discharge, commonly called a U.D. It means she has been discharged from the Navy as an undesirable, and her discharge papers will state that it is under conditions other than honorable and without satisfactory service. In certain circumstances she may face trial by General Court-Martial.

Answer these questions for yourselves . . . if you were discharged from the Navy for committing a homosexual act . . . , what kind of a job would you be able to get? The person hiring you would investigate and find out that you were not the type of person who would be a good risk as an employee. Government employment is impossible. You may lose virtually all rights as a veteran under both Federal and State legislation. You would probably be reduced to getting a job of such low level and so undesirable that your employer wouldn't bother to investigate.

What would you tell your family and friends? Or the man you hope someday to marry? Could you tell them that you were discharged from the Navy as an undesirable, or were Court-Martialed for abnormal sex practices? These facts have an unpleasant way of coming out, no matter how much you try to hide them.

The families, parents, and friends of women who have been discharged from the Navy for homosexual acts write tearful letters to the Navy Department in Washington, D.C., begging for relief from the type of discharge they have received. They claim the Navy has branded them as homosexuals, and because of this they find it difficult to earn a living, or find an acceptable young man for dating, companionship, or possible marriage. Actually, the Navy has not branded these women. They have branded and disgraced themselves, and no relief is possible. Women who engage in homosexual acts cannot and will not be tolerated by the United States Navy. . . .

If a homosexual makes an approach to you, stay away from her. If you have evidence of homosexual acts report them to the proper authorities. . . .

Remember, the fine friendships between normal, decent women is not the thing I'm referring to today. The many wholesome friendships formed in the Naval service are one of the finest influences in barracks and social life. These friendships are of great value to the Navy woman, both while in the service and in civilian life when she has returned to her home. The annual reunion celebration of Navy women throughout the United States every year gives some concept of the importance of such friendships. It is good for young women coming into the service to use their petty officers as guides and models of service life. Be wise in your choice of friends. Be alert and avoid emotional pitfalls.

Finally, all of us should be very proud to be women serving in the United States Navy, but let us be sure that we retain as much of our basic femininity as possible. We are not competing with the men; we are supplementing and complementing them. We must take pride in the kind of things women do well, that of setting a high standard of conduct by living in accord with the moral beliefs of our society.

May I now present Doctor _____ , Medical Corps, U.S. Navy, who will speak to you on the medical aspects of homosexuality.

MEDICAL OFFICER'S PRESENTATION (WAVE RECRUITS)

The medical officer, particularly one that specializes in psychiatry, is interested in homosexuality as an abnormal form of human behavior. . . .

Generally speaking, homosexual activity is the manifestation of failure on the part of the individual to grow up sexually, which leads to personality disorders in adult life. This is true whether the individual be exclusively homosexual or only a "dabbler." . . . What you have done in your younger and developing life is not to be taken as placing you in a position of the person under discussion today, or to be in a position of danger. To draw a comparison, it is not that you wet the bed as a child but do you wet the bed today.

By virtue of the fact that you are now in the Navy, you are considered grown-up and adult behavior is expected of you. If such behavior is not forthcoming, you will be held accountable. . . .

Several common misconceptions exist about homosexuality and it is these misconceptions which lead people into trouble. One such misconception is that it is easy to identify a practicing female homosexual by her masculine mannerisms and characteristics. This is not true. Many practicing female homosexuals are quite feminine in appearance and some are outstandingly so. There are probably more female homosexuals who are completely feminine in appearance than there are female homosexuals who are masculine in appearance.

Another common misconception is that those who engage in homosexuality are safe from acquiring venereal disease. This also is not true, as both gonorrhea and syphilis can be readily contracted through sexual relations with females as well as through sexual relations with males. Reports from various clinics reveal one out of every four male and female patients admitted with syphilis acknowledged homosexual contacts as the source of their infection. Practicing homosexuals are notoriously promiscuous and not very particular in whom they pick up, infected or otherwise.

A third misconception is that homosexuals are born and not made. This idea leads to the beliefs, first, that an individual who is not born a homosexual can participate in homosexual acts without danger and, second, that nothing can be done medically for the confirmed homosexual. Neither of these beliefs is true. Treatment is available for even the confirmed homosexual but this is not an obligation of the Navy Medical Corps. As to the other belief, repeated dabbling in homosexuality in late adolescence as well as in adulthood can and frequently does constitute the making of a homosexual. Some who start as "dabblers" or "experimenters" progress steadily to become exclusively homosexual in their behavior. Experimentation, therefore, aside from being an infringement on social as well as Navy standards, is dangerous in its own right.

In this entire problem, the medical officer has a two-fold interest: first, and uppermost, he is a naval officer and has an interest in the Navy as a whole. It is his duty to help eliminate disturbing and undesirable factors from the Naval service, such as confirmed homosexuals. In the second place, as a physician and a psychiatrist, he offers his experience and knowledge of behavior disorders in helping those who are concerned about this problem. In this latter capacity, he maintains an open door attitude to all, and he is available for interview at your request.

May I now present Chaplain who will speak to you on the social, moral and spiritual aspects of homosexuality.

CHAPLAIN'S PRESENTATION (WAVE RECRUITS)

The Chaplain's primary concern with the problem of homosexuality is its relationship to the individual's social, moral and spiritual life. . . .

Homosexuality Destroys a Woman's Social Status and Her Social Future
I do not feel I have to emphasize to you how delicate a structure is a woman's good name, or how easy it is to tarnish or destroy it.

A single act, or an association, may brand a woman as a sexual pervert. Society allows women more emotional demonstrations in public than it allows men. Women friends may embrace and kiss each other as they meet in public without causing suspicion or starting a whispering campaign. Such displays of emotion and friendship, however, must always be within good taste.

By her conduct a Navy woman may ruin her chances for a happy marriage. Friends should be chosen with great care. Friendships are best when they are carefully formed on the basis of similar ages and interests. . . .

To get entangled with homosexuality means three things: (1) The woman gambles with the possible destruction of her social life and future marriage; (2) She will become the target of other homosexuals; (3) All normal, decent people who know, or even who strongly suspect the facts will have nothing to do with her.

Homosexuality Destroys a Woman's Character

Homosexuality is a social offense, and is named a felony by law. . . . People who engage in homosexuality fear exposure for there is always a witness (the other person). It is not possible to live under constant tension and fear, without seriously weakening one's moral fiber, mental and emotional stability.

Homosexuality destroys a woman's personal integrity. Little by little, the individual becomes more deeply entangled in the homosexual web. At first she wonders how it all happened. She reacts with confusion, shame and fear. She rationalizes that she was only a passive partner; that she really did not do anything. But she knows better. Then she faces the possibility of blackmail. She finds it easier to submit to homosexuality than to fight against it.

Experience indicates that the odds are heavy against her ever quitting. She slowly deteriorates in character, losing her power of will, and her integrity. Thus the deterioration and destruction of character and integrity are the end results of homosexuality. Even such gross crimes as robbery, suicide and murder often grow out of homosexuality.

Homosexuality Destroys a Woman's Spiritual Values and Her Spiritual Life

Moral and ethical codes reaching far back into history are against any form of homosexuality. It is universally condemned by all religions. All nations who have given way to the practice of homosexuality have fallen and it is against the law of all civilized nations. The guilt associated with homosexuality is a barrier between the individual and God.

The Creator has endowed the bodies of women with the noble mission of motherhood and the bringing of human life into the world. Any woman who violates this great trust by participating in homosexuality not only degrades herself socially but also destroys the purpose for which God created her.

In Conclusion

Let me emphasize the following:

It is important to recognize danger. It is foolish to expose yourself. Good sportsmanship and courage are never proved by taking unnecessary risks, flirting with danger, or "taking a chance!" Homosexuality is dangerous in all of its phases. The woman who takes any chances with it demonstrates only her own stupidity, never her courage or smartness.

We do not wish to alarm you about homosexuality, nor do we intend anything that we say in this lecture to lead you to believe that an unmarried woman who does not engage in sexual practices with men is homosexual. She is, on the contrary, a sensible person. Sex was created for the married state and true happiness can best be found through marriage and a home.

We are confident that you will go on through life using common sense and self-discipline.

We would also like to emphasize again the need of avoiding vicious gossip and rumors accusing or implying that someone is a homosexual or engaging in homosexual acts. Before engaging in such talk or spreading such dastardly gossip about anyone, I would suggest that you think of two things. First, think of the terrible harm that may come to this girl and her family because of you. And secondly, ask yourself—How would I feel if someone were to spread such vicious rumors about me?

If you are actually approached by one of these people or if you strongly suspect something that is out of line, talk the matter over with someone who can do something about it without harming someone who may be innocent. Your WAVE officer, your Medical officer and Chaplain are always available for personal counsel. If you wish to discuss this presentation just given, please feel free to contact any of us who have given it or any of the above mentioned officers. Thank you for your attention.

Letters from Lesbian WAFs to American Civil Liberties Union, 1951

Feb 15, 1951

Dear Sir,

I'm not sure whether the following is included in the absence of Civil Liberties but if it isn't I think it should be. I recently joined your organization not consciously connecting it with my predicament at the time, but when I saw inked in at the bottom of your "welcome to membership" note the statement that you were glad to have an Air Force girl with you I couldn't resist telling you about this situation—I would like any comments or suggestions you have to offer.

I enlisted in the Air Force in [the summer] of '49 and am about to receive an Undesirable Discharge. Seems I am guilty of lewed [sic] and lacivious [sic] behavior—this constitutes homosexuality in their eyes—they have been having a housecleaning and work thusly: Down at Keesler about 11 girls were called in and questioned as to their alleged homosexuality by the OSI—Office of Special Investigation—the girls being sick of the worry and strain of being under suspicion and being promised by a very likable chap Capt _____ of the OSI that they would receive General Discharges if they confessed all proceeded to do so and after confessing were informed that it wasn't enough to incriminate only themselves—they must write down also someone else with whom they had homosexual relations—this done they waited and at the end of January they were all out with Undesirables—I was named in one of these statements and when the records got up here was called in by the OSI. Before I said anything I was read the 24th Article of War where you don't have to testify against yourself and told also that I might have an attorney with me during this questioning—that seems fair enough but their scare technique is such that you don't quite believe what you hear—he tells you that you don't have to say anything, but does it in such a way that you are sure if you don't the consequences will be little short of fatal.

As far as the attorney is concerned—who could afford a civilian one and I didn't know until it was too late that I had a officer on the base at my disposal—so I stupidly went ahead and made a statement to the effect that I had had such relations with this individual—that the relationship had ended and that never before or since had anything of that nature occurred. If I had been aware of the base attorney at my disposal I would of course been advised to say nothing and they would have had to prove every allegation—as it was I just hung myself out of fear. The papers then went to the Judge Advocates office where he reviewed them and recommended an Undesirable Discharge which I was asked to sign a request for and refused—I requested a courts martial but am not very hopeful of that.

My objections to this whole procedure are many—first of all in the recruiting office no indication is given that lesbians are undesirable or considered so to the service—their job is to fill a quota and that's all they do. This alone would have saved many people a good deal of heartbreak. Once in and aware of the govt attitude in this regard there is no way out except that of having your reputation ruined and the chances of a future job nil—if you were to go and confess the type of discharge would be the same. No consideration is given to your quality of work or dependability—whether you seduce every girl in sight or whether you were once seduced and have since been dating and staying far away from the whole business. The OSI encourages you to spy on the other girls and to list girls who are friends and who might be engaging in homosexual relations—and they say they want facts! No consideration is given to the vast amounts of money expended on outfitting and training girls for work only to be discharged at great financial loss to the govt. The Air Force Regulation on this matter AFR 35-66 is the strictest ever and contains such gems as . . . if it is thought that a conviction by courts martial cannot be obtained then Washington shall direct the discharge—it provides that anyone with homosexual tendencies may be discharged—and who among us is without such? For every 10 girls they are discharging they recruit 20 more who will be put through basic and through tech school and then discharged and over and over again.

There seems to be no way to fight this thing—those who decide your fate are in Washington and never see you—if they knew the cost in morale of their troops—the nervous wear and tear on the individual—I wonder if they would think twice. A big wheel comes to visit the base and turns in a good report—how does he know the great percentage of airmen living in fear—waiting from day to day for the call from the OSI. I don't mean to sound childishly dramatic—perhaps it's my own amazement that such a situation exists in this country—this wasn't what we learned in school—our govt tells us how well she has done by the Indian and the foreign nation, but where is one speck of regard for the individual govt employee? No doubt you have had experience with this situation when it came up in the State Dept—here was the last place I expected a rotten deal—I am furious at my ineptness at fighting this thing—somehow I should have been aware of the resources at my disposal—but I am more angry that they should be necessary—that such an unreasonable and unrealistic attitude should prevail—the personal heartbreak where my parents are concerned coupled with the job prejudice in civilian life adds up to one hell of a mess. They have discharged married girls for this also—frankly I'm at my wits end and am writing this in the hope that you will have some suggestion or thought on the matter. Have you any info on what kind of jobs those so branded can obtain? I understand Russia has started rejecting homosexuals for military service—is this a clue?

Thank you for your time spent in reading this.

Sincerely,

——————

. . . .

16 Mar. '51

Dear Sirs,

A friend of mine, Cpl. ————, has been telling me a lot about your organization and your continual and magnificent fights for justice in this country. I would very much like to be a part of such a group. Perhaps my interest is greater right at this time than it would have been previously because I have just been separated from the United States Air Force in a manner that I personally feel to have been less than legal. If I may take a few minutes leeway, I'd like to explain the situation to you.

I enlisted in the WAF [in early] 1949. I took my basic training at Lackland AFB. While I was there, I met a girl with whom I became very friendly, and our friendship continued during our basic training. After graduating from basic, we had a party in San Antonio, and it was at this time that I first realized that the girl with whom I'd been associating was a homosexual. For reasons too numerous to state here, this knowledge did not terminate our friendship. We were both shipped to Keesler AFB, Biloxi, Miss. where our relationship, which was of a homosexual nature, continued. Because of strong guilt feelings, and various other psychological repercussions, I broke off our friendship in the Thanksgiving season of that year (1949). I was attending Radio Operator's school there in Biloxi and remained there until the following March, when I graduated with a Superior rating from aforementioned school. From Thanksgiving 1949 until March 1950, I had no further contact with this girl.

I was sent to Wright-Patterson AFB in March, '50. As soon as I was settled in my job, I started seeing the base psychiatrist, Capt. _____, in an effort to get my mental set straightened out. He, very obligingly, took me on as a patient.

Sometime in December, 1950, I received a letter from this homosexual girl, saying that she had been questioned by the O.S.I. (Office of Special Investigation), and had signed a statement to the effect that she had had homosexual relationships with me "several times." I had an opportunity to read her statement later, and most of what she said was true. Her sins were those of ommission [sic]; she neglected to state that she had had relations with two other girls after I "walked out" on her. Another [In other] words, she had a grudge to pay back. I was very much worried about this letter and took it in to Capt. _____ [the base psychiatrist]. He told me not to bother about it, because his word meant a lot more than that of a disgruntled lesbian.

I was called in by the OSI office in our base about two weeks later. I explained to them truthfully what had happened, and thought that would be the end of it. Such was not the case. I was called in by our Troop Commandant about the middle of February and he asked me if I wanted to request an Undesirable discharge — (it seems that this saves the AF a lot of money.) I refused to sign the request and asked for a court-martial.

My squadron called me the 23rd of February and told me to start clearing the base — I was to be discharged the following week. My appeal for a trial had been refused under the following section of AFR 35-66 (Regulation concerning discharge of homosexuals) "when conviction by courts-martial is unlikely, the Secretary of the Air Force may direct discharge administratively." I was given a General Discharge from the AF February 28 [1951]. This discharge, under honorable conditions, simply means that I am refused forever the right to wear the uniform of my country; that I may never hold a position of trust in this country because I am a "bad security-risk." Anytime I want to apply for a Civil Service job, it will be right there. With a little less honesty, with a little less integrity, I could have bluffed my way through it!

I was the fourth girl to be discharged thusly on Wright-Patterson, there were eleven at Keesler and I can't get the figures from Lackland.

It's too late to help me at all in this mess, but there are about twenty girls left there at Wright-Patterson who live in constant terror of the telephone. Theirs is no small problem. If we were given any consideration as individuals, it would be a different matter. But nobody asked my Squadron Commander about my character, nobody asked my work unit if I did my work well. (They, by the way, when I asked them for a recommendation for a civilian job, told me to write my own if I was in any way displeased with theirs—they recommended me without qualification.) To all this no attention was paid. To Washington, I was a non-entity with a homosexual contact. I ask you, for all those girls left, is this fair? Is it in keeping with the principles we shout so loud? How efficient can our armed forces be, with this sort of psychological warfare raging within? As an individual, I'm powerless; as an organization, can you help them?

Sorry to have sputtered on so long. I'm still rather incensed at the situation.

Thanks for your attention,

—————

San Francisco, Calif.

· ·

April 4, 1951

Dear Miss ————,

I can well sympathize with your plight, but unfortunately, there is no violation of civil liberties involved in the policy of the Army that homosexuals of either sex must be discharged from the Army.

So you see, there is really nothing we can do about whether the Army is sensibly handling the matter or whether they could more sensibly handle it by furnishing medical treatment to the parties concerned, is not for us to say.

Your friend Corporal ———— wrote us about the same problem in a letter dated February 15th. . . . The only suggestion that I can have on this matter is a purely practical one—doubtless social stigma will follow both of you if the present situation continues; the only way of alleviating it that I can think of is to submit yourself to medical treatment if you really desire to abandon homosexual relations.

Sincerely yours,

_____

Staff Counsel

. . . .

April 23, 1951

Dear Mr. _____,

Received your letter dated April 4, and wish to thank you so much for your attention. Believe me, I fully understand that you are unable to help in straightening out our situation. The cause of homosexuals is a decidedly unpopular one. My letter to the ACLU was merely a shot in the dark. I am one of the luckier ones, with an understanding family, but two of the girls discharged for homosexuality have committed suicide and one other has disappeared completely. These girls, you understand, are all girls who never ran into homosexuality until they entered the service.

I was able . . . to influence our Commanding officer to hold a squadron meeting and explain to the girls their rights under the Articles of War. She was shortly thereafter relieved of her position. Maybe it's a coincidence.

I've written to ex-corporal _____ and sent her your letter. I know full well that my grateful thanks may be extended from both of us. We are both proud to be members of the ACLU and wish you continued success in your very fine work.

Very sincerely yours,

_____

NOTES

1. Senate Committee on Expenditures in Executive Departments, _Employment of Homosexuals and Other Sex Perverts in Government_, 81st Cong., 2d sess., 1950. For a discussion of the "homosexual scare" during the McCarthy era, see John D'Emilio, _Sexual Politics, Sexual Communities: The Making of a Homosexual Minority in the United States, 1940–1970_ (Chicago: University of Chicago Press, 1983), 40–53.

2. Headline reprinted in _ONE Magazine_, April 1954, 16–17. See also Lee Mortimer, _Washington Confidential Today_ (New York: Crown, 1952), and Jack Lait and Lee Mortimer, _U.S.A. Confidential_ (New York: Crown, 1952).

3. Exclusion of homosexuals and lesbians from all government jobs was specified in

Eisenhower's Executive Order 10450, issued on April 27, 1953, printed in the *New York Times*, April 28, 1953, 20. For a detailed analysis of federal policies, see John D'Emilio, "The Evolution and Impact of Federal Antihomosexual Policies during the 1950s" (report prepared for the National Gay Task Force, New York, 1983).

4. Statistics on military discharges on grounds of homosexuality may be found in Colin J. Williams and Martin S. Weinberg, *Homosexuals and the Military* (New York: Harper and Row, 1971), 31–36, 45–47, 53. The statistics are not broken down by gender.

5. U.S. Navy, "Report of the Board Appointed to Prepare and Submit Recommendations to the Secretary of the Navy for the Revision of Policies, Procedures and Directives Dealing with Homosexuals, 21 December 1956–15 March 1957," Captain S. H. Crittenden Jr., chairman, 40–41 (hereafter cited as Crittenden Report).

6. On women during World War II and after, see Karen Anderson, *Wartime Women: Sex Roles, Family Relations, and the Status of Women during World War II* (Westport, Conn.: Greenwood Press, 1981); William H. Chafe, *The American Woman* (New York: Oxford University Press, 1972), chaps. 6–8; and Mary P. Ryan, *Womanhood in America*, 2d ed. (New York: New Viewpoints, 1979), chaps. 5–6.

7. "Sex Hygiene Course, Officers and Officer Candidates, Women's Army Auxiliary Corps," May 27, 1943, War Department Pamphlet no. 35-1 (Washington, D.C.: Government Printing Office, 1943). Quotations are from "Lecture I: Introduction," 3–4, and "Lecture V: Homosexuality," 24–29.

8. On lesbians in the U.S. military during World War II, see Allan Bérubé, "Coming Out Under Fire," *Mother Jones* 8, no. 11 (February/March 1983): 23–29, 45, and "Marching to a Different Drummer," *Advocate*, no. 328 (October 15, 1981), 20–25, reprinted in *Powers of Desire: The Politics of Sexuality*, edited by Ann Snitow, Christine Stansell, and Sharon Thompson, 88–99 (New York: Monthly Review Press, 1983).

9. Lectures are from the Crittenden Report, vol. A, app. 23, "Samples of Standard Indoctrination Lectures."

10. Crittenden Report, Board Report, 42–43. These pages of the Board Report include a chronology of events that led to the implementation of the indoctrination program on the subject of homosexuality.

11. Program guidelines are from Bureau of Naval Personnel, "Proposed Modifications to Recruit Training Curriculum" and "Proposed Procedure for Implementing Program of Indoctrination of Naval Personnel at Naval Training Centers as to Subject of Homosexuality," approved for implementation in Secretary of the Navy to Chief of Naval Personnel, November 14, 1952, all included in Crittenden Report, vol. A, app. 22, "Instructions for Committee on Indoctrination and Education."

12. The letters are from General Correspondence, vol. 16, 1951, ACLU Papers, Princeton University, Princeton, N.J.

13. On the military's use of administrative discharges, see Clifford A. Dougherty and Norman B. Lynch, "The Administrative Discharge: Military Justice?," *George Washington Law Review* 33 (1964): 498–528, and Jerome A. Susskind, "Military Administrative Discharge Boards: The Right to Confrontation and Cross-Examination," *Michigan State Bar Journal* 46 (1965): 25–32.

14. On the position of the ACLU concerning homosexuality and civil liberties, see Herbert Levy to William Klausner, April 17, 1953, and Levy to Mrs. Thomas Manly Dillingham, September 20, 1955, General Correspondence, vol. 55, 1953, and vol. 27,

1955, respectively, ACLU Papers, Princeton University. The text of the statement "Homosexuality and Civil Liberties," adopted by the ACLU board of directors on January 7, 1957, may be found in *Civil Liberties*, March 1957.

15. For more information on the DOB, see Del Martin and Phyllis Lyon, *Lesbian/Woman* (San Francisco: Glide Urban Center Publications, 1972), and D'Emilio, *Sexual Politics, Sexual Communities*.

PART III

A Working-Class Intellectual

Personal Reflections on Identities

Caught in the Storm
AIDS and the Meaning of Natural Disaster

The AIDS epidemic hit Bérubé in the most immediate way when his partner, Brian Keith, was diagnosed with AIDS and died in 1987. In this essay, Bérubé writes of the need to grieve and mourn as well as to acknowledge the horrific human cost of the epidemic. At the same time, he takes strong issue with those who try to impose meaning on the tragedy. Some of the responses to AIDS, he argues, continued a long historical tradition of scapegoating gay men for their sexual desires. Instead, he sees AIDS as "a profound tragedy" and mourns the loss of "our old shelters" where, through sexual expression, gay men had found warmth, companionship, pleasure, and community. "Caught in the Storm" is the first of several long essays that Bérubé composed in which he mined his personal experience for broader insights into both the past and the present. He published it in Out/Look, *a Bay Area publication with a national reach that was founded in 1988, just as the AIDS epidemic was leading to a revival of radical critiques of American society and more militant gay activism.*

> Strong wind destroy our home. Many dead, tonight it could be you. . . .
> Somebody sings, Somebody cries why, why, why?
> — *Paul Simon*, "Homeless"

When I look at the AIDS epidemic without turning away, I find myself asking questions about the meaning of my life and my death. I remember asking these same questions in the 1950s as a devoutly Catholic adolescent. In those days, I was first coming to terms with what were to me the abstractions of war, the Holocaust, and Hiroshima. Now, in my early forties and no longer a practicing or believing Catholic, I face the reality of my lover Brian's death last year, my own tentative survival, the AIDS/ARC diagnoses or positive HIV antibody statuses of most of my close male friends, and the deaths of many other good friends. Where I live in San Francisco, our mayor tells us that

Originally published in *Out/Look*, Fall 1988, 8–19.

Annette Bérubé created the AIDS quilt square for Brian. Courtesy of the Allan Bérubé Collection at the GLBTHS, San Francisco.

twice as many local men have died of AIDS than were lost from this city on the combined battlefields of World War I, World War II, Korea, and Vietnam.

The questions I now ask are the most profound I know: "Why was it Brian who got AIDS and died?" "Why not me?" "Why is AIDS attacking so many of us?" "Why now?" I want to make sense of this awful tragedy. I want it somehow to be worth the suffering, to know that some good will come of it. I want to console those who are sick and comfort them, to reassure them and myself that it's going to be all right and they are not going to die. I want to make things better, to give advice, to save lives.

My deepest fears are that I cannot stop things from getting even worse, that more harm than good will come of this epidemic, that there is no comfort or consolation, that I cannot prevent my friends from dying, that I won't be able to bear more loss. I want to salvage some good, some meaning, some hope from the wreckage of this storm. I want to know why.

Yet I'm troubled by answers I hear that try to bring the tragedy of AIDS under control. These answers explain that AIDS is attacking gay men now for a reason, that it exists to teach us a lesson, that we have created AIDS, that it chooses us or that we choose it, or that it has inherent meanings and benefits that can compensate for so much loss.

People offer these explanations and reassurances to try to rescue us from our helplessness, our fear, and our loss. "Keep busy," they say. "Cheer up!" "Get angry." "Don't mourn, organize!" They try to deny the tragedy of so many deaths by calling AIDS a "learning experience," a "golden opportunity," a "gift," or a "blessing in disguise." These attempts to protect us from our pain usually go unchallenged because they are often camouflaged with good intentions. They can lie hidden within consolations; they can be disguised by a well-meaning but patronizing desire to give us shortcuts to hope.

At this year's AIDS memorial march in San Francisco, one of the few public rituals we have created to grieve together as a community, it was as if sadness and grief themselves were our enemies, lurking in the shadows and in our hearts, threatening to destroy us as individuals and as communities. Many marchers, including myself, became totally preoccupied with the business of trying to protect our lighted candles from the cold wind. A large group in front of us kept silence at bay by singing Broadway show tunes. At the rally following the procession, hardly any speaker addressed our pain, our fear, our anger, or our loss. Instead, we heard political victory speeches, upbeat songs, and a jubilant litany of cities where similar AIDS memorials were being held around the world, without an acknowledgment of the tragedy that makes such marches necessary. My friends and many others I talked to that night went home early. We had the uneasy feeling that this well-meaning rally, which was supposed to have been a memorial to those who have died, instead had ritualized our fears and had failed to "give" us hope.

Individual denial—which some hospice workers call terror management —is one important way to cope with multiple loss. But ethical issues are raised when anyone, individually or collectively, imposes their own denial on others. Ethical boundaries are crossed when people try to save rather than support those of us who, against all odds, try to face painful truths. As a surviving partner, it hurts each time someone denies the tragedy of Brian's untimely death and the depth of my own sadness by explaining that there are compensations that somehow make it all worthwhile. Reassurances based on these compensatory benefits—whether political, moral, or spiritual—deny us survivors our inconsolable loss. Attempts to rescue us from our grief deny us survivors the particular strength and hope that we gain by facing our worst fears and moving on.

After he was diagnosed, Brian and I tackled the troubling "why" questions together, struggling ourselves between hope and grief, between explanations and acceptance. Brian was a British biochemist; I'm an American historian. He had dedicated his working life to understanding how plants grow and flower; I've dedicated mine to understanding how human sexuality changes over time. We both grew up in working-class families where disasters as well as once-in-a-lifetime opportunities, such as scholarships to college, seemed to happen by chance, completely outside our control. Both of us mistrusted organized religions. But Brian's skepticism, his scientific questioning, and his matter-of-fact approach toward his illness gave him a clarity and acceptance that seemed spiritual at times.

Why was the HIV destroying Brian's body? His science told us that viruses, like storms and plagues of locusts, are experienced by humans as natural disasters but are not evil forces intent on causing misery. If the virus had any "purpose" or "interest" at all, it was to thrive and reproduce. As a therapeutic experiment, I tried to get us both to visualize the virus as an evil enemy that we wanted to destroy, but it didn't work. The best we could do was to think of it as a rude, unwelcome intruder whom we screamed at to "get out of our house!" That tapped into my anger and made me cry, which brought Brian and me even closer to each other. But we couldn't find ways to blame the virus.

Why did the virus get into Brian's body and not into mine? I found myself telling friends how unfair this was because Brian had never gone to the baths and I had gone often. Then I realized that by saying this, I was making the mistake of assuming that it would have made more sense or have been more just if I had gotten AIDS instead of Brian. In fact, we both had been very careful sexually beginning in 1983 when the first safe sex guidelines were issued. I lucked out, Brian didn't. Was that the only reason he was going to die? Was that it? Yes, he kept telling me. Bad luck. And the government's neglect.

Many times I sat silently next to Brian, crying, with no answers for why this was happening to him or to me. Yet I knew in my bones that we were creating an intimacy that, paradoxically, gave our lives meaning as each loss and each minute went by and as he peacefully came closer to a death that he fully expected would end his existence forever. With Brian, I learned how to live well without the answers I ached for.

Like many other disasters, this epidemic is a part of nature that devastates our lives and makes us wonder why. Yet AIDS is nothing more or less than a disease that is killing human beings. It is a natural event that exists because it exists. While HIV itself may have no inherent meaning or purpose, the ways that Brian and I responded to its presence in his body made all the difference in the world. We realized that the power to create or destroy meaning was in us, not in the virus. While the virus had the power to kill without intent, we had the power to create meaning out of our responses.

It is tempting to use AIDS the disease, like other parts of nature, as if it were an open book of blank pages on which each of us can write lessons, morals, and answers. Because AIDS creates life-and-death situations, the statements we write in this book are about the meanings of our lives and our deaths. This task of creating meaning for ourselves is profoundly personal, and its outcome is as varied as our individual lives. It's also a terrifying task during an epidemic, because no matter how many pages we fill, no matter how many explanations we create, there are always more empty pages. Each blank page, each new person dying, makes us face again, with fear and disbelief, the unjust suffering, the random deaths, and the unanswered questions that this disaster leaves in its path. It is always painful for me to open this book, put down my pen, look at its blank pages without turning away, and sit quietly or cry. But continuing to grieve in this way—letting go of my need for answers, feeling the sadness and loss, and then moving on—is one of the best ways I have learned to respond to this epidemic.

The Names Project quilt helps me go through this process within a larger community. Like the Vietnam War Memorial and the AIDS memorial marches, visiting the quilt is a ritual that allows many of us to remember and grieve together in the face of incomprehensible loss. Each panel holds unique meanings for the survivors that are intensely personal. But sewn together into a patchwork quilt, they create a work of folk art that has no center, no limit, no one meaning, and no easy answers. In fact, several panels consist solely of questions scrawled onto cloth. We can walk inside this quilt, by ourselves or holding each other, as we do each day inside this epidemic. We have created in this quilt a response, a memory, and a shared intimacy that each gives meaning to what we are going through. By unfolding the quilt on the Mall during our March on Washington, our communities created a rare public ritual that joined our hope with our grief. AIDS did not empower us to do this; we empowered ourselves.

There are two different ways to respond to the "why" questions we ask about AIDS. Their differences are not between religious and secular, the political right and left, antigay and gay, but in the ways each assigns meaning to misfortune. One response offers answers; the other accepts uncertainties and dwells in the place between the questions and the answers. When people respond with answers, they are likely to explain why AIDS happens at particular times to particular people and what AIDS teaches us. They can cause harm when their definitive answers keep people from finding their own meanings, blame people for their illness, or fill the silences in which people can face their fears and grieve. When people respond to the tragedy of AIDS without answers, they are likely to challenge moral explanations and open up the possibility of wondering, listening, and being silent together. But without answers, people can feel isolated, helpless, and without direction.

Each of these kinds of responses has ethical implications. The stories we tell each other about why particular people do or do not get AIDS have tremendous power. They touch real lives with real consequences and have the potential for framing some of the most profound experiences in a person's life. Even our most casual comments or reassurances—"You should have loved yourself better" or "There must be a reason why your son is suffering"—can be fragments of a moral framework which, if we could see it whole, we might not condone. It is important for us, as individuals and as communities, to examine our assumptions and begin openly discussing with each other the ethics of how we ask and answer questions that assign meaning to other people's misfortune.

If we could strengthen our ability to live with unanswered questions, it would help us define such an ethical framework. This could reduce the power of this disease by deflating its overblown meanings. It could also lift from people with AIDS the weight of interpretations that reduce diverse and complex lives to moral, spiritual, or political lessons. In the process, we could clear away for ourselves a safe breathing space wherein we could find relief from the constant pressure to address the "why" questions about AIDS.

I feel the urgency of this task because the more dominant response to AIDS is to explain exactly what it means. It is difficult enough for each of us in these times to find meaning for our own lives and deaths. But some people, wishing either to comfort and advise or to blame and exploit people with AIDS, have taken on the task of assigning their own meanings to other people's illnesses. They give ready-made or unexamined answers to the most troubling personal question, "Why me?" by reducing it to "Why you?" "Nothing is more punitive," wrote Susan Sontag, who herself has survived cancer, "than to give disease a meaning—that meaning invariably being a moralistic one. Any important disease whose causality is murky, and for which treatment is ineffectual, tends to be awash in significance." In our communities today, AIDS means too much.

The answers we are offered cut across the boundaries of politics, religion, and sexual orientation and teach us lessons about AIDS: Gay men should have known better; AIDS is the inevitable result of the sexual revolution; The "gay plague," the "gay cancer," the "gay disease" was created by the "gay lifestyle"; AIDS exists to open us up to the spiritual aspects of our lives; AIDS exists because God is punishing homosexuals, drug users, prostitutes, and the sexually active for their sins; AIDS is nature's revenge against those who have declared war on nature and from whom nature is exacting an awful retribution; or that AIDS exists for a host of other reasons. The implication of all these explanations, as well as the systems of meaning they represent, is that people get AIDS because they live bad or incomplete or unbalanced lives.

To make matters worse, people who use AIDS to teach us lessons use people with AIDS as their lesson books. They place on people with AIDS the unfair burden of being scapegoats, moral examples, or the original "patient zeros." Others of us, sometimes without realizing it, use people with AIDS to inspire: We expect people with AIDS to serve us as models of courage, as our spiritual teachers or moral guides, people who have the answers or, in the words of Elisabeth Kübler-Ross, are "catalysts" who set in motion "wonderful world changes." People living with AIDS have enough business to take care of without being burdened involuntarily with the task of inspiring us or teaching the rest of us how to live morally or die correctly.

While some people tell us that the virus chooses people to teach us moral or spiritual lessons, others tell us that people infected with HIV choose this disease. Every few weeks I'm exasperated to hear yet another person explain that people with AIDS have created their illness, either literally or spiritually. A gay spiritual counselor writing in the *Sentinel*, one of San Francisco's gay newspapers, believes that we all choose our illnesses and deaths. "Potentially fatal situations," he explains, "such as car wrecks, cancer operations, rape, food poisoning, suicide and even AIDS . . . are all ways in which we express our death urge."[1] Louise Hay, in her 1987 book *You Can Heal Your Life*, explains that many gay men have "created a destructive lifestyle" that is "monstrous" and, as a result, have "created a disease called AIDS" which is a "monstrous disease."[2] Elisabeth Kübler-Ross, in her 1987 book *AIDS: The Ultimate Challenge*, wonders if "our AIDS patients, children and adults alike, chose to contribute their short life spans on planet Earth to help us open our lives, to raise our consciousness, to open our hearts and minds, and to finally see the light."[3] Other popular articles and books have promoted the theory that people choose AIDS because they somehow need it to give their lives purpose, balance, or completion.[4]

An even more disturbing explanation is that "gay people" choose AIDS because we are a "chosen people." This interpretation links AIDS with the belief that all gay men and women have a unique spiritual mission. A columnist summarizing the philosophy behind a gay metaphysical spiritual center in San Francisco writes that the "gay community—as a collective consciousness—has chosen to experience AIDS first in this country as a learning experience to open closed hearts and fearful minds, so that we can return to our ancient roles as healers, shamans, priests and priestesses of society."[5] AIDS, then, makes us into a chosen people; it is the special "path" through which gay men and women are meant to become more spiritually evolved and thus fulfill our "ancient roles" as healers of the world.

AIDS does not choose people, and people don't choose AIDS. Despite the increasing popularity of what homeopathic educator Dana Ullman has called "wellness macho"—"the mistaken assumption that each of us has universal knowledge of the present and the future and that each of us is so strong and mighty that we can successfully avoid or defend against any stress, infection or environmental assault"—we do not choose everything that happens to us. There are some things over which we have no control. I see this most clearly when I think of AIDS as just one of many meaningless but devastating natural disasters. Ever since Brian was diagnosed, I have compared AIDS to a tornado to remind myself and my friends how the puzzling randomness of disasters can make us ask questions that don't have answers.

A tornado unexpectedly touches down on a small midwestern town. Some people find safety in a shelter or basement, while others driving in cars or without shelters are caught in the storm. Many people die. Families wonder why their homes were hit; surviving spouses question why their lives were spared. Why did the tornado hit this particular town at this particular hour and kill these particular people? How were they different from the survivors? Did they unconsciously want to die? Was it just bad luck or fate or God's will? Some survivors' questions project onto the tornado a personality and a will. Did it strike with a purpose? Did the tornado intend to teach the townspeople a lesson? What were they supposed to learn? Was it that the dead might not have had to die if they had lived differently? Was it merely that death can strike anyone at any time without warning? Or was it that no one should ever live where strong winds blow?

No matter how careful we are, living in today's world means living in the path of unpredictable winds over which we have little control but which can threaten our lives. We are aware of the risks of living in cities built on earthquake faults or in the paths of tornadoes, of flying in jets, of walking on city streets at night, of making love. We take precautions, yet some of us still die. We want explanations for their deaths as much as we want to postpone our own. But the goals of leading a risk-free life, of creating a cocoon of total safety, or of being certain that one's death will not be random are unattainable. Every day we take ordinary risks with no guarantee that we will survive.

The AIDS epidemic places gay men in a frightening dilemma because it has taken the safety out of our shelters from another deadly storm. Many of us first came out into a fiercely antigay climate of hate, fear, violence, and shame that threatened us with the force of a natural disaster. We found partial refuge in our lovemaking with each other and in the shelters that made our sexuality safe: our bedrooms, our bars, our bathhouses and cruising places. While the age-old storm of homophobia still rages on, the new storm of AIDS—the panic as well as the disease—takes the safety out of our old shelters by attacking our bodies, our lovemaking, and our sexual institutions. How do you rationally weigh risks when your shelters seem to threaten your life? What is remarkable is not that gay men were slow to change our sexual behavior, but that we so quickly built and occupied a new shelter to protect us from both of these storms: safe sex.

Those of us who led sexual lives before AIDS did not know that it was transmissible until 1982. No one had safe sex guidelines until May 1983, when our gay and lesbian communities began a process of education and risk reduction that by 1987 led to virtually no new sexually transmitted infections among gay men in San Francisco and dramatic declines in other cities. We each have developed our own methods for reducing sexual risks, knowing that some activities are safer than others, weighing them against a range of other needs.

Taking small risks, which are on the same order as other daily risks in our lives, does not mean that we want the worst outcome to happen. Even those few who knowingly took the greatest risks, or made mistakes, or were not able to make the best decisions because of alcohol or drugs and therefore increased their chances of infection, were not choosing AIDS. We all are ultimately responsible for our actions, but sometimes chance events occur that are beyond our control and that radically change the consequences of what had never been such life-threatening activities.

The tragedy of AIDS is not that so many people live such desperate lives that they choose to die of AIDS. It is that so many people are dying random deaths for no reason other than that they took the kinds of risks we all take in order to lead meaningful lives. Taking risks and losing is not the same as choosing to die.

Choice and responsibility are important issues for many people facing this epidemic. But the act of telling people with AIDS that they chose their disease—a notion that one does not have to accept in order to take responsibility for one's health and well-being—can have damaging effects. People who are sick, especially when treatments don't stop the course of their illness, unnecessarily ask themselves, "What is wrong with me? Why did I want to get sick and die? How are my attitudes creating a fertile ground for AIDS? Why can't I choose life?" And if we are convinced that most people with AIDS really choose to get this virus, then it can be argued that they alone are to blame for their illness and they, not society, must pay the price.

All people with AIDS, regardless of the risks they did or did not take, deserve our respect and our care. They have a right to determine for themselves how to respond to this disease without anyone assuming that they chose AIDS to rescue them from their bad lifestyles or to complete their lives. The burning moral issue in this epidemic is not how to judge who did or did not choose their illness so that we can separate the innocent from the guilty. It is rather how we all choose to respond to people who are living with AIDS and HIV.

Another troubling response that gives excessive meaning to AIDS is gratitude. This feeling is based on the perception that AIDS is happening now because our individual or collective pasts were immature, sinful, sick, or spiritually impoverished. In this scenario, AIDS is characterized as the savior. It is assigned meaning because it forces us to grow up, it is our salvation from sin, it cures us from a deeper psychological illness, or it rescues us from spiritual death.

Some gay men's gratitude toward AIDS, and the larger society's perception that AIDS is making gay men grow up, relies on the "Peter Pan" stereotype of gay men. In the old days, the story goes, gay men used to be uncaring, unthinking, irresponsible, and self-destructive adolescents who were obsessed with quick sex, partying, drugs, dancing, youth, and beauty. The bathhouse and the disco are the current symbols for this pre-AIDS lifestyle. The Peter Pan stereotype describes our lives before AIDS as so hopelessly compulsive that only massive deaths could change us. Some people explain that this pre-AIDS lifestyle (a distorted caricature of our real lives) was itself an illness that inevitably led to AIDS or was actually cured by AIDS.

Now, thanks to AIDS, literary bookstores replace bathhouses, country-western bars replace discos, dinner parties replace cruising, commitment replaces casual encounters, community service replaces partying, and monogamy replaces promiscuity. The media has been quick to report the news that AIDS finally has forced Peter Pan to act like an adult. The *San Francisco Examiner* publishes an article entitled "The Castro Grows Up," and the *New York Times* reports that AIDS has made the Castro district go through a "sort of maturation" from adolescence to adulthood.[6] The lesson is that AIDS has improved our lives.

The press also has given prominent coverage to stories about gay men who are grateful to AIDS for changes in the gay community and in their own lives. Both the mainstream and gay media highlight their reports of gay men's gratitude with glowing superlatives that read like advertisements for AIDS. "AIDS is the most wonderful thing that has ever happened in my life," proclaims a provocative cover of *Image*, the *San Francisco Examiner* Sunday magazine, quoting a gay "victim" of AIDS.[7] "AIDS was the best thing that ever happened to me" is another quote featured in a sidebar to an interview with a person with AIDS in the *Bay Area Reporter*, a San Francisco gay newspaper.[8] Shortly after Gay Games founder Tom Waddell's death, the *Examiner* published his thoughts on what he called "the enormous beneficial effect" that AIDS has had on the gay community. "I think that if it hadn't been AIDS, something would have happened to the movement, the way it was going was so bizarre. . . . It didn't know what it was doing, except that it kept talking about sexual freedom. . . . Something was going to happen, and it turned out to be AIDS. . . . AIDS has transformed the gay community."[9]

The interest of the media in reporting the "maturing" of gay male communities reflects their disapproval of our sexual lives and is only the most recent version of a stereotype that caricatures gay men as immature boys who never grew up into responsible heterosexuals. The depth of the gratitude gay men publicly express toward AIDS may measure how much we have internalized the Peter Pan stereotype of our lives, our regrets about past years when we took each day for granted, and how desperately we want some good to come out of this senseless tragedy.

While AIDS does not exist to teach us a lesson or to save us from ourselves, many of us have decided to respond to this epidemic by making changes in our lives. We take responsibility for our past actions and accept the consequences without self-hate. We educate each other about safer sex and other safe practices. We ask for help and offer it. We demand the services we deserve from our governments. We learn how to live well in the present. We pay more attention to our health and explore all possible treatments. We celebrate our lives together. We face each other's deaths and our own. We remember, grieve, and hope. We respond to AIDS as we would to other life-threatening situations—by reorganizing our lives and taking care of each other.

It is important to remember that when we make these changes, we are the same people we were before AIDS. Our strength and power do not originate in this disease but grow out of who we were as individual men and women, as families, as friends, and as communities before the HIV entered some of our bodies. We face a new situation, and we are making new decisions every day to deal with this epidemic. But we don't have to fall into the trap of thanking AIDS for saving us from our pasts.

AIDS is a profound tragedy, not a golden opportunity. It is neither an exterminating angel who came into our lives to punish us nor a guardian angel come to offer us the chance to be born again. If we have anyone to thank for the changes we have made, it is ourselves and each other, not AIDS. We deserve the credit. We can be proud of who we are now, and of what we are doing, without making the present seem better than it is by painting a bleak Dorian Gray portrait of our past. The caricature of our past doesn't do justice to the depth and maturity of our lives before AIDS, including the sexual creativity that has enabled us to protect ourselves and each other by eroticizing safe sex. Nor does gratitude toward AIDS take into account the physical pain, the multiple losses, the discrimination, the antigay violence, the isolation, and the cruel accusations that tear us apart today.

Few of us respond to this epidemic without fear and confusion, without love, without anger, and without aching to know why. It is the rough patchwork of all of our responses, not the disease itself, that gives meaning to our lives as we weather this terrible storm.

As I write these words, I fill up blank pages in the open book of AIDS. But there are more empty pages staring back at me, the most troubling questions that still haunt me: Why did Brian have to die? Why have I survived this long? Why are my friends still dying?

I step back, take a breath, and rather than look for answers, I look inside and take stock of where I am. I accept that AIDS the disease has no intent, no meaning, and no purpose. I'm learning how to let go of my need to make sense of this epidemic and my need for explanations that console. I'm beginning to live with the randomness of Brian's death and the deaths of so many other good people. I'm learning that I can better face these realities by grieving the losses I feel. I learned from Brian that, without reassurances and answers, it was sufficient for me to stop talking, sit with him silently, try to make him comfortable, touch him, listen, or cry. I value all of these private moments of grief, peace, and acceptance.

Then I look at my relationships with other people. I am able to continue doing my history work inside this epidemic only with the support and encouragement of others. I have my ability to remember Brian and to grieve his death with our friends and family. I have the Names Project quilt, when it is displayed, where I can go to remember Brian and everyone else I've lost. I have people with whom I can share my senses of humor, irony, silliness, camp, and weird jokes, qualities that hold despair at bay and get us through the worst times. I have ways to engage in lusty, loving sex without transmitting or being exposed to the virus. I have the companionship of my bereavement support group of gay men whose lovers also have died. I have my outrage and outrageousness that allow me to transform my grief into action and to protest with others the cruel injustices. I have my friends who are living with HIV and AIDS who ask for, accept, and offer me help. And I've salvaged some hope.

These are pieces of my life which don't always fit together. But they are helping me to create who I am, to give my life meaning during this epidemic, and to begin facing my death in my own way whenever it comes, even though I will never know why I was born, lived, and died on this earth.

January–July 1988

Acknowledgments

I wish to thank Jeffrey Escoffier for our New Year's Day talk over afternoon tea at Sweet Inspirations in San Francisco, where we shaped some of these thoughts and he encouraged me to put them down on paper. I am also indebted to the Forget-Me-Nots (my civil disobedience affinity group) and to many friends for our discussions and their constructive criticism and encouragement while I struggled to write this essay. And especially I thank Brian Keith.

NOTES

1. Julian Baird, "Embracing Life: Loving Death," *San Francisco Sentinel*, June 17, 1988, 15.

2. Louise L. Hay, *You Can Heal Your Life* (Santa Monica: Hay House, 1987), 137–39.

3. Elisabeth Kübler-Ross, *AIDS: The Ultimate Challenge* (New York: Macmillan, 1987), 12.

4. See Mona Charen, "Dangers of Positive Thinking: Upbeat Cruelty," *San Francisco Chronicle, This World*, June 19, 1988, 3; Michael Bronsky, "The Meaning of AIDS Explored in Four New Books," *Advocate*, November 24, 1987, 47–51; Dana Ullman, "Getting Beyond Wellness Macho: The Promise and Pitfalls of Holistic Health," *UTNE Reader*, January/February 1988, 68–73; Marlys Harris, "Shirley's Best Performance," *Money*, September 1987, 160–78.

5. Van R. Ault, "Metaphysical Center Opens on Castro Street," *San Francisco Sentinel*, April 17, 1987, 16.

6. Jayne Garrison, "The Castro Grows Up," *San Francisco Examiner*, January 31, 1988,

A1; Robert Lindsey, "Where Homosexuals Found a Haven, There's No Haven from AIDS," *New York Times*, July 15, 1987, 10. See also Dawn Garcia, "Straights Moving into the Castro," *San Francisco Chronicle*, August 1, 1988, A1.

7. *San Francisco Examiner, Image*, June 26, 1988.

8. Rex Wockner, "Michael Callen: Taking His AIDS Diagnosis to the Top 40," *Bay Area Reporter*, July 7, 1988, 26.

9. Paul Moor, "Gay Olympian in His Own Words," *San Francisco Chronicle*, July 13, 1987, 41. This superlative has migrated to articles about businesses that profit from AIDS. "AIDS is the best thing that ever happened to the life insurance industry," proclaimed a sidebar to an article in the business section of the *San Francisco Chronicle* entitled "Insurers See New AIDS-Test Benefits," July 18, 1988, C2.

Intellectual Desire

Bérubé used this keynote address at the first queer studies conference in Quebec as an opportunity to think deeply about his own roots. Using class, ethnicity, and race as lenses through which to understand not only his own life but, in some ways, the broader contours of gay experience, he argues that gay as a social category can never stand alone. "Class and racialized ethnic histories," he asserts, "shape our languages, our sexual desires and relationships, our psychologies, our writings, and our intellectualities." He writes honestly and feelingly about the "sentimental nostalgia" that pulls him to study the past as a way to restore an emotional wholeness to life.

In 1992 I was invited to present one of two keynote addresses at La Ville en Rose: Le premier colloque Québécois d'études lesbiennes et gaies—the First Quebec Lesbian and Gay Studies Conference—held in Montreal that November. Nicole Brossard, the lesbian-feminist *québécoise* poet, novelist, and essayist, presented the other address. We were paired up as speakers for a reason. The conference organizers as a group included both anglophones and francophones, and their goal was to create an event that brought together lesbian and gay studies in Canada's two official languages. The conference was held at two locations: Concordia University in the predominantly English-speaking West End and L'Université du Québec à Montréal in the predominantly French-speaking East End (near Le Village—the gay center of the city). Nicole Brossard presented her address in French, and I presented mine in English; both were simultaneously translated into the other language.

I was invited because, since the late 1970s, I've written and spoken about lesbian, gay, and bisexual social and political history, especially in my book *Coming Out Under Fire: The History of Gay Men and Women in World War II*. But I was invited also because I'm an anglophone Franco-American of Quebec ancestry, an independent historian who could try to speak across some

Originally published in *GLQ* 3, no. 1 (February 1996): 139–57.

Allan's *Mé-mère*, Donalda
Bérubé, Aldenville, Mass.,
1950s. Courtesy of the Allan
Bérubé Collection at the
GLBTHS, San Francisco.

boundaries—between Franco-American and French Canadian, anglophone and francophone, United States and Canada, the university and the "community," literary studies and the social sciences. My audience included people in all these categories, but I especially wanted to speak to those intellectuals at the conference who, like myself, were from working-class backgrounds or were in their family's first generation to go to college. (Quebec's modern, secular, public colleges date only from the Quiet Revolution in the 1960s.) I also wanted to use this occasion to see if I could weave together apparently separate strands of my own life—my white Franco-American ethnicity, my class migration, my homosexuality, and my intellectuality—and identify the desires that surround and sometimes connect them. And I wanted to do this without hiding the romantic, even sentimental, longing to go home that this first visit to Montreal had aroused in me.

This is a revised version of what I said.

· · · · · ·

When I accepted the invitation to address you at this First Quebec Lesbian and Gay Studies Conference, I knew that I was being offered a chance to return to what novelist and essayist Salman Rushdie has called an "imaginary homeland." "My Quebec" is the place my ancestors came from but to which I've never traveled except in my imagination. The thought of such a home-coming forced me to look across the distances I've traveled and the boundaries I've crossed to get here. How did I—a Franco-American kid raised rural and working class in New England, whose earlier family history included no self-identified intellectuals or homosexuals—how did I learn how to become this new thing: a gay community-based historian who lives in a gay "ghetto" in San Francisco? I'm not going to answer this question with the happy-ending narrative of a coming-out story. Instead, I want to describe how both my homosexual and my intellectual desires have moved me across class boundaries and how this movement places me within a long tradition of ethnic migration and assimilation. And I want to show how I use history to calm my anxieties about living in the borderlands where I've ended up, one of which is the world of lesbian and gay intellectuals.

At the core of my anxiety about being a gay intellectual is a dilemma: Books, ideas, and a college scholarship provided the class escape route that gave me the resources to come out with pride as a gay man. But the middle-class educational and gay worlds I entered haven't helped me overcome the shame of having used my intellectual work to escape my Franco-American working-class origins. When class, race, and ethnicity are not part of that work, studying with other gay and lesbian intellectuals can actually increase my anxiety. I worry that I'll pass as something I'm not. Or I worry that I'll fall into wearing my class origins as a badge of courage rather than use them to improve our thinking.

Class escape stories tell what happens when you get out of the class you grew up in and enter one of higher status. They reveal unresolved conflicts about what you have lost and gained. They expose the anguish of leaving a home you can't return to while not belonging where you've ended up. These dislocations deepen what have been called the "hidden injuries of class" (Sennett and Cobb). Many of us from poor or working-class backgrounds experience these injuries when we are the first generation to go to college, as I was, even if we drop out before graduating, as I did—from class panic, lack of money, and unfulfilled homosexual desires. The injury is the belief that we've deserted our people by going away to serve our more desirable benefactors, who would use us for their ends and seduce us into abandoning our own.

My gay and intellectual journeys across ethnic and class lines have too often felt like a desertion. Yet my own migration patterns—going to college, coming out, moving west—continue a tradition in which at least four generations of my family also migrated across boundaries between nations, languages, cultures, and classes, leaving them unsure of where they belonged. Never undertaken lightly, our migrations put us in serious conflict with structures of power that were not our own. We used old strategies to survive and even invented new ones, some of which worked, while others boomeranged, threatening our safety and well-being. The injuries I've sustained along the way have been, to use James Baldwin's words, the price of my ticket out, just as there was a heavy price for the escape routes my family took before me.

My family's itinerary followed a larger map of French migration around North America, what Franco-American scholars have called a "tortured geography." Imagine trying to connect the dots of the many disconnected French worlds (past and present) just inside the United States: Woonsocket, Rhode Island; Manchester, New Hampshire; Lowell, Massachusetts; Lewiston, Maine; Lafayette, Louisiana; Frenchtown, Montana; Wildwood, New Jersey; Hollywood, Florida; Kankakee, Illinois; Ste. Genevieve, Missouri. They form a far-flung archipelago connected only by what have been called "fragile alliances spanning distant and disparate communities" (Waddell and Louder 350). Not only is our French North American geography tortured, but so are the names that we have called ourselves or were hurled at us: Frenchy, Frog, Creole, Acadien, Metis, Franco, Coonass, Lard-Eater, Dumb Frenchman. "They say that you are a *Québécois*," observed Jean Morisset, a Franco-American geographer, "that others are *Fransaskois, Martiniquais,* Cajun, Canuck, *Haïtien, Franco-Tenois,* French-Cree" (Morisset 340). My generation in the United States grew up calling ourselves "French Canadian," but people always asked us "Where in Canada were you born?" We now call ourselves "Franco-American," but people ask us "From where in France?" or make jokes about canned spaghetti. No common name fits.

"We bear the names of the itineraries we have traveled and the rivers we have navigated," explains Morisset (340). My Uncle Laury—from the French "Laurent," he'd remind us, not from the English "Lawrence"—was named after the great river, the St. Laurent, the lifeline of Quebec. Our French North American names, life stories, and writings are the living records of wherever our explorations, expulsions, and migrations have taken us—along great rivers and lakes, from our conquest of native peoples to our defeat and colonization by the English, and even to losing a sense of ourselves and our history. Displacement and invisibility often characterize us. The Acadians became the Cajuns after the English forcibly deported them from the maritime provinces to the English colonies and then to Louisiana in the 1700s. Jack Kerouac made his itinerary his life work when he wrote *On the Road* after leaving his native Frenchtown in Lowell, Massachusetts.

Our anglicized American names hide their Franco origins: White (LeBlanc), Greenwood (Boisvert), Fisher (Fourcier). Our writers describe us as a people with "a fractured culture, a culture that emerges in little bursts, a culture in which those to whom it belongs barely recognize themselves" (Dubois 69). Or we are "a people in the process of becoming an endangered species, suffering from loss of memory" (Dubois 71). Or we are "a people who have traditionally had nothing to say, who have been too far down the social ladder and too weighted with frustrations to make works of art" (Homel 87). Or as "an America that knows no name" (Morisset 337). Or as no longer a people at all.

Silenced, forgotten, lost, sold, abandoned, translated into English, absorbed, deported, or conquered, still often poor or working class, keeping to ourselves, staying out of sight, on the move. And ashamed of ourselves. "Where does our incredible sense of shame come from?" asks the geographer (Morisset 339, 346), as if shame itself were a river you could see cutting across our internalized French maps of North America.

The history of working-class Francos trying to survive in a fiercely Anglo North America in so many ways resonates with the emotional history of homos trying to survive in a fiercely hetero world. It was only a matter of time before I'd see and feel these connections between class, ethnicity, and sexuality, then use my intellect to make sense of them. My own life's itineraries—coming out across sexualities, becoming a working-class intellectual in middle-class worlds, moving to California—all distanced me from my Franco-American family of origin. Yet it is our common history of migration that I and my Franco ancestors share most profoundly, crossing borders generation after generation for over three centuries on this continent as we searched for ways to survive, creating new selves in the process.

More than a hundred years ago, in the 1870s and 1880s, my great-grandparents left Trois-Rivières and Saint Pascal in Quebec to live and work in the United States. This was not a pleasure trip. They moved because the small farms they were allowed to own could no longer support their large families. They were part of a huge exodus that lasted until the 1920s, in which hundreds of thousands of French Canadians moved south to find jobs during New England's industrial boom. They were lured away from Quebec by mill owners' agents sent north across the border to recruit cheap manual labor for the mills that grew up all along New England's great rivers: the Connecticut, Merrimack, Penobscot, and Androscoggin.

My ancestors—the Bérubés, LeBlancs, Fleurys, and Boisverts—moved from Quebec to Aldenville, a village between Holyoke and Chicopee, Massachusetts, on the Connecticut River. For three generations the women and girls worked in the nearby textile mills, or as domestic workers in middle-class Yankee homes, or as mothers and homemakers in their large Catholic families. The men and boys worked as manual laborers in the surrounding brickyards, paper mills, and machine shops. Both envied and derided by folks back home in Quebec, and despised at the bottom of the white ethnic hierarchy in New England, these immigrants were of two minds about being in the United States. Fearful of losing their culture in a hostile Yankee land, they were fortified by their nearness to Quebec. While many did go back home to visit their families, most stayed in their new *Québec d'en bas* (Quebec down below). There they took the strategies of *la survivance* they had developed in Quebec against English domination—defending church, language, and family—and adapted them to this new country. In Aldenville they formed a *P'tit Canada*, as their "cousins" did in nearly every other industrial city in New England. Their little Frenchtown reconstructed the institutions of French Quebec as barricades against assimilation in the United States: barricades against the English language, Protestantism, and the dominant Irish Catholic Church hierarchy. In Aldenville, three generations of my family lived totally French lives and kept French Canadian customs at home, in church, at the parish schools, in the shops, and on the porches and in the backyards of their tenement "blocks." Their vision for these Little Canadas was to create something new: a particular way to remain French in the United States, to be American in French. "You are 'Americans, yes!'" wrote Jacques Ducharme, a novelist from Holyoke, trying to articulate this vision to those Francos who were adopting English as their language, "but '*nous sommes Américains.*'"[1]

The limited Anglo imagination attacked this Franco refusal to assimilate by challenging their whiteness. Yankees called these French Canadian immigrants in New England "The Chinese of the East"—*Les Chinois de l'Est*—comparing the self-contained Frenchtowns to the Chinatowns on the West Coast (Lafleur). "It is said that there are more French-Canadians in New England than there are in Canada," complained a *New York Times* editorial a century ago. "It is next to impossible to penetrate this mass of protected and secluded humanity with modern ideas. . . . No other people," the *Times* went on, "except the Indians, are so persistent in repeating themselves. Where they halt they stay, and where they stay they multiply and cover the earth." These French Canadian migrants had not yet securely earned the privileges of whiteness in the United States. Well into the twentieth century, public-school teachers ordered Franco-American students to "speak white" when they were overheard talking to each other in their French mother tongue. Such racist forms of ethnic shaming, when combined with the promise of white race privilege because of their European ancestry, but despite their own Native American/First Nation ancestors, intensified the desperation of these Franco immigrants to achieve and defend their own American whiteness.[2]

In the 1930s my grandparents and their six children were forced to leave Aldenville because of the Great Depression. Unable to support themselves on factory wages alone, they reversed earlier Franco-American migration patterns and moved from the city back to a farm in a rural Yankee town fifteen miles away. There they survived by raising and hunting their own food, while the women made the Franco rural dishes that I grew up on as a child: our homemade maple syrup poured over snow, stewed tomatoes and fresh corn on the cob, *sauce blanche* (flour, milk, and hard-boiled eggs poured over bread or potatoes), wild venison and pheasant, and *tourtières*—Christmas meat pies. Isolated from their *P'tit Canada* as their parents had been isolated from Quebec, they found themselves surrounded by Yankee farmers, attending Mass at an unfriendly Irish Catholic church, and having to speak English while shopping in town. Although all six children had gone to the French parish school, L'École Sainte Jeanne D'Arc, in Aldenville, my father, the youngest, now had to attend the town's English-speaking public high school, where his Yankee teachers failed him in French, his mother tongue, because he did not speak it properly.

My family, unable to defend themselves with the community resources they'd had in Aldenville, devised other strategies to get out from under the social stigma of being a French minority in a Yankee town. One strategy was to tell racist jokes to bond with others in their all-white but now ethnically mixed worlds. They were trying to ease the pain of being called "Dumb Frenchmen" by stigmatizing those who had been excluded from their whiteness. Another strategy was to "marry up" into Irish, Italian, and even two steps up into Protestant Yankee families, and to raise my generation as the first to grow up speaking English. Learning to forget French was slow and painful in our family, as each generation was taught that our "lousy" French was not worth speaking. I as a gay man now make a living speaking and writing in English because my family was shamed into silencing their French. At first my aunts and uncles survived by staying close to home (my father and uncle built houses on the family farm), but eventually most of them moved away, even to other states. Slowly, they abandoned their traditional strategies of *survivance*—the trinity of large family, Catholic church, and French language—in order to survive as their world changed around them.

This bilingual, ethnically mixed extended family was the rural working-class world into which I was born in 1946. I was the seventh grandchild but the first with both a French mother, Lorraine Tétreault, and a French father, Ronald Bérubé. Even in the 1950s I grew up feeling in my family an almost magnetic pull back to Aldenville, a place I'd never been. On Sundays after Mass, my grandmother, my *mé-mère*, would prepare a big dinner and, still wearing her Sunday dress under her apron, would sit on the front porch waiting for company to arrive from Aldenville with gossip and lively French conversation. When company did come, which was often, I caught glimpses of how full of vitality their *P'tit Canada* had been. And after they went home, I saw *Mé-mère's* melancholy pining as she was lost in the memories of a place she'd never wanted to leave.

It's still difficult for me to say the word *mé-mère* in public. It was a private Franco-American family word spoken only at home, not found in French dictionaries, that we always translated as "grandmother" when speaking to outsiders. It was one of a small category of words so charged with power they had to be said in hushed tones, with shame or reverence, or never at all. As Catholics, we had to bow our heads when we said "Jesus." By the second grade, I knew that our casual use of the word "nigger" marked our family as low-class, ignorant, and prejudiced. "Fuck" was dirty and obscene. The French language as we spoke it was like these words—a mark of shame, difference, or ignorance. "Homosexual" fit right in. When I first read this word in books, I had to make a deliberate decision to actually speak it aloud. When I did (to myself), it felt like the other words had felt in my mouth: my voice held back in a whisper, tongue and lips not quite completing each sound within it. This word "homosexual" exposed more about me than I wanted anyone to know—even a priest. Growing up Franco, but ashamed to speak our French, gave me the practice I needed in not saying this word that was so often on the tip of my tongue.

As much as my father loved the farm, which had been his mother's prison, he had to leave it to give his own family the nice things and secure life he wanted for us. My father was the first child in the family to escape assembly-line factory work. He got out by earning a radio operator's license in night school and getting work in broadcasting, achieving the minor status that came with this skilled blue-collar job. But in 1950, when I was three, my mother died in childbirth, a too-common fate among Franco-American women. Their bodies, and those of their many babies who died at birth, were the casualties of yet another line of Franco self-defense, a part of *la survivance* called the "revenge of the cradle"—making large families so they wouldn't die out as a people. *Mé-mère* and *Pé-père* took me in. My father went to Manhattan for two years, where he found new opportunities in early television broadcasting and married a working-class, Polish American Catholic woman from Brooklyn.

My just-married parents moved us all into a tiny house trailer, a cramped eight-by-thirty-six-foot space that eventually held a family of six. For years we moved around, unhitching our mobile home in blue-collar trailer parks named "Sunnyside" in Connecticut and "Sunset" in New Jersey. They were trying to save money to buy a real house and acquire the security, comfort, and leisure time that was their vision of a better life—a vision they acquired from reading *Better Homes and Gardens*, the bible for postwar migrants into the expanding white middle class.

It was during grade school, when we lived in a trailer park in Bayonne, a multiracial blue-collar town in New Jersey, that my desires for other boys awakened but were not fulfilled. I was drawn to boys whom I fantasized as my brothers (I was the oldest child, with three younger sisters). From the start, my erotic desire for "brotherness" was shaped by class. The moments I felt it most strongly were when I was in other boys' homes, something my parents strictly prohibited. I visited a schoolmate who lived on a wooden barge docked nearby on Newark Bay and felt an erotic charge of sympathy for him in his poverty. A boy in another trailer park took me inside his trailer when his parents were at work. When we peed together in his tiny bathroom, I wanted to pee with him again as brothers. And when I visited a schoolmate who lived up the street in a house—a real building with rooms, doors, and an upstairs—I fantasized that I lived there with him, sharing a bedroom and being able to close the door. Eroticizing other boys, up, down, and across these working-class hierarchies, entering their homes and imagining being alone there with them when I had no privacy at home, wanting them close to me forever as my brothers: These were desires that only later in college did I dare to name "homosexual."

An intellectual desire awakened in me as well. I knew no one, other than my teachers, who had gone to college or who made a living working with ideas. Yet in the *Encyclopaedia Britannica*, which my parents bought on credit from a door-to-door salesman who worked the trailer park, and in the collection of classical music records they bought in weekly installments at the supermarket and played on a hi-fi my father had built from a do-it-your-self kit, I envisioned a different world full of poetry, literature, great music, philosophy, and art.

As my desire to find that world grew, I began to imagine the escape routes that might get me there. One of these pointed inward as I tried to create that world on my own. I became a bookworm who didn't like sports—that particular kind of male sissy who is teased in his working-class family for putting on airs by burying himself in books, the "smart one" who thinks he is no longer "one of us." With so many of us packed into this little trailer, it was hard to write or even read much. But each summer, when we went back to stay with my *mé-mère* and *pé-père* on the family farm, I found the solitude to read books and write poetry. I returned to the trailer with memories and dreams of going back to the farm that kept my imagination alive. My moving back and forth between the trailer park and the farm taught me early on that I could survive a difficult present by reminiscing about the past and dreaming about the future. This survival strategy has shaped my imagination ever since. It has infused my writing with a sentimental nostalgia that's still hard to overcome, but also with a utopian idealism that keeps me going through hard times.

I also imagined escape routes that pointed outward. I built a radio, and every night I would hide under the covers wearing my father's klunky World War II headphones, searching the dial for the distant crackle of the classical music station WQXR, from New York City. College was as far on the intellectual horizon as my limited vision could reach — a place where people like me could talk about art, literature, and ideas. My parents warned me over and over that if I wanted to go to college I'd have to win a scholarship because they didn't have the money to send me. In my nightly prayers I asked God to let us move to a town with good schools and to let me win a scholarship. And I became a student obsessed with reading and studying: no straight A's, no scholarship, no college education, no exit.

At the same time, I saw in my father what I might become if I couldn't escape by going to college. Although he was brilliant at making the most of being trapped, my father's ingenuity couldn't rescue him from the working-class traps themselves. A cautious, self-effacing, honest man, and a meticulous worker terrified of getting caught making mistakes, my father's life was shaped by the ethnic and class shame that came with his living in "their" worlds, forced to speak "their" languages. He spent his life behind the scenes, running the machinery that broadcast other people's voices and faces to television sets across North America. His need to justify his existence by satisfying his bosses, and his sacrifice of himself through hard work to make our lives better, slowly killed him with a lifetime of stomach ulcers and finally with cancer. I knew that the same traps could kill me, too — unless I got out.

For two years, my first years in high school from 1960 to 1962, my parents' middle-class dream did come true. They bought a new four-bedroom, colonial-style house in a New Jersey suburb and decorated it with new colonial furniture and new wall-to-wall carpeting and even bought a new Plymouth station wagon to put in our two-car garage. They finally had a better home *and* garden. For the first time, I could proudly bring a friend over to my house for dinner. And I got my own bedroom and the good school I'd prayed for.

Our modern, suburban, 99 percent white high school placed me in college-track classes, segregated from the vocational-track students. I'd felt lucky to be let into their honors classes, but I was always on guard, never quite sure I belonged in their world, afraid that it was only a matter of time before they would discover their mistake and send me "down" to the vocational track. But I held my own with a desperately good academic performance and a compulsion to join any extracurricular activity that would look great on a scholarship application form.

The crisis came in my sophomore year, when my father was offered a low-level management position at work that he turned down, he said, because he didn't want the responsibility of supervising other workers. But there was more to his refusal than class panic over becoming "one of them." The distance he had traveled—away from his French working-class family, their farm, and the land—was now so far from where he'd started that he began to lose the ground beneath his feet. He wanted to go home. My parents sold their dream house and bought the Massachusetts family farm, where my dad had grown up, from my *pé-père*, who continued to live with us there after my *mé-mère* died. My dad found a job at a local television station in Springfield for half his former wages, and after his union lost a critical strike, his income steadily declined.

My prospects for college now looked grim. The public high school in this mill town rarely sent anyone to a "good" university. My mother tells me that I cried for days at the thought of not going to college (I've blocked out all memory of this). I was rescued by the local, third-rate private boys' academy, which accepted me as a day-student "townie." Every morning and afternoon I hitched a ride between the farm and town on the public grade-school bus, humiliated to be sitting there, a teenage bookworm dressed up in a sports jacket and tie, surrounded by screaming farm kids who must have thought I had dropped in from Mars. Luckily, I was rescued again, this time by a young, friendly, and handsome American history teacher (whom I had a crush on). With his guidance and connections, he helped me win a rare senior-year scholarship to a prestigious college-preparatory boarding school fifty miles away.

I was about to enter an elite world my parents knew little about, while their income was rapidly falling. The class divide between me and my family was growing wider and deeper.

I arrived at prep school with a mixture of fear and awe, feeling as if I had been invited into the homes of the rich. This was the world that could give me the escape and the culture I wanted, yet it made me acutely aware of my "lower" class background. I earned my keep by washing dishes, setting tables, and serving students in the dining room; I performed well in classes; and I even wrote poetry and a play about my alienation that won a *Reader's Digest* creative writing award. During summer session, when I worked in the school's kitchen to earn money for college, I was housed with five other scholarship boys[3] in the basement of the same dormitory I'd lived in as a student. But now a locked door separated us from the well-to-do students upstairs. As workers, we were forbidden to visit or even talk to the students. But during time off from our fourteen-hour workday, we were graciously allowed to attend their general lectures, which that year were about the history of utopian socialism!

Here I was, a Franco-American, raised in a French family, learning French for the first time from Protestant, English-speaking teachers in this upper-class Yankee school—nice teachers who agreed that I was wise not to have learned "bad" French at home. This was proper Parisian French they taught me—"French from France," as Franco-Americans called it in English—a language my *mé-mère* used to love to hear spoken, as she loved touching fine Parisian lace, and as I enjoyed art and poetry—beautiful things that the well-to-do took for granted and which we could only dream about with envy.

This all-male Protestant school was nearly all white, and rumor was that it had quotas for no more than twenty-five Catholics and twenty-five Jews. It was there that I stopped going to Mass and left the Catholic Church, opening a door toward someday acting on my homosexual desires without having to confess my sins to a priest. I became intrigued with liberal Protestantism and especially my Protestant classmates—young white men who seemed so confident and in control, who looked good and knew how to dress in good clothes, and whose school had been so generous to let me in, for which I felt too much gratitude.

I knew that their attractive prep-school world wasn't really mine. I was their guest. Yet I no longer belonged at home, either. When my parents came to visit me, I was stunned to see them through the eyes of a different class. Despite my homesickness for them, I was embarrassed by what was now their old station wagon, their sturdy rather than tasteful clothes, and the down-to-earth way they talked. Who was I becoming? And where was I going?

My desire to belong in an intellectual world—which in this school taught us to take whiteness, upper-class privilege, and maleness for granted—aroused a new but secret and often sexual desire for these smart, well-to-do, articulate men. I wanted to have them, I wanted to be them, and I wanted to be wanted by them. And so my homosexual desires began to split into two directions. They moved horizontally, toward working-class men like myself and the scholarship boys I worked with in the kitchen, whom since childhood I had eroticized as brothers and now associated with my past and my family. My homo desires also moved vertically, up toward my "betters," who seemed to have what I lacked and who I believed had the authority to give me self-respect, verify my respectability, and offer me another escape route into a better, more secure future.

This class split in my homosexual desires continued to structure my love relationships for years. In the 1980s I decided to stop having any middle-class boyfriends for a while. I partnered only with men who were raised working class so I could begin to step outside and examine the dynamics of my cross-class desires. Yet I wondered how much my new relationships with working-class men were also shaped by my having moved as a guest into middle-class worlds. Was my desire for working-class guys now an expression of a middle-class sexual attraction to the "other," an attraction absorbed from my "betters"? Or was it an expression of an erotic, romantic longing to come home? Or was it both—a hybrid mix of same-class and cross-class desires?

I graduated from prep school in 1964 with honors and won a work/study scholarship to the University of Chicago as an English major. My entering class was still nearly all white (98 percent) but now only two-thirds rather than 100 percent male. During the economic boom of the 1960s, the gratitude and indebtedness I and too many other poor or working-class students felt for winning scholarships to private colleges reflected our desperation to scramble through these temporarily open doors.[4] Our scholarships were attempts by our elite benefactors not only to be generous but also to mine us for what they often condescendingly praised us for—our "freshness" and "vitality," our "passion" and "original thinking"—and then to train us and even trap us with loans and enormous debts into serving their institutions. We usually made their lives richer rather than enriching those of our own people, whose sacrifices had gotten us as far as they could. This is how the mill owners had mined Quebec and the *P'tit Canadas* for the cheap manual labor of my family years before, and how my European ancestors had mined the native peoples of North America for their resources, land, and culture.

My parents and *Pé-père* were of two minds about where my college education was taking me. They wanted me to "better" myself. But they didn't want me to become a "stuffed shirt," to think or act as if I were better than they were. I knew these were the risks: that I might betray them by abandoning them in their difficult lives while fulfilling their own dreams of self-improvement and escape. This is a core dilemma that many working-class intellectuals often face alone: By pursuing our intellectual desires, we risk becoming like our own and our parents' class "enemies"—those who would rescue us only to use us for their ends while looking down on those whom they left behind.

I tried to figure out how to resolve this class dilemma and still keep up with the demands of a hyperacademic college curriculum. Convinced that I had nothing intelligent to say compared to the articulate students around me, I never spoke a word in any of my courses. Then, in 1968, I faced more serious crises, all in April. One crisis involved riots and police repression: explosions of grief, anger, and fear after the assassination of Dr. Martin Luther King Jr., followed by the declaration of martial law in Chicago and the closing of our campus in a citywide curfew. Another crisis was set off when, a week after the riots, I said, "I have a homosexual problem," to the man I was in love with and had to deal with the consequences on my own. As my grades plummeted in the wake of these and other incidents and the university punished me by changing my scholarship to a loan, I faced a new class panic as well: I didn't know how I was ever going to pay back the debts. I dropped out. Like my father, who had panicked in the suburbs, I felt the ground disappearing beneath my feet and wanted to go back home. But home wasn't where I could come out. So I moved to Boston.

College, and bull sessions with students I hung out with after I dropped out, taught me two new languages. One was the shop talk of intellectual work: educated talk that made you feel either smart or stupid, depending on how you performed and who you were. The other language was political. At its best it gave us a way to analyze systems of oppression and take action, although usually from a white middle-class perspective, rather than from the perspective of a scholarship student. At its worst it was show-off talk about talk itself, as if talk alone were the same as action. I wanted to learn how to use both these new languages because they let me understand and discuss ideas I needed. But they also conflicted with a native language I had learned at home, a language that spoke through action and held a deep mistrust of educated talk that doesn't come through when times get tough. And now that I'd dropped out of school with big debts and no money, my times were getting tough.

One of the things I used my educated languages for was to come out. By 1970 I'd read psychology and sociology articles and some gay liberation literature, and I'd gone to Student Homophile League meetings at MIT. I'd learned how to talk politically and intellectually about my own and other people's homosexuality. But when I finally went home to come out to my parents, I ended up reopening old wounds of class rupture between us. They accepted my being gay. But they heard me describing my homosexuality in the language of those more powerful and more educated than they were, and they saw my homosexuality as one more indication that I had entered elite worlds that were changing me beyond recognition. Through me they saw "gay" as college educated—and I couldn't deny it, since, in my middle-class worlds, that's what I had learned, too. Yet I was trying to appropriate that educated language (such as "homophobia" and "sexual orientation") so that its words would become "ours" as well. I wanted these ideas to belong to me, to my family, and even to my class of origin, so we could use them to make our lives better, too.

In 1973 I discovered a gay community when I visited San Francisco for the first time. I saved some money and moved there a year later. Living in a gay male hippie commune in the Haight-Ashbury district, I saw other gay men settling in the more affluent Castro district, building a gay neighborhood that was called both a "mecca" and a "ghetto." As Aldenville had been created by French Canadian immigrants a century earlier out of their memories of Quebec, "The Castro" was being created out of new dreams by "sexual migrants."[5] Uprooted from my own class and ethnic backgrounds, and attracted by the openness of gay life in San Francisco, I was a sexual migrant, too. I was intrigued by the ability of these mostly white gay men in the Castro to build a new identity, their own gay politics, and their own neighborhood. I wanted passionately to belong to that gay community. These men were constructing what I grew up so aware of losing—an extended family and an ethnic-like community with a culture and language all its own. In their neighborhood, gay could be ordinary. I hung out in the Castro a lot. In 1979 I worked with others to create our own activist/intellectual version of community, the San Francisco Lesbian and Gay History Project, a study group that became the home base for my work as a gay historian for over ten years.

These attempts at community building, and the broader lesbian and gay movement, helped me transform my gay shame into gay pride and gave me the support I needed to make a living as a "community-based" gay historian. But I hadn't overcome the shame from my own class escape, ethnic erasure, and white-skin privilege. Gay pride showed me this was possible, but it was too often a substitute for the specific work on class, ethnicity, and race I had yet to do.

The ideas of gay community, gay politics, and gay studies were built partly by white, middle-class-identified, college-educated gay men on a belief that homosexuality could and should stand alone as the organizing principle for our lives and work—as if our homosexualities had not been significantly shaped by our race, gender, and class. Many lesbians and people of color told us that much of what we created with the resources we had—money, education, connections, professional skills—reproduced the race and gender hierarchies of the larger society. What I experienced most directly as a white gay man with little money and no college degree was how the gay community reproduced class hierarchies. There were many gay restaurants, disco parties, conferences, resorts, and bathhouses I couldn't afford. And I didn't have the income to live in the Castro.

It's a mistaken idea that gay community or gay activism or gay studies can stand alone as "gay." They all were made possible by past civil rights, ethnic, class, and women's struggles, and by those who enjoyed many forms of institutionalized power and privilege. The white, male, and middle-class separation of "gay" from these other struggles and histories is one of the many predictable outcomes of a larger process of Americanization that I know too well from my family's class and ethnic history. The newcomer's desire to belong fully—as American, or white, or middle class, or college educated, or gay—tempts many of us to join others in scrambling up ladders beyond and even on the backs of those on the lower rungs. Moving closer to the top, we're encouraged to believe we got there on our own. We're taught to forget those on the bottom, or regretfully leave them behind, or romanticize them, or look down on them with pity or disdain, or study them to get PhDs. In my life, I find myself both on the higher and lower rungs of many ladders.[6] I've climbed up through access to a privileged and systematically exclusive private education, fractured and interrupted as it was. At the same time I've endured the painful injuries of class, and of ethnic and sexual shame. The hurt is what drove me so passionately toward creating a supportive gay life and community; the privileges gave me the resources to do it. So long as we white, educated gay men in queer studies do not investigate, then incorporate into our work, the class, race, and gender structures that shape our own intellectual pursuits—keeping our histories buried as if they were something "not gay" or "not intellectual"—I will never be able to think that our work is "real," as my mother would say, or relevant to the lives of those we have left behind or left out.

I know what it's been like to improve my lot by leaving my working-class background. But in the last few years I've been exploring what an alternative route might have been. I've been doing a community-based history of the Marine Cooks and Stewards Union, a left-wing, multiracial maritime union on the West Coast that included lots of openly gay working-class men. I've created a slide show about what they did that I take to union halls, labor conferences, and community colleges, as well as to private universities. I was inspired to do this work by a former member of the union now in his late seventies, a gay Franco-American whose family name was anglicized from Blais to Blair when they crossed the Canadian border to live in Minnesota at the turn of the century. Mickey Blair and other former members of the Marine Cooks and Stewards Union are teaching me how they, as gay working-class men, improved their lot by moving in solidarity with their class, rather than by leaving it.[7]

My interest in the queer, multiracial, working-class history of this union is also part of the magnetic pull back to the past that haunts me as it has haunted at least four generations of my family. It's expressed in my intellectual desire to bridge the distances I've traveled that still make me feel so dislocated in the present, and to search the past for answers, solutions, maps, and useful strategies that might make things better for those still in my class of origin. For my father the pull back was the homesickness that made him return to the family farm. From that farm my *mé-mère* longed for her French community in Aldenville. There her parents looked back toward their homes in Quebec. My gay history work, paradoxically, grows out of my desire to break this chain of longing, so that I can finally arrive here, now, in this place in North America, as I am and as we are, fully belonging, with all the disconnected fragments of my life finally put together into an integrated, dignified whole. This utopian vision of the future mirrors the most romantic visions of lost, imaginary homelands.

My desire to realize this dream of wholeness at first drew me to Catholicism, then to having a college education, then to embracing the identity politics of gay liberation, then to going west, then to "reclaiming" my ethnic roots. But none of these could ever make my dream come true. I'm learning from others in similar situations to accept and constructively use the distances and dislocation, my double vision and two-mindedness, and my homosexual desires up, down, and across class lines. This is where I've ended up as a gay working-class intellectual and as a Franco-American, too. The "America in between" that the geographer Morisset names as the Franco's location on this continent is also my home base as a gay writer and historian (Waddell and Louder 348).

I do my work now in the borderlands between social classes, between the university and the community, between heterosexual and homosexual, between educated speech and down-to-earth talk, between Franco-American and Québécois, between my family and the gay community, between the past and the present. This is a land where I make visits home, then leave again; a land where I maintain long-distance relationships and enjoy one-night stands; where, without a BA, I teach in an elite university, then enter a maximum-security prison because the men inside have asked me to talk to them about gay history; where I am my family's historian because they know I've published gay history; and where on my bedroom wall I hang my *mé-mère*'s rosary beads next to my Tom of Finland leatherman print. These temporarily bridged distances and unexpected combinations have become a workshop in which it seems possible to make the gay, intellectual, working-class, and Franco-American parts of myself reinforce each other, rather than split me apart.

What I've tried to do in this talk is describe one particular white gay man's history from the inside in a way that focuses on class, ethnic, and educational migration, rather than on coming out. But the danger in describing a working-class life from the inside is the temptation to frame one's narrative within a "rhetoric of hardship"—a storytelling strategy that tries to mitigate class oppression by appealing to the sympathy and generosity of the more fortunate. This rhetorical strategy is very seductive because it reshapes working-class lives into stories of courageous struggle against impossible odds. It may be the working-class equivalent of using the coming-out story as an appeal for heterosexual understanding and acceptance. But the class hardship narrative only reinforces class hierarchies in the telling. Even as it makes visible and validates the lives of working-class people, and evokes sympathy from middle-class listeners, it reduces us to either victims or heroes. Our lives become satisfying dramas of suffering that end in inspiring victory or poignant tragedy.[8] I've tried to resist this temptation and to use the stuff of my life to understand a much larger historical process: how class and racialized ethnic histories shape our languages, our sexual desires and relationships, our psychologies, our writings, and our intellectualities.

I want to speak for a minute to those of you who were taught that intellectual work belonged to your "betters," not to you. Whenever we've entered middle-class worlds, especially those of "higher" education, many of us have had to pass, and still pass, as one of "them"; we've been invited in as guests; or we've even trespassed in without invitation. The risks of this cross-class movement are great. *Class passing* forces us to erase our own history. It makes us afraid that someone will find out the truth about us and kick us out. Being treated as a guest—as a scholarship student in college, as a member of the "community" invited to attend an academic conference, or as a scholar without a degree asked to give a university lecture or keynote address—seems to demand our gratitude and indebtedness in return. Guest status can make us afraid of being disinvited, expelled, or humiliated if we say or do the wrong thing. *Class trespassing*, the deliberate violation of class boundaries—going where we are not wanted, bringing up class when we are not asked—can get us caught and punished, then sent back to where we came from.

While I can now proudly call myself gay without feeling the shame I once knew, it's still not easy to call myself an intellectual without feeling like an impostor. But none of us can do our best work until we believe that the life of the mind really does belong to us, from the pleasures of theoretical analysis and brilliant insights to the way an idea can save lives. When we who are independent scholars, or the first generation to go to college, or avid readers and writers, do claim our intellectualities as our own, we become a force to be reckoned with. Among our most valuable resources are the abilities to see the familiar in new ways, to question privileged assumptions, and even to use our intellects to dismantle the powerful systems that cause the class injuries we know too well.

Coming here to this conference, I am completing a circle of migration that my great-grandparents began when they left Quebec over a century ago. I now see that their escape route was not destined to be a one-way trip for our family. They left hoping that factory work in the United States would help them survive as French Catholic families. I've come back because I'm gay and intellectual and Franco-American—and I wanted to see what happens if I connect these three parts of my life. I'm awed when I realize that my great-grandparents could never have imagined my being here with all of you today, creating with each other something new in North America: a *québécois* way of doing lesbian, gay, and bisexual studies, which is a project I want and need to be a part of.

After visiting Montreal for the first time these last two weeks, I'm pleased to discover that this place, including this conference, is not the sentimental Quebec of my imaginary homeland, not "My Own Private Quebec." You are full of more contradictions than I could ever have imagined from so great a distance. Because of that, you make me feel a little more at home.

Acknowledgments

I wish to thank Smoky Cormier, Jeffrey Escoffier, Lisa Kahaleole Chang Hall, David Halperin, Ross Higgins, Jonathan Ned Katz, Robert Mercer, Peter Nardi, Susan Raffo, Gayle Rubin, Robert Schwartzwald, Bill Walker, Tom Waugh, and many other friends and family members, including my sister, Annette Bérubé, and my mother, Florence Bérubé, whose encouragement, conversations, reading of drafts, or memories helped solidify my ideas, clarify my writing, and correct inaccuracies. My thinking and writing in this talk were also inspired by the work of Dorothy Allison, James Baldwin, Chrystos, Amber Hollibaugh, bell hooks, Audre Lorde, Biddy Martin, Cherríe Moraga, Minnie Bruce Pratt, Richard Rodriguez, David Plante, Steven Riel, Mab Segrest, Barbara Smith, and Carolyn Kay Steedman. I also read special "class" issues of various periodicals: *Gay Community News* (January 21, 28, February 4, 1990); *Lesbian Ethics* 4, no. 2 (Spring 1991); *Sinister Wisdom* 45 (Winter 1991/92); and *Bridges: A Journal for Jewish Feminists and Our Friends* 3, no. 1 (Spring/Summer 1992). Other versions of this talk were presented on the panel "Writing Working Class" at the 1991 Out/Write Lesbian and Gay Writers Conference in San Francisco and at the Summer 1994 Crossing Boundaries lecture series at Portland State University in Oregon.

NOTES

1. "But We Are *Américains*" (Dion-Levesque 261). See also Ducharme.

2. Concerning the public-school teachers' injunction, see Ford. There is a small but growing body of literature on the history of American whiteness. See, for example, Morrison and Roediger.

3. I first read about the "scholarship boy" in Rodriguez's chapter titled "The Achievement of Memory" (41–73). Rodriguez describes reading about the scholarship boy in Hoggart 238–49.

4. On the situation of working-class male scholarship students from this generation who became academics, see Ryan and Sackrey.

5. On sexual migration, see Rubin 286.

6. I wish to thank Lisa Kahaleole Chang Hall for our conversations about looking both up and down the hierarchies of power in which we are located. See Hall 170.

7. Paul Lauter, echoing Emma Goldman, has described people raised working class as those "who, to advance their conditions of life, must move in *solidarity* with their class or must leave it" (16, emphasis in original).

8. On working-class storytelling strategies within and across class hierarchies, see, for example, Robinson, Olsen and Shopes, and Fox.

WORKS CITED

Baldwin, James. *The Price of the Ticket: Collected Nonfiction, 1948–1985.* New York: St. Martins, 1985.

Dion-Levesque, Rosaire. "Jacques Ducharme." In *Silhouettes Franco-Américaines,* 261–64. Manchester, N.H.: Publications de l'Association Canado-Américaine, 1957.

Dodge, William, ed. *Boundaries of Identity: A Québec Reader.* Toronto: Lester, 1992.

Dubois, René Daniel. "October 1990." In Dodge 63–73.

Ducharme, Jacques. *The Shadows of the Trees: The Story of French Canadians in New England.* New York: Harper, 1943.

Ford, Royal. "Cultural Resolution: Franco Americans Struggle to Preserve Their Heritage." *Boston Globe*, October 28, 1994, 1, 16.

Fox, Pamela. *Class Fictions: Shame and Resistance in the British Working-Class Novel, 1890–1945*. Durham: Duke University Press, 1994.

"The French Canadians in New England." Editorial. *New York Times*, June 6, 1892, 4.

Hall, Lisa Kahaleole Chang. "Compromising Positions." In *Beyond a Dream Deferred: Multicultural Education and the Politics of Excellence*, edited by Becky W. Thompson and Sangeeta Tyagi, 162–73. Minneapolis: University of Minnesota Press, 1993.

Hoggart, Richard. *The Uses of Literacy: Aspects of Working-Class Life, with Special Reference to Publications and Entertainment*. 1957. Reprint, New York: Oxford University Press, 1970.

Homel, David. "The Way They Talk in *Broke City*." In Dodge 85–88.

Lafleur, Normand. *Les "Chinois" de l'Est*. Ottawa: Éditions Leméac, 1981.

Lauter, Paul. "Working-Class Women's Literature: An Introduction to Study." *Radical Teacher* 15 (1980): 16–26.

Morisset, Jean. "An America That Knows No Name." In Waddell and Louder 337–47.

Morrison, Toni. *Playing in the Dark: Whiteness and the Literary Imagination*. New York: Vintage, 1992.

Olsen, Karen, and Linda Shopes. "Crossing Boundaries, Building Bridges: Doing Oral History among Working-Class Women and Men." In *Women's Words: The Feminist Practice of Oral History*, edited by Sherna Berger Gluck and Daphne Patai, 189–204. New York: Routledge, 1991.

Robinson, Lillian S. "Working/Women/Writing." In *Sex, Class, and Culture*, 223–53. Bloomington: Indiana University Press, 1978.

Rodriguez, Richard. *Hunger of Memory: An Autobiography*. New York: Bantam, 1992.

Roediger, David. *Toward the Abolition of Whiteness*. New York: Verso, 1994.

———. *The Wages of Whiteness: Race and the Making of the American Working Class*. New York: Verso, 1991.

Rubin, Gayle. "Thinking Sex: Notes for a Radical Theory of the Politics of Sexuality." In *Pleasure and Danger: Exploring Female Sexuality*, edited by Carol Vance, 267–319. Boston: Routledge, 1984.

Rushdie, Salman. *Imaginary Homelands: Essays and Criticism, 1981–1991*. New York: Penguin, 1992.

Ryan, Jake, and Charles Sackrey. *Strangers in Paradise: Academics from the Working Class*. Boston: South End, 1984.

Sennett, Richard, and Jonathan Cobb. *The Hidden Injuries of Class*. New York: Knopf, 1972.

Waddell, Eric, and Dean R. Louder. "The Search for Home in America." In *French America: Mobility, Identity, and Minority Experiences across the Continent*, edited by Waddell and Louder, 348–58. Translated by Franklin Phillip. Baton Rouge: Louisiana State University Press, 1993.

Sunset Trailer Park

WITH FLORENCE BÉRUBÉ

In this expanded version of a talk he presented in 1997 at an academic conference called "The Making and Unmaking of Whiteness," Bérubé continued his autobiographical exploration of class and race as categories that shape our daily experience. In dialogue with his stepmother, he recalls his family's years living in a New Jersey trailer park, including the gradations of status within that community. The essay also provides insight into the origins of Bérubé's aspirations for class mobility, which included his parents' hopes for their children and the chance opportunities that entered his life. Here and elsewhere in his personal writing, Bérubé locates himself in a borderland between classes. He continues to try to balance his nostalgia for the past with the recognition of the painful realities of working-class life.

"I cried," my mother tells me, "when we first drove into that trailer park and I saw where we were going to live." Recently, in long-distance phone calls, my mother—Florence Bérubé—and I have been digging up memories, piecing together our own personal and family histories. Trailer parks come up a lot.

During the year when I was born—1946—the booming, postwar "trailer coach" industry actively promoted house trailers in magazine ads like this one from the *Saturday Evening Post*:

TRAILER COACHES RELIEVE SMALL-HOME SHORTAGE
THROUGHOUT THE HOUSE-HUNGRY NATION
Reports from towns and cities all over the United States show that modern, comfortable trailer coaches—economical and efficient beyond even the dreams of a few years ago—are playing a major part in easing the need for small-family dwellings. Returning veterans (as students or workers), newlyweds, and all others who are not ready

Originally published in *White Trash: Race and Class in America*, edited by Matt Wray and Annalee Newitz, 15–39 (New York: Routledge, 1997).

Allan outside the family trailer, 1950s. Courtesy of the Allan Bérubé Collection at the GLBTHS, San Francisco.

for—or can't locate—permanent housing, find in the modern trailer coach a completely furnished (and amazingly comfortable) home that offers the privacy and efficiency of an apartment coupled with the mobility of an automobile.

When I was seven, my parents, with two young children in tow, moved us all into a house trailer, hoping to find the comfort, privacy, and efficiency that the "trailer coach" industry had promised. But real life, as we soon discovered, did not imitate the worlds we learned to desire from magazine ads.

Dad discovered Sunset Trailer Park on his own and rented a space for us there before Mom was able to see it. On our moving day in January 1954, we all climbed into our '48 Chevy and followed a rented truck as it slowly pulled our house trailer from the Sunnyside Trailer Park in Shelton, Connecticut, where we lived for a few months, into New York State and across Manhattan, over the George Washington Bridge into New Jersey, through the garbage incinerator landscape and stinky air of Secaucus—not a good sign—then finally into the Sunset Trailer Park in Bayonne.

A blue-collar town surrounded by Jersey City, Elizabeth, and Staten Island, Bayonne was known for its oil refineries, tanker piers, and navy yard. It was a small, stable, predominantly Catholic city of working-class and military families, mostly white with a small population of African Americans.

When we moved there, Bayonne was already the butt of jokes about "arm-pits" of the industrial Northeast. Even the characters on the TV sitcom *The Honeymooners*, living in their blue-collar world in Brooklyn, could get an easy laugh by referring to Bayonne. "Ralph," Alice Kramden says to her husband in one episode, "you losing a pound is like Bayonne losing a mosquito." My mom was from Brooklyn, too. A Bayonne trailer park was not where she wanted to live or raise her children.

Along with so many other white working-class families living in fifties trailer parks, my parents believed that they were just passing through. They were headed toward a *Better Homes and Gardens* suburban world that would be theirs if they worked hard enough. We moved to Bayonne to be closer to Manhattan, where Dad was employed as a cameraman for NBC. He and his fellow TV crewmen enjoyed the security of unionized, wage-labor jobs in this newly expanding media industry. But they didn't get the income that people imagined went with the status of TV jobs. Dad had to work overtime nights and on weekends to make ends meet. His dream was to own his own house and start his own business, then put us kids through school so we would be better off and not have to struggle so much to get by. My parents were using the cheapness of trailer park life as a stepping-stone toward making that dream real.

As Dad's job and commuting took over his life, the trailer park took over ours. We lived in our trailer from the summer of 1953 through December 1957, most of my grade school years. And so I grew up a trailer park kid.

Sunset Trailer Park seemed to be on the edge of everything. Bayonne itself is a kind of land's end. It's a peninsula that ends at New York Bay, Kill Van Kull, and Newark Bay—polluted bodies of water that all drain into the Atlantic Ocean. You reached our trailer park by going west to the very end of Twenty-fourth Street, then past the last house into a driveway where the trailer lots began. If you followed the driveway to its end, you'd stop right at the waterfront. The last trailer lots were built on top of a seawall secured by pilings. Standing there and looking out over Newark Bay, you'd see tugboats hauling barges over the oil-slicked water, oil tankers and freighters carrying their cargoes, and planes (no jets yet) flying in and out of Newark Airport. On hot summer nights the steady din of planes, boats, trucks, and freight trains filled the air. So did the fumes they exhaled, which, when mixed with the incinerator smoke and oil refinery gasses, formed a foul atmospheric concoction that became world-famous for its unforgettable stench.

The ground at the seawall could barely be called solid earth. The owner of the trailer park occasionally bought an old barge, then hired a tugboat to haul it right up to the park's outer edge, sank it with dump-truck loads of landfill, paved it over with asphalt, painted white lines on it, and voila!—several new trailer lots were available for rent. Sometimes the ground beneath these new lots would sink, so the trailers would have to be moved away until the sinkholes were filled in. Trailers parked on lots built over rotten barges along the waterfront—this was life on a geographic edge.

It was life on a social edge, too—a borderland where respectable and "trashy" got confused.

. . . . . .

"Did you ever experience other people looking down on us because we lived in a trailer park?" I ask my mom.

"Never," she tells me.

"But who were your friends?"

"They all lived in the trailer park."

"What about the neighbors who lived in houses up the street?"

"Oh, they didn't like us at all," she says. "They thought people who lived in trailers were all lowlife and trash. They didn't really associate with us."

In the 1950s, trailer parks were crossroads where the paths of poor, working-class, and lower-middle-class white migrants intersected as we temporarily occupied the same racially segregated space—a kind of residential parking lot—on our way somewhere else. Class tensions—often hidden—structured our daily lives as we tried to position ourselves as far as we could from the bottom. White working-class families who owned or lived in houses could raise their own class standing within whiteness by showing how they were better off than the white residents of trailer parks. We often responded to them by displaying our own respectability and distancing ourselves from those trailer park residents who were more "lower class" than we were. If we failed and fell to the bottom, we were in danger of also losing, in the eyes of other white people, our own claims to the racial privileges that came with being accepted as white Americans.

In our attempt to scramble "up" into the middle class, we had at our disposal two conflicting stereotypes of trailer park life that in the 1950s circulated through popular culture. The respectable stereotype portrayed residents of house trailers as white World War II veterans, many of them attending college on GI loans, who lived with their young families near campuses during the postwar housing shortage. In the following decades, this image expanded to include the predominantly white retirement communities located in Florida and the Southwest. In these places, trailers were renamed "mobile" or "manufactured" homes. When parked together, they formed private worlds where white newlyweds, nuclear families, and retirees lived in clean, safe, managed communities. You can catch a glimpse of this world in the 1954 Hollywood film *The Long, Long Trailer*, in which Lucille Ball and Desi Arnaz spend their slapstick honeymoon hauling a house trailer cross-country and end up in a respectable trailer park. (The fact that Arnaz is Cuban American doesn't seriously disrupt the whiteness of their Technicolor world—he's assimilated as a generally "Spanish" entertainer, an ethnic individual who has no connection with his Cuban American family or community.)

A conflicting stereotype portrayed trailer parks as trashy slums for white transients—single men drifting from job to job, mothers on welfare, children with no adult supervision. Their inhabitants supposedly engaged in prostitution and extramarital sex, drank a lot, used drugs, and were the perpetrators or victims of domestic violence. With this image in mind, cities and suburbs passed zoning laws restricting trailer parks to the "other side of the tracks" or banned them altogether. In the fifties, you could see this "white trash" image in B-movies and on the covers of pulp magazines and paperback books. The front cover of one "trash" paperback, *Trailer Park Woman*, proclaims that it's "a bold, savage novel of life and love in the trailer camps on the edge of town." The back cover, subtitled *Temptation Wheels*, explains why trailers are the theme of this book.

> Today nearly one couple in ten lives in a mobile home—one of those trailers you see bunched up in cozy camps near every sizable town. Some critics argue that in such surroundings love tends to become casual. Feverish affairs take place virtually right out in the open. Social codes take strange and shocking twists. . . . "Trailer Tramp" was what they called Ann Mitchell—for she symbolized the twisted morality of the trailer camps. . . . This book shocks not by its portrayal of her degradation—rather, by boldly bringing to light the conditions typical of trailer life.

This image has been kept alive as parody in John Waters's independent films; as reality in Hollywood films such as *Lethal Weapon*, *The Client*, and *My Own Private Idaho*; and as retro-fifties camp in contemporary postcards, posters, T-shirts, and refrigerator magnets.

I imagine that some fifties trailer parks did fit this trashy stereotype. But Sunset Trailer Park in Bayonne was respectable—at least to those of us who lived there. Within that respectability, however, we had our own social hierarchy. Even today, trying to position ourselves into it is difficult. "You can't say we were rich," as my mom tries to explain, "but you can't say we were at the bottom, either." What confused things even more were the many standards by which our ranking could be measured—trailer size and model, lot size and location, how you kept up your yard, type of car, jobs and occupations, income, number of kids, whether mothers worked as homemakers or outside the home for wages. Establishing where you were on the trailer park's social ladder depended on where you were standing and which direction you were looking at any given time.

To some outsiders, our trailer park did seem low class. Our neighbors up the street looked down on us because they lived in two- or three-family houses with yards in front and back. Our trailers were small, as were our lots, some right on the stinky bay. The people in houses were stable; we were transients. And they used to complain that we didn't pay property taxes on our trailers but still sent our kids to their public schools.

On our side, we identified as "homeowners" too (if you ignored the fact that we rented our lots), while some people up the street were renters. We did pay taxes, if only through our rent checks. And we shared with them our assumed privileges of whiteness—theirs mostly Italian, Irish, and Polish Catholic, ours a more varied mix that included Protestants. The trailer park owner didn't rent to black families, so we were granted the additional status of having our whiteness protected on his private property.

The owner did rent to one Chinese American family, the Wongs (not their real name), who ran a Chinese restaurant. Like Desi Arnaz, the presence of only one Chinese family didn't seriously disrupt the dominant whiteness of our trailer park. They became our close friends as we discovered that we were almost parallel families—both had the same number of children, and Mrs. Wong and my mother shared the same first name. But there were significant differences. Mom tells me that the Wongs had no trouble as Asian Americans in the trailer park, only when they went out to buy a house. "You don't realize how discriminatory they are in this area," Mrs. Wong told my mother one day over tea. "The real estate agents find a place for us, but the sellers back out when they see who we are." Our trailer park may have been one of the few places that accepted them in Bayonne. They fit in with us because they, unlike a poorer family might have been, were considered "respectable." With their large trailer and their own small business, they represented to my father the success he himself hoped to achieve someday.

While outsiders looked down on us as trailer park transients, we had our own internal social divisions. As residents we did share the same laundry room, recreation hall, address, and sandbox. But the owner segregated us into two sections of his property: left courtyard for families with children, right courtyard for adults, mostly newlyweds or retired couples. In the middle were a few extra spaces where tourists parked their vacation trailers overnight. Kids were not allowed to play in the adult section. It had bigger lots and was surrounded by a fence, so it had an exclusive air about it.

The family section was wilder, noisier, and more crowded because every trailer had kids. It was hard to keep track of us, especially during summer vacation. Without having to draw on those who lived in the houses, we organized large group games—like Red Rover and bicycle circus shows—on the common asphalt driveway. Our activities even lured some kids away from the houses into the trailer park, tempting them to defy their parents' disdain for us.

We defended ourselves from outsiders' stereotypes of us as lowlife and weird by increasing our own investment in respectability. Trashy white people lived somewhere else—probably in other trailer parks. We could criticize and look down on them, yet without them we would have been the white people on the bottom. "Respectable" meant identifying not with them, but with people just like us or better than us, especially families who owned real houses in the suburbs.

My mom still portrays our lives in Bayonne as solidly middle class. I'm intrigued by how she constructed that identity out of a trailer park enclave confined to the polluted waterfront area of an industrial blue-collar town.

"Who were your friends?" I ask her.

"We chose them from the people we felt the most comfortable with," she explains. These were couples in which the woman was usually a homemaker and the man was an accountant, serviceman, or salesman—all lower middle class, if categorized only by occupation. As friends, these couples hung out together in the recreation hall for birthday, Christmas, and Halloween costume parties. The women visited each other every day, shared the pies and cakes they baked, went shopping together, and helped each other with housework and babysitting.

"There was one woman up the street," my mom adds, "who we were friends with. She associated with us even though she lived in a house."

"Who didn't you feel comfortable with?" I ask her.

"Couples who did a lot of drinking. People who had messy trailers and didn't keep up their yards. People who let their babies run around barefoot in dirty diapers. But there were very few people like that in our trailer park." They were also the boys who swam in the polluted brine of Newark Bay and the people who trapped crabs in the same waters and actually ate their catch.

When we first entered the social world of Sunset Trailer Park, our family found ways to fit in and even "move up" a little. Physical location was important. Our trailer was first parked in a middle lot. We then moved up by renting the "top space"—as it was called—when it became available. It was closest to the houses and farthest from the bay. Behind it was a vacant housing lot, which belonged to the trailer park owner and separated his park from the houses on the street—a kind of "no-man's-land." The owner gave us permission to take over a piece of this garbage dump and turn it into a garden. My dad fenced it in, and my mom planted grass and flowers which we kids weeded. Every year the owner gave out prizes—usually a savings bond—for the best-looking "yards." We won the prize several times.

Yet the privilege of having this extra yard had limits. With other trailer park kids we'd stage plays and performances there for our parents—it was our makeshift, outdoor summer stock theater. But we made so much noise that we drove the woman in the house that overlooked it crazy. At first she just yelled "Shut up!" at us from her second-story window. Then she went directly to the owner, who prohibited the loudest, most unruly kids from playing with us. After a while we learned to keep our own voices down and stopped our shows so we, too, wouldn't be banned from playing in our own yard.

My mom made a little extra money—$25 a month—and gained a bit more social status by working for the owner as the manager of his trailer park. She collected rent checks from each tenant, handled complaints, and made change for the milk machine, washers, and dryers. "No one ever had trouble paying their rent," Mom tells me, adding more evidence to prove the respectability of our trailer park's residents.

Our family also gained some prestige because my dad "worked in TV" as a pioneer in this exciting new field. Once in a while he got tickets for our neighbors to appear as contestants on the TV game show *Truth or Consequences*, a sadistic spectacle that forced couples to perform humiliating stunts if they couldn't give correct answers to trick questions. Our neighbors joined other trailer park contestants who in the fifties appeared on game shows like *Beat the Clock*, *Name That Tune*, *You Bet Your Life*, and especially *Queen for a Day*. The whole trailer park was glued to our TV set on nights when our neighbors were on. We rooted for them to win as they became celebrities right before our eyes. Even the put-down "Bayonne jokes" we heard from Groucho Marx, Ralph Kramden, and other TV comics acknowledged that our town and its residents had at least some status on the nation's cultural map.

My dad wasn't the only trailer park resident who gained a little prestige from celebrity. There was a musician who played the clarinet in the NBC orchestra. There was a circus performer who claimed he was the only man in the world who could juggle nine balls at once. He put on a special show for us kids in the recreation hall to prove it. There was a former swimming champion who lived in a trailer parked near the water. Although he was recovering from pneumonia, he jumped into Newark Bay to rescue little Jimmy who'd fallen off the seawall and was drowning. He was our hero. And there was an elderly couple who shared a tiny Airstream with twenty-four Chihuahua dogs—the kind pictured in comic books as small enough to fit in a teacup. This couple probably broke the world's record for the largest number of dogs ever to live in a house trailer. You could hear their dogs yip hysterically whenever you walked by.

Trailer park Chihuahua-dog collectors, game show contestants, circus performers—lowlife and weird, perhaps, to outsiders, but to us, these were our heroes and celebrities. What's more, people from all over the United States ended up in our trailer park. "They were well-traveled and wise," my mom explains with pride, "and they shared with us the great wealth of their experience." This may be why they had more tolerance for differences (within our whiteness, at least) than was usual in many white communities during the fifties—more tolerant, my mom adds, than the less-traveled people who lived in the houses.

· · · · · ·

Dangers seemed to lurk everywhere. To protect us, my parents made strict rules we kids had to obey. They prohibited us from playing in the sandbox because stray cats used it as their litter box. We weren't allowed to walk on the seawall or swim in Newark Bay, in which little Jimmy had nearly drowned and whose water, if we swallowed it, would surely have poisoned us. And they never let us go on our own into anyone else's trailer—or house—or bring any kids into ours.

"Why did you make that rule?" I ask my mom after wondering about it for years.

"Because there were lots of working couples," she explains, "who had to leave their kids home alone with no adult supervision. We didn't want you to get into trouble by yourselves."

But I did break this rule. Once the Chihuahua-dog couple invited me inside their Airstream to read the Sunday comics with them. I went in. But I was so terrified by the nonstop, high-pitched barking, the powerful stench, and my own act of disobedience that I couldn't wait to get back outside.

At other times I visited schoolmates in their homes after school. One was a Polish kid who lived two blocks away in a slightly nicer part of town. His house made me think his family was rich. They had an upstairs with bedrooms, a separate kitchen and dining room, a living room with regular furniture, doors between rooms, a basement, and a garage. I fantasized about moving into his house and sharing a bedroom with him as my brother.

When I visited an Italian boy who lived in a downtown apartment, I learned that not everyone who lived in buildings was better off than we were. Their smelly entry hall had paint peeling from the cracked walls and a broken-down stairway. I was afraid to go upstairs. I visited another schoolmate who lived with his grandfather and a dog inside the Dickensian cabin of a deserted barge on the docks at Newark Bay. They heated their cabin with wood scavenged from the piers and vacant lots nearby. I felt sorry for him because he seemed like the orphans we prayed for in church who had something to do with "alms for the poor." I visited a boy who lived in another trailer park. He was an only child who was home alone when his parents were at work. I envied his privacy and dreamed about us being brothers, too. At times, I'd even go down to the seawall to watch the bad boys swim in Newark Bay.

Alone like that with other white boys in their homes or by the water, I sometimes felt erotic charges for them—affectional desires that moved up, down, or across our class positions in the form of envy, pity, and brotherliness. Only years later did I learn to identify and group all these feelings together as a generic "homosexual" attraction. Yet that "same-sex" reading of those erotic sparks erased how they each had been differentiated by class and unified by race during my disobedient excursions around Bayonne. Even today, a predominantly white gay identity politics still regards race and class as nongay issues, refusing to see how they have fundamentally structured male homoerotic attractions and socially organized our homosexual relationships, particularly when they're same-class and white-on-white.

I wasn't the only person around who was a little queer.

"Did I ever tell you about the lesbian couple who lived in the trailer park?" my mom asks me.

"No, Ma, you never did."

I'm stunned that after all these years, she's just now telling her gay historian son about this fabulous piece of fifties trailer park dyke history coming right out of the pages of her own life!

"They were the nicest people," she goes on.

Grade school teachers. One taught phys. ed., the other taught English. Military veterans. They lived in a trailer bigger than ours over in the adult section. I forget their names, but one dressed like a woman and the other dressed like a man. The woman who dressed like a woman had a green thumb. She kept her trailer filled with houseplants and took good care of them. She did all the housekeeping—the inside work. The woman who dressed like a man did the outside work—waxed the trailer, repaired their truck. In their yard she built a beautiful patio with a rose arbor and a barbecue—did all the cement work herself. They threw barbecue parties there in the summer—with finger food, hamburgers, and wine. They were lots of fun.

I'm as intrigued by Mom's description of a "woman dressed like a woman" as I am by her description of a "woman dressed like a man." The logic of seeing the butch partner acting like the man led to Mom seeing the femme partner acting like the woman, rather than just being a woman. Yet this female couple created a domestic relationship that was familiar enough for my parents and their friends to accept as normal. And like the Wongs, their class respectability—in the form of good jobs, large trailer, and well-kept yard—seemed to make up for differences that in other neighborhoods might have set them apart.

"Did you know then that they were lesbians?"

"Oh yeah," Mom says. "We never talked about it or used that word, but we all knew. They were a couple. Everybody liked them. Nicest people you'd ever want to meet!" The protection of not having their relationship named as deviant allowed these women to fit into our trailer park world.

It was another woman from the adult section who helped nurture my own incipient queerness. On one of the rare nights when my parents splurged by going to the movies, this woman babysat for us. An expert seamstress, she spent her time with us sewing outfits for my sister's Ginny Doll. I was jealous. "Boys can have dolls, too," she reassured me. Sitting on our sofa with me right next to her eagerly watching her every move, she pieced together a stuffed boy-doll for me (this was years before Ken or GI Joe appeared), then sewed him little pants and a shirt. When my parents saw this present, they let me keep him. For a while I cherished this peculiar toy—a handmade gift that acknowledged my own uniqueness. But before long, "unique" evolved into "weird" and even "queer." My boy-doll embarrassed me so much that I threw him away.

My parents' protective rules were based on an important truth. Whenever I went into other people's houses and trailers, or when they came into ours, I did find myself getting into trouble—queer trouble, too.

· · · · · ·

Let's Look Inside . . .

No one who has not actually BEEN INSIDE a modern trailer coach can fully appreciate the roominess, convenience and downright comfort to be found there. (A 22-foot trailer is longer than most BIG living-rooms!) Study the illustrations on this page. Imagine yourself seated on that soft couch . . . using that efficient kitchen . . . hanging your clothes in spacious closets . . . going to sleep on that well-sprung bed. Here is good living, coupled with freedom from unnecessary obligation and expense—in A HOME OF YOUR OWN!

—1946 *Trailer Coach* magazine ad

House trailers were a lot like cars—metal shells built on wheels, manufactured on assembly lines, that varied by price, style, width, and length. As companies produced new models, old ones grew outdated and depreciated in value. If you lived in one trailer for a long time, you lost status, like driving around in an old, run-down car while this year's newer, shinier, spiffier models passed you by. The older your trailer got, the more important it was that you did what you could to "keep it up."

Living in our house trailer was like living in a big car. Ours was an eight-by-thirty-six-foot Pacemaker that had been manufactured around 1950. Post-streamline in style but predating the fifties "popu-luxe" fins, it was enamel-painted in a two-tone design—maroon body and top with a cream band around the middle at window level. In the summer it felt like an oven as the sun beat down on our metal roof, until we bought an air conditioner to save us from baking to a crisp. In the fall we were terrified of hurricanes and tornadoes. Like schoolyard bullies, these windstorms have an uncanny ability to seek out all vulnerable trailers in their path so they can turn them over, tear them apart, or crush them under fallen trees.

Inside we had three "rooms." At the front was a living-dining-kitchen area; in the middle, the bedroom; and at the back, the kids' room with two bunk beds and a tiny bathroom. There were no real doors separating these areas, because each was a passageway to the next. We had a small TV set in the front room. The rest of our "furniture" was built in: beds, dressers, couch, cabinets, lighting. Freestanding furniture was a status symbol we didn't enjoy—except for our Formica dinette set and a plastic-covered rocking chair. Stored in the closets, under the beds, and behind things were folding items—a spare chair, a card table—that we brought out whenever company came. Everything was tiny, compact, multipurpose, and convertible. Even today, the lavatories at the rear of jet planes give me an eerie sense of déjà vu.

We quickly adjusted to the restrictions of our cramped living space. Before my mom married, she had made extra money as a piano teacher, so she wanted to teach me piano, too. But no piano would ever fit in our trailer. So she rented a small accordion—we pretended it was a little piano—and sent me to the Police Athletic League up the street to take lessons from a retired policeman. On rainy Saturdays our parents made us go to the all-day kiddie matinee at the local movie theater, which we loved. This was to get us out of the trailer so we wouldn't drive Mom crazy in that small space. One Christmas my parents gave me a plastic toy house trailer as a present. The roof came off, and inside the layout was identical to our own. It contained a little white family of four, just like ours. This toy was the logical extension of the miniaturization of our lives. And it was small enough to fit in the tiny, tightly packed space under the bunk beds that was reserved for our toys.

In 1955 my mom gave birth to a baby girl. When the baby outgrew her crib, our trailer developed its own housing shortage. My parents' solution was to put my new sister in my bunk bed and put me in their own bed. When they were ready to go to sleep, they moved me to the couch in the front room. Before long, I could wake up in the morning with no memory of having been moved. That's how I started sleepwalking. One night I got out of bed, walked into the front room, and told my parents, who were watching TV, that I had to go to the bathroom. "So go," they said. I turned around, walked over to the refrigerator—which was only slightly smaller than our bathroom—and slowly opened the door. "No!" my parents yelled as they jumped up to stop me from peeing all over the food in the fridge.

In those days I had a recurring dream that I'd found a hidden door in our trailer that opened to a tiny stairway leading up to a space no one knew about which I claimed as my own secret room. Dreams, fantasies, and disorientation were all ways to rearrange the immovable furniture and expand the diminutive interior of our house trailer, which seemed to get smaller as our family grew in size and we kids got bigger.

Most of the trailer park's children went to Roosevelt Grade School, up the street and behind the Police Athletic League. This public school, like Catholic schools, required boys to dress up in uniforms, in our case, a white shirt and tie. But a dress code to make working-class students look respectable did not cover up other differences that were still visible among us.

It was at Roosevelt School in the second grade that I first had African American classmates. When I told my mom about these students by using the n-word, she warned me never to say that word again and to use the word "colored" instead. This is my first memory of being taught to respect people of other races. But the lesson didn't extend far enough for me to learn where the black students lived. I knew it wasn't in our neighborhood. The social distance between our white lives in the trailer park and the lives of the black students in Bayonne remained too great for me to cross, even in my disobedient visits into other boy's homes.

More than once our school used white students—including me—to extend that racial distance. One Easter week Roosevelt School decided to put on a children's fashion show for the parents. The producers of the show, who were from a downtown department store, auditioned the students to see who they'd like to use as fashion models. I was among the chosen few because, as they said, I had "dark features"—this in a school with African American students whose "features" were darker than mine but who were not chosen to be fashion models. My school granted me fashion status for my dark features—hair, eyes, and skin—but only because I was white. When I walked down that runway in the school auditorium, I was mortified. Modeling clothes in public was stuff that sissy boys did, and to make things worse, I was wearing clothes my parents couldn't really afford to buy. Exactly whose fantasies was our school's fashion show acting out, anyway?

White kids from the houses, trying to position themselves as better than us trailer park kids, experimented with ways to challenge us as not "white enough" or even not "really white." My own dark "features" made me vulnerable to their name-calling. During the summers, I ran around the trailer park barefoot and shirtless in shorts—a slip in my parents' commitment to respectability—so my skin reached a dark tan. One day, some white boys from up the street cornered me in the alley beside our recreation hall and started pushing me around. They might have called me a sissy or a host of other names, but this time they taunted me with racial epithets. "Look at the nigger-boy," I remember one boy saying as he hit me. "Naw, he's just a monkey-boy," the other mocked back. They hit me until I denied that I was either of these, then let me run home crying. My experience as the target of their racism was mild compared to what black children had to deal with at school from these same boys. Yet these bullies successfully taught me—a "dark" white child living in a trailer park—that other whites who looked down on us because of where we lived could call my whiteness into question. Ashamed, I kept these and other social injuries to myself, channeling them into desires to learn how to act and look more white and to find other ways to move up and out of this life that more and more felt like a trap I had to escape.

School seemed to offer me the best way out. When I was in the fourth grade, a white university student came by the trailer park to talk to my parents. He was doing a study for his thesis, he told them, and would like their permission to give me and my sister psychological and intelligence tests, for which they would be charged nothing at all. Was he studying the psychology and intelligence of the white working class? Did he pick us because we were in a trailer park or in a blue-collar town? No one remembers. Dad called the university to make sure he was legit; then my parents agreed to let us be part of his study.

A few days later he came by again. I got in his car, and he drove me to a house in another part of Bayonne where we went upstairs into a dark garret. For hours I described ink blots, put blocks into holes, drew stick figures on paper, and made up stories about what was happening in pictures he showed me. As he drove me back home, we passed by a big street sign for a loan company, and he warned me, "Never, ever borrow money from those people!" I never did.

He reported to my parents that our test results indicated we would do well in school and that we were college material. "It was that young man's tests," my mom now explains to me, "that first got us thinking about how we could find a way to send you kids to college."

· · · · · ·

My parents' dreams of someday buying a house, starting a small business, and sending the kids to college were the engines that drove their lives. They pinched pennies, bought cheaply or did without, and developed such schemes for making a little extra money as managing the trailer park or entering contests for the best-looking yard. Saving to buy a house was always their first priority. Next came putting us through school and starting the small business, like our friends who had their own Chinese restaurant, that would get them where they wanted to go with some security and independence.

"It always seemed like a constant struggle," Mom tells me. "You couldn't take a breather long enough to feel like you were getting ahead." She budgeted every cent. She did our back-to-school and other kinds of shopping at John's Bargain Stores, Two Guys from Harrison, and Robert Hall—where the "values go up, up, up," and the "prices go down, down, down," because they've got "low overhead," as their radio jingle went. My sisters wore hand-me-down clothes from each other, our older cousins, and me. We did our part by studying hard in school to get good grades. Illnesses, uninsured dental work, strikes at NBC, a broken-down car, and an exploded hot water heater periodically set their savings plan back to zero or even less.

In 1957 my mother gave birth to another baby girl. Now there were six of us in our little home, pushing our living space to the breaking point. There was no denying that the longer we stayed put, the more we were slipping down rather than moving up. We were a large family packed into a small trailer that looked older every day compared to the brand-new models that surrounded it. These were two- and even three-bedroom "mobile homes," ten feet wide and fifty feet long, with chrome exteriors, screened-in porches, even double-deckers with an upstairs sleeping "loft."

"When the new mobile homes were pulled into the park," my mom tells me, "we'd all go over to the lot and watch them set up—not just the women, but the men, too! Sometimes they'd invite us inside to show us what they had—big kitchens, regular furniture, even a step up from the kitchen to the living room, like a split-level house. Dad would say, 'Boy, they've sure come a long way since we bought ours.' Then we'd go back to our old trailer, envious."

On Sunday drives we'd visit model homes at the housing developments that were sprawling all over the New Jersey suburbs in the late fifties. These were almost as exciting as going to Disneyland. Our fantasies went wild as we imagined ourselves living in four-bedroom homes with dens, two-car garages, and lots of space in layouts packaged as Split-Levels, Colonials, Ranches, or Cape-Cods. On Sunday nights we drove back to Sunset Trailer Park. These new homes were too expensive for us to afford.

My parents wanted to buy a house so badly that they, like other upwardly mobile working-class adults, took a real estate course to learn how to make money selling houses. They never managed to sell any, but they did learn how the housing market worked. One day they found an ad for a cheap, run-down mansion at the edge of a nearby suburb. It had been on the market as a "White Elephant" for over a year because no one wanted a big old Victorian house during the fifties craze for suburban newness. Combining their savings with a loan from a real estate broker's acquaintance, they scraped together enough money for a down payment, sold the trailer, and finally moved into their own house. The whole trailer, we wrote our relatives, could fit into our new front hallway.

Finally we'd escaped the trailer park to begin what became our brief entry into white middle-class suburban life. The dramatic change was exciting yet awkward for me, as I mistakenly believed that we'd arrived in the land of the rich and famous. For my first day as the new kid in school, I dressed up in my Sunday hat, suit, and tie, expecting to fit into the wealthy world I'd imagined. Instead, to my horror, I became the laughingstock of the schoolyard. Hearing my foreign-sounding last name (we were "French Canadian" in the fifties, "Franco-American" now) and seeing me in my peculiar outfit, the other students somehow got the idea that I'd migrated to their suburb all the way from Peru. I denied this but knew right away that to fit into this new world, I had to keep my trailer park past a tightly guarded secret.

It took me a long time to figure out where we'd ended up. But I knew enough to take advantage of the rare opportunities that this high-caliber school system now offered me.

Our suburban dream world lasted only a few years. By 1962 Dad left his job as NBC began replacing its technical crews with automated machinery. My parents sold the house and moved back to Massachusetts to live with Dad's father on the family farm. There they tried to start a small-business bookkeeping service, but it never brought in enough money to live on. When Dad got seriously ill without health insurance and couldn't work, Mom took a job in a local mascara brush factory earning $45 a week. Although they tried very hard, my parents never did save enough to send any of us to college.

"You were smart," my mom tells me now. "Getting a good education was your way out." When in 1964 I graduated from high school with honors and did win a full college scholarship to the University of Chicago, she adds, "you kept up your part of the bargain." The bargain, I think, was that if they worked hard enough and I studied hard enough, we would all succeed. But in 1968, during my senior year, I dropped out of college. A crisis hit me in April as I started to confront my homosexuality before gay liberation, faced class panic when I was rejected for graduate school and didn't know what came next, feared for my own life as I witnessed murders on the streets during the Chicago riots following the assassination of Dr. Martin Luther King Jr., and decided to resist the draft rather than fight in Vietnam. The world was coming apart around me, yet I blamed myself for not working hard enough to keep up my part of the bargain. "You had only one chance to get out and you blew it," I remember thinking at the time, still missing the truth that, for both me and my parents, the bargain itself had been a lie.

· · · · · ·

As the distance from the trailer park grew in years, miles, and class, I began to manipulate my memory of that world so that it carried less shame. In college I met other scholarship students who adapted to our new middle-class surroundings by working their lower-class origins into cool, competitive, "class escape" stories in which they bragged about how far they'd come. I joined in, "coming out" about my trailer park past. Having grown up in Bayonne made my stories—and my ascent—even more dramatic.

By the nineties, a pop culture, retro-fifties nostalgia resurrected and then commodified the artifacts of trailer park life, reworking their meanings into a campy "trash" style. So I unearthed my own trailer park past once again, this time learning how to take an ironic, parodic, "scare quotes" stance toward it, even using it at times as a kind of white trash cultural—and sexual—currency. I now collect old paperback books, souvenirs, and magazine ads having to do with fifties trailer parks. I love the stuff. And I'm glad that the current fascination with white trash icons, like house trailers, has opened up a public discourse big enough to include my own queer, working-class, trailer park voice. Today I can use that voice—and its identity—to challenge the class-based stereotypes that hurt real people. And I can enjoy the pleasures of campy nostalgia along with the pleasures of cross-class sex experienced from many sides. Now that there's a new "rock 'n roll fag bar" in San Francisco called White Trash, I get to wonder what I'd wear, who I'd want to be, and who I'd want to pick up if I went there.

But sometimes it's hard for me to distinguish the camp from the painful realities around which it dances. Ironic distancing has served me as a lens through which I've been able to re-view my trailer park past with less shame. But it has so distorted my vision that I misremember the "reality" of that part of my life. I've caught myself actually believing that we and our neighbors all had fabulous plastic pink flamingoes in our yards. I am sure—and so is my mom—that none of us ever did.

Lately I've searched flea markets for a plastic house trailer just like the one I had as a child. Today it would be a valuable collector's item, and my desire to find it is partly as a collector. But I also want to see it again because it once pointed this working-class boy's way out of being embarrassed about how his family lived, showing him that their trailer park life was respectable enough to be made into a mass-produced toy.

Recently, at a gay gift shop on Castro Street in San Francisco, I bought a T-shirt that says "Cheap Trailer Trash" over a picture of a fifties trailer that's identical to the one I grew up in—except, of course, it has a pink flamingo. I now can be both cool and authentic when I wear this shirt. When people say, "I like your shirt," I get to say, "Thanks. And it's true, too." When some start telling me their own stories of growing up in trailer parks, I can feel us bond around this weird nineties identity that's built on shared—if distorted—memories rather than on current realities. Sometimes we slip into playing the old class-positioning game. "What kind of trailer did you live in? How wide and how long? How big was your family? Did you own or rent your lot? Did you call it a mobile home? How long did you live there? What kind of trailer park was it? What part of town was it in?" In an inverted form of social climbing, the player with the trashiest past gets to be the winner of this game. We can do this because the distance from our former lives gives us room to play with old degradations as contemporary chic. But back then, actually living inside a trailer park, those who won the game were the ones who got out for good. Nowadays, trailer park folks still try to get out by playing games—not as TV game show contestants, like our neighbors in the fifties who made fools of themselves for prizes, but as "guests" on so-called "trash" talk shows, like Geraldo, Richard Bey and Jenny Jones, who "win" celebrity, but no prizes, if they can act out the real dramas of their lives as trashy stereotypes, reassuring viewers that it's someone else who's really on the bottom.

The whole country looks more like a trailer park every day. As our lived economy gets worse, more jobs are becoming temporary, homes less permanent or more crowded, neighborhoods unstable. We're transients just passing through this place, wherever and whatever it is, on our way somewhere else, mostly down.

"I get really scared sometimes," my mom tells me, "that the old days are coming back." She means the Great Depression days she knew in her childhood, and the trailer park days I knew in mine.

I get scared, too. Without any academic degrees, and with the middle dropping out of the book publishing world as it's dropping out of everything else, I find it increasingly difficult to survive as a writer. As I approach fifty, I see how closely my economic life history resembles that of my parents as I'm pushed around the edges of lower-middle-class, working-class, and "new Bohemian" worlds. Lately, I've been having a perverse fantasy that if times get too tough, I can always retire to a trailer park, maybe in Bayonne.

. . . . . .

A few years ago, I actually went back to visit Bayonne, which I hadn't seen since 1957. I wanted to check my distorted fantasies against a tangible reality, to go back "home" to this source of memories that I mine for insights as I try to understand and fight the race and class divisions that are still tearing our nation apart. I asked my friend Bert Hansen to go with me for support because he also grew up white, gay, and working class. I didn't wear my "Trailer Park Trash" T-shirt that day. We took the Path train from Christopher Street in Greenwich Village over to Jersey City, rented a car, and drove out to Bayonne.

To my surprise the trailer park was still there, along with every house, store, bar, and restaurant that used to be on our block, all still run by the same families. This was a remarkable testament to the death-defying—and too-often life-threatening—stability of this blue-collar town, despite the enormous social and economic odds working against it.

With my camera in hand, I walked into the trailer park and around both courtyards, taking pictures of the same lots we'd lived in four decades ago.

The place was run down now; many lots were empty and littered with car parts and old boards; almost no one was around. A man washing his car in front of his house up the street told me that the trailer park had just been sold to a condo developer. People who worked in Manhattan, he said, would be moving in because it would be cheaper and convenient for commuting. Up the street Roosevelt Grade School and the Police Athletic League buildings were still standing but closed. Slated for demolition, the school was surrounded by chain-link fence and barbed wire until a new one could be built.

When I walked around the trailer park one last time to take my final pictures, two white boys on bicycles suddenly appeared from around a corner. They followed us, keeping their distance, wary and unfriendly, as if protecting their territory from intruders. Watching them watching me, I realized that the distant memory of my boyhood in this trailer park, which was coming alive as I stood there, was now their hard reality. At first glance they seemed really poor. As a kid who never felt poor, did I sometimes look like they do to outsiders? Surely these boys were much worse off than I had been. They seemed hostile, but why should they be friendly toward me—a total stranger taking pictures of their trailers? I could be there to steal their possessions, or to expose their poverty to outsiders, or to design the condos that would replace their house trailers, forcing them to move against their will. Or I might be a graduate student earning an academic degree, wanting to use them as working-class subjects, like the grad student who came here so long ago to give me and my sister intelligence tests, for free, then disrupting our lives by telling us that our high scores might offer us a way out.

I can still see these two boys looking at me as if I am some kind of spy, which indeed I am. I don't belong here anymore. Their days belonging here are nearly over, too.

November 1995

How Gay Stays White and
What Kind of White It Stays

Bérubé intended this talk as a critical commentary on the state of gay male politics and community life. Reflecting upon experiences that were overtly political (his work with the Campaign for Military Service in 1993) as well as personal (his gay men's HIV-negative support group), he investigates how race gets constructed, seemingly without intentionality but with profound consequences. The whiteness of "gay male" as a social category has significant implications for how the agenda of a movement gets set, what kind of successes and limitations a movement has, and who reaps the benefits from a politics of sexual identity.

The Stereotype

When I teach college courses on queer history or queer working-class studies, I encourage students to explore the many ways that homosexuality is shaped by race, class, and gender. I know that racialized phantom figures hover over our classroom and inhabit our consciousness. I try to name these figures out loud to bring them down to earth so we can begin to resist their stranglehold on our intelligence. One by one, I recite the social categories that students have already used in our discussions—immigrant, worker, corporate executive, welfare recipient, student on financial aid, lesbian mother—and ask students first to imagine the stereotypical figure associated with the category and then to call out the figure's race, gender, class, and sexuality. As we watch each other conjure up and name these phantoms, we are stunned at how well each of us has learned by heart the same fearful chorus.

Whenever I get to the social category "gay man," the students' response is always the same: "white and well-to-do." In the United States today, the

Originally published in *The Making and Unmaking of Whiteness*, edited by Birgit Rasmussen, Eric Klineberg, Irene Nexica, and Matt Wray, 234–65 (Durham: Duke University Press, 2001).

Sergeant First Class Perry Watkins speaking at the funeral of Leonard Matlovich, 1988.
Photograph © 2010 JEB (Joan E. Biren).

dominant image of the typical gay man is a white man who is financially better off than most everyone else.

My White Desires

Since the day I came out to my best friend in 1968, I have inhabited the social category "gay white man." As a historian, writer, and activist, I've examined the gay and the male parts of that identity, and more recently I've explored my working-class background and the Franco-American ethnicity that is so intertwined with it. But only recently have I identified with or seriously examined my gay male whiteness.[1]

Several years ago I made the decision to put race and class at the center of my gay writing and activism. I was frustrated at how my own gay social and activist circles reproduced larger patterns of racial separation by remaining almost entirely white. And I felt abandoned as the vision of the national gay movement and media narrowed from fighting for liberation, freedom, and social justice to expressing personal pride, achieving visibility, and lobbying for individual equality within existing institutions. What emerged was too often an exclusively gay rights agenda isolated from supposedly nongay issues, such as homelessness, unemployment, welfare, universal health care, union organizing, affirmative action, and abortion rights. To gain recognition and credibility, some gay organizations and media began to aggressively promote the so-called positive image of a generic gay community that is an upscale, mostly male, and mostly white consumer market with mainstream, even traditional, values. Such a strategy derives its power from an unexamined investment in whiteness and middle-class identification. As a result, its practitioners seemed not to take seriously or even notice how their gay visibility successes at times exploited and reinforced a racialized class divide that continues to tear our nation apart, including our lesbian and gay communities.

My decision to put race and class at the center of my gay work led me as a historian to pursue the history of a multiracial maritime union that in the 1930s and 1940s fought for racial equality and the dignity of openly gay workers.[2] And my decision opened doors that enabled me as an activist to join multiracial lesbian, gay, bisexual, and transgender groups whose members have been doing antiracist work for a long time and in which gay white men are not the majority—groups that included the Lesbian, Gay, Bisexual, and Transgender Advisory Committee to the San Francisco Human Rights Commission and the editorial board of the now-defunct national lesbian and gay quarterly journal *Out/Look.*

But doing this work also created new and ongoing conflicts in my relationships with other white men. I want to figure out how to handle these conflicts as I extend my antiracist work into those areas of my life where I still find myself among gay white men—especially when we form new activist and intellectual groups that once again turn out to be white. To do this I need "to clarify something for myself," as James Baldwin put it when he gave his reason for writing his homosexual novel *Giovanni's Room* in the 1950s.[3]

I wanted to know how gay gets white, how it stays that way, and how whiteness is used both to win and attack gay rights campaigns.

I want to learn how to see my own whiteness when I am with gay white men and to understand what happens among us when one of us calls attention to our whiteness.

I want to know why I and other gay white men would want to challenge the racist structures of whiteness, what happens to us when we try, what makes me keep running away from the task, sometimes in silent despair, and what makes me want to go back to take up the task again.

I want to pursue these questions by drawing on a gay ability, developed over decades of figuring out how to "come out of the closet," to bring our hidden lives out into the open. But I want to do this without encouraging anyone to assign a greater degree of racism to gay white men, thus exposed, than to other white men more protected from exposure, and without inviting white men who are not gay to more safely see gay men's white racism rather than their own.

I want to know these things because gay white men have been among the men I have loved and will continue to love. I need them in my life and at my side as I try to make fighting racism a more central part of my work. And when students call out "white" to describe the typical gay man, and they see me standing right there in front of them, I want to figure out how, from where I am standing, I can intelligently fight the racist hierarchies that I and my students differently inhabit.

Gay Whitening Practices

Despite the stereotype, the gay male population is not as white as it appears to be in the images of gay men projected by the mainstream and gay media, or among the "out" men (including myself) who move into the public spotlight as representative gay activists, writers, commentators, and spokesmen. Gay men of color, working against the stereotype, have engaged in long, difficult struggles to gain some public recognition of their cultural heritages, political activism, and everyday existence. To educate gay white men, they've had to get our attention by interrupting our business as usual, then convince us that we don't speak for them or represent them or know enough about either their realities or our own racial assumptions and privileges. And when I and other gay white men don't educate ourselves, gay men of color have done the face-to-face work of educating us about their cultures, histories, oppression, and particular needs—the kind of personal work that tires us out when heterosexuals ask us to explain to them what it's like to be gay. Also working against their ability to put "gay" and "men of color" together in the broader white imagination are a great many other powerful *whitening practices* that daily construct, maintain, and fortify the idea that gay male means white.

How does the category "gay man" become white? What are the whitening practices that perpetuate this stereotype, often without awareness or comment by gay white men? How do these practices operate, and what racial work do they perform?

I begin by mining my own experience for clues.[4] I know that if I go where I'm surrounded by other gay white men, or if I'm having sex with a white man, it's unlikely that our race will come up in conversation. Such racially comfortable, racially familiar situations can make us mistakenly believe that there are such things as gay issues, spaces, culture, and relationships that are not "lived through" race, and that white gay life, so long as it is not named as such, is not about race.[5] These lived assumptions, and the privileges on which they are based, form a powerful camouflage woven from a web of unquestioned beliefs—that gay whiteness is unmarked and unremarkable, universal and representative, powerful and protective, a cohesive bond. The markings of this camouflage are pale—a characteristic that the wearer sees neither as entirely invisible nor as a racial "color," a shade that allows the wearer to blend into the seemingly neutral background of white worlds. When we wear this everyday camouflage into a gay political arena that white men already dominate, our activism comes wrapped in a *pale protective coloring* that we may not notice but which is clearly visible to those who don't enjoy its protection.

I start to remember specific situations in which I caught glimpses of how other gay whitening practices work.

One night, arriving at my favorite gay disco bar in San Francisco, I discovered outside a picket line of people protesting the triple-carding (requiring three photo IDs) of gay men of color at the door. This practice was a form of racial *exclusion*—policing the borders of white gay institutions to prevent people of color from entering. The management was using this discriminatory practice to keep the bar from "turning," as it's called—a process by which a "generically gay" bar (meaning a predominantly white bar) changes into a bar that loses status and income (meaning gay white men with money won't go there) because it has been "taken over" by black, Latino, or Asian gay men. For many white owners, managers, and patrons of gay bars, only a white gay bar can be *just* gay; a bar where men of color go is seen as racialized. As I joined the picket line, I felt the fears of a white man who has the privilege to choose on which side of a color line he will stand. I wanted to support my gay brothers of color who were being harassed at the door, yet I was afraid that the doorman might recognize me as a regular and refuse to let me back in. That night, I saw a gay bar's doorway become a racialized border, where a battle to preserve or challenge the whiteness of the clientele inside was fought among dozens of gay men who were either standing guard at the door, allowed to walk through it, or shouting and marching outside. (The protests eventually made the bar stop the triple-carding.)

I remember seeing how another gay whitening practice works when I watched, with other members of a sexual politics study group, an antigay video, *Gay Rights, Special Rights*, produced in 1993 by The Report, a religious right organization. This practice was the *selling* of gay whiteness—the marketing of gays as white and wealthy to make money and increase political capital, either to raise funds for campaigns (in both progay and antigay benefits, advertising, and direct-mail appeals) or to gain economic power (by promoting or appealing to a gay consumer market). The antigay video we watched used racialized class to undermine alliances between a gay rights movement portrayed as white and movements of people of color portrayed as heterosexual. It showed charts comparing mutually exclusive categories of "homosexuals" and "African Americans," telling us that homosexuals are wealthy, college-educated white men who vacation more than anyone else and who demand even more "special rights and privileges" by taking civil rights away from low-income African Americans.[6] In this zero-sum, racialized world of the religious right, gay men are white; gay, lesbian, and bisexual people of color, along with poor or working-class white gay men, bisexuals, and lesbians, simply do not exist. The recently vigorous gay media promotion of the high-income, brand-loyal gay consumer market—which is typically portrayed as a population of white, well-to-do, college-educated young men—only widens the racialized class divisions that the religious right so eagerly exploits.

During the 1993 Senate hearings on gays in the military, I saw how these and other whitening practices were used in concentrated form by another gay institution, the Campaign for Military Service (CMS).

The Campaign for Military Service was an ad hoc organization formed in Washington, D.C., by a group composed primarily of well-to-do, well-connected, professional men, including billionaires David Geffen and Barry Diller, corporate consultant and former antiwar activist David Mixner (a personal friend of Bill Clinton), and several gay and lesbian civil rights attorneys. Their mission was to work with the Clinton White House and sympathetic senators by coordinating the gay response to hearings held by the Senate Armed Services Committee, chaired by Sam Nunn. Their power was derived from their legal expertise, their access to wealthy donors, and their contacts with high-level personnel inside the White House, Senate, and Pentagon. The challenge they faced was to make strategic, pragmatic decisions in the heat of a rapidly changing national battle over what President Clinton called "our nation's policy toward homosexuals in the military."[7]

The world in and around the CMS that David Mixner describes in his memoir, Stranger among Friends, is a network of professionals passionately dedicated to gay rights who communicated with Washington insiders via telephone calls, memos, and meetings in the White House, the Pentagon, and private homes. Wearing the protective coloring of this predominantly white gay world, these professionals entered the similarly white and male but heterosexual world of the U.S. Senate, where their shared whiteness became a common ground on which the battle to lift the military's ban on homosexuals was fought—and lost.

The CMS used a set of arguments they called the *race analogy* to persuade senators and military officials to lift the military's antigay ban. The strategy was to get these powerful men to take antigay discrimination as seriously as they supposedly took racial discrimination, so they would lift the military ban on homosexuals as they had eliminated official policies requiring racial segregation. During the Senate hearings, the race analogy projected a set of comparisons that led to heated disputes over whether sexual orientation was analogous to race, whether sexual desire and conduct were like "skin color," or, most specifically, whether being homosexual was like being African American. (Rarely was "race" explicitly discussed as anything other than African American.) On their side, the CMS argued for a qualified analogy—what they called "haunting parallels" between "the words, rationale and rhetoric invoked in favor of racial discrimination in the past" and those used to "exclude gays in the military now." "The parallel is inexact," they cautioned, because "a person's skin color is not the same as a person's sexual identity; race is self-evident to many whereas sexual orientation is not. Moreover, the history of African Americans is not equivalent to the history of lesbian, gay and bisexual people in this country." Yet, despite these qualifications, the CMS held firm to the analogy. "The bigotry expressed is the same; the discrimination is the same."[8]

The military responded with an attack on the race analogy as self-serving, racist, and offensive. They were aided by Senator Nunn, who skillfully managed the hearings in ways that exploited the whiteness of the CMS and their witnesses to advance the military's antigay agenda. Working in their favor was the fact that, unlike the CMS, the military had high-ranking officials who were African American. The chairman of the Joint Chiefs of Staff, Gen. Colin L. Powell, who opposed lifting the ban, responded to the CMS with the argument that the antigay policy was not analogous to racial segregation because "skin color" was a "benign characteristic" while homosexuality constituted conduct that was neither benign nor condoned by most Americans.[9] Another African American army officer, Lt. Gen. Calvin Waller, Gen. Norman Schwarzkopf's deputy commander and the highest-ranking African American officer in Operation Desert Storm, attacked the race analogy with these words: "I had no choice regarding my race when I was delivered from my mother's womb. To compare my service in America's armed forces with the integration of avowed homosexuals is personally offensive to me."[10] Antigay white senators mimicked his outrage.

During the race analogy debates, the fact that only white witnesses made the analogy, drawing connections between antigay and racial discrimination without including people of color, reduced the power of their argument and the credibility it might have gained had it been made by advocates who had experienced the racial discrimination side of the analogy.[11] But without hearing these voices, everyone in the debate could imagine homosexuals as either people who do not experience racism (the military assumption) or as people who experience discrimination only as homosexuals (the progay assumption)—two different routes that ultimately led to the same destination: the place where gay stays white, the place where the CMS chose to make its stand.

According to Mixner's memoir, the Senate Armed Services Committee "had asked CMS to suggest witnesses."[12] As gay gatekeepers to the hearings, the CMS utilized another whitening practice—*mirroring*. This is a political strategy that reflects back the whiteness of the men who run powerful institutions to persuade them to take "us" seriously, accept "us," and let "us" in because "we are just like you." From the witnesses they selected, it appears that the CMS tried to project an idealized image of the openly gay service member that mirrored the senators' racial makeup and their publicly espoused social values and sexual mores—the image of the highly competent, patriotic, sexually abstinent, young, male officer who had earned the right to serve with a proud record and therefore deserved equality. The CMS selected for the gay panel a group of articulate and courageous veterans—all white men, except for one white woman.[13] Cleverly, Senator Nunn's staff selected a panel of African American ministers opposed to lifting the ban to precede the gay white panel, so that both sides constructed and participated in a racialized dramatic conflict that reinforced the twin myths that gay is white and African Americans are antigay.

Missing was the testimony of service members whose lives bridged the hearings' false divide between black and gay—veterans who were both African American and lesbian, gay, or bisexual. In this context, a significant whitening practice at the hearings was the exclusion of Sgt. Perry Watkins as a witness. Watkins was an openly gay, African American veteran considered by many to be a military hero. Kicked out of the army as a homosexual shortly before his retirement, he successfully appealed his discharge to the Supreme Court, becoming what one attorney called "the first out gay soldier to retire from the Army with full honors."[14]

To my knowledge, there is no public record of how or why the CMS did not invite Watkins to testify.[15] (This is another privilege that comes with whiteness—the ability to make decisions that seriously affect people of color

and then protect that decision-making process from public scrutiny or ac-
countability.) Sabrina Sojourner, who recalls that she was the only African
American at the CMS among the nonsupport staff, told me that she "got
moved further and further from the decision-making process" because she
"brought up race," including the problem of the racial dynamic set up by
presenting only white witnesses to testify.[16]

There was a moment when I was personally involved with this process.
As the author of *Coming Out Under Fire: The History of Gay Men and Women
in World War II*, I was asked by the CMS to prepare to fly from California
to Washington to testify, but my appearance was not approved by the Senate staff, who allowed no open homosexuals to testify as expert witnesses.[17]
During a phone conversation with a white CMS staff member, I remember
getting up the courage to ask him why Watkins wasn't a witness and was
told that "Perry is a difficult personality." I didn't push my question any further, getting the message that I shouldn't ask for complicated explanations
during the heat of battle and deferring to their inside-the-Beltway tactical
decisions, thus forfeiting an important opportunity to seriously challenge
Watkins's exclusion. More instances of this painful struggle over Watkins's
participation in and around the hearings must have been going on behind
the scenes.[18] Watkins believed he was shut out because he was a "queeny"
African American.[19]

It seems that the CMS considered Watkins to be the opposite of their ideal
witness. His military story was indeed more complicated than the generic
coming-out story. During his 1968 induction physical exam in Tacoma,
Washington, he had openly declared his homosexuality, checking "Yes" to
the written question "Do you have homosexual tendencies?" and freely describing his sexual experiences to the induction psychiatrist. But the army
drafted him nevertheless because it needed him to fight in Vietnam, along
with other mostly working-class African American men, who, by 1966, ac-
counted for 20 percent of U.S. combat deaths in that war, when African
Americans made up 11 percent of the U.S. population and 12.6 percent of
U.S. troops in Vietnam. Journalist Randy Shilts, who later interviewed Watkins, reported that Watkins believed "the doctor probably figured Watkins
would . . . go to Vietnam, get killed, and nobody would ever hear about it
again."[20] So Watkins's story was not a white narrative. "If I had not been
black," he told Mary Ann Humphrey in an oral history interview, "my situation would not have happened as it did. . . . Every white person I knew from
Tacoma who was gay and had checked that box 'Yes' did not have to go into
the service."[21] Watkins's story resonated more with how men of color experience antigay racism in the military than with the story so many white ser-

vicemen tell. That white narrative begins with how a gay serviceman never experienced discrimination until he discovered his homosexuality in the service and ends with his fighting an antigay discharge, without referring to how he lived this experience through his whiteness. But Watkins explicitly talked about how he lived his gay military experience through race. "People ask me," he explained, "'How have you managed to tolerate all that discrimination you have had to deal with in the military?' My immediate answer to them was, 'Hell, I grew up black. Give me a break.'"[22] Watkins had also, while in the military, danced and sung on U.S. army bases as the flamboyant "Simone," his drag persona; as a veteran he was HIV-positive; and in some gay venues he wore body piercings in public.[23]

Nevertheless, Watkins's testimony at the hearings could have struck familiar chords among many Americans, including working-class and African American communities, as the experience of someone who was real rather than an *ideal*. His story was so compelling, in fact, that after the hearings he was the subject of two films and a segment of the television news magazine 20/20.[24] But the story of his military career—which he so openly lived through race (as an African American), sexuality (had a sex life), and gender (performed in drag)—seems to have been considered by the CMS as too contaminated for congressional testimony and too distracting for the personal media stories that were supposed to focus only on the gay right to serve.

Watkins's absence was a lost opportunity to see and hear in nationally televised Senate hearings a gay African American legal hero talk about his victory over antigay discrimination in the military and expose the racist hypocrisy of how the antigay ban was in practice suspended for African Americans during wartime. The lack of testimony from any other lesbian, gay, or bisexual veteran of color was a lost opportunity to build alliances with communities of color and to do something about the "(largely accurate) perception of the gay activist leadership in Washington as overwhelmingly white."[25] Their collective absence reinforced another powerful myth that, even in a military population that is disproportionately African American and Latino, the representative gay soldier is a white officer, and the most presentable gay face of military competence is a white face.

As the hearings progressed, some CMS activists, speaking in public forums outside the hearings, took the race analogy a step further by promoting the idea that the gay rights movement was *like* the civil rights movement. During the hearings, those who argued the race analogy had drawn parallels between racist and antigay bigotry and discrimination. But those who extended the race analogy to the civil rights movement analogy had to take several more steps. First, they had to reconceptualize the civil rights movement. They took a multiracial movement for human equality and human rights, which included many lesbian, gay, and bisexual activists, and changed it into a nongay, black movement for African American racial equality. Next, they had to imagine the gay movement as a white movement for homosexual rights rather than as a multiracial movement that grew out of and continued the work of the civil rights movement. Then they could make the analogy between these two now-separated movements—one just about race, the other just about homosexuality. The last step was to symbolically recast gay white men in the roles of African American civil rights leaders. These moves tried to correct a problem inherent in such whitening practices as excluding people of color and the wearing, mirroring, and selling of gay whiteness. Because such practices draw directly on the privileges of whiteness, they do not on their own carry much moral weight. The extended race analogy compensates for this weightlessness by first invoking the moral authority of the civil rights movement (while erasing its actual history), and then transferring that unearned moral authority to a white gay movement, without giving anything back. At its worst, the race analogy can become a form of historical erasure, political cheating, and, ultimately, a theft of cultural capital and symbolic value.

David Mixner's memoir reveals how the extended race analogy was used in and around the CMS. When President Clinton, at a press conference, revealed that he wouldn't rule out separating homosexuals from heterosexuals within the military, Mixner first interpreted Clinton's comments as condoning gay segregation, then began equating it with racial segregation. Mixner's account of what happened next does not include attempts to seek advice from or build alliances with people whose histories include long struggles against legal segregation. This despite solid support for lifting the ban from civil rights veterans, including Coretta Scott King and Roger Wilkins; the Black Lesbian and Gay Leadership Forum; the Congressional Black Caucus (including Ron Dellums, chairman of the House Armed Services Committee and a former marine who eventually held House hearings to counter Nunn's Senate hearings); and, in public opinion polls, a majority of African Americans (in contrast to a minority of white Americans).[26] Mixner instead describes a series of decisions and actions in which he invokes scenes from the history of racial segregation and the civil rights movement and appears to be reenacting those scenes as if he were a gay (white) version of a black civil rights leader.

A telling moment was when Mixner asked his friend Troy Perry, a gay white minister who founded and heads the gay Metropolitan Community

Church (MCC), to let him use the Sunday pulpit at the MCC cathedral in Dallas as a "platform from which to speak." Covered by network television, Mixner delivered a sermon to the nation about the gay "road to freedom." In his sermon he referred to the military's antigay policy as "ancient apartheid laws" and charged that "Sam Nunn is our George Wallace" and that "bigotry that wears a uniform is nothing more than a uniform with a hood." He angrily warned President Clinton, cast as antigay segregationist, that "with or without you we will be free. . . . We will prevail!"[27] Shortly after the sermon, Tracy Thorne, a gay white navy veteran who had courageously faced verbal abuse at the Senate hearings and who flew to Dallas to support Mixner, said out loud what had been implied by Mixner's words and actions. David Mixner "could be our Martin Luther King, no questions asked," Thorne told a reporter from a gay newspaper.[28]

Such dramatic race-analogy scenarios performed by white activists beg some serious questions. Are actual, rather than "virtual," people of color present as major actors in these scenarios, and if not, why not? What are they saying or how are they being silenced? How is their actual leadership being supported or not supported by the white people who are reenacting this racialized history? And who is the "we" in this rhetoric? Mixner's "we," for example, did not account for those Americans—including lesbian, gay, bisexual, or transgender activists from many racial backgrounds—who did not finally have or indeed need "our own George Wallace" or "our own Martin Luther King." "Martin Luther King is the Martin Luther King of the gay community," Dr. Marjorie Hill, board president of Unity Fellowship Church and former director of the New York City Mayor's Office for Lesbian and Gay Issues, has pointedly replied in response to those who were looking for King's gay equivalent. "His lesson of equality and truth and non-violence was for everyone."[29] If the gay rights movement is already part of the ongoing struggle for the dignity of all people exemplified in the activism of Dr. Martin Luther King Jr., then there is no need for gay equivalents of Dr. King, racial segregation, or the civil rights movement. If the gay rights movement is not already part of the civil rights movement, then what is it? Answering this question from a white position with the race analogy—saying that white gay leaders and martyrs are "our" versions of African American civil rights leaders and martyrs—can't fix the problem and ultimately undermines the moral authority that is its aim. This use of the race analogy ends up reinforcing the whiteness of gay political campaigns rather than doing the work and holding on to the dream that would continue the legacy of Dr. King's leadership and activism.[30]

What would the gay movement look like if gay white men who use the race analogy took it more seriously? What work would we have to do to close the perceived moral authority gap between our gay activism and the race analogy, to directly establish the kind of moral authority we seek by analogy? What if we aspired to achieve the great vision, leadership qualities, grassroots organizing skills, and union solidarity of Dr. Martin Luther King Jr., together with his opposition to war and his dedication to fighting with the poor and disenfranchised against the deepening race and class divisions in America and the world? How could we fight, in the words of U.S. Supreme Court Justice Harry A. Blackmun, for the "fundamental interest all individuals have in controlling the nature of their intimate associations with others," in ways that build a broad civil rights movement rather than being "like" it, in ways that enable the gay movement to grow into one of many powerful and direct ways to achieve race, gender, and class justice?[31]

These, then, are only some of the many whitening practices that structure everyday life and politics in what is often called the "gay community" and the "gay movement"—making *race analogies*; *mirroring* the whiteness of men who run powerful institutions as a strategy for winning credibility, acceptance, and integration; *excluding* people of color from gay institutions; *selling* gay as white to raise money, make a profit, and gain economic power; and daily wearing the *pale protective coloring* that camouflages the unquestioned assumptions and unearned privileges of gay whiteness. These practices do serious damage to real people whenever they mobilize the power and privileges of whiteness to protect and strengthen gayness, including the privileges of gay whiteness, without using that power to fight racism, including gay white racism.

Most of the time, the hard work of identifying such practices, fighting racial discrimination and exclusion, critiquing the assumptions of whiteness, and racially integrating white gay worlds has been taken up by lesbian, gay, bisexual, and transgender people of color. Freed from this enforced daily recognition of race and confrontation with racism, some prominent white men in the gay movement have been able to advance a gay rights politics that, like the right to serve in the military, they imagine to be just gay, not about race. The gay rights movement can't afford to "dissipate our energies," Andrew Sullivan, former editor of the *New Republic*, warned on the Charlie Rose television program, by getting involved in disagreements over nongay issues such as "how one deals with race . . . how we might help the underclass . . . how we might deal with sexism."[32]

But a gay rights politics that is supposedly color-blind (and sex-neutral and classless) is in fact a politics of race (and gender and class). It assumes, without ever having to say it, that gay must equal white (and male and economically secure); that is, it assumes white (and male and middle class) as the default categories that remain once one discounts those who as gay people must continually and primarily deal with racism (and sexism and class oppression), especially within gay communities. It is the politics that remains once one makes the strategic decision, as a gay activist, to stand outside the social justice movements for race, gender, or class equality, or to not stand with disenfranchised communities, among whom are lesbian, bisexual, gay, or transgender people who depend on these movements for dignity and survival.

For those few who act like, look like, and identify with the white men who still run our nation's major institutions, for those few who can meet with them, talk to them, and be heard by them as peers, the ability to draw on the enormous power of a shared but unacknowledged whiteness, the ability never to have to bring up race, must feel like a potentially sturdy shield against antigay discrimination. I can see how bringing up explicit critiques of white privilege during high-level gay rights conversations (such as the Senate debates over gays in the military), or making it possible for people of color to set the agenda of the gay rights movement, might weaken that white shield (which relies on racial division to protect)—might even, for some white activists, threaten to "turn" the gay movement into something less gay, as gay bars "turn" when they're no longer predominantly white.

The threat of losing the white shield that protects my own gay rights raises even more difficult questions that I need to "clarify . . . for myself": What would I say and do about racism if someday my own whiteness helped me gain such direct access to men in the centers of power, as it almost did during the Senate hearings, when all I did was ask why Perry Watkins wasn't testifying and accept the answer I was given? What privileges would I risk losing if I persistently tried to take activists of color with me into that high-level conversation? How, and with whom, could I begin planning for that day?

Gay white men who are committed to doing antiracist activism as gay men have to work within and against these and other powerful whitening practices. What can we do, and how can we support each other, when we once again find ourselves involved in gay social and political worlds that are white and male?

Gay, White, Male, and HIV-Negative

A few years ago, in San Francisco, a friend invited me to be part of a new political discussion group of HIV-negative gay men. Arriving at a neighbor's apartment for the group's first meeting, I once again felt the relief and pleasure of being among men like me. All of us were involved in AIDS activism. We had supported lovers, friends, and strangers with HIV and were grieving the loss of too many lives. We didn't want to take time, attention, and scarce resources away from people with AIDS, including many people of color. But we did want to find a collective, progressive voice as HIV-negative men. We wanted to find public ways to say to gay men just coming out that "we are HIV-negative men, and we want you to stay negative, have hot sex, and live long lives. We don't want you to get sick or die." We were trying to work out a politics in which HIV-negative men, who are relatively privileged as not being the primary targets of crackdowns on people who are HIV-positive, could address other HIV-negative men without trying to establish our legitimacy by positioning ourselves as victims. When I looked around the room I saw only white men. I knew that many of them had for years been incorporating antiracist work into their gay and AIDS activism, so this seemed like a safe space to bring up the whiteness I saw. I really didn't want to hijack the purpose of the group by changing its focus from HIV to race, but this was important because I believed that not talking about our whiteness was going to hurt our work. Instead of speaking up, however, I hesitated.

Right there. That's the moment I want to look at—that moment of silence, when a flood of memories, doubts, and fears rushed into my head. What made me want to say something about our whiteness and what was keeping me silent?

My memory took me back to 1990, when I spoke on a panel of gay historians at the first Out/Write conference of lesbian and gay writers, held in San Francisco. I was happy to be presenting with two other community-based historians working outside the academy. But I was also aware—and concerned—that we were all men. When the question period began, an African American writer in the audience, a man whose name I later learned was Fundi, stood up and asked us (as I recall) how it could happen, at this late date, that a gay history panel could have only white men on it. Awkward silence. I don't trust how I remember his question or what happened next—unreliable memory and bad thinking must be characteristics of inhabiting whiteness while it's being publicly challenged. As the other panelists responded, I remember wanting to distance myself from their whiteness while my own mind went blank, and I remember feeling terrified that Fundi would address me directly and ask me to respond personally. I kept thinking, "I don't know what to say, I can't think, I want to be invisible, I want this to be over, now!"

After the panel was over I spoke privately to Fundi. Later, I resolved never to be in that situation again—never to agree to be on an all-white panel without asking ahead of time why it was white, if its whiteness was crucial to what we were presenting, and, if not, how its composition might be changed. But in addition to wanting to protect myself from public embarrassment and to do the right thing, that writer's direct challenge made me understand something more clearly: that only by seeing and naming the whiteness I'm inhabiting, and taking responsibility for it, can I begin to change it and even do something constructive with it. At that panel, I learned how motivating though terrifying it can be as a white person to be placed in such a state of heightened racial discomfort—to be challenged to see the whiteness we've created, figure out how we created it, and then think critically about how it works.[33]

In the moment of silent hesitation I experienced in my HIV-negative group, I found myself imagining for the first time, years after it happened, what it must have been like for Fundi to stand up in a predominantly white audience and ask an all-white panel of gay men about our whiteness. My friend and colleague Lisa Kahaleole Hall, who is a brilliant thinker, writer, and teacher, says that privilege is "the ability not to have to take other people's existence seriously," the "ability not to have to pay attention."[34] Until that moment I had mistakenly thought that Fundi's anger (and I am not certain that he in fact expressed any anger toward us) was only about me, about us, as white men, rather than also about him—the history, desires, and support that enabled him to speak up, and the fears he faced and risks he took by doing it. Caught up in my own fear, I had not paid close attention to the specific question he had asked us. "The problem of conventional white men," Fundi later wrote in his own account of why he had decided to take the risk of speaking up, "somehow not being able, or not knowing how, to find and extend themselves to women and people of color had to be talked through. . . . My question to the panel was this: 'What direct skills might you share with particularly the whites in the audience to help them move on their fears and better extend themselves to cultural diversity?'"[35] I'm indebted to Fundi for writing that question down, and for starting a chain of events with his question that has led to my writing this essay.

I tried to remember who else I had seen bring up whiteness. The first images that came to mind were all white lesbians and people of color. White lesbian feminists have as a movement dealt with racism in a more collective way than have gay white men. In lesbian and gay activist spaces I and other gay white men have come to rely on white lesbians and people of color to raise the issue of whiteness and challenge racism, so that this difficult task has become both gendered as lesbian work and racialized as "colored" work. These images held me back from saying anything to my HIV-negative group. "Just who am I to bring this up?" I wondered. "It's not my place to do this." Or, more painfully, "Who will these men think I think I am? Will they think I'm trying to pretend I'm not a white man?"

Then another image flashed in my mind that also held me back. It was the caricature of the white moralist—another racialized phantom figure hovering in the room—who blames and condemns white people for our racism, guilt-trips us from either a position of deeper guilt or holier-than-thou innocence, claims to be more aware of racism than we are, and is prepared to catalog our offenses. I see on my mental screen this self-righteous caricature impersonating a person of color in an all-white group or, when people of color are present, casting them again in the role of spectators to a white performance, pushed to the sidelines from where they must angrily or patiently interrupt a white conversation to be heard at all. I understand that there is some truth to this caricature—that part of a destructive racial dynamic among white people is trying to determine who is more or less responsible for racism, more or less innocent and pure, more or less white. But I also see how the fear of becoming this caricature has been used by white people to keep each other from naming the whiteness of all-white groups we are in. During my moment of hesitation in the HIV-negative group, the fear of becoming this caricature was successfully silencing me.

I didn't want to pretend to be a white lesbian or a person of color, or to act like the self-righteous white caricature. "How do I ask that we examine our whiteness," I wondered, "without implying that I'm separating us into the good guys and bad guys and positioning myself as the really cool white guy who 'gets it' about racism?" I needed a way to speak intelligently from where I was standing without falling into any of these traps.

I decided to take a chance and say something.

"It appears to me," I began, my voice a little shaky, "that everyone here is white. If this is true, I'd like us to find some way to talk about how our whiteness may be connected to being HIV-negative, because I suspect there are some political similarities between being in each of these positions of relative privilege."

There was an awkward pause. "Are you saying," someone asked, "that we should close the group to men of color?"

"No," I said, "but if we're going to be a white group I'd like us to talk about our relationship to whiteness here."

"Should we do outreach to men of color?" someone else asked.

"No, I'm not saying that, either. It's a little late to do outreach, after the fact, inviting men of color to integrate our already white group."

The other men agreed, and the discussion went on to other things. I, too, didn't really know where to take this conversation about our whiteness. By bringing it up, I was implicitly asking for their help in figuring this out. I hoped I wouldn't be the only one to bring up the subject again.

At the next month's meeting there were new members, and they all appeared to be white men. When someone reviewed for them what we had done at the last meeting, he reported that I'd suggested we not include men of color in the group. "That's not right," I corrected him. "I said that if we're going to be a white group, I'd like us to talk about our whiteness and its relation to our HIV-negative status."

I was beginning to feel a little disoriented, like I was doing something wrong. Why was I being so consistently misunderstood as divisive, as if I were saying that I didn't want men of color in the group? Had I reacted similarly when, caught up in my own fear of having to publicly justify our panel's whiteness, I had misunderstood Fundi's specific question—about how we could share our skills with other white people to help each other move beyond our fear of cultural diversity—as an accusation that we had deliberately excluded women and men of color? Was something structural going on here about how white groups respond to questions that point to our whiteness and ask what we can do with it?

Walking home from the meeting, I asked a friend who'd been there if what I said had made sense. "Oh yes," he said, "it's just that it all goes without saying." Well, there it is. That is how it goes, how it stays white. "Without saying."

Like much of the rest of my gay life, this HIV-negative group turned out to be unintentionally white, although intentionally gay and intentionally male. It's important for me to understand exactly how that racial *unintentionality* gets *constructed*, how it's not just a coincidence. It seems that so long as white people never consciously decide to be a white group, a white organization, a white department, so long as we each individually believe that people of color are always welcome, *even though they are not there*, then we do not have to examine our whiteness because we can believe it is unintentional, it's not our *reason* for being there. That may be why I had been misunderstood to be asking for the exclusion of men of color. By naming our group as white, I had unknowingly raised the question of *racial intent*—implying that we had intended to create an all-white group by deliberately excluding men of color. If we could believe that our whiteness was purely accidental, then we could also believe that there was nothing to say about it because creating an all-white group, which is exactly what we had done, had never been anyone's intent, and therefore had no inherent meaning or purpose. By interrupting the process by which "it just goes without saying," by asking us to recognize and "talk through" our whiteness, I appeared to be saying that we already had and should continue to exclude men of color from our now very self-consciously white group.

The reality is that in our HIV-negative group, as in the panel of the Out/ Write conference and in many other all-white groupings, we each did make a chain of choices, not usually conscious, to invite or accept an invitation from another white person. We made more decisions whether or not to name our whiteness when we once again found ourselves in a white group. What would it mean to make such decisions consciously and out loud, to understand why we made them, and to take responsibility for them? What if we intentionally held our identities as white men and gay men in creative tension, naming ourselves as gay *and* white, then publicly explored the possibilities for activism this tension might open up? Could investigating our whiteness offer us opportunities for reclaiming our humanity against the ways that racial hierarchies dehumanize us and disconnect us from ourselves, from each other, and from people of color? If we took on these difficult tasks, how might our gay political reality and purpose be different?[36]

When I told this story about our HIV-negative group to Barbara Smith, a colleague who is an African American lesbian writer and activist, she asked me a question that pointed to a different ending: "So why didn't you bring up the group's whiteness again?" The easy answer was that I left the group because I moved to New York City. But the more difficult answer was that I was afraid to lose the trust of these gay men whom I cared about and needed so much, afraid I would distance myself from them and be distanced by them, pushed outside the familiar circle, no longer welcomed as white and not belonging among people of color, not really gay and not anything else, either. The big fear is that if I pursue this need to examine whiteness too far, I risk losing my place among gay white men, forever—and then where would I be?

Pale, Male—and Antiracist

What would happen if we deliberately put together a white gay male group whose sole purpose was to examine our whiteness and use it to strengthen our antiracist gay activism?

In November 1995, gay historian John D'Emilio and I tried to do just that. We organized a workshop at the annual Creating Change conference of activists put on that year in Detroit by the National Gay and Lesbian Task Force. We called the workshop "Pale, Male—and Anti-Racist." At a conference of over 1,000 people (mostly white but with a large number of people of color), about 35 gay white men attended.[37]

We structured the workshop around three key questions: (1) How have you successfully used your whiteness to fight racism? (2) What difficulties have you faced in doing antiracist activism as a gay white man? And (3) what kind of support did you get or need or wished you had received from other gay white men?

Before we could start talking about our successes, warning lights began to flash. You could sense a high level of mistrust in the room, as if we were looking at each other and wondering, "Which kind of white guy are *you*?" One man wanted to make sure we weren't going to waste time congratulating ourselves for sharing our white privilege with people who don't have access to it or start whining about how hard it is to work with communities of color. Someone else wanted to make sure we weren't going to guilt-trip each other. Another said, "I'm so much more aware of my failures in this area, I can't even see the accomplishments."

But slowly, once all the cautions were out in the open, the success stories came out. About fighting an anti–affirmative action initiative. About starting a racism study group. About getting a university department to study why it had no teaching assistants who were students of color. About persuading a gay organization in Georgia to condemn the state's Confederate flag. "What keeps me from remembering," I wondered, "that gay white men publicly do this antiracist work? Why can't I keep their images in my mind?"

One possible answer to my question appeared in the next success story, which midway made a sharp turn away from our successes toward how gay white men can discipline each other for standing on the "wrong" side of the color line. A man from Texas, Dennis Poplin, told us about what happened to him as the only white man on the board of the San Antonio Lesbian and Gay Assembly (SALGA), a progressive, multiracial lesbian and gay alliance. When SALGA mobilized support that successfully canceled a so-called gay community conference whose planning committee was all white—this in a city that was 65 percent Latina/Latino—a "community scandal" exploded, as he put it, "about political correctness, quotas, [and] reverse racism." A local newspaper, which was run by gay white men, started attacking SALGA. When a white reporter asked a man of color from SALGA why the group's board had no white men on it, and he replied that Dennis was on the board, the reporter said, "He's not white."[38]

Right away the men in the workshop started talking about the difficulties they'd had with other gay white men. "I find myself like not even knowing who it's safe to bring it up with," one man said. When he tries to talk about race, another said, "I'm just met with that smug, flippant, 'I'm tired of hearing about [all that].'" Others talked about fears of being attacked as too "PC."

At the "risk of opening a whole can of worms," as he put it, another man moved the discussion away from us to our relationships with white lesbians and people of color. Some men talked about how tired they were of being called "gay white men," feeling labeled, then attacked for who they were and for what they tried to do or for not doing enough; about having to deal with their racism while they didn't see communities of color dealing with homophobia; and about how after years of struggling they felt like giving up. Yet here they all were at this workshop. I began to realize that all our frustrations were signs of a dilemma that comes with the privileges of whiteness: having the ability to decide whether to keep dealing with the accusations, resentments, racial categorizations, and other destructive effects of racism that divide people who are trying to take away its power, or, because the struggle is so hard, to walk away from it and do something else, using the slack our whiteness gives us to take a break from racism's direct consequences.

Bringing this dilemma into the open enabled us to confront our expectations about how the antiracist work we do should be appreciated, should be satisfying, and should bring results. One man admitted that he didn't make antiracist work a higher priority because "I [would have to face] a level of discomfort, irritation, boredom, frustration, [and] enter a lot of [areas where] I feel inept, and don't have confidence. It would require a lot of humility. All these are things that I steer away from."

Over and over the men at the workshop expressed similar feelings of frustration, using such phrases as "We tried, but . . . ," "No matter what you do, you can't seem to do anything right," and "You just can't win." These seemed to reflect a set of expectations that grew out of the advantages we have because we are American men and white and middle class or even working class—expectations that we can win, that we should know how to do it right, that if we try we will succeed.

What do we—what do I—expect to get out of doing antiracist work, anyway? If it's because we expect to be able to fix the problem, then we're not going to be very satisfied. When I talk with my friend Lisa Kahaleole Hall about these frustrations, she tells me, "Sweet pea, if racism were that easy to fix, we would have fixed it already." The challenge for me in relation to other gay white men—and in writing this essay—is to figure out how we can support each other in going exactly into those areas of whiteness where we feel we have no competence yet, no expertise, no ability to fix it, where we haven't even come up with the words we need to describe what we're trying to do. For me, it's an act of faith in the paradox that if we, together with our friends and allies, can figure out how our own whiteness works, we can use that knowledge to fight the racism that gives our whiteness such unearned power.

And whenever this struggle gets too difficult, many of us, as white men, have the option to give up in frustration and retreat into a more narrowly defined gay rights activism. That project's goal, according to gay author Bruce Bawer, one of its advocates, is "to achieve acceptance, equal rights, and full integration into the present social and political structure."[39] It's a goal that best serves the needs of men who can live our gayness through our whiteness and whose only or most important experience with discrimination is as homosexuals. James Baldwin, who wrote extensively about whiteness in America, noticed long ago the sense of entitlement embedded in a gay whiteness that experiences no other form of systematic discrimination. "You are penalized, as it were, unjustly," he said in an interview. "I think white gay people feel cheated because they were born, in principle, into a society in which they were supposed to be safe. The anomaly of their sexuality puts them in danger, unexpectedly."[40]

The gay rights project that grows out of the shocking experience of being cheated unexpectedly by society because one is gay defines the gay political problem in its narrowest form. One solution is to get back the respect one has learned to expect as a white man. Some prominent, well-connected activists do this by educating the men who run our nation's powerful institutions, using reasoned arguments to combat their homophobia and expose discrimination as irrational—a strategy that sometimes does open doors but mostly to those who look and behave like the men in power. I have heard some of these activists express a belief that less privileged members of the "gay community" will eventually benefit from these high-level successes, but this would happen apparently without the more privileged having to do the work of fighting hierarchies that enforce race, class, and gender inequality. Their belief in a kind of "trickle-down" gay activism is based on the idea that powerful men, once enlightened, will generously allow equality to flow from the top to those near the top and then automatically trickle down to those down below. An alternative belief in "bottom-up activism" is based on the idea that, with great effort, democratic power must more slowly be built from the bottom up, and out, experimenting with more equal power relations along the way by creating links of solidarity across the divides of difference. Some gay white men explicitly reject, as nongay, this broader goal of joining activists who stand and work at the intersections of the many struggles to achieve social justice and to dismantle interlocking systems of domination. In the narrow world of exclusively gay "integrationist" activism, which its advocates privilege as the site of "practical" rather than "Utopian" politics,[41] college-educated gay white men have a better chance of knowing what to say and how to be heard, what to do and how to succeed within existing institutions. Because, when antigay barriers and attitudes are broken down but no other power relations are changed, we are the ones most likely to achieve "full integration into the present social and political structure." All it takes sometimes is being the white man at the white place at the white time.

When John and I asked the workshop participants our last question—"What would you need from each other to be able to continue doing antiracist work?"—the room went silent.

When push comes to shove, I wondered, holding back a sense of isolation inside my own silence, do gay white men as *white* men (including myself) have a lasting interest in fighting racism, or will we sooner or later retreat to the safety of our gay white refuges? I know that gay white men as *gay* men, just to begin thinking about relying on each other's support in an ongoing struggle against racism, have to confront how we've absorbed the antigay lies that we are all wealthy, irresponsible, and sexually obsessed individuals who can't make personal commitments, as well as the reality that we are profoundly exhausted fighting for our lives and for those we love through years of devastation from the AIDS epidemic. These challenges all make it hard enough for me to trust my own long-term commitment to antiracist work, let alone that of other gay white men.

Yet at this workshop we created the opportunity for us to see that we were not alone, to risk saying and hearing what we needed from each other in fighting racism, and to assess what support we could realistically hope to get. We wanted the opportunity to complain to another gay white man, to be held and loved when we get discouraged or feel attacked, whether justifiably or not. We wanted understanding for all the frustrations we feel fighting racism, the chance just to let them out with a gay white man who knows that it's not our racism he's supporting but the desire to see it and together figure out what to do next, so we won't give up or run away. We wanted other gay white men to take us seriously enough to call us on our racist shit in ways we could actually hear without feeling attacked. And we wanted to help each other lift at least some of the work and responsibility of supporting us from the shoulders of our friends and coworkers who are white women or people of color.

As time ran out at the workshop, I asked everyone to think about another difficult question: "Who is the gay white man who has had more experience than you in supporting other gay white men who are fighting racism, and who you can look to for advice on how to do it well?" "I think the more interesting question," one man answered, "is how many of us don't have anyone like that." We looked around at each other, wondering if any of us could name someone, until somebody said, "It's us."

Staying White

By trying to figure out what is happening with race in situations I'm in, I've embarked on a journey that I now realize is not headed toward innocence or winning or becoming not white or finally getting it right. I don't know where it leads, but I have some hopes and desires.

I want to find an antidote to the ways that whiteness numbs me, makes me not see what is right in front of me, takes away my intelligence, divides me from people I care about. I hope that, by occupying the seeming contradictions between the "antiracist" and the "gay white male" parts of myself, I can generate a creative tension that will motivate me to keep fighting. I hope to help end the exclusionary practices that make gay worlds stay so white. When I find myself in a situation that is going to stay white, I want to play a role in deciding what kind of white it's going to stay. And I want to become less invested in whiteness while staying white myself—always remembering that I can't just decide to stand outside of whiteness or exempt myself from its unearned privileges.[42] I want to be careful not to avoid its responsibilities by fleeing into narratives of how I have been oppressed as a gay man. The ways that I am gay will always be shaped by the ways that I am white.

Most of all, I want never to forget that the roots of my antiracist desires and my gay desires are intertwined. As James Baldwin's words remind me, acting on my gay desires is about not being afraid to love and therefore about having to confront this white society's terror of love—a terror that lashes out with racist and antigay violence. Following both my gay and antiracist desires is about being willing to "go the way your blood beats," as Baldwin put it, even into the heart of that terror, which, he warned, is "a tremendous danger, a tremendous responsibility."[43]

Acknowledgments

This is an expanded version of a personal essay I presented at the Making and Unmaking of Whiteness conference at the University of California at Berkeley in April 1997. I want to acknowledge that my thinking has grown out of conversations with many friends and colleagues, including Nan Alamilla Boyd, Margaret Cerullo, John D'Emilio, Arthur Dong, Marla Erlien, Jeffrey Escoffier, Charlie Fernandez, Dana Frank, Wayne Hoffman, Amber Hollibaugh, Mitchell Karp, Jonathan Ned Katz, Judith Levine, William J. Mann, David Meacham, Dennis Poplin, Susan Raffo, Eric Rofes, Gayle Rubin, Sabrina Sojourner, Barbara Smith, Nancy Stoller, Carole Vance, and Carmen Vasquez; the editors of this collection, especially Matt Wray and Irene Nexica; the participants in the "Pale, Male—and Anti-Racist" workshop at the 1995 Creating Change conference in Detroit; Lisa Kahaleole Hall and the students I joined in her San Francisco City College class on Lesbian and Gay Communities of Color; and the students in the courses I taught at the University of California at Santa Cruz, Portland State University, Stanford University, and the New School for Social Research.

NOTES

1. "Caught in the Storm: AIDS and the Meaning of Natural Disaster," *Out/Look: National Lesbian and Gay Quarterly* 1 (Fall 1988): 8–19; "'Fitting In': Expanding Queer Studies beyond the *Closet* and *Coming Out*" (paper presented at Contested Zone: Limitations and Possibilities of a Discourse on Lesbian and Gay Studies, Pitzer College, April 6–7, 1990, and at the Fourth Annual Lesbian, Bisexual, and Gay Studies Conference, Harvard University, October 26–28, 1990); "Intellectual Desire" (paper presented at La Ville en Rose: Le premier colloque Québécois d'études lesbiennes et gaies [First Quebec Lesbian and Gay Studies Conference], Concordia University and the University of Quebec at Montreal, November 12, 1992, published in *GLQ: A Journal of Lesbian and Gay Studies* 3, no. 1 [February 1996]: 139–57, reprinted in *Queerly Classed: Gay Men and Lesbians Write about Class*, edited by Susan Raffo, 43–66 [Boston: South End Press, 1997]; "Class Dismissed: Queer Storytelling across the Economic Divide" (keynote address at the Constructing Queer Cultures: Lesbian, Bisexual, and Gay Studies Graduate Student Conference, Cornell University, February 9, 1995, and at the Seventeenth Gender Studies Symposium, Lewis and Clark College, March 12, 1998); "I Coulda Been a Whiny White Guy," *Gay Community News* 20 (Spring 1995): 6–7, 28–30; "Sunset Trailer Park," in *White Trash: Race and Class in America*, edited by Matt Wray and Annalee Newitz, 15–39 (New York: Routledge, 1997).

2. *Dream Ships Sail Away* (forthcoming, Houghton Mifflin). [The book was unfinished at the time of Bérubé's death.—Eds.]

3. Richard Goldstein, "'Go the Way Your Blood Beats': An Interview with James Baldwin (1984)," in *James Baldwin: The Legacy*, edited by Quincy Troupe, 176 (New York: Simon and Schuster/Touchstone, 1989).

4. Personal essays, often assembled in published collections, have become an important written form for investigating how whiteness works, especially in individual lives. Personal essays by lesbian, gay, and bisexual authors that have influenced my own thinking and writing about whiteness have been collected in James Baldwin, *The Price of the Ticket: Collected Nonfiction, 1948–1985* (New York: St. Martin's, 1985); Cherríe Moraga and Gloria Anzaldúa, eds., *This Bridge Called My Back: Writings by*

Radical Women of Color (Watertown, Mass.: Persephone Press, 1981); Cherríe Moraga, *Loving in the War Years* (Boston: South End Press, 1983); Audre Lorde, *Sister Outsider* (Freedom, Calif.: Crossing Press, 1984); Elly Bulkin, Minnie Bruce Pratt, and Barbara Smith, *Yours in Struggle: Three Feminist Perspectives on Anti-Semitism and Racism* (Brooklyn: Long Haul Press, 1984); Essex Hemphill, ed., *Brother to Brother: New Writings by Black Gay Men* (Boston: Alyson, 1991); Mab Segrest, *Memoir of a Race Traitor* (Boston: South End Press, 1994); Dorothy Allison, *Skin: Talking about Sex, Class, and Literature* (Ithaca, N.Y.: Firebrand, 1994); and Becky Thompson and Sangeeta Tyagi, eds., *Names We Call Home: Autobiography on Racial Identity* (New York: Routledge, 1996).

5. For discussion of how sexual identities are "lived through race and class," see Robin D. G. Kelley, *Yo' Mama's Dysfunktional!* (Boston: Beacon, 1997), 114.

6. Whiteness can grant economic advantages to gay as well as straight men, and gay male couples can sometimes earn more on two men's incomes than can straight couples or lesbian couples. But being gay can restrict a man to lower-paying jobs, and most gay white men are not wealthy; like the larger male population, they are lower middle class, working class, or poor. For discussions of the difficulties of developing an accurate economic profile of the "gay community," and of how both the religious right and gay marketers promote the idea that gay men are wealthy, see Amy Gluckman and Betsy Reed, eds., *Homo Economics: Capitalism, Community, and Lesbian and Gay Life* (New York: Routledge, 1997).

7. David Mixner, *Stranger among Friends* (New York: Bantam, 1996), 291. For accounts of how the CMS was formed, see Mixner's memoir and Urvashi Vaid, *Virtual Equality: The Mainstreaming of Lesbian and Gay Equality* (New York: Anchor, 1995). Preceding the ad hoc formation of the CMS in January 1993 was the Military Freedom Project, formed in early 1989 by a group composed primarily of white feminist lesbians. Overshadowed during the Senate hearings by the predominantly male CMS, these activists had raised issues relating the military's antigay policy to gender, race, and class—specifically, that lesbians are discharged at a higher rate than are gay men; that lesbian-baiting is a form of sexual harassment against women; and that African American and Latino citizens, including those who are gay, bisexual, or lesbian, are disproportionately represented in the military, which offers poor and working-class youth access to a job, education, and health care that are often unavailable to them elsewhere. See Vaid, *Virtual Equality*, 153–59.

8. "The Race Analogy: Fact Sheet Comparing the Military's Policy of Racial Segregation in the 1940s to the Current Ban on Lesbians, Gay Men and Bisexuals," in *Briefing Book*, prepared by the Legal/Policy Department of the Campaign for Military Service, Washington, D.C. (1993).

9. Quoted from the *Legal Times*, February 8, 1993, in Mixner, *Stranger among Friends*, 286. Professor of history and civil rights veteran Roger Wilkins, responding to Powell's statement, argued that "lots of white people don't think that being black is benign even in 1993" (Mixner, *Stranger among Friends*, 286).

10. Henry Louis Gates Jr., "Blacklash?," *New Yorker*, May 17, 1993.

11. For brief discussions of how the whiteness of those making the race analogy reduced the power of their arguments, see Gates, "Blacklash?," and David Rayside, *On the Fringe: Gays and Lesbians in Politics* (Ithaca, N.Y.: Cornell University Press, 1998), 243.

12. Mixner, *Stranger among Friends*, 319.

13. The gay service members on this panel were former staff sergeant Thomas Pannicia, Sgt. Justin Elzie, and Col. Margarethe Cammermeyer. See Margarethe Cammermeyer, with Chris Fisher, *Serving in Silence* (New York: Penguin, 1994), 299. Other former gay service members who testified at the hearings were Sgt. Tracy Thorne and PO Keith Meinhold. Active-duty lesbian, gay, or bisexual service members could not testify without being discharged from the military as homosexuals, a situation that still exists under the current "don't ask, don't tell" military policy.

14. Mary Dunlap, "Reminiscences: Honoring Our Legal Hero, Gay Sgt. Perry Watkins, 1949–1996," *Gay Community News*, Winter 1996, 21.

15. In his memoir, *Stranger among Friends*, Mixner makes no mention of Watkins.

16. Author's personal conversation with Sabrina Sojourner, October 19, 1998.

17. An expert witness who was white, male, and not a gay historian was allowed to introduce a brief written synopsis of historical evidence from my book. I was one of the white men working with the CMS behind the scenes and from afar. Early in the hearings, Senator Edward Kennedy's staff asked me to compile a list of questions for him to ask during the hearings. In July, after the hearings were over and the "don't ask, don't tell" policy had been adopted, I submitted to the House Armed Services Committee written testimony, titled "Historical Overview of the Origins of the Military's Ban on Homosexuals," that critiqued the new policy and identified heterosexual masculinity, rather than the competence or behavior of homosexual service members, as the military problem requiring investigation. And I sent the CMS a copy of a paper I had given in April, "Stripping Down: Undressing the Military's Anti-Gay Policy," that used historical documents and feminist analysis to argue for investigating the military's crisis in heterosexual masculinity. In all these writings, I was trying, unsuccessfully, to get the CMS and the Senate to adopt a gender and sexuality analysis of the military policy; I used race and class analysis only to argue that the antigay policies disproportionately affected service members who were people of color and/or working class.

18. After Watkins's death in 1996 from complications due to HIV, Mary Dunlap, a white civil rights attorney who for years had followed his appeal case, in a tribute addressed to him, called him a "generous, tireless leader" who expressed "open and emphatic criticism and unabashed indictment of the racism of those among us who so blatantly and hurtfully excluded your voice and face and words from the publicity surrounding the gaylesbitrans community's challenge to 'Don't Ask, Don't Tell' in the early 90s" (Dunlap, "Reminiscences," 21).

19. Shamara Riley, "Perry Watkins, 1948–1996: A Military Trailblazer," *Outlines*, May 8, 1996.

20. Randy Shilts, *Conduct Unbecoming: Gays and Lesbians in the U.S. Military* (New York: St. Martin's, 1993), 50, 65; Mary Ann Humphrey, *My Country, My Right to Serve* (New York: HarperCollins, 1990), 248–57. Statistics are from D. Michael Shafer, "The Vietnam-Era Draft: Who Went, Who Didn't, and Why It Matters," in *The Legacy: The Vietnam War in the American Imagination*, edited by D. Michael Shafer (Boston: Beacon Press, 1990), 69.

21. Humphrey, *My Country*, 255–56.

22. Ibid.

23. Dunlap, "Reminiscences"; Shilts, *Conduct Unbecoming*, 155–56; Humphrey, *My Country*, 253–54.

24. A 1996 documentary film, *Sis: The Perry Watkins Story*, was coproduced by Chiqui Cartagena and Suzanne Newman. On the 20/20 segment and a feature film on Watkins that was in preproduction, see Jim Knippenberg, "Gay Soldier Story to Be Filmed," *Cincinnati Enquirer*, December 23, 1997.

25. Rayside, *On the Fringe*, 243.

26. Keith Boykin, *One More River to Cross: Black and Gay In America* (New York: Anchor, 1996), 186–92.

27. Mixner, *Stranger among Friends*, 301–2, 308–10.

28. Garland Tillery, "Interview with Top Gun Pilot Tracy Thorne," *Our Own*, May 18, 1993.

29. Quoted from the documentary film *All God's Children*, produced by Dee Mosbacher, Frances Reid, and Sylvia Rhue (Women Vision, 1996). I wish to thank Lisa Kahaleole Hall, Stephanie Smith, and Linda Alban for directing me to this quotation.

30. One way to measure how much moral authority the race analogy tries to take from the civil rights movement and transfuse into a predominantly white gay movement is to see what moral authority remains when the race analogy is removed. David Mixner would be the David Mixner of the gay movement, the military's antigay policy would be a form of antigay bigotry, and Sam Nunn would be "our" Sam Nunn. Or, to reverse the terms, other movements for social change would try to gain moral authority by using a "gay analogy," declaring that their movement was "like" the gay movement. These moves do not seem to carry the moral weight of the race analogy.

31. Quoted from Justice Blackmun's dissenting opinion in the U.S. Supreme Court's 1986 *Bowers v. Hardwick* decision. See "Blackmun's Opinions Reflect His Evolution over the 24 Court Years," *New York Times*, March 5, 1999. I wish to thank Lisa Kahaleole Hall for the conversation we had on October 24, 1998, out of which emerged the ideas in this essay about how the civil rights movement analogy works and is used as a strategy for gaining unearned moral authority, although I am responsible for how they are presented here.

32. "Stonewall 25," *The Charlie Rose Show*, Public Broadcasting System, June 24, 1994. I wish to thank Barbara Smith for lending me her videotape copy of this program.

33. For Fundi's reports on this panel and the entire conference, see "Out/Write '90 Report," pt. 1, "Writers Urged to Examine Their Roles, Save Their Lives," *San Diego GLN*, March 16, 1990, 7; "Out/Write Report," pt. 2, "Ringing Voices," *San Diego GLN*, March 23, 1990, 7, 9; and "Out/Write Report," pt. 3, "Arenas of Interaction," *San Diego GLN*, March 30, 1990, 7–9.

34. Lisa Kahaleole Chang Hall, "Bitches in Solitude: Identity Politics and Lesbian Community," in *Sisters, Sexperts, Queers: Beyond the Lesbian Nation*, edited by Arlene Stein, 223 (New York: Plume, 1993), and in personal conversation.

35. Fundi, "Out/Write Report," pt. 3, pp. 7, 9.

36. I wish to thank Mitchell Karp for the long dinner conversation we had in 1996 in New York City during which we jointly forged the ideas and questions in this paragraph.

37. I have transcribed the quotations that follow from an audiotape of the workshop discussion.

38. I wish to thank Dennis Poplin for allowing me to use his name and tell this story.

39. Bruce Bawer, "Utopian Erotics," *Lambda Book Report* 7 (October 1998): 19–20.

40. Goldstein, "'Go the Way,'" 180.

41. Bawer, "Utopian Erotics," 19–20.

42. I wish to thank Amber Hollibaugh for introducing me to this idea of "staying white" during a conversation about how a white person can be tempted to distance oneself from whiteness and escape the guilt of its privileges by identifying as a person of color. I was introduced to the idea that white privilege is unearned and difficult to escape at a workshop called "White Privilege" conducted by Jona Olssen at the 1995 Black Nations/Queer Nations Conference, sponsored by the Center for Lesbian and Gay Studies at the City University of New York. See also Peggy McIntosh, "White Privilege: Unpacking the Invisible Knapsack," *Peace and Freedom*, July/August 1989, 10–12.

43. Goldstein, "'Go the Way,'" 177.

PART IV

A Labor Historian

Queering Work and Class

Class Dismissed

By the mid-1990s, Bérubé was deeply involved in his research on the Marine Cooks and Stewards Union. Beyond the reflections and writing it provoked about how class shaped his own life experience, this work also pushed him to think deeply and analytically about how class operates in society. Here, in an address to an academic queer studies conference, he moves back and forth between historical episodes and personal experience as ways of illustrating the pervasiveness of class, even as class often gets dismissed in the United States as inconsequential. Bérubé calls for making class central to how queer scholars frame their work. He asks tough questions of himself and others, including "Whose [class] position do I want to make stronger by doing my intellectual work?"

We acknowledge that we are here today
because of something someone did before we came.
— *Bernice Johnson Reagon*, in her 1978 song "Fannie Lou Hamer"

1. Situated Knowledge

Sociologists used to talk about situational homosexuality. Perhaps I'm a situational homosexual. Most of what I know and how I think has grown out of the situations I have been in. Moving around. Checking out what's going on and trying to understand how it got to be that way with me in it. Situated knowledge.

· · · · · ·

I walk into a building, down a hallway, into a room.
   This one's in a public school, or inside a health clinic, or it's the broad expanse of a factory floor.
I walk into histories and conversations here that are already in progress.
   Or it's a welfare office. A restaurant. An apartment house.

Keynote Address for "Constructing Queer Cultures," a conference sponsored by the Program in Lesbian, Bisexual, and Gay Studies at Cornell University, February 1995.

Poster for the National Maritime Union, 1930s. Courtesy of the Allan Bérubé Collection at the GLBTHS, San Francisco.

I'm entering a complex field of classed relations while they are being racialized, gendered, sexualized, partly in response to my presence.

A private university. State prison. Hotel.

From my point of view, and for the moment, all the class relations operating in this room seem to intersect in me, yet I know this is simultaneously true for everyone else in this room.

Prep school chapel. Cruise ship kitchen. Broadway theatre lobby.

I have to read these class relations instantly but carefully even as I'm trapped in them and move through them.

Police station. Department store. Art gallery.

I activate these class relations and alter them even as they are shaping me, cutting me off and then reconnecting me to other people, marking who I am.

Cocktail party. Army base. Real estate office.

There are many people in this particular building.

Bank. Bathhouse. Homeless shelter.

I know some of these people; most of them are complete strangers.

Laundry. Supermarket. Airport.

They each have stories about why they are in this place right now.

Subway. Nursing home. Public restroom.

They have stories about what they have learned to do with what has been done to them in this place.[1]

Locker room. Beauty salon. Union hall.

Stories that reveal the deep intelligence of people who are acutely aware of their surroundings, people who know how to read situations that they are in.[2]

· · · · · ·

How do we negotiate our journeys through these endless rooms, these social structures, these institutions? And who are we each time we make it back out that door, go down the street, and inevitably walk into the next building, the next conversation? What are the stories we tell each other about how we move through these fields of class relations when we are not the ones on top and yet are not the ones on the absolute bottom—stories told with a purpose as if the telling itself could point our way out from under?

There are so few opportunities to talk about class in public, especially in queer situations, that you feel like you have to fit everything in because this will be the only chance you will ever have in your entire life. You know what I mean? I'm going to resist this impulse to include everything and instead talk in different ways about one particular thing I know a lot about: the telling of queer stories by working-class men about entering rooms and buildings where other men catch us in their own fields of class relations. And I'll probably rant and rave a little along the way.

2. Divas

It's the late 1930s, a cool fall afternoon in Manhattan. Ralph Ellison, a young man who had just abandoned his music studies at the Tuskegee Institute and who would eventually write the novel *Invisible Man*, is making his way through the tenements of San Juan Hill, an African American neighborhood that was later bulldozed and replaced with the Lincoln Center for the Performing Arts. Ellison is collecting signatures on a petition for the Federal Writers' Project. "Starting on the top floor of the building," he wrote forty years later, "I had collected an acceptable number of signatures, and having descended from the ground floor to the basement level, was moving along the dimly lit hallway toward a door through which I could hear loud voices. They were male Afro-American voices," Ellison continues, "raised in violent argument. . . . Reaching the door, I paused, sounding out the lay of the land before knocking to present my petition. . . . Being myself a slum dweller," he explains,

> I knew that voices in slums are often raised in anger, but that the
> *rhetoric* of anger, being in itself cathartic, is not necessarily a prelude
> to violence. . . . No, I hesitated because I realized that behind that door
> a mystery was unfolding . . . a joke designed to assault my knowledge
> of American culture and its hierarchical dispersal. . . . For the angry
> voices behind the door were . . . locked in verbal combat over which of
> two celebrated Metropolitan Opera divas was the superior soprano!
> . . . They were describing not only the sopranos' acting abilities but
> were ridiculing the gestures with which each gave animation to her
> roles, and they shouted strong opinions as to the ranges of the divas'
> vocal equipment.

Ellison finally gets up the courage to knock on the door. The voices go silent, there's rustling of chairs, and the door opens slowly. Peering inside he sees "four huge black men [sitting] sprawled around a circular dining-room table, looking toward me with undisguised hostility." They are coal haulers, and they are sitting next to the coal fire drinking whiskey. They ask him what he wants; he tells them he has a petition for the Writers' Project he'd like them to sign. They each read the petition and carefully sign it. "There you go," the last man says. "Having our names on there don't mean a thing, but you got 'em."

Ellison stands there, trying to unravel the mystery of these men.

"What else do you want?" one of the men shouts.

"I'd like to ask you just one more question."

"Like what?"

"Like where on earth did you gentlemen learn so much about grand opera?"

"For a moment he stared at me with parted lips," Ellison recalls,

> then, pounding the mantelpiece with his palm, he collapsed with a
> roar of laughter. As the laughter of the others erupted like a string
> of giant firecrackers I looked on with growing feelings of embarrass-
> ment and insult, trying to grasp the handle to what appeared to me to
> be an unfriendly joke. Finally, wiping coal-dust-stained tears from his
> cheeks, he interrupted his laughter long enough to initiate me into
> the mystery.

"Hell, son," he laughed, "we learn it down at the Met, that's where. . . . Strip us fellows down and give us some costumes and we make about the finest damn bunch of Egyptians you ever seen. Hell, we been down there wearing leopard skins and carrying spears or waving things like palm leafs and ostrich-tail fans for *years*!"

Ellison joins them now in laughing at what he calls "the hilarious American joke that centered on the incongruities of race, economic status and culture. . . . The men were products of both past *and* present" he observes, "both coal heavers *and* Met extras; were both workingmen *and* opera buffs. . . . The joke," he concludes, "sprang from my attempting to see them by the light of social concepts that cast less illumination than a lump of coal."[3]

3. The Marine Cooks and Stewards Union and the Triangular Conversation

Ralph Ellison was himself a working-class opera buff who attended whenever he could save up enough money. He was also a member of the Cooks and Stewards Division of the National Maritime Union. He joined the union in World War II when he went to sea in the merchant marine, working as a cook and beginning to write fiction between shifts in the kitchen.

The men and women in the Marine Cooks and Stewards Unions on both coasts from the 1930s to the 1950s developed a working-class movement dedicated to racial equality and economic justice. Together they transformed an all-white, all-male racist union into one that was mostly men of color, that included great numbers of visible "queens," and that integrated women into the workforce. Their record on gender politics wasn't as good in this primarily male workforce, yet by 1949 they had dedicated themselves to a goal of equality of the sexes. To learn from their history, I've been listening to their stories, reading their writings, and studying the images they created of themselves and their society. Some of their names may be familiar to you, but I'm certain you do not know them as members of the same maritime union: Langston Hughes, Woody Guthrie, Cisco Houston, Jack Kerouac, Allen Ginsberg, Ralph Ellison, Ted Rolfs, Revels Cayton, the gay porn artist BLADE, the lesbian photographer Honey Lee Cottrell, and, as honorary members, W. E. B. DuBois and Paul Robeson. This is a mighty queer category of cultural workers, but not all of them, of course, were queers. All of them did, however, knowingly work among and struggle with queers.

In the 1980s, when I was researching my book on World War II, several veterans asked me to consider doing a history of the Marine Cooks and

Stewards Union, which they had joined after they were kicked out of the military for being homosexuals. "You know," one former member, Stephen Blair, told me, "what many of you younger people are trying to do today as queers—what you call inclusion and diversity—we already did it 50 years ago in the Marine Cooks and Stewards Union. We did it in the labor movement as working-class queens with left-wing politics, and that's why the government crushed us, and that's why you don't know anything about us today—our history has been totally erased." At first I was skeptical about believing that this could have happened. But as I talked to more people who were in this union, I saw that they had indeed done something extraordinary, that here was a group of working-class people who had organized a movement around many identities, many oppressions. "Did you know," a straight Finnish American woman told me who was the union's entire office staff in Portland, Oregon, "that our union really welcomed the gay cooks and stewards?" This was before I had even had a chance to ask her the gay question. "We had a lot of pretty terrific queens in that union," bragged a straight white man in San Francisco. "I went to sea at 16 in the 1930s and they really taught me how to survive." A straight African American official in the union told me, "In 1936 we developed this slogan: It's anti-union to red-bait, race-bait, or queen-bait. We also put it another way: If you let them red-bait, they'll race-bait, and if you let them race-bait, they'll queen-bait. That's why we all have to stick together." That was their way, he explained, of building solidarity out of the realities of who they were.

As I meet the gay men who were in this union, I realize that many will talk to me because I am from a working-class background, and because I am not doing this work for a degree. And they are talking to me because they have their own agenda of setting the public record straight. In 1991, Karen Olsen and Linda Shopes, in an anthology on the feminist practice of oral history,[4] wrote about the power dynamics that occur when scholars from working-class backgrounds return to do oral history interviews with working-class women and men. "It seems," they observed,

> that the people we interview are quite aware of class differences in this society and also know that the middle-class world we represent does not understand or respect their way of life. They see their role in the interview as instructing us about those differences so that we can then communicate them to the middle-class audience of students, readers, and policymakers they presume we have access to. Thus the interview relationship might properly be viewed as a triangular one: the interviewee, us, and the larger society. . . . The researcher is cast

in the role of mediator. . . . [They] assume that we know the necessary procedures for setting the public record straight. . . . They seem concerned that we "get it right." . . . Some have told us directly, "Put that in your book," or "That will make a good story."

"By entrusting us with their stories," they conclude, "working-class informants have given us the responsibility of presenting and interpreting their lives in arenas of public discourse to which they themselves have little access."

These elderly working-class men and women from the Marine Cooks and Stewards Union tell me their stories, teach me as their student, instruct me as the researcher to get it right, recognize my power, and expect me to use it in middle-class worlds to set the public record straight and to take their histories into places they can't go: buildings, rooms, conversations. "Tell them what we did," they are saying to me, "tell them our government and the shipowners destroyed us for doing it. We even wrote books, articles, had our own intellectuals, our own newspapers, songs, artwork, meeting places, strikes, demonstrations, poetry. Tell them our history was stolen from us because no one knows we were there. Tell them why. Use your power to help us get it back." Every time I talk to them, each of you is potentially present in their room as they speak, because they expect me to use my influence to make you the third point in our triangular conversation.

Yet the members of this union also know they are teaching me an even greater intellectual responsibility than just carrying their message across into middle-class worlds. Because the work they started fifty years ago is still unfinished business—the work of strengthening the position of those who are on the receiving end of class oppression. This is why I have worked their history into a slide show that I take into union halls and workplaces. As times are getting harder, the insights the members of the Marine Cooks and Stewards Union had so long ago become even more useful today. They understood back then that the only real change will come out of a solidarity that can reach across and dismantle the hierarchies of race, class, gender, and sexuality—a solidarity that can engage intellectuals, activists, working people, and artists in its struggle. But the history this union teaches us also has a more frightening lesson: that whoever really does create this solidarity will be seen as a threat and targeted for destruction by the most powerful institutions the world has ever known.

How can studying what they did and wrote help us widen the field of queer studies so that it includes working-class intellectuals and cultural workers? And why is this kind of task especially important now?

4. Hard Times

Bulletin: This Just In: In the last twenty years the United States has been going through an accelerating wage and income gap that is unprecedented. And this is not just a recession, folks, it's a deep shift in the economic structure. Here's a quick rundown of what's been going on.

The 1980s saw the largest transfer of wealth to the richest 1 percent of the population in our nation's history. The ranks of the rich and the poor are steadily growing, while the ranks of middle- and working-class households are shrinking fast. Most people are working more hours at lower wages with fewer benefits, while the rich have never had it so good. Union membership is falling at an alarming rate as the government takes away the rights to organize and strike. Salaries for corporate executives are doubling, while wages go down for corporate employees *if* they are lucky enough not to be laid off by the thousands. High-paying blue-collar manufacturing jobs are disappearing, while the bulk of new jobs are as cashier, clerk, waitress, and hospital cleaner. Fewer people are owning homes, while rents go up. Income taxes have gone way down for the richest 5 percent and gone up for the rest of the workforce. Family household income remains stable only because women are working more hours including overtime. People are losing their health insurance coverage at the rate of 100,000 a month. More children and full-time workers (nearly one in five) are living below the poverty line since the War on Poverty began in 1964. The minimum wage has reached a forty-year low in terms of buying power. The next generation is expected to be worse off than their parents. This widening gap between the haves and the have-nots is deeply racialized and gendered. The Census Bureau, for example, reports that "white households are 10 times wealthier than black households and 8 times wealthier than 'Hispanic' households," with those headed by African American women owning the least.

According to [President Clinton's] Labor Secretary Robert Reich, "America [now] has the most unequal distribution of income of any industrialized nation in the world." All services and institutions are now being split into two parallel tracks—one public, the other private. These splits have already hit education, police protection, housing, health care, transportation, even television. Public services and institutions for the "have-nots" are in rapid decline, while the business of privatizing them for the "haves" is booming even as they become more expensive. There are no forces in our society strong enough to reverse this alarming trend. In fact, the Republican Party's Contract with America is designed to accelerate it, threatening to split our nation apart.

The prison system is booming while our schools are falling apart. Three years ago the imprisonment rate in the United States became the largest in the world, with over 1 million people behind bars. The national prison population—which is disproportionately male, African American, and Latino—has doubled since 1980 and tripled since 1970, while crime rates have generally dropped or remained stable. What's going on here? Ten years ago in California the budget for prisons was only half that of higher education and there were half as many prisoners as there were students in the University of California. Last month the California prison budget outstripped the budget for higher education, and the UC and state prison populations are now the same. In five years the prison population is projected to be more than twice the UC student population. California has created thousands of new jobs for correctional employees, while it cuts thousands of jobs in higher education.

While prisons multiply, education for poor and working-class students is in a free-fall decline. Students in public high schools and community colleges see their buildings deteriorate, budgets shrink, retiring faculty not replaced, janitors laid off. Teachers have to buy students' supplies with their own money, while libraries close, extracurricular activities are eliminated, classrooms are overcrowded. Students in state colleges see their fees and tuition double, then triple, and their financial aid dwindle, while the annual cost of attending private colleges skyrockets. Higher education is rapidly becoming what is being called a "two-tier" system—an expensive private system for the haves and a deteriorating, shrinking system for the have-nots. The situation seems to be out of control. We now return to our regularly scheduled program, which is now in progress. Stay tuned for further developments.

5. Bad Timing

What does this massive redistribution of wealth and widening class divide have to do with queer studies? It just happens to be the twenty-year moment when a gay rights movement and the field of queer studies have both emerged. There's no inherent reason why queer studies and gay politics would not reproduce the racialized class inequality and confusion that structure the larger society. But unfortunately, we can't enjoy the luxury of standing on the sidelines as innocent bystanders. We have been implicated. While queer studies has mostly ignored the economy and queer activists promote our "community" as the hottest marketing niche around, the religious right has been *explaining* why this economic decline is happening. They name exactly who is to blame and exactly where families should direct their growing class and race resentments. The right has racialized queers as white and then positioned us among the elites who have been accumulating money, cultural capital, special rights, and privileges. Queers could care less about those in the "working middle class" who are in economic free-fall, they say, and we are even benefiting from the material conditions that are hurting the "middle class." Together with the "burden" that welfare mothers, immigrants, African American men, and the homeless have put on "taxpayers," we have "caused" both the economic and "moral" decline in America and are the reason why so many people are losing control of their lives.

From what class positions do we defend ourselves against charges that we constitute an economic elite? How have our activists responded to the right-wing politics of racialized class resentment? And how have we in queer studies, located as we are within the institutions of higher education, used our power and resources to analyze the dynamics and consequences of this widening class divide both inside and outside queer worlds?

Too often I hear responses like this one from last Sunday's *New York Times*: "Surveys by gay publications and the U.S. Census Bureau show that gay people have a collective $514 billion in yearly expendable income and take vacations more than any other single demographic group."[5] Or I see queer studies conference programs with almost no papers or panels that explicitly and analytically deal with class on any level—never mind panels of working-class queer scholars who are doing work about and for working-class queers—a reasonable idea which itself seems almost beyond imagining.

6. The Class Struggle within My Own Queer Psyche

Sometimes I have this internal dialogue between the middle-class and working-class parts of myself. "Queer studies," working-class me says to myself, "sure looks to me like a field created by, about, and for middle-class and upper-class queers. Perhaps queer studies is inevitably situated within the most elite academic institutions in the United States, *and* it is totally irrelevant to poor and working-class queers, or intellectuals outside academia."

"Well there's nothing particularly queer about this," middle-class me responds, "because in this postmodern, post-Marxist world, class no longer exists as a useful concept either in popular culture, where the most interesting forms of resistance are now located, or in theorizing, especially in the United States. Class categories themselves are essentialist, trapped within discourses of authenticity and experience; they are mechanistic, deterministic, unqueer, and have a disreputable history of associating with whiteness, maleness, and heterosexist assumptions."

"Yes but are these good enough reasons for throwing the baby out with the bathwater?" working-class me replies. "Why do people even here at Cornell University, for example, and in other private universities as well as in unions and community colleges, invite me to talk about my class-based scholarly work? I can't believe it's only what Henry Abelove has campily called a 'nostalgia for vulgar Marxism' that has emerged in this post–Cold War era. On some level we at least suspect that we can't totally dismiss class in queer studies, or we wouldn't be standing here, you and me, talking like this, right?"

"But exactly *how* do we *not* dismiss class?" middle-class me asks myself. "What do we *do* with it? What *is* class in the nineties? Who is in *what* class? How is *class* related to queer studies? How can we talk about class identities when we're busy fracturing and disrupting binary polarities and coherent identities altogether?"

"Be careful," working-class me interrupts, "or you'll be arguing class right out of existence again. Class is certainly one of the toughest—perhaps *the* toughest—issues to talk about in public," working-class me goes on, trying to get a grip on this phenomenon of class dismissal while it's right here in the room.

Think about it—take any group of queer scholars—how much do you know about their sexual interests and desires, and how much do you know about their income, wealth, and class background? What's the major taboo operating here—economic or sexual? The public discourses surrounding class are characterized by silence and denial, dismissal and willful confusion, fabricated life histories, romantic nostalgia, secret desires, guilt, defensiveness, anger—and that's just for starters. And it's even tougher to talk about how class is always simultaneously racialized, gendered, and sexualized, and then to dislodge class discourse from its historic associations with whiteness, maleness, and heterosexuality. It's not that class is necessarily always *the* core issue. But that doesn't mean it's not there. It's *always* there. I never said it would be easy. But too often class is the proverbial elephant in the room that everyone agrees not to notice. Not noticing class, in fact, has developed into one of the finest of American arts. And by the way, the language your queer theory friends use some-times seems to be a class-positioning move designed to scare the rest of us away.

"That was a low blow," middle-class educated me responds. "I admit queer theory talk can become needlessly obscure, but you know as well as I do that since we both were kids you've wanted the words and languages to express the complex feelings and thoughts that help you understand the complicated situations you're always finding yourself in. Perhaps a useful way out of class denial," middle-class me goes on, trying to be helpful, "would be to find ways to at least temporarily place class at the center of queer studies, and use it as one of our lenses through which we examine queer subjects. Perhaps even placing working-class positionality at the center of our inquiry."

"Oh yes, I like any metaphor that places working class at the center," working-class me responds. "I'm so sick of that tired old metaphor of ver-ticality—you know, the one that talks about 'upward mobility,' the 'lower classes' and the 'upper classes,' and the 'lower-middle, middle-middle, and upper-middle class?' That worn-out ladder needs to be taken down and chopped up for firewood. Looking up at my betters all the time has given me a chronic stiff neck."

"One thing at a time here," middle-class me cautions. "We can't change everything all at once."

"OK, I'll be patient. Now, do you remember," working-class me asks, get-ting kind of excited now,

> how we read years ago in E. P. Thompson's *Making of the English Working Class* that class is not a static structure but is the dynamic interaction of human relations, and he actually used lover relation-ships to illustrate his point? You can't have lovers without a relation-ship, he said, just like you can't have class without class relations. Class is something that people do with and to each other. Well there's a door open wide enough for even queer studies to drive right on in. We could take his cue and begin a queer study of the ways that class happens in particular situations in particular relationships, as well as how it happens in texts and representations, including the stories we tell each other. As Ralph Ellison discovered in his very queer diva story, we would then have a new angle of vision that would let us see everything differently. We might even enjoy, in Ellison's words, "the hilarious American joke that centers on the incongruities of race, eco-nomic status and culture."

"Well you inspire me to get a little bolder here," middle-class me responds, now that the discussion has moved into more familiar territory. Eve Sedg-wick, in her introduction to *Epistemology of the Closet*, observed that the homo-hetero binary is central to the study of Western culture. We might dare to alter her words to frame an observation on queering class that we both might agree on: We could say that "an understanding of virtually any aspect of modern queer culture must be, not merely incomplete, but damaged in its central substance to the degree that it does not incorporate a critical analysis of modern class relations."[6]

"Perfect, that's terrific, and I couldn't agree with you more," working-class me exclaims. "Now let's get down to work."

7. The Shape of Some Queer Working-Class Stories

Fifteen years ago Audre Lorde told an audience attending a colloquium at Amherst College that "even the form our creativity takes is often a class issue."[7] Historians Carolyn Steedman and Pamela Fox[8] have observed that some of the most common working-class written genres have been personal narratives (including essays and autobiographies), realistic novels and stories, and people's histories. Audre Lorde has identified poetry as "the most economical" of art forms, "the one which is the most secret, which requires the least physical labor, the least material, and the one which can be done between shifts, in the hospital pantry, on the subway, on scraps of surplus paper. As we reclaim our literature," she adds, "poetry has been the major voice of poor, working class, and Colored women."[9] These and other cultural critics have also been identifying the narrative structures that working-class authors frequently use within these larger genres.

Class displacement stories, solidarity stories, class discovery stories, stories of self-exposure told up the class hierarchy. These four narrative forms are often used as strategies to work, disrupt, manipulate, and reveal class relations. Class displacement stories by poor and working-class writers—especially the "class escape" story—are about what happens when one gets out of the class world one grew up in and enters a world of higher status—poor migrating into working class, working class migrating into middle class, middle class migrating into upper class worlds. These stories—such as those told by scholarship boys or girls, including queer boys and girls, about being the first in one's family to go to college on a full scholarship—reveal unresolved conflicts and ambivalence about what one has lost and gained, along with the anguish of leaving a home you can't return to while not belonging where you have ended up.

Class displacement stories about traveling up the class hierarchies often describe the experiences of passing in others' worlds as one of them, or being invited in as a visitor or as a guest, or even trespassing into places where you haven't been invited and where you don't "belong." The risks of these cross-class movements are great. *Passing* forces us to erase our past and makes us afraid that someone will find out the truth about us and kick us out. Being treated as a *guest*—whether as a scholarship student in college, a member of a gay dinner party at an expensive restaurant, or, as I often am, a guest lecturer on gay history at an elite private university—seems to demand our gratitude and indebtedness in return. It can make us afraid of being disinvited, expelled, or put in our place if we say or do the wrong thing. *Trespassing*—the deliberate violation of class boundaries, going where we are not wanted, talking about class when we are not asked—can make us afraid of being caught and punished, sent back to where we came from, put in our place.

Solidarity stories, on the other hand, are about how the unlikeliest people find ways to stick together. They express a desire for, and show the way toward, healing the wounds of class oppression and displacement through collective action, including the possibility that even the displaced person can return home. Working-class solidarity stories sometimes even include queers to demonstrate how far the embrace of solidarity can reach, how even an injury to a queer can be an injury to all.

Here's a queer working-class solidarity story passed down from a straight father to a straight son and then passed on to me. In October 1993 I was asked by a teacher at San Francisco City College if I would present my slide show on the Marine Cooks and Stewards Union to his labor studies class. A lesbian in his class, he told me, had seen it in Oakland at the Lesbian/Gay/Bi Caucus's Solidarity Conference, which had been held at the union hall of Local 250, Service Employees International Union. I agreed and presented the slide show to a class of mostly heterosexual union members, who loved it and asked great questions and made good comments. During the discussion I was trying to explain to the class what "reading beads" meant, with little success. Toward the end of the class, a middle-aged, Asian American longshoreman asked if we had time for him to tell a story that his father had told him (his father was also a longshoreman). Of course we had time, I said. Years ago, he began, a gay longshoreman in his father's crew, whose name was Eli, threw a lunch party for all the guys on the dock, to which Eli brought his lover. When someone started playing a radio he had brought, Eli and his lover started dancing together. Then Eli's lover jokingly asked this man's father to dance, too. "Sorry," he replied, "but I don't party that way." All this time a tourist has been standing near the pier, watching. Suddenly he walks over to the group and shouts out to Eli, "Hey, you, are you one of those goddam HOMOSEXUALS?" Eli looks up, stops dancing, and slowly walks over to the tourist, with twenty longshoremen following close behind. Eli stops, puts his hand on his hip, and says very loudly: "Honey, that's not what you called me last night when you gave me that blowjob!" The terrified tourist turned right around and started to run away. "Is that what you mean by reading beads?" the student asks me. I reply, "I think you should be teaching this class." After we stop laughing, I ask him if I can use his story, and he says, sure, go ahead and use it. And now all of you know it, too.

Solidarity stories. And class displacement stories.

And class discovery stories, too. These are usually top-down narratives, looking down the ladder of verticality from higher up, discovering what has been hidden from the higher classes, what you get when you "study down" the class hierarchy, as feminist scholars have called it. Barbara Ehrenreich writes in her book *Fear of Falling* that middle-class mainstream media periodically breaks through its class denial and "discovers" with "huge, crude astonishment" that "a vast segment of the population [is] not middle class." What follows is a series of travels and explorations into poor and working-class territories to discover and bring back stories about what has been hidden from view. This is the crudest form of the class discovery story. Much more sympathetic is Ralph Ellison's Diva story that I told: He does travel down the tenement stairs into the basement and deeper into the coal haulers' room, but his discovery of their enjoyment of high opera makes them all laugh with each other at the absurd expectations that the hierarchies themselves produce, a kind of camp "reading" of class. Sometimes a class discovery story looks up the ladder of class hierarchies, as the storyteller reads the beads of those at the top. Maids, room stewards, waiters, and bellhops on luxury liners and in hotels routinely dish the dirt with each other about the private lives of the passengers and guests to whom they give their personal service and far too many smiles in return for wages and tips.

It is in the self-exposure stories, however, as Pamela Fox observes in her new book *Class Fictions*, where working-class narrators address those who have power over them most directly and even in anger. "You see," these narrators say, "THIS is what's been done to us, THESE are the lives we've been forced to live, THIS is what it's like." Realism in these stories, she reminds us, is not a sign of backwardness or lack of sophistication, but a logical strategy from this position. The rage of self-exposure stories, Fox reminds us, is easy to romanticize as resistance, but the powerlessness of their class position ensures that they end up displaying shame as well, particularly the humiliation of having to expose one's debasement to get any attention. Yet the self-exposure narrative is one of the most enduring working-class storytelling strategies, especially when your audience has the power to change your circumstances when you yourself do not.

8. Washington State Reformatory

It's October 1982. I'm living in a collective household of relatives and friends in San Francisco, paying cheap rent and working part time as a temp-typist, which gives me the time to put together a slide show on Lesbian and Gay Americans during World War II and to begin writing my book. I get a call from John Sheets in Seattle, who asks me if I'll bring my slide show to the campus of the University of Washington as a benefit for the Lesbian Heritage Project. I agree and we start making plans.

A few days later I get a call from Larry Anderson in Seattle, who I had not talked to since we were in the greater orbit of Gay Male Liberation and the Fag Rag Newspaper Collective in Boston in 1970. "The gay prisoners at Washington State Reformatory," he asks, "want to know if you'll do your slide show for them inside, since you're going to be in the area. Of course they can't pay you anything." My heart starts to beat fast with the fear of entering a maximum security prison as a gay man. Nevertheless, I agree, wondering what I'm getting myself into, and we start making plans.

Over the next few weeks the implications of this agreement become clearer. The prison's "Community Resource Coordinator" sends me a clearance form to sign. "Have you ever been arrested?" it says. "Do you have any relationship with a resident at Washington State Reformatory? Who has invited you?" I need to list in detail the equipment I'll need because I'm told that "checking the equipment through the metal scanner will be quite time-consuming."

Larry Anderson calls a week or so later to tell me that my clearance has been approved, and we start a difficult conversation that goes on for weeks. He and John are the outside contacts for the gay prisoners, who call their group the Sexual Minority Prisoners Caucus—one of the few of its kind in any state prison system in the country. Larry tells me it's too dangerous for me to go in alone, so he'll accompany me. I'm relieved. Meanwhile, the University of Washington group schedules the slide show on campus at the Friends Service Center. They arrange for sign language interpretation; child care; the serving of coffee, tea, and cookies; and an announcement in the *Seattle Gay News*.

As soon as I arrive in Seattle a week later, I learn that there's been a problem at the prison. When administrators in the State Department of Corrections learned that I was bringing in slides, they immediately disapproved my clearance to enter the prison. The associate superintendent of treatment explained why in a letter. "Of extreme concern to me," he wrote, "is the sensitivity of this issue in relationship to its viewing within a Washington prison and what consequences it might have for members of the S[exual] M[inority] P[risoners] C[aucus] or other inmates. If any of the other resident groups," the superintendent went on, "such as the Black Prisoners Caucus, the Chicanos, [or] Indians of All Tribes, requested that they be authorized a slide presentation depicting heterosexual sex or nude pictures of women, their request would [also] be denied."

What to do. Larry gets on the phone and uses his contacts inside to explain that this is a *history* slide show, not a *sex* slide show, and he begins to arrange a compromise. Prison officials agree to send a staff person out to preview the campus showing. This staff person turns out to be a woman who arrives with her female roommate, and our "gaydar" goes into high gear. After the showing she tells me how much she was moved by my presentation and said she would definitely recommend that the inmates should see it, too.

At 8:00 A.M. the next morning the prisoners are told they are going to see the show that night. But at 10:30 our previewer calls to tell us it's off, she's real upset, can't go into the reasons why. Larry spends the afternoon negotiating with prison officials over the phone. He gets them to agree to at least let me come into the prison without the slides, only the script.

Larry and I sit down to talk. I'm angry and frustrated at the prison officials and relieved that here is a way out of this increasingly terrifying situation. "I see no reason to go inside now," I tell him, "because the script is almost useless without the slides." I was thinking about the integrity of my presentation. "Take some time to think about it," Larry replies, and we spend hours talking. Wise and practical, he explains that bringing in the script is also a way to bring in flyers for the show, which the prisoners could keep for themselves and put up in their cells. It would be worth it for that alone. I realize that I had come this far, and as scared as I was, I did want to see this through. So I decide to go in.

Larry starts to prepare me for my first visit inside a maximum security prison. One of the worst parts of being inside, he explains, is the total boredom, no contact with the outside world, the chipping away of any dignity one might have, the constant threat of violence, the absolute sense of defeat and powerlessness, being forced to live in an acute state of lack and total need. So first, two important rules. The men will ask you to do a million favors, so don't make any promises you can't keep. Don't say yes or even maybe unless you mean it and can follow it through. They don't need anyone gay from the outside lying to them with all the rest. And second, don't ask anyone why he is there. They'll tell you if they want you to know. As we talk, I realize that the most important thing I had to offer these men was my refusal to let the prison officials keep me away, and my following through on the original "yes" I had spoken over the phone so many weeks ago.

As it gets dark, Larry drives us to the prison in the pouring rain. We are cleared at the gate, park in the lot, get out of the car, and run up to the front doors, me holding tight the folder that covers my script, my identity. Through more doors to the search area, where they take our coats, empty our pockets of money, driver licenses, keys, then pat us down. There's supposed to be a memo waiting for us authorizing me to take in my script, but no one can find it. So they take the script away from me, too, as well as my pen and my single piece of paper. We have nothing with us but our clothes and each other. Moving ahead of us in line during these visitors' hours are religious groups bringing in books, guitars, movie projectors, art supplies, etc. We see and understand what's happening here.

Once we are cleared, two guards lead us through several barred gates that are opened and then locked behind us, until they finally lead us into the sally port, then step back behind a gate which they close and lock between us. They stand there watching us, smirking, ready to enjoy what will happen to us without their protection—Larry with his dangling earrings, me a scholar without my papers. We are waiting there in this open area for two gay prisoners to come down from the classroom and meet us. Through a far door some naked men covered with mud and shouting run into the corridor from the yard where they have been mud-fighting in the rain. They shake their bodies, attracting other prisoners who gather around them hooting, hollering, and punching them in the arms and on the butt. I try to imagine myself invisible. Then huge doors open from an auditorium where a movie has just ended, and what seems to be the entire prison population fills the corridor where we are waiting. They are killing time before they have to go back to their cells. No guards in sight. Just then the two gay prisoners arrive to escort us to a classroom. We were as glad to see them as they were to see us. One of our escorts is black and one is white. Larry turns to me and whispers that there's been racial tension in the prison and the gay prisoners know that it would only increase these tensions to have two white or two black gay prisoners escort us—a white man and a black man—through the general prison population. These men know what they are doing, I realize, and I'm glad they're there to protect us.

By now, of course, the whole prison population knows that Larry and I are queer. As we slowly walk through the two long corridors and up the stairway full of prisoners, we are whistled at, hooted at, pinched, and poked—the four "girls" on parade. I peer under the stairway and notice two men necking, who see us and smile. Other men are holding hands. My God, I think to myself, the sexual energy in this place is like the state mental hospital I worked in as a teenager to pay my way through college, or like a bathhouse that's not supposed to be gay.

When we get to the classroom, and the door is locked behind us by the guard outside, I relax a little in the company of this roomful of men who have been waiting for us. For the next hour they tell me the history of how they came together as a group, then catalog the endless harassments that have come down on them. They started as a gang of queens who were tired of being raped by other prisoners and together vowed to kill anyone who raped any of their "sisters." A recent split had taken place in the group; most of the queens had left, and now the remaining members were mostly "gay" men who were trying to bring the queens back in. The prison system was trying to break their Sexual Minority Prisoners Caucus, they explained. The guards were suddenly separating couples who had been together for years, and half of their members were already locked up in the hole. So the prison's refusal to let my slide show go on was part of this larger crackdown. The men tell me how they had talked over how to respond to the crackdown. If they fought back, they would lose everything they had—their organization, their lovers, and their friends as they were split up one by one and locked in the hole. But if they didn't fight back, they would also lose everything they had. So they were going to fight back.

I listen to their stories, then talk briefly. I tell them I had wanted to do the slide show for them, but the prison officials wouldn't let me. I thank them for asking me and say that I wanted to tell them this in person rather than have them hear it from a prison guard or not know why. That's why I was there even without the script. For a minute no one says anything as we look at each other and look down at the floor. In the awkward silence a few of us fight back tears as we feel the meanings of the "yes" in what I had just said. I start to do some quick thinking, try to decide how my gay intellectual work could possibly be useful in this situation. I start to tell them stories I have learned from gay veterans about how they helped each other survive when their government rounded them up and locked them into queer stockades because they were gay. Someone asks me if I was in the military. I tell him no, I was a conscientious objector and a draft counselor. Then they start to tell me stories about being in the military, fighting in Vietnam, living as gay veterans.

The guard opens the door and tells us it's time to leave. Most of the men go with us to escort us back to the front gate. As we're walking, a guard comes out of nowhere, grabs the man I'm talking to, slaps handcuffs on him, and takes him away to the hole. "You *see*," the others whisper to me, "this is what's going on all the time in here!" I want to know why *this* man? Because he was talking to *me*? Because of something else? For a moment I am flushed with the powerless feeling of not having anyone to ask, not getting any answers, not even deserving any answers, the possibility of never knowing why. "You *see*?" the man next to me says again. "*This* is what it's like. *This* is what they're doing to us."

As I pass back out the locked gates, one of the men who told me he grew up in San Francisco's Tenderloin waves to me and says, "Hey, say hello to the Tenderloin for me!" I say, "Ok, I will!" A week later, back home in San Francisco, I walk through the Tenderloin and, slightly embarrassed, I stand still, remember that day in the prison, then shout loud enough so my voice echoes from the buildings, "Hey, Ricardo says hello!"

9. The Magnetic Pull of Middleclassness

In the United States, the idea of "middleclassness" is used as a powerful disciplinary practice that confuses class relations, denies the existence of class, silences intelligent discussion, thwarts class solidarity and cross-class cooperation, and mobilizes racial resentments. In our nation, the advocates of middleclassness tell us, there is no class because everyone is middleclass. Middleclass is everyone who has more than the homeless and less than Donald Trump. We are the middle 90 percent of the population. "Middleclass" is used as a code word for ordinary Americans, the average family, the white male swing vote, anyone who works for a living, people of color who have benefited from affirmative action, everyone born in the United States, people with family values, Christians, all heterosexuals, all the leaders of the lesbian and gay movement. Middleclass is the neutral ground where there is no class warfare, no class division, no class struggle, no class consciousness. We are all individuals on this middleclass map, all potential millionaires waiting, working and hoping for our lucky break or our just reward. There is just no way to get a strong foothold to step outside the unity of this middleclassness that we're all supposed to be a part of. Middleclassness hides the vast power of the ruling class and obliterates the unique situations of those who are located in less powerful class positions. And, what's worse, it instills within us both the desire and the language with which we can erase ourselves as anything other than middleclass.

10. The Fundraising Dinner

It's the early nineties, and I've published my book *Coming Out Under Fire: The History of Gay Men and Women in World War II.* I get a call from a gay organization which raises money for gay-positive political candidates. They ask me if I would create a special slide show on the gay history of San Francisco to be presented at their annual fundraising dinner at the Sheraton Palace Hotel in downtown San Francisco. We brainstorm, negotiate a fee of $500 plus expenses, and I agree. For the next few months I do research, take new slides, write many drafts of scripts, and rehearse the final presentation. I bill the organization for my expenses and receive my first check. I'm happy being this kind of public historian for the gay community.

It's a few days before this Annual $150-A-Plate, Black Tie, Gala Dinner, to which all the pro-gay politicians of northern California have been invited to make their appearance. I talk with the group's representative on the phone about what I should wear. I say I already have a black tie and a black three-piece suit that my lover, before he died of AIDS, bought for me and which I have never had a chance to wear. There's an awkward silence.

"Black Tie doesn't mean black tie," he corrects me. "It means tuxedo."

Another awkward silence. How was I supposed to know this? I think to myself. Aren't there other ways to learn these things without being humiliated? He rescues the moment and says, "We'll make an appointment with you to be measured for a rental."

Another silence forces me to ask the next difficult question. "Who's going to pay for it?"

"We will," he replies, and it seems the matter is settled for now.

It's the night of the Gala Dinner. I arrive early and work with the technicians setting up the sound and projection equipment in the ballroom where the event will take place. Setting up always makes me nervous and edgy. I see the waiters—both men and women—rushing around setting up the tables. They're nervous, too. Many of them seem gay, and most of them are people of color. I make friendly eye contact with one or two but don't bother them because they are busy at work. I look around for anyone I might recognize, because several of my friends (and former boyfriends) work as waiters in downtown hotels.

I go upstairs to the room that has been rented for us. My tuxedo is waiting, and we start getting dressed. Now I'm having fun. Some more men arrive, and we all become queens putting on our drag for the great ball, dressing up and posing for each other, looking good. We leave the room and walk through the hall and down the stairs that lead to the lobby outside the ballroom. As I descend the stairway into the lobby, all I can see for as far as I can see are hundreds of white men dressed in tuxedos—Black Tie, as it were. I'm terrified, and my first impulse is to flee. I've never been in a situation like this before. I don't belong here, I hear voices saying in my head; I don't know how to act here, I want to go home.

I start to think fast on my feet. Okay, I say to myself, you have two choices: Either you're going to be intimidated, freak out, shut down, feel bad, smolder in anger, play the outsider, get cynical and bitter and sarcastic, or—I pause while I try to imagine what the other choice might be. Okay, I'll pretend I'm a spy, or maybe I'll be an anthropologist who has been sent to a faraway land to observe the indigenous rituals of an exotic culture and then report back to his own people. I laugh. This could be fun. I keep reminding myself that I was invited to be here, I am a guest, some of these men have even come to see me because of my work. And then I suddenly remember that I am middleclass, too,—right?—so I should be able to fit right in here. No problem.

I'm escorted into the ballroom and seated at a table with ten other men. The other tables have been bought by groups, organizations, circles of friends—I calculate the cost at $1,500 a table. I look around and notice some white women who are politicians sitting at some tables—and two tables of lesbians who have been active in political organizations. I see one table that's mostly men of color—I recognize several as outreach and educational staff from AIDS organizations. I realize that I was wrong to read this crowd as uniformly well-to-do. Many are here on complimentary tickets, or [were] paid for by community-based organizations, or are working-class dates of their well-to-do boyfriends. Including the men at my table. Well isn't this interesting, I think to myself, a whole roomful of racialized and gendered class relations—waiters, boyfriends, guest speakers, award recipients, complimentary invitees on one side (where nearly all the people of color are), with the hosts, organizers, politicians, sponsors on the other side (where most of the white people are). The normal middleclassness of gay life.

The man on my left interrupts my thoughts as he turns to me and asks the inevitable class-positioning question, "What do you do?" Okay, Bérubé, remember, you're being a spy here, you're passing.

"I teach at UC Santa Cruz," I reply. I *was* teaching a course at Santa Cruz on queer history, although I was making it sound as if I were tenured faculty instead of a visiting instructor brought in from the community.

"That's a beautiful campus," he says.

"Yes, I love the hour and a half drive down there twice a week—it's one of the most beautiful routes in the country."

"It takes you an hour and a half to get there? It takes me a little more than an hour."

"Well, it takes me an hour and a half." Passing is getting a little more difficult here.

"What kind of car do you have?" he asks, not so innocently. My mask is about to slip off.

"A used 1985 Toyota Tercel," I say slowly and firmly.

"Oh," he replies, "no wonder."

"Why, what kind of car do you have?"

"A bmw," he says casually.

"Oh," I reply, "no wonder," trying to imitate the best of Roseanne's sarcasm. I feel sorry for his boyfriend sitting next to him. But then he wouldn't be here if this weren't what he wanted. And that's cool—he knows what he wants and he knows how to get it.

Hours later, after too many awards and too many politicians, and after too many guests had gone home exhausted, I did my slide presentation to a warm reception. A few days later I sent in my invoice for the $500 fee for doing the show, didn't hear back, so I called to gently remind them that I hadn't received the check yet.

"You know," I hear on the other end of the line, "everyone was donating their services that night because it was a fundraising event and we didn't quite reach our goal."

Now I'm beginning to get a little peeved. "Excuse me"—I'm thinking to myself—"but exactly *who* was donating their services that night—the waiters, the kitchen staff, the cooks, the dishwashers and potscrubbers, the laundry workers, the maids, the cab drivers, the dry cleaners, the doormen, the sound technicians, and all the other workers who actually *produced* this fundraising event?" Why is he asking me to donate my services after the fact? Is it because he doesn't know how to place me?

I find myself suddenly perched on a fence that feels very familiar. He's making me choose which side I'm on. I can choose the status of gay donor but lose my hard-earned money, or I can take the money but lose gay status. Decide! Are you with *us*—the gay community—or with *them*—the paid help? Position yourself! Maybe this is how you are invited to move up the class hierarchy?

I collect myself and reply, "*I* was not donating my services. I was doing my work and this is how I make my living. I need the money to pay my bills." I'm proud to be in such good company on this side of the fence. But why does it still feel so humiliating? How come I'm once again forced to ask for the money owed me for doing my work? It feels like I'm begging, when the entire fundraising dinner was itself a ritualized form of middleclass respectable begging. I begin to wonder if I'll ever be able to say these things out loud without losing my gay credentials.

He says he'll send me the check, tells me how much everyone loved my presentation, and thanks me for the fine work I've done. The next week, to celebrate my birthday, I go with my sister and brother-in-law, Annette and José, to Gay Bingo Night in the basement of the Most Holy Redeemer Church in the Castro, where each week working-class Catholics raise thousands of dollars for the AIDS hospice and winners voluntarily donate their prize money back to rounds of applause. We don't win anything, and we still have a good time.

11. The Rhetoric of Hardship

The temptation in describing a gay working-class life from the inside, as I am trying to do, with all its fractures of displacement and privilege, especially within an institution of higher learning such as this, is to frame one's narrative within what might be called the "rhetoric of hardship." This rhetorical strategy tries to defuse class hostility by appealing to the sympathy and generosity of the more fortunate, reinforcing existing class hierarchies in the process and producing more class shame. The rhetoric of hardship is very seductive because it repackages working-class life into the story of courageous struggle against impossible odds. But even as it seems to validate the lives of working-class people and evokes sympathy from more well-to-do listeners, the hardship narrative reduces us to either victims or heroes, and our lives to satisfying dramas of suffering that end in inspiring victory or poignant tragedy. I am trying to resist this temptation and instead examine how class can shape our languages, our sexual desires, our psychologies, our writings, our intellectualities, and the stories we tell. And not always from within class categories, but as an attempt to complicate them as well.

. . . . . .

Reading situations that we are in.
Classed situations.
Racialized class.
And gendered class.
Situational homosexuals.
Situated knowledge.

. . . . . .

Thinking fast on our feet to survive these situations, trying to remember or forget them, knowing ourselves through them, using our bodies in them, talking and writing about them, romanticizing them or making them all too real, trying to understand how they got to be that way with us in them, and how we can work together to change them, and even how we can escape them on our own leaving all the others behind.

. . . . . .

Displacement.
Solidarity.
Discovery.
Self-exposure.

. . . . . .

Having to reveal the shame inside the anger and not being able to help it. Trying to take back the dignity that was rightly ours and which they took away from us.

. . . . . .

Set the record straight.
Get it right.
Tell them what we did.
What we learned to do with what was done to us.

. . . . . .

In the last two years, as I've entered middle age, I've been asking myself the most difficult question that one can ask about one's intellectual work: So what? What and who is this work for? An obvious answer is that it's for me—I love this work and I want to keep making my living doing it. But there's more here to answer for, still the old injuries of race and class that have yet to be healed, while new ones are inflicted. So here's the hardest way I know of to ask myself this question: Whose position do I want to make stronger by doing my intellectual work?

NOTES

1. Paraphrasing of a quote from Herbert Gutman on labor history.

2. I'm indebted to Lisa Hall for sharing her writings with me and for our conversations on reading situations as well as texts.

3. Ralph Ellison, "The Little Man at Chehaw Station: The American Artist and His Audience," *American Scholar* (Winter 1977–78), reprinted in Ralph Ellison, *Going to the Territory* (New York: Vintage, 1986), 3–38.

4. Karen Olsen and Linda Shopes, "Crossing Boundaries, Building Bridges: Doing Oral History among Working-Class Women and Men," in *Women's Words: The Feminist Practice of Oral History*, edited by Sherna Berger Gluck and Daphne Patai, 189–204 (New York: Routledge, 1991).

5. Monique P. Yazigi, "Gay Dollars on the Road," *New York Times*, February 5, 1995, city section, 4.

6. Eve Kosofsky Sedgwick, *Epistemology of the Closet* (Berkeley: University of California Press, 1990), 1.

7. Audre Lorde, *Sister Outsider* (Freedom, Calif.: Crossing Press, 1984), 116.

8. Pamela Fox, "De/Re-fusing the Reproduction-Resistance Circuit of Cultural Studies: A Methodology for Reading Working-Class Narrative," *Cultural Critique*, no. 28 (Fall 1994): 53–74; Pamela Fox, *Class Fictions: Shame and Resistance in the British Working-Class Novel, 1890–1945* (Durham: Duke University Press, 1994).

9. Audre Lorde, "Age, Race, Class, and Sex: Women Redefining Difference," in *Sister Outsider*, 114–23.

"Queer Work" and Labor History

As Bérubé immersed himself in labor history in order to provide deep context for his study of the Marine Cooks and Stewards Union, he confronted the absence of analyses of what he came to call "queer work." "How do jobs become queer?" he wondered. How do people find such jobs? Are there political ramifications to the queering of some workplaces? He brought such questions, as well as his initial speculation about them, to a labor studies conference in San Francisco as a way to provoke further thought and investigation.

It's January 1936. Jim Vieira, a senior at Mission High School in San Francisco, is working the 3:30 to midnight shift in a restaurant, earning extra money to pay for his family's living expenses. He's an effeminate young man with no friends who buries himself in books when he gets home from work. One day a customer in the restaurant, noticing that Vieira is a good waiter, starts up a conversation with him that gets around to ships and the sea.

"A liner is coming in tomorrow," the man says. "How would you like to work on a ship?"

"Well, I've never even been aboard one," young Vieira replies.

"That's all right," the man says. "I'll give you a letter to the head of the Marine Cooks and Stewards Union and maybe he'll have a job for you. Go down there in the morning."

Jim is fascinated by this invitation to go to sea. So he takes the man's letter over to the union hall and gets his first "trip card." The next day he's onboard the *Malolo*, a Matson liner headed out the Golden Gate, working as a scullion washing dishes. After a few days out at sea, the chief steward moves him above deck as a bellboy, and by the end of the summer, he's worked his way up to first-class room steward. He brings food to the passengers in the suites and does up their rooms. And he's receiving good tips for his fine service.

Keynote address for 22nd Annual Southwest Labor Studies Conference, San Francisco State University, February 1996.

Allan Bérubé and Stephen "Mickey" Blair, 1990s. Courtesy of the Allan Bérubé Collection at the GLBTHS, San Francisco.

Even on his first trip out, young Vieira notices that there's something a little queer about the stewards. "In the galley," he recalls, "or in the dining room, when there weren't any passengers around, all the stewards called each other by girls' names." When he gets up the nerve to ask them why they did this, they say, teasing him, "Why, doesn't everybody do it?" He begins to notice that the stewards department has lots of other gay men and boys like himself. "I can't say the stewards were 100 percent gay," Jim Vieira tells me, "but say 65 percent to 70 percent—and everybody knew it!" In those days on the Matson liners, gay meant white, because the company hired only white men, except for the few laundry workers, who were Chinese or Japanese.

Some gay stewards called themselves "queens." Queens are open, daring, and know how to take care of themselves. "When you liked them," explains Pete Brownlee, a straight waiter who also worked on the Matson liners, "you always called them a queen."

On some ships there are queens who reign supreme. There's the Honolulu Queen, and Miss MacDonald, and Mother Shannon, and Miss Effie, and Miss Leprosy, and Grace Line Gertie, and Toto Le Grand, and Lady Agatha, and many, many more. When in the late 1930s the Marine Cooks and Stewards Union begins to racially integrate the white liners, black queens also come aboard, with names like Madame Queen, and the African Queen, and Black Beauty, and the Black Orchid. In private, the queens and other gay stewards call each other "waitresses" or "stewardesses," and they address each other as union "sisters" as well as union "brothers."

"We didn't use the word 'gay' on the ships," Jim Vieira says. "No, it was always girls' names, or 'Miss'—Miss Cook, Miss McCormick, Miss Blair. Or they'd give them theatrical names—Hedy Lamarr, and names like that. The ugliest waiter of all was called Hedy Lamarr. The captain even called him Hedy Lamarr! It was 'Get her!' and 'Tell your sister come pick up those eggs!'—that sort of thing."

So many stewards on the Matson liners are gay that the ships themselves earn queer nicknames among seamen. They call the *Lurline* the "Queerline," the *Matsonia* the "Fruit-sonia," and the *Mariposa* the "Mary-posa" or "Fairy-posa." Seamen on freighters call Matson's liners the "fruit boats" or the "fruit ships." The Marine Cooks and Stewards Union, which represented the stewards department, also developed a queer reputation among merchant seamen, who sometimes called it the "Marine Cooks and Fruits," as well as other names.

During those early months of 1936, young Vieira found himself doing what might be called "queer work"—that is, work which is performed by, or has the reputation of being performed by, homosexual men or women—in this case, gay men. [The word "queer" in those days was derogatory. I'm calling this work "queer" because I want to emphasize the stigma that was attached to it.] Queer work included jobs for which gay men were supposed to be especially well suited. The stewards who did queer work on the passenger liners were the pastry chefs, waiters, caterers, bedroom stewards, pursers, wine stewards, florists, hairdressers, and telephone operators.

In recent years, labor historians have been looking at how work has been *gendered* as women's work or men's work; how work has been *racialized*, such as colored work or white work; and how work has been *ethnicized*, such as Irish work, Chinese work, etc. Since at least the nineteenth century, work has increasingly been *"homosexualized"* as queer work, or "heterosexualized" as straight work or even antigay work, such as military service, which still excludes open homosexuals by federal law.

Understanding queer work can help open labor history to new areas of study. This concept can help us put the lives and struggles of lesbian, gay, and bisexual workers into labor history, as well as those of heterosexual coworkers who stood with them as allies. And it can help us better understand how the growing homosexualization and heterosexualization of the workplace has affected all workers, regardless of their sexuality.

The first reference to queer work in the United States that I'm aware of is a poem published in *Vanity Fair* in 1860 as a parody of Walt Whitman's

Song Of Myself. This poem makes fun of those white men who worked as "counter-jumpers"—that was slang for salesmen in dry goods and department stores who sold fabric to ladies—a word that later became one of many derogatory terms for gay men. "I am the Counter-jumper," the parody begins, "weak and effeminate,"

> I love to loaf and lie about dry-goods.
> I loaf and invite the Buyer.
> I am the essence of retail. . . .
> I am . . . the box of silks fresh from France. . . .
> I am the creature of weak depravities;
> I am the Counter-jumper;
> I sound my feeble yelp over the woofs of the World.[1]

Other references to queer occupations have popped up over the years. In 1907, a newspaper reported a police raid of an African American drag dance in St. Louis where men were dressed up in gowns and called each other by women's names. Most of these men were employed by white families as butlers, cooks, and chauffeurs—service work in which these queens made a living and possibly got to know each other. In 1927, a Los Angeles psychiatrist wrote that the "choice of occupation" among homosexuals "is to a considerable extent determined by [their] homosexuality. . . . Thus," he observed, "we find many engaged in dressmaking, millinery, beauty parlor work, crocheting, embroidery; others work at window trimming, or in drapery, picture and art shops; still others are to be found among painters, sculptors, musicians, actors; others again in the army, navy, police, and among prison guards, male nurses, masseurs, and public bath attendants."

During World War II, U.S. military officials began to generalize about what special talents they believed gay male soldiers possessed and what job classifications typically included them. "In the military," wrote two navy doctors who studied gay sailors as their patients, "we find homosexuals in the capacities of hospital corpsmen, yeomen and chaplain's assistants." An army psychiatrist similarly concluded that gay soldiers had "considerable talent in stenographic, musical, clerical and special service [entertainment] activities," but they were "lacking in temperament and skills necessary to the combat soldier."

All women who served in the army and Marine Corps during the war had to deal with the public perception that their military units were full of "mannish women" or "dykes." Soldiers most likely to be stereotyped as lesbians were those working in the most masculine assignments, which one team of medical officers listed as "plumbers, welders, mechanics, carpenters, parachute riggers, truck drivers, chauffeurs, guards, radio operators, electricians, plane dispatchers [and] signalmen." Most of these jobs were restricted to white women; African American women were generally assigned to "women's" work that was also "colored" work—doing housekeeping, kitchen, and laundry duties. Queer work for women in the military, then, was both gendered as "men's work" and racialized as "white work."

Ever since the counter-jumper poem was published in 1860, queer work stereotypes have flourished in the workplace, in literature, and in popular culture, including radio shows and Hollywood films. Help me out here —what are some of the stereotypes of queer work for *women* that you've heard of? I've made my own little list: gym teachers, settlement house workers, ambulance drivers in World War I, tennis players, professional golfers, auto mechanics, police officers, bodybuilders, carpenters and other women in the trades, camp counselors, nuns, prison guards and wardens, teachers and administrators in women's colleges and girls' boarding schools, taxi drivers, school bus drivers, feminist movement leaders, nursing administrators, African American blues singers, and of course UPS loaders and truck drivers, like Newt Gingrich's lesbian sister, Candace Gingrich.

What are the stereotypes of queer work for men that you've heard of? My own list: fashion designers and models, interior decorators, costume and set designers, dressmakers, antique dealers, florists, window dressers, hotel desk clerks, Catholic priests, ballet dancers, hairdressers, beauticians, word processors, receptionists, church organists, gospel choir directors and singers, figure skaters, travel agents, male strippers, congressional aides, day care workers, archivists, librarians, graphic designers, landscape designers, tour guides at theme parks, real estate salesman in San Francisco, personal secretaries like Mr. Smithers on the Simpsons, and virtually all men other than ministers working in the wedding industry. (I think I've dated most of these men at one time or another.)

I myself have done lots of queer work, as a nurses' aide, temporary typist, receptionist, waiter, and, of course, gay historian.

Many but not all of these jobs are filled by people who are crossing gender roles: jobs where men do women's work and women do men's work, or where effeminate men and masculine women can make a living. Queer work also includes jobs in same-sex environments, especially where women live with women and men live with men, like colleges, jails, and the military. Queer work for men also includes both personal service jobs—like waiters—and work that focuses on the decorative, designing, and self-expressive arts. Queer jobs range from working class to middle class, but they're usually marginal to the primary labor force.

Like all stereotypes, these jobs don't represent the work that's performed by everyone who is gay, lesbian, or bisexual. And lots of people doing these jobs are definitely not gay. But the history of how these stereotypes emerged and how people who did queer work used them is a critical part of both lesbian and gay history and labor history. Too often, people think of gay and lesbian life as taking place off the job in bars or in the bedroom. And too many middle-class gay activists have tried to distance themselves from the gay hairdresser and lesbian truck driver, while straight labor historians have either ignored queer work or have been careful not to offend us by bringing it up. As a result, our collective silence about queer work has impoverished both gay history and labor history.

The history of queer work carries a rich legacy. It hands down to us the many strategies that past generations developed for making a living as openly lesbian and gay workers, for creating a gay social life and work culture on the job, and even for building a labor movement that protected them as workers who were assumed to be gay.

We don't yet have a theory that describes how and explains why certain jobs get stereotyped as queer work, or how these jobs function in the economy and even have been organized into unions. But today I'd like to raise just a few questions and make some observations about what I think queer work means for labor history.

. . . . . .

Exactly how do jobs become queer?

To begin answering this big question, we'd have to look at how each particular queer job also became racialized and gendered. Let's look at Jim Vieira's experience on the Matson liners. When he first went to sea in 1936, the stewards department, which was mostly white, was already pretty queer. A Matson official once told Vieira that his company preferred having gay men working as stewards because, as he said, "If it wasn't for these boys, who else would we get to do that kind of women's work—to turn down the beds and lay out ladies' nightgowns?" But on land in trains, hotels, and wealthy homes, this same service work was often "colored" work. So what the Matson official also meant was "What other white men are we going to get who'll do this colored work on our all-white crews?"

White men owned the shipping companies, were the officers on the ships, headed the unions, and worked in the "trades" in the engine room and on the deck. Chinese and Japanese men worked in the laundry room. When the Cooks and Stewards Union integrated African American and Filipino men onto the white ships in the late 1930s, they at first worked mostly below deck in the kitchens, galleys, and storerooms, but not in the suites or dining rooms. When Matson allowed one or two white women to work on the ships at all, it was as nurses and telephone operators. None of these jobs had reputations as queer work.

The queer work on the ships generally was the work that only white men did "on stage" working with the passengers—as waiters, pursers, room stewards, and bartenders. As a result, white gay men on the liners learned to racialize gay as white. "There were gay cooks, too," one white gay steward recalls, "gay bakers, gay butchers, gay everything. [Not the laundrymen?]—no, the laundrymen were usually Chinese." But this simple "checkerboard" scheme, as it was called, hides important exceptions. Some of the Chinese stewards *were* known to be gay, though they were not doing queer work. And the Alexander liners, which had all-black stewards departments, also had many gay stewards, who, according to one former steward on these ships, mostly did queer work as waiters and room stewards. But neither the black stewards departments nor their "colored" stewards union had the queer reputations that the white stewards did.

This rough sketch raises many questions. How long before Jim Vieira went to sea in 1936 did white gay men start congregating in the stewards departments? Although Chinese men's work was often feminized by white men, why wasn't it also homosexualized as queer work? Under what conditions did Chinese, Japanese, Filipino, and "colored" work become queer work, if at all, and by whose standards? As the union opened more jobs to men of color on the Matson liners, did the white queer work become less queer or did it attract more gay men of color? When women became waitresses, did their presence make dining room service less queer or more attractive to lesbians?

It will be a huge but important task to unravel the elaborate, interconnected, ever-changing historical process by which queer work on the ships and in hundreds of other workplaces has been racialized, gendered, and classed.

. . . . . .

How do people find queer work and how do they make these jobs their own?

When workers were fired for being lesbian or gay, they still had to work, so they looked for other jobs where they might fit in. Some, like Jim Vieira, stumbled into queer jobs by accident. Others were actually pushed into queer work by those who fired them. When in 1943 David Barrett was kicked out of the navy for being gay, his officer advised him, "You're going to have a lot of trouble finding a job with this on your record. The only people who will hire you now are the Marine Cooks and Stewards." So Barrett went right over to the union hall and signed up.

From at least the turn of the century, more films, jokes, songs, cartoons, novels, and gossip made fun of people who did queer work. Gay and lesbian workers could cleverly use these insults as signposts to identify what work was queer. These jobs acted as magnets that attracted even more lesbian or gay workers while repelling those who didn't want to work among such people. That's how some jobs end up predominantly queer.

During World War II, for example, a few white women were assigned to work as truck drivers and vehicle mechanics in the Motor Transport units of the Women's Army Corps (WAC) and Women Marines. These jobs were so desirable and carried such a powerful stereotype as queer work that many lesbians were drawn to them. One lesbian veteran told me that the women in *her* motor transport unit were all "butchy-acting with short haircuts, smoking cigarettes with the cupped hand and drinking beer from the bottle." These women kept a dog-eared copy of *The Well of Loneliness*, a lesbian novel, hidden under the seat of a certain truck. A resident WAC counselor observed that one "boyish-appearing girl . . . cut her hair short" as soon as she started driving trucks, and she joined other couples who walked arm-in-arm at night and danced together in the base's service club. For a while, these women created their own lesbian world on the job.

· · · · · ·

How does queer work fit into society?

At its worst, queer work is a stigmatized ghetto, a trap that confines lesbian and gay workers to a few acceptable jobs. This work is supposed to be all we are good for and all we are allowed to do until we aren't needed any more. When we're told to "stay in our place," these are the places we're supposed to stay. Queer work controls our movement through the workforce by containing us in nonthreatening jobs. It can make us easy targets for ridicule, harassment, or even violent attacks. The motor transport lesbians were tolerated because the military needed them for the war effort. But as soon as the war ended, they were rounded up, interrogated, and then kicked out with bad discharges in terrifying antilesbian purges.

In a world in which gay men and lesbians were supposed to always remain invisible, silent, and isolated, queer work *was* a trap, but one that we ingeniously transformed into our own little refuge. It was one place where we could make a living without always having to hide that we were gay. We gradually realized that if you put all the queer jobs together, they not only added up to a sizable workforce but showed us how successful we already were at carving out, job by job, our own place in the economy. It was in queer jobs where many of us first discovered that we weren't alone. It's where we first learned how gay people can cover for each other and even create camaraderie in the workplace. Here we could sometimes use our own language, make up secret codes, and give each other campy nicknames. We sometimes privately dished the hostile straight people we served or, daring each other to be more open, even mocked them to their faces. "My dear," whispered one gay waiter to a woman whose husband was giving him a hard time, "it seems that your butch girlfriend here [pointing to her husband] thinks that she's a real man." Or as a gay flight attendant told an overdemanding male passenger, "Honey, I'm here to save your ass, not kiss your ass."

· · · · · ·

Can queer work be political?

People in queer jobs do not necessarily belong to gay organizations, identify with the gay movement, or even talk about being gay. Yet they are hardly in the closet, because doing queer work makes everyone assume that you are gay, and it surprises them if you tell them you're not.

Doing queer jobs forced workers to develop the fine art of self-defense. Sometimes a brilliant wisecrack can do the trick. But people doing queer work also defended themselves collectively. When they formed unions, they were developing an early form of gay activism. This came decades before the more middle-class and white homosexual movement emerged in the 1950s. While the gay movement has organized around the idea that homosexuality itself constituted their primary political identity, these workers used their unions to improve their lives as homosexuals, sometimes fighting for racial equality at the same time.

The Marine Cooks and Stewards was one of the unions that early on organized men who did queer work. This union had started out in 1901 as a white men's union dedicated to the exclusion of Asian and black workers. But by the time Jim Vieira went to sea in 1936, it was full of left-wing activists, some openly gay and/or men of color, who were beginning to racially integrate the white liners. As they succeeded, the union's queer reputation took on a new twist. Instead of just being called the "Marine Cooks and Fruits," now they were being called "a third red, a third black, and a third queer." Some of its members, of course, were all three.

Most men in the Marine Cooks and Stewards had to come to terms with their changing membership and reputation. At stake was their dignity as seamen who were treated as riff-raff, who were doing "women's work," who were men of color or worked with men of color, who were gay or worked with queens, and who were communists or worked with communists. In the 1930s, these men were going way out on a limb. But through their collective struggle, they built a solidarity that bridged many of their differences. They even came up with a slogan. One version, recalls Revels Cayton, a straight, African American former steward now in his late eighties, went like this: *It's anti-union to red-bait, race-bait, or queen-bait!* Another version of their slogan, he tells me, went like this: *If you let them red-bait, they'll race-bait, and if you let them race-bait, they'll queen-bait. These are all connected, and that's why we have to stick together!*

You could see this new solidarity at work below deck among the crew. "Frank Bowers was one of the toughest queens I ever met," Mickey Blair, a white gay former steward, tells me. "One time a crew member came through the food line while Miss Bowers was serving, and he says to her, 'Put some food on there, you fruit!' And Miss Bowers pulls back and says, 'Why did you call me a fruit?' And he says, 'Because you *are* a fruit!' Well! Miss Bowers grabs a big soup ladle and, boy, she slaps him right across the head. 'Now,' she says, 'you son-of-a-bitch, I bet I'm the meanest fucking fruit you ever saw'—and I mean she drew blood. He didn't dare report her. That's the way Frank Bowers would do it, so you didn't fuck with the Marine Cooks and Stewards," Blair explains. "That was his form of militancy."

Their straight coworkers found ways to stand up for the queens, too. "You want to know about my union?" asks Pete Brownlee, a white heterosexual steward. "The most important thing was not that we had gays. It was that an injury to one *was* an injury to all—and we practiced it. We took care of each other. If someone hurled an insult at a black steward," he says, a queen would stand there until he took it back. Or if he insulted a queen, a black steward would stand there until he took it back. "To them," Brownlee went on about the hostile crew members, "our union was all queers. They didn't even have the courtesy to call us homosexuals—they called us queers. So you had to kick the shit out of a few guys once in a while. I kicked the shit out of a couple guys on the ship—you just *had* to do it. They would torment you, do a lot of stupid shit. So 'fuck you!' we said. We knew that our union would back us."

What would we learn if we began to uncover other histories of people who did queer work? How do the traditions of queer work wind their way through our whole economy and social fabric? From nineteenth-century counter-jumpers to the sales clerks now working at Macy's. From the WAC truck drivers in World War II to Candace Gingrich. From nineteenth-century African American drag dances to openly gay black fashion designers, like Willi Smith, who died of AIDS a few years ago. Why did legislators in the McCarthy era identify the State Department, the military, the maritime trades, and the women's prison system as "havens for homosexuals," then conduct government witch hunts to root them out? And what is the history of the many other unions besides the cooks and stewards that have organized people who do queer work—men who work as flight attendants, department store clerks, nurses' aides, telephone operators, and waiters, and women who work as nurses, librarians, pilots, mechanics, telephone linepersons, and UPS truck drivers?

The fact that queer work has a history of being unionized gives me some hope in these hard times. We can use it to challenge the religious right's twin stereotypes of the antigay working man and his family pitted against the rich homosexual who enjoys special rights and privileges. And we can use it to fight our own twin myths that gay people are not working class, and that unions are not gay. The history of organized queer work reclaims the powerful legacy left us by lesbian and gay workers and their straight allies who worked and built unions together long before I was born. That legacy offers me the gift of seeing myself in history as a gay unionist from a working-class background. And it strengthens my own belief that a grassroots labor activism that is multiracial and pro-gay is not only possible but can help us survive the economic disaster that is currently tearing our nation apart.

Mickey Blair, a gay former steward who just turned seventy-nine, tells me that he still dreams about militant democratic unions, like the Marine Cooks and Stewards, with openly gay leadership and members, that are dedicated to racial equality, economic justice, and solidarity across many lines. "We already proved that it could be done, so it's not just a dream," he tells me. "We can do it again," he says, "only we have to do it differently this time." That's why every few weeks for the last twelve years, Mickey Blair has called me long-distance from Seattle just to make sure I haven't given up, to make sure I'm still working to uncover and make public the history of what he and his gay coworkers accomplished so many years ago.

NOTE

1. Jonathan Ned Katz, *Gay American History* (New York: Thomas Crowell, 1976), 655 n. 133.

Trying to Remember

Although Bérubé never finished his book on the Marine Cooks and Stewards Union, he did produce several incomplete drafts, each one approaching the material in a different way. In this selection, drawn from a draft he wrote in 2003, he experimented with using a first-person voice to present this history. He injects himself, the interviewer, into the narrative, thus allowing readers to see something of how he worked as an oral historian. The approach gives this account of labor struggles in the 1930s and 1940s an immediacy as it draws the reader into the lives and homes of these historical actors. The excerpt illustrates Bérubé's commitment to preserving the stories of an older generation of gay activists, many of whom have died since he conducted his interviews.

I first met Stephen "Mickey" Blair, who called himself a working-class queen, in 1983 at his home in Seattle. A former boyfriend of mine, Chip Parker, and his lover, Gregg Kasner, introduced us. My friends knew I wanted to talk to older gay men, as I called them, who sailed as merchant seamen. I'd heard fantastic stories about how, from the 1920s into the 1950s—the golden age of luxury liners—hundreds of "queens," as they called each other, sailed in the stewards departments of the big passenger ships, put on drag shows for their shipmates, became active in their multiracial unions, and were even elected as union leaders. Legends too outrageous to believe, I thought. But I needed to know for sure, because I wanted them to be true.

My memory takes me back to the morning we first meet. Stephen, who spent decades serving meals to passengers and crew, cooks me what he calls a "whore's breakfast"—scrambled eggs, bacon, sausages, pancakes with maple syrup, strawberries, muffins, toast, coffee, and orange juice—which he spreads out for me banquet-style on his kitchen table.

"It's what the girls ate to get their energy back after a long night's work," he explains, then suddenly remembers one of his stories. This one's about

Unpublished manuscript, 2003.

MCSU members Frank McCormick and Ted Rolfs. Courtesy of the Allan Bérubé Collection at the GLBTHS, San Francisco.

Frank Bowers, a queen he worked with in the stewards department of the coastal passenger ships run by the Alaska Steamship Line.

"Miss Bowers would always get the whores going from Seattle up to Alaska for the season," he begins. "One time, a group of girls and their madam called him to their table." Stephen performs the women summoning the waiter by clapping his hands three times.

"Miss Bowers—he was blocky and short and tough—walked over to see what the women wanted.

"'Good morning ladies, how many in your party?'

"'Well there's six of us,' they said, 'six old whores!'

"'No, no,' he said, 'SEVEN!—*I'm* here now!'

"I tell you," Stephen laughs, "that fucking dining room would rock and roll!"

Stephen had lived in this West Seattle house—one of the only places he ever felt at home—with his life partner, Frank McCormick, from the 1960s until Frank succumbed to lung cancer in 1977 at the age of eighty.

"Frank died in my arms at the table here," he tells me.

At first, Stephen doesn't talk much about Frank. Each time he says his partner's name, he grows quiet, then changes the subject. But over the years, his story of their relationship slowly comes out, sometimes in a single detail, other times in outbursts of praise or tears.

"I met Frank during the '36 seamen's strike in San Francisco," Stephen tells me one afternoon. Frank had found work as a waiter on the luxury liners of the Matson Line after being kicked out of the navy for allegedly making an advance at a fellow sailor. As a member of the Marine Cooks and Stewards Union, he organized seamen's support for the 1934 longshoremen's strike on the West Coast. During the national seamen's strike in 1936, Frank, who then was thirty-nine, was organizing strike activities when nineteen-year-old Stephen came to San Francisco looking for work, after also being kicked out of the military on homosexual charges.

"I was in disgrace," Stephen tells me. "I couldn't go home. My family back in Duluth was absolutely horrified. They made it clear that they'd be happy if I didn't come around."

Stephen heard that the Marine Cooks and Stewards Union could get him work on the ships. But when he went down to 86 Commercial Street, just off the Embarcadero, to sign up at the union hall, he was told there weren't any jobs because all the men were on strike. In the hall, he happened to hear a voice coming from another room. When he peeked in, he saw a short, thin man with a pencil-line mustache giving a speech—one that the union later published as the pamphlet *A Plea from the Sea: An Open Letter to the American Congress . . . and The Public*. (Stephen saved the pamphlet for the rest of his life as a cherished memento of their first day together.) Frank's dramatic voice (between voyages he performed speaking roles in Hollywood films) and his message mesmerized the teenage boy.

"At the turn of the century," Frank McCormick explained to the nation's landlubbers and the passengers of the world, "the stereotype sailor was an illiterate, cursing, colorful figure, who never got beyond the waterfronts with their bars and tattoo shops. He always came ashore with a parrot or a monkey. He was supposed to be unmarried but had many loves. This conception is as out of date . . . as would be a present day buggy-whip factory in Detroit.

"The sea . . . develops a particular kind of man," McCormick continued.

When ashore, we feel uncomfortable until we get out on the sea once more. We belong there. We may not always understand you who live on land in superior comfort and more civilized conventions. . . . We wait for you to serve you as passengers, and millions can testify that we have done so in the past with satisfaction and courtesy. . . . You are always our guests. We are glad that this is so. . . . But please don't forget that we were cradled in Dubuque, Iowa; Oshkosh, Wisconsin; and New York City. So we are of you and a part of you—and never fail to observe you. . . . Like you, [we] have golden dreams for the future. . . .

"If you work ashore on an eight or nine hour basis," he explained,

you are not also required to remain in the shop, or factory, or office where you are employed, to eat and sleep there for weeks at a time, such as we do on a ship. Neither are you subject to call for emergencies at any hour within those weeks. Nor are you denied all recreation except reading and conversing during that time, such as we are on a ship. Nor are you required to act instantly and spontaneously, at a given signal, to do all that is humanly possible to stave off the complete and utter destruction of all life. . . . Were you ever in a shipwreck? If not, pray God you may never be. The helplessness, the extremity of the human soul under such a condition does not admit of description. . . . Is it any wonder that we object to further restrictions of our time and liberty and freedom?

Stephen never forgot Frank's speech.

"I kept thinking about it," he tells me, "and the more I thought of it, the more I thought about Frank, his writing and lovely speaking voice. I knew nothing about labor unions in those days. He's the one who taught me. I'll show you the picture of when he became the vice president of the Congress of Industrial Organizations in California as the head of Marine Cooks and Stewards."

Smitten by this older, experienced seaman, Stephen introduced himself.

"I remember he and I sitting down and how he looked at me and how I looked at him, feeling something neither one of us had ever felt before. I know I'm speaking for him. He's not here to speak for himself. I don't think I'm being undue. I hope I'm not. But there was that, you know, seeking each other out. I had not come out yet and he was out but wasn't; quite ungay, I would say, and yet gay. Does that make any sense?"

"It does," I said.

"I didn't know about me too much, but I knew he was gay. He made no bones about it. Oh he would camp! I kept thinking, 'He's honest, and I'm dishonest. He is clear, and I'm clouded.' And the closer we got, the clearer it became that I had a very deep love for this man and he had a very deep love and respect for me. Now mind you, nothing had gone on here. We did not go to bed with each other, we were just very much taken with one another. From the beginning, I wanted to be in his presence, he wanted to be in mine.

"I've never really found the words to describe what was between him and me," Stephen says.

I think camaraderie was primary, but yet there were so many other elements to that relationship. With twenty years' difference between us, there was an admiring and yet there was this "equus," this equality. Hours would go by when we didn't even speak—we were just happy that the other one was there. Yet there was communication all that time, without speaking. It was very, very intense—a different kind of a love, but a deep one. Certainly a homosexual one, but a whole lot more. Bit by bit, this worked into a loving friendship, and from there it blossomed. When Frank and I set up housekeeping together, we really were married. We were very devoted to each other and very devoted to that union and that union was devoted to us. I don't know what you call that. There is no name for it. It's just—it was there, it was a great gift. Frank was a mentor, he was my friend, he was the family I never had. It's empty now without him.

As Stephen comes to trust me enough to tolerate my sometimes naive questions, we become friends, then, over the course of our fourteen-year friendship, family for each other.

"Now listen to your mother, because this is important," he tells me during one visit. "You don't know it yet, but you are the mirror."

I'm not sure what he means.

At first I think that he wants me to tell his gay life story, make sure to get it right, and reflect it back to him so he can see himself in the mirror of history. I've been a community-based gay historian and activist for a long time. I know how to do this.

But that's not it.

"My dear," he says when I ask him to be more specific, "you have to figure it out by finding the stories. *You* have to do it, because you're like me—no college degree, French-Canadian, working class, queer—and people like us have been treated like nobodies. We weren't supposed to know our history. They stole it from us. But it's ours, darling, and we can steal it back. You know where to look for it. What you find will show you where you're going and what you have to do."

It takes me a long time to realize that what Stephen wants from me is more difficult, and riskier, than preserving his life story for future generations.

From not only his words but the way he looks into my eyes and squeezes my hand and talks about Frank, I sense that he is challenging me to take a journey through some hazardous, class-infested waters, and that he's offering to serve as my guide. Find the maps you'll need, I hear him say, and go where they take you. Then come back to tell the story of what you learned. Tell it in a way that pulls together the unlikeliest listeners, so they can see their own power and commitment to each other reflected back in their history and in each other's eyes, as when mirrors reflect mirrors, into infinity. Make the way you tell the story, and the way people come together to hear it, resemble where you all could be at journey's end.

I'm not sure I know how to do this. But because I love this man, I decide to try.

Every time I visit Stephen in Seattle, from the day we meet until his death at the age of eighty in 1997, I find myself waxing poetic about "working people working together," as the AFL-CIO union slogan says. With me as his audience, he feels free to get on his campy soapbox and orate with the grandest revolutionary gestures. We know we are hopeless romantics. But we sing our homemade rhapsodies to sustain each other in a world that doesn't want us powerful enough to make our dreams of economic democracy come true.

"Stephen," I say, sometimes with a kiss, "you're such a god damn drama queen."

"Dramatic as hell," he says, "but real—like you, my dear. Tell them what really happened."

. . . . . .

I've never worked in the stewards department of any passenger ship or merchant vessel. But I've sailed as a passenger on a luxury liner (a weekend cruise-to-nowhere from New York's West Side piers on Cunard's *Queen Elizabeth 2*), and, as a scholarship boy, I waited tables and washed pots and pans in the kitchen of an upper-class New England prep school. I've never been on strike for better pay and conditions. But I'm a member of a union (National Writers Union, Local 1981 of the United Auto Workers), and I've walked picket lines to support other unions in their strikes. I've never worked on the docks or found refuge in seamen's bars, pool halls, or rooming houses. But, looking for sexual intimacy, I've cruised the gay bars, bathhouses, alleys, and deserted piers that in the 1970s lined the waterfronts of America's port cities. I didn't live through the revolutionary labor uprisings of the Great Depression or the global catastrophe of World War II. But the magnetic fields of these events pulled my childhood back toward them with such force that they've become the focus of my life's work as writer and historian.

I've begun to realize that my desire for history comes from a painful, dislocated place inside me. It's there that I feel seduced by the power of events I haven't lived through that promise me the kind of unifying experience I've longed for all my life. My historical research is itself a journey from that place into the past, a passionate search for stories of social struggles that, in the retelling, might give me the chance to recover a wholeness and sense of belonging I believe I once had but lost. The loss grew with each of too many family moves, temporary jobs, and evictions by gentrifying landlords; getting caught up in the violence of racial segregation, race riots, and the crisis of the military draft; and feeling displaced by my class escape into upper-class schools, along with the accumulated grief of long-distance relationships that failed and the sudden deaths of family, friends, and lovers by senseless murder, war, and even political assassination, and from the disintegration of cancer and AIDS. By searching for a past when people pulled together to fight such threats despite their differences, then pulling that experience back with me into the present, I think I've been trying to rebuild a sense of myself that's not isolated, that's instead connected to a multifaceted, cross-generational "we" made so strong it can't be destroyed by the destructive forces that have torn my own life apart.

One of my earliest memories of feeling dislocated, trapped, and alone was growing up in a trailer park at the ragged edge of one of America's industrial ports. The big bang of 1950s upward mobility splintered my large, extended, Franco-American working-class family into separate nuclear units that scattered to places as far apart as Massachusetts and California. In 1953, when I was seven years old, my parents, to get closer to better-paying jobs, split away from our small-town New England family farm to settle temporarily in a racially segregated trailer park in Bayonne, New Jersey—the "armpit of the nation," as New Yorkers called it.

In Sunset Trailer Park, house trailers were parked on gravel that had been dumped onto sunken barges. This landfill process minutely extended into Newark Bay the western edge of Bayonne's waterfront: nine miles of oil and chemical refineries, train yards, military terminals, piers, dry docks, and ferryboat slips that surrounded three sides of this "Peninsula of Industry," as our city proudly called itself. To the north, Bayonne was anchored to the continent at Jersey City. To the west were Newark Airport and the freight docks of Elizabeth. To the south, across Kill Van Kull, were the ferry terminals, ship repair yards, and tugboat docks of Staten Island's North Shore. To the east, beyond a skyline of massive oil tanks over which loomed Miss Liberty's rear end, a high-class Manhattan flaunted her necklace of luxury-liner piers and her skyscraper crown.

On summer afternoons I snuck out to the far end of a dangerously rotting wooden dock, from which I watched ships sail up and down Newark Bay. No luxury liners, just beefy tugboats pushing barges. Or the occasional freighter sliding out of a pier and down the drab green waterway, then disappearing under the grand suspended arch of the Bayonne Bridge to sail through the narrows and on to foreign ports across the Atlantic Ocean.

A house trailer was no luxury waterfront condo. Our family of six was packed tightly into an eight-by-thirty-six-foot tin can—a boatlike metal container enclosing an alley of "rooms" divided only by plastic folding doors. Within its narrow confines, my sisters and I ate meals and did homework on a miniature dinette, teased and pushed each other out of the way, walked in our sleep, heard muffled crying in the night. Somehow, our parents had sex without us knowing.

It was in this landlocked vessel, not at sea, that I first experienced something like the rhythms and perils of maritime life. On sunny summer days, the trailer's sheet-metal hull was baked hot enough to make a drop of water sizzle. The industrial air we breathed was laced with poisonous gases spewing from oil refinery smokestacks and the funnels of passing tankers. When hurricanes slammed the Jersey shore, my parents locked the windows and prayed the trailer wouldn't be crumpled by violent winds or swept, shipwrecked, into the polluted waters of the bay. On hot foggy nights I climbed into my upper bunk, ratcheted open the tiny oval porthole at my feet, and fell asleep to a chorus of waterfront lullabies—horns and whistles broadcast live from nearby buoys, boats, and bridges.

I escaped to worlds far from our trailer park not by sailing away but by reading books. In our blue-collar grade school, named after the first President Roosevelt, our geography textbooks (so old they were themselves historic documents) introduced me to the world's peoples, places, and things, located on colorful maps of the five continents and the seven seas. The story that geography books told us was deeply racial and romantic: photographs, maps, and words meant to take white kids to faraway lands to meet exotic peoples around the globe. The story they told was also Depression-era practical, showing us how people obtain the food, clothing, shelter, and fuel they need to survive, how people communicate with each other, and how they move over great distances. "Why do people travel?" asked the frayed schoolbook.

> In order to secure the things necessary to supply our daily needs, people must go from place to place . . . for different parts of the world produce different things.
>
> We have freight as well as passenger service on the water and it is very important. But for this, there could be no exchange of products between countries separated by the ocean. Great freight steamships carry to other lands some of the things which we have to sell and bring to us things which we do not produce. . . .
>
> Name the things brought to the United States on freight ships. . . .
>
> But it is not simply to secure and exchange the necessities of life that people travel. A few persons do this for the many who stay at home. Many journey to see different lands and peoples. . . .

Standing there by myself at the end of that rotting dock, I didn't know I was part of a long tradition. For centuries, outsiders who've been knocked around this violent continent have been pushed and pulled to every place where land's end meets water's edge. Eyes turned away from the past, they looked to the horizon, as I did, trying to see a future that might offer a way out of their difficult lives. Nor did I know if there was a place for me among the people from different countries and of different "races" who mistrusted each other in this blue-collar port that was hardly my hometown, didn't even know where they came from or what work they did to supply their daily needs. I didn't know what cargo the ships carried past my lookout, or where they were sailing, or who was working in their crews, or how those men lived above deck and below, or what they might dream at night, lying in their bunks so close to the bodies of other sleeping men.

What I did know (with more longing than certainty), as I buried myself in books about the past and other lands, or wandered out to the waterfront, or watched boys swim disobediently in the oil-slicked waters of the bay, or walked streets where people who lived in houses looked down on us as trailer park trash, or envied Negro girls skipping rope together in the school-yard—what I did know was that I needed to make my own way out, so I could find the place where someone like me might belong.

· · · · · ·

"I would like to work with you," Revels Cayton, former longshoreman and seaman, tells me.

We've been put in touch by Gene Vrana, the librarian and archivist at the International Longshore and Warehouse Union in San Francisco. Vrana told me Revels Cayton sailed as a steward on the liners and served as a union official. He told Revels Cayton I was taking a community-based rather than academic approach in a book I'm writing, with a focus on gay stewards. Cayton was interested, so on this September afternoon in 1994, he has invited me into his home—a spacious fifties-modern house in San Francisco's Diamond Heights—so we could meet and talk.

Revels Cayton offers me a mug of coffee. His wife has gone out, he says, but he will introduce me to her when she comes home.

"Are you married?"

I hesitate. "No . . . I'm gay myself."

Silence.

After decades of gay activism, I'm still vulnerable to this fear of coming out. I'm particularly afraid that if older straight union men find out I'm gay, they'll refuse to talk to me and I'll have to go away without hearing their stories. It's no idle fear—union men I've called have hung up on me without telling me why. That fear grows stronger when I try to cross the lines that separate races and generations and sexualities all at once, as I am now doing, talking with this eighty-seven-year-old, married, African American man.

I try to read his silence. He seems to be reminiscing.

"There were lots of gay stewards," he tells me, "on Matson's big white ships."

I've also seen this happen. Merchant seamen and longshoremen try to remember the queens they worked and lived with on the ships so their memories can bridge the distance between their married lives and my gay life.

"Were most of the gay stewards on those ships white?" I begin.

"All the stewards were white on the Matson ships," Mr. Cayton patiently explains.

"Take Frank McCormick," he says. "You could tell he was gay right away by his mannerisms and how he used gay language and phrases. It was right there—obvious. He could do funny imitations of anyone. He'd be angry at some phony, so he would mimic him. He could pick out everything that was funny, crazy, wrong about this guy. He'd just make you laugh."

As we talk, Cayton measures his words between long pauses, drifting in and out of memory, rationing a voice made raspy by age and illness.

He leads me upstairs, using cane and handrail to ease his way. He wants to show me family portraits hanging on his office wall.

Here is his mother, Susie Revels, and her father, Hiram Revels, who, after Reconstruction, became the first Negro United States senator, from Mississippi. And here is his father, Horace Cayton, born into slavery in Mississippi, who published a Republican newspaper in Seattle, where the Caytons moved at the turn of the century.

Then Revels Cayton leads me on a slow journey back down two flights to the basement, where he shows me a photograph on another wall: crowds of union men parading up Market Street during the 1936 San Francisco maritime strike.

"I was marching that day," he tells me.

He pulls from a shelf a three-ring notebook, opens it to show me photographs of passenger steamships: the *H. F. Alexander, Emma Alexander, Ruth Alexander, Dorothy Alexander*. In the 1920s and 1930s this family of "Alexander Boats" (which Admiral Line founder H. F. Alexander named after his wife, Ruth; his daughter, Dorothy; his mother, Emma; and himself), carried passengers up and down the West Coast and employed only African American stewards in their crews.

"I worked on those liners," he tells me.

Then he pulls out a dissertation by Richard Stanley Hobbs, "The Cayton

Legacy," about his family's history. He says I should read it because it will answer basic questions that he then won't have to answer himself. He's conserving his limited energy.

A few days later I come back with my list of questions. We go to work—only months, it turns out, before he dies—trying to rescue some nearly lost stories with the help of his photographs, a dissertation, my copies of old newspaper clippings, and the flickering light of Revels Cayton's memory.

· · · · · ·

Today I am visiting Dan Rolfs.

Seventeen years ago, in 1980, Dan's brother Ted was serving me jasmine tea in the carefully tended Japanese-style garden of his San Francisco Richmond district home, where at seventy-three he was enjoying his retirement.

Back then, I was interested in Ted's memories of gay life in San Francisco for a book I was writing on gay and lesbian GIs in World War II. Now I want to know more about his life as a merchant seaman and longshoreman. But Ted Rolfs died seven years ago.

I remembered that Ted had shown me a photo album, which I hoped had not been lost or destroyed. When one of Ted's friends told me that Ted's brother Dan was still living in San Francisco and might have some of Ted's belongings, I called Dan on the telephone. He invited me to meet him at his home—a house perched on the hillside above Ghirardelli Square, with a grand view across the Golden Gate of the Marin Headlands.

"The album is somewhere down in the garage," Dan reassures me as he welcomes me inside. "But I don't know exactly where."

I tell him about my work, then we talk about Ted.

"Can we see if we can find the album?" I ask.

"If you've got time. It could take a while."

Dan leads me downstairs and points to piles in a dark corner. "It's in there. Those are all of Ted's belongings. You can look through them, if you want. I'll be upstairs."

As I begin to unpack a mound of old cardboard boxes and paper bags, I'm amazed by what I find: hundreds of photos, letters, clippings, notebook journals, 1930s strike cards and union membership books, 78 rpm voice recordings from World War II, and, yes, the photo album. Rummaging through the papers, I happen to pick up a 1984 letter to Ted from Bill Bailey, a legendary 1930s maritime union activist whom I've seen interviewed in documentary films about labor history:

"I had a talk with Al Richmond the other day," Bailey writes, about the contribution made by the gay members of the waterfront unions. Their contribution has always been swept under the carpet or locked up in a closet so few ever got the recognition or love that they merited and earned. Mother nature is now working against us and our memories are fading ever so slowly. . . . The struggles, the wins and losses, the wave of respect and depths of humiliations, the inner sufferings that the gay members went through has never been put down on paper. Don't you think that those gays who were members of the maritime unions, especially the Marine Cooks and Stewards, and the great things they accomplished to improve our conditions—and the sacrifices many made in the war effort—don't you think, Ted, that this should be put down on paper? . . . It is a historical fact and must be made part of our maritime heritage. Who is better suited for writing such a piece of history than a man who lived through it all and contributed to it, namely Ted Rolfs? Ted, will you give this some thought, please, and let's help to break down another myth about human beings who gave their very best to make our conditions the best in the world?

Leafing through more letters and notebooks, I see Ted's life story begin to take shape, the way I imagine archaeologists piece together the history of a forgotten village from shards of pottery its people left behind.

Dan comes back downstairs carrying a tray of cookies and hot chocolate for me. As I look up at him, I have to wipe away tears that are blurring my vision.

"Ted saved everything!" I say. "He was the archivist of his own life."

Then I realize it's time to bring up a delicate subject.

"Would you think about, someday, maybe in your will, donating Ted's materials to a public archives, possibly the lesbian and gay archives here in San Francisco?"

"Do you think they'd really be interested in Ted's stuff?"

"I know they would. I can come back at another time to sort the materials into boxes."

Dan thinks it over for a moment.

"Could you maybe take them with you today?" he says. "It would be great to have them out of my garage. You see, I'm selling the house and moving into a smaller place."

Then it hits me. If I'd come here just a few weeks later, Ted's papers might not have survived the move.

A familiar chill shivers my body: How many vital stories will no one ever know are missing?

· · · · · ·

Ted and Dan Rolfs, Revels Cayton, Stephen Blair, and Frank McCormick all belonged to the Marine Cooks and Stewards Union (MCS). The MCS organized the men—and in later years the women—who worked in the stewards departments of United States vessels that sailed the Pacific Ocean. On the passenger liners these men made up the "hotel" service staff: waiters, cooks, pastry chefs, bakers, messmen, pantrymen, porters, room stewards, wine stewards, bellhops, janitors, hairdressers, laundrymen, smoking-room attendants, and bartenders.

White men in San Francisco had formed the MCS union in 1901, meeting secretly in the back room of a waterfront saloon. They came together to protect their jobs from what their constitution called "competition from alien and inferior races." By this they meant Chinese and Japanese seamen, whom shipowners, to increase their profits, hired in Asia at lower wages than they paid white men. During the great Depression-era maritime strikes—the longshoremen's strike of 1934 and the seamen's strike of 1936—communists and other young radicals who joined the Marine Cooks and Stewards Union transformed it into one of the most democratic, racially integrated unions in the United States. At the same time, it developed a reputation as a union full of "queers." "A third red, a third black, and a third queer!" mocked its enemies at the time. During the military buildup of World War II the MCS membership grew from 3,000 to 19,000. Many of these civilians were killed, wounded, or shipwrecked at sea, at a casualty rate higher than any branch of the military service. Taking a leadership role in postwar campaigns for waterfront and maritime unity, the MCS won wage increases and improved conditions and aggressively fought for racial and gender equality for its members. Mounted over its job board in its San Francisco union hall was this motto and commitment: "Equality in hiring regardless of race, religion, national origin or political affiliation." In 1950 it was one of the unions kicked out of the Congress of Industrial Organizations (the CIO) in a McCarthy-era anticommunist purge. By the mid-fifties the MCS was destroyed under a barrage of anticommunist and antihomosexual attacks spearheaded by state and federal agencies, the Coast Guard, shipowners, newspapers, and rival unions.

I want to know why so many queens were working in the stewards departments of the passenger ships. But more importantly, I want to know exactly how merchant seamen, who were once so divided and pitted against each other, were able to put together, beginning with the 1934 strike, a multiracial union with a sense of solidarity large enough to embrace and protect even the most obvious queens.

The maritime workers I meet are old enough to remember the 1936 seamen's strike. But they're too young to remember the earlier turning point: the 1934 waterfront rebellion that led to the largest general strike in United States history, setting the stage for some of the most important union victories of twentieth-century America. Who, I wonder, knows what happened?

Stephen Blair often told me that his life partner, Frank McCormick, played an important role in the 1934 strike. But when I ask him if he remembers what Frank actually did, he says he can't remember, reminding me that it was two years before they first met.

"Ask Jimmy Vieira" he says. "He was good friends with Frank. Jimmy would be better on that than me."

· · · · · ·

Jim Vieira has decorated every level surface of his San Francisco Tenderloin apartment with porcelain figurines he's collected during his travels around the world. On a warm autumn day in 1994, this short, handsome, seventy-six-year-old Portuguese American man, whom Stephen Blair has asked to talk to me, offers me a glass of Diet Pepsi, then apologizes for serving me a piece of Sara Lee coffee cake. As a steward who's proud of a life devoted to impeccable personal service, he's letting me know that this presentation is not up to his high standards. I tell him he's making me feel right at home. He says it's hard to recall things that happened so long ago, but he'll do his best.

"I was a scullion on the *Malolo*," he begins, going back to the time he first went to sea, just a few months before the 1936 seamen's strike. At fifteen Jimmy had run away from home in Mendocino to San Francisco, where his aunt took him in. After school each day, he worked in a restaurant to pay for his living expenses, then came back to his aunt's Mission district home, studying sometimes until two in the morning. "I was so eager to read and find out things," he tells me. "See, my people are not educated people. We had the Bible in the house and that was it."

One day a customer in the restaurant, noticing how hard this young man worked, started up a conversation.

"A liner is coming in tomorrow," the man said. "How would you like to work on a ship for the winter?"

"I've never been aboard a ship," Jimmy replied.

"I'll give you a letter to take to the head of the Marine Cooks and Stewards Union and maybe he'll have a job for you. Go down there in the morning."

The next day Vieira went to the union hall and was issued his first "trip card," which permitted him to work one round trip on one ship in a single, specified job. Within hours he was onboard the *Malolo*, sailing through the Golden Gate toward the Pacific Ocean.

Vieira suddenly found himself living and working on the lower decks of an upstairs/downstairs, Depression-era world of passenger luxury. As the company's first modern liner, this "Flying Fish Queen" of the Matson fleet (*malolo* is the Hawaiian word for "flying fish," explained magazine ads) carried only first-class passengers—650 of them—who were housed on seven decks, the wealthiest guests enjoying one of sixteen luxury "lanai" suites, with a telephone in every room.

In the grand dining saloon of the *Malolo*, stewards seated guests at tables "laden with delicious fresh produce of tropic climes and sunny California," prepared by cooks and messmen in an up-to-date, all-electric galley. Two motion picture theaters made her the favorite liner of film stars who traveled from the Hollywood dream factory across "the path of dreams come true," said the ads, toward a white vacationer's paradise on the island of Oahu. At Honolulu's Aloha Tower, where the *Malolo* docked at the Matson pier, Matson's band, the Royal Hawaiians, serenaded new arrivals to the strains of "Aloha Oe" as they were escorted to Matson's tropical-pink hotels—the Moana and the Royal Hawaiian—located on the palm-lined beach at Waikiki.

"Scullion meant washing dishes," Jimmy Vieira explains. "I was very thin, and seventeen years old, and this seemed a mountainous job. The sea was rough—it was wintertime—and I was getting sick. I had to learn everything, start from scratch. We worked hard. When you were finished, you went back to your fo'c'sle, and if you could sleep, you went to sleep, and did the same thing the next day. At sea you don't have a day off, because there was only one crew member for each job. So if you happened to get sick—why then other people had to do your work, although they weren't paid extra. There was no such thing as overtime.

"The quarters we had," he says,

slept forty waiters, or room stewards, in one fo'c'sle. You had a bunk next to somebody else's. You had a locker by your bed, or far from your bed sometimes, and that's where you kept your things—throw your clothes in the locker or hang them near your bunk. In the *Malolo* the crew quarters were aft, below the water line, over the engine room. They had blowers aimed down from the upper deck and you got air that way. You had to get used to that—and the heat. If you set your shoes on the deck when you went to bed, in the morning they'd be curled up. The toes were meeting the heels from the heat!

It was frightful. I was young. I didn't realize that the quarters could be improved. It was very cruel at that time for the crew. But not for the profits of the company.

On his first day "pearl diving," as seamen call dishwashing, Vieira overheard men in the galley refer to each other as "girls."

"Why do you do that?" he asked them.

"Well, everybody does that," they said.

"I was flabbergasted," he tells me.

It was all new to me. But I suppose it was my destiny. I was extremely effeminate, so I fit the pattern well. I thought I was a girl, as a child. They called me Sissy Jim at school in Mendocino.

I didn't have any name yet, but most of them did. The cooks in the galley—one was named Hedy Lamarr. Ugliest person in the world! They were so funny. One of the cooks would say, "Hedy, come pick up this omelette before it gets cold!" or "Tell Hedy to bring over some more of that fruit!" And Hedy would do it, and nobody raised an eyelash. It was as natural as could be. Even the captain called him Hedy Lamarr!

Within hours Jim discovered that the *Malolo* was "full of gay people. The stewards department—everywhere. I can't say they were 100 percent, but say 65 to 70 percent gay, and everybody knew it! Nobody thought anything of it.

"I had never been around anybody like that," he tells me, "any queens. I didn't even know what the word meant. We didn't use the word 'gay.' No. It was girls' names. Or Miss. Or belle. Or queen. Or they'd give them theatrical names like Hedy Lamarr. That was the way it was on the ships."

"Did you have a girl's name?" I ask.

"I was Mimi, for a short while," he says, a little shy. "It didn't last, though. I was never teased on the ships for being effeminate," he's quick to add. "No, no, never! But I was taught by many not to be so effeminate. It was just natural to me so I had to learn how to hold my hand. Keep your hand in your pocket if you can, if you have to have the broken wrist. And lower your voice."

"Why?"

"Because they didn't want us running around like that. I wasn't even aware of it, but they made me aware of it. I had a great deal of good help on the ship. But in the galley, or in the dining room, when there weren't any passengers around, all the stewards had a girl's name.

"We were birds of a feather, you might say.

"The gay ones would have parties," he continues. "They'd get in drag and have a little show. That was on trips to Australia, but the quick runs to Hawaii and back they didn't have the time. On the Australian run the pace was slower."

"Everybody knew about the queens," he says. "If somebody was on the make for a certain person, and that person wasn't interested, he'd just say so. The word got around, 'Joe Blow is not interested. Forget him.' And that was the end of that.

"A lot of married men on the ships would maybe have a regular queen, use somebody's room. But on the Matson ships, we were so busy, we worked so hard, we didn't have much time for that, except to drink in the fo'c'sle when we finished work."

Among the stewards in the crew, he explains, "there wasn't any such thing as prejudice about that sort of thing. It was completely accepted. Nobody would think you were a lesser person because you were gay. They would ashore, but not on the ship. The reason we had to learn to tolerate each other was because we lived very closely. We slept only, say, three feet away from another person, or the berth right beside him. We had to get along. So we did."

"Why were so many queens on the big liners?" I ask.

"It was the way it had to be," he says. "The chairman of the board of the Matson company once said at a meeting that 'if it wasn't for the boys, who would we get to do that kind of work—to turn the beds down and lay out ladies' bed jackets and nightgowns? That's traditionally women's work. You can't expect longshoremen to do that.'

"There were gay cooks, too," Vieira adds, "gay bakers, gay butchers, gay everything. Porters, laundrymen—no, the laundrymen were usually Chinese. They weren't gay. But they'd scream with us anyway. Or just laugh."

At first, I'm delighted to hear Jim Vieira confirm that lots of queens worked on the Matson liners. The rumors, it seems, are true. But the more I listen to his stories, my delight begins to fade. A simple gay story about lots of queens working as stewards on the big ships is turning into a complicated story about men, women, and race. Queens worked on Matson liners, Vieira believes, because the company refused to hire women, and somebody had to do the "women's work," which a "real man" wouldn't do, so the queens did that work. African American men might have been allowed to perform the same personal service, as they did on the Alexander Boats and on Pullman sleeping cars on land, but the Matson Line didn't hire Negro men. Chinese men might have been allowed to do the same work, as they did in the stewards departments of the Dollar liners, but the Matson Line didn't hire Chinese men, except to work in the laundry rooms, where queens did not work because they were not Chinese. Longshoremen did not do stewards' work because they considered themselves real men, as did men who worked in the engine rooms and on the decks, which meant, on the West Coast docks and liners, that they were white men. Women's work, real men's work, white work, Negro work, Chinese work, queen's work: all isolated traps that, although they offered people work during an economic depression, kept them each in their separate places, too divided by their differences to help each other out of any predicament they might actually have in common.

When I ask Jimmy Vieira if he knows anything about what Frank McCormick did during the 1934 strike to build unity out of these divisions, he says, "Ask Stephen Blair. He can tell you."

. . . . . .

"A lot of our friends were queens."

Lillian Kaufman, a retired nurse who is recovering from a serious operation (she will pass away two years later), is talking to me from her bed, where she is lying against a bank of pillows. She's invited me to sit at the foot of her bed. I've placed my tape recorder on the blankets between us. Her daughter, Laura, also a nurse who is active in her union, is sitting on a chair nearby.

I've come to visit Mrs. Kaufman at her Seattle suburban home on this summer day in 1995 at the suggestion of Joe Doyle, a New York City maritime historian. He told me that Lillian and her husband, Sid, both worked on the *Lurline* and other luxury liners and were active in the Marine Cooks and Stewards Union. Some years ago, Joe had interviewed Lillian and Sid and three of their shipmates during a reunion at the Kaufman's home. They had reminisced together, he told me, about the queens who worked with them on the liners. Since then Sid has passed away, but Lillian, despite her difficult state of health, has agreed to tell whatever she can remember about working on the big ships.

Lillian Kaufman grew up working class and Catholic in Jersey City, New Jersey. She first met Sid in 1938, when he returned to New Jersey after fighting with the Abraham Lincoln Brigade in the Spanish Civil War. Lillian had become good friends with Sid's sister, who kept bragging about how wonderful he was. When they first met, they hit it off and, before long, married each other.

Sid first went to sea, he told his new wife, as a young teenager in the late 1920s, working as a cabin boy on Danish vessels. By the early 1930s he was employed in the stewards departments of luxury liners docked in Hoboken, including the *Leviathan*, on which he worked as a plate washer in the kosher galley alongside dozens of queens.

"The *Leviathan* had a working alleyway," he had told Joe Doyle, "it was a mile long!—called 'Broadway.' So the night before arrival in port, at eleven o'clock, the ship's bars and everything else are closed. All the waiters and room stewards—all the swishy ones—had gotten their tips from the passengers. And they would go in drag up and down Broadway, wearing these imported, flashy Japanese kimonos, and heavy hairdresses with combs in them, Spanish mantillas. That was a sight!"

In the 1940s the couple worked on the *Avalon* and *Catalina*, passenger ships that ferried tourists between the Los Angeles port of Wilmington and the resort hotels on Catalina Island—Sid as concession stand clerk, Lillian as ship's nurse. In 1952 they began working together on the *Lurline*.

"Do you remember working with any of the gay stewards?" I ask Lillian.

"Paul Boyles was a gay steward," she says. "Riff-Raff Rolfs was, too."

"Did you ever know Frank McCormick?"

"Yes, I knew Frank McCormick. He was a tall, skinny man. Fact of the matter is, I rented him my apartment when I left San Francisco, and he lost half my stuff. We figured we'd be back in a year, but it didn't work out that way. Frank got discouraged and went off to sea. It was a furnished place, and whatever we left just got lost.

"I knew about William Brandhove. He was a rather vicious one. He tried to implicate homosexuals and in a very bad way."

"How did he do that?"

"Making accusations against them."

Her replies to my questions get shorter as Lillian begins to tire. So we break for lunch—bowls of Campbell's tomato soup that Laura prepares for us and serves on a card table she sets up in the bedroom for her mother's comfort.

When lunch is over and the table is cleared, Laura, to my delight, carries a box into the room and from it spreads out unorganized piles of Sid's letters and photographs that we begin to explore together.

"You look in these envelopes," Lillian says, "and you find things down in the bottom that you don't think are there at all."

"This has a list of ships," says Laura, "and years, but I don't know if it means anything."

"It was the ships he was on," says her mother.

We take turns reading the document out loud.

"SHIPS. ONE: *S.S. Baymead*, 1934," I begin.

"And the *Leviathan*, 1934," Lillian says.

"THREE was *S.S. Ancon*, 1934–35," I continue. "FOUR is *S.S. President Hayes*, 1935–36. FIVE is *S.S. President Wilson*, 1936–37. SIX is *S.S. Monroe*, 1939. SEVEN is *S.S. Manhattan*, 1940. EIGHT is *S.S. Texas*, 1940. NINE is *S.S. Panama*, 1940."

During the war, Lillian says, Sid worked as a steward on the *Lurline* after it was converted to a troop ship in San Francisco.

"We used to watch from Coit Tower," she says, "looking for the *Lurline* coming in. The wives who had husbands on it used to call each other when they saw it coming. They wouldn't mention the name of the ship because of the warning: Loose Lips Sink Ships. They'd just say, 'Your husband's home,' and you'd know."

We start looking through the letters.

"Here's the '36 maritime strike," Lillian says.

"Here he's writing about Bill Rolfs," I say. "That's Ted Rolfs."

"Riff-Raff," she translates.

"Did you know Riff-Raff?"

"Sure. He's a very nice guy."

"He died a couple of years ago," I tell her.

Lillian picks up the pile of photographs. There are pictures of Sid's ships, his family members, and press photos from the Marine Cooks and Stewards Union. Among them I see a familiar face.

"That's Frank McCormick and Sid together!" I exclaim.

The two friends are standing outside the MCS union hall on Pearl Street in New York City. It's during World War II, because there's another shot of them inside the same hall, with a calendar on the wall showing "September 1944." And there's another photo of the two of them inside the office, posing at their desks.

Lillian, Laura, and I spend the afternoon looking through more letters and photos, which Lillian lends me so I can make copies for my research and to donate to the maritime archives in New York City. As I'm getting ready to leave, after I've packed up my notebook and tape recorder, Lillian has one more thing to tell me.

"Gay men went to sea," she explains, "because they could find equality there."

"I remember Frank McCormick."

On this bright, February afternoon in 1997, I've come to Miriam Johnson's house atop one of the many winding streets in San Francisco's Bernal Heights. We're sitting at her kitchen table, where she serves me a supper of home-baked bread, mashed potatoes, and meatloaf with ketchup—one of my favorite dishes, I tell her.

"I didn't know Frank that well," she says, as I struggle to hide my disappointment. "I remember his appearance. He was grey-haired. If I could draw him—but I can't draw, you know."

"I could show you a photo," I say, hoping it will spark memories.

"Is he dead?"

"Yeah, he died in the '70s."

"Jesus Christ, they're all dead."

Miriam Johnson is acutely aware that, having been only fifteen in 1934, she is one of the few participants in the longshoremen's strike who is still alive. In that year, she spent her days and nights at the kitchen table listening to lively debates among the bohemians, leftists, and militant seamen her mother invited into their O'Farrell Street apartment.

"My mother housed everybody," she tells me. "There were nights when I had no place to sleep. Homeless kids from the boxcars would come over to take a bath. She would walk miles so she could buy five-cent groceries and cook meals for them. I ironed clothes for them. I didn't know what the word 'lonely' meant. For me to be alone now, and I am terribly alone now, it's very hard. Our house was full of people."

Among the radicals who gathered at the kitchen table was a young seaman, Harold Johnson, who would later become her husband and from whom she is now separated but still a close friend.

"Harold was one of those men—the clean, beautiful seaman."

The talk was mostly about politics and union organizing. How to replace the company-run longshoremen's union with one more democratic. How to make the Marine Workers Industrial Union, formed by members of the Communist Party, a racially integrated alternative to the whites-only seamen's unions. White communists, it seems, were among the few white people working to integrate the waterfront.

"I was very young," Miriam tells me, "I didn't know the issues. I was just terribly excited."

Miriam can't remember if Frank McCormick ever came to their home. But his name makes her recall that he was an important leader in a union she now thinks of as gay. "In the Marine Cooks and Stewards," she says, "it was no question about the femininity, the homosexuality, the talk, the conversation, the appearance, the gestures, the stories they told you. There were an awful lot of gay guys. I mean, openly gay guys. The *Lurline* crew, the *Mariposa*, the *Monterey*, and some of the President ships of the Dollar Line, were heavily gay, and that was clear. Most of the big ships that required better waiters, more elegant service, and people who knew more about being charming and stuff like that. Go to a fancy restaurant. Aren't the waiters gay?"

"Still!" I laugh.

"It would've been nice to have seen one woman there, by the way" she adds. "There were no women at all."

"In the more blue-collar unions," she continues, referring to the deck-hands, firemen, and longshoremen, "these guys were too masculine for you to get the idea about them. But you knew that some had lovers. Or that they pursued guys, or that they were attracted to guys. You didn't call them gay. It didn't have the same connotation as in the Marine Cooks and Stewards, who were clearly and openly gay, see? But you knew. Just as I knew about Bill Caves."

"Caves?" I ask.

"Oh, Bill Caves!" she says. "'Butch queen'—that's what queens on the ships called men like him. There was nothing effeminate about him. He was very tough. His knuckles were all broken and he could tell you the date and type of battle in which he broke each one. I mean, he was the epitome of the tough deckman, you know?"

I can't believe Miriam actually knew Bill Caves. I'd heard his name mentioned as a gay merchant seamen and union activist, but he died years ago without leaving any record, it seems, of what he had accomplished.

"Can you tell me what you remember about Bill Caves?" I ask.

"As a matter of fact," Miriam says, "my husband was shipmates with him on the *President Hoover*. It was the first ship to hit port after the longshoremen went on strike on May 9th, 1934. The seamen's strike committee began at our house with Caves there. We were very fond of him. He told great stories. Nervous. A very colorful man, very hell-bent on the strike. I don't know what happened to him. As the seamen got more involved in the strike, they left the little confines of my mother's kitchen.

"Now Caves drove my husband crazy," she confides, "because he kept making overtures to him."

"What do you mean?"

"During the strike Harold went home to see his mother in Seattle. He was sleeping and his mother came in and kissed him and he landed a punch on her."

"On his mother?"

"Sent her flying across the room—a tiny little woman—because he thought she was Bill coming on to him again!

"Harold had quite a bit of experience with that," Miriam adds. "He was very sought-after by men because he was quite handsome—a boyish, beautiful, Icelandic man. Brown-eyed, and light brown hair, not fair but not dark. Sun-kissed. I can't tell you that he always fought it off!" she laughs. "He would certainly not tell me. He might tell you more. I'll call him to see if he'll speak to you."

· · · · · ·

Harold Johnson, who in his late eighties lives north of San Francisco in Sebastopol, can talk on the phone for only a few minutes—throat cancer (which will take his life a year after we talk) makes it hard for him to speak. But, he says, he enjoys his memories of the old days. I ask him if he can tell me what it was like to work on the Dollar liners before the big strike of 1934.

He was twenty-one in 1932 when he first went to sea, he says, working as a deckhand, ordinary seaman, on the *President Grant*. He and other white seamen were being hired on the docks of Seattle and San Francisco by shipping masters who gave preference to members of the company-run Waterfront Employers' Union, which blacklisted union activists. The Dollar liners served passengers who made up what Johnson calls the "Oriental trade"—Christian missionaries and businessmen traveling between the United States and Asian ports—along with white vacationers on round-the-world cruises. Most of the stewards on the *President Grant* had been Chinese men hired by Dollar "out of Canton through Hong Kong," he says, but by the time he came aboard, the company was finally following government orders to replace the Chinese men in the crew with white American citizens like himself, who were being given job preferences during the Depression. The awful working conditions on Dollar Line ships so angered Johnson that he risked his job by starting to talk union with his shipmates. He even joined the tiny but militant Marine Workers Industrial Union (MWIU).

"It was all reds," he says of the MWIU, "mostly white men, but a few Filipino, Chinese, and black seamen." These men, who were hired during white strikes as scabs, were excluded from the Sailors' Union of the Pacific, whose membership was all white.

In the fall of 1933, Harold Johnson started working on the Dollar's newest luxury liner, the *President Hoover*, where he became buddies with a ship-mate, Bill Caves—a fellow deckhand, able-bodied seaman, who was old enough to be his father.

Caves was "a good hand on ships," Johnson tells me, "a real tough character, built like a football player." Caves had a "lot of savvy" about the ways of rank-and-file seamen. He was also "a homosexual," Harold adds, "completely obsessed with me, for one. Drove me nuts. He was after me all the time.

"There was always somebody homosexual on the Dollar ships," Harold Johnson adds. "It's all men in the fo'c'sle, sailing together all the time. Sort of life that attracts homosexuals."

No Race-Baiting, Red-Baiting, or Queer-Baiting!
The Marine Cooks and Stewards
Union from the Depression to the Cold War

As he did with his research on passing women, gay bathhouses, and World War II, Bérubé put together a lecture illustrated with slides that he gave dozens of times around the country. This version of his talk on the Marine Cooks and Stewards Union provides an overview of the project. Its title suggests perhaps the key lesson that he extracted from this history: that solidarity across lines of difference is possible and necessary. Here was a working-class union that was multiracial, multiethnic, queer-inflected, and politically radical. In the Depression, its members drew strength from the unity they forged in the struggle to improve wages and working conditions.

The *Lurline* is about to embark on her maiden voyage from San Francisco to Honolulu. Among her passengers is William P. Roth, the president of the Matson shipping line. He's accompanied by his wife, Lurline Matson Roth, after whom the ship is named, and their twin teenage daughters. Joining them are other business executives, government officials and their families, and society women and teenage debutantes. On later voyages many celebrities also sail on the *Lurline* to Hawaii—Amelia Earhart, Shirley Temple, George Burns, and Gracie Allen. As the Roths and other passengers walk up the gangway, they can see longshoremen down below busily loading their trunks along with the ship's supplies.

The *Lurline* is the queen of the Matson Company's new quartet of luxury liners. Her sister ships are the *Mariposa*, the *Malolo*, and the *Monterey*—the grandest American passenger liners sailing the Pacific Ocean. They have been nicknamed the "white ships" because their hulls are painted a dazzling white that makes them stand out with a "gleaming radiance" on the blue Pacific waters.

Text of a lecture with slides, 1996.

MCSU member Scotty Ballard. Courtesy of the Allan Bérubé Collection at the GLBTHS, San Francisco.

The Matson liners also stand out with another kind of whiteness. The purser and the rest of the service staff who politely greet the Roth family, carry their luggage, and lead them along the corridors to their first-class suites are white men and boys. So are the longshoremen and the officers and crew of the ship. These workers are white because Mr. Roth's policy is to hire only white men. The maritime unions have their own "whites only" policies, too.

It's noon—departure time. The last of the *Lurline*'s 700 passengers has come aboard. The *Lurline* slides out from Pier 32 to begin her long voyage to the Hawaiian Islands, the South Seas, and Asia. In travel brochures and magazine ads, the Matson Company has constructed a colorful fantasy world in which smiling Hawaiian women and men invite white tourists to their islands, which Matson partly owns and which the United States has colonized as its territory. Matson dominates the entire Hawaiian tourist trade—from the piers in San Francisco to the Royal Hawaiian Hotel on the beach at Waikiki.

Mr. Roth is gambling that there are still enough people with money during the Depression to pay for the expensive luxury cruises that will make his new ocean liners profitable. The round-trip fare for a two-week cruise starts at $250. A lanai suite, with its private, glass-enclosed deck opening out on the sea, costs up to $2,400. His gamble is paying off. Even these luxurious lanai suites were sold out months ago.

This maiden voyage of the *Lurline* is reserved for first-class passengers. Their "A" deck deluxe suites have two double bedrooms, a living room, maid's room, dressing room, and private bath. Passengers swim in outdoor pools, play tennis, shoot clay pigeons, enjoy deck games, and exercise in the gymnasium. As they play, they're entertained by hula dancers and Hawaiian ukulele singers. They lounge in deck chairs or relax in the Veranda Cafe while they sip pineapple cocktails. They eat dinner in the grand, air-conditioned dining room, where waiters seat them at intimate tables, then hand them menus covered with sensual paintings of native Hawaiians. After dinner, passengers move to the dance pavilion, where they sway long into the night to the strains of Hawaiian melodies played by Hawaiian musicians. Some couples wander onto the decks for romantic moonlit strolls in the warm Pacific air.

"Here is every aspect of luxurious living," promises Matson's travel brochure. "And naturally the service is just as impeccable as the whole conception of this maritime existence."

Far below deck, where passengers never go, the stewards who provide this impeccable service are living a very different "maritime existence." Most of the 350 members of the *Lurline*'s crew work in the stewards department. They are usually all men but occasionally two or three women work as nurses or stewardesses. Many stewards will never see the light of day while the *Lurline* is at sea because they are forced to live and work below the waterline with no portholes or fresh air. They sleep in hot, cramped quarters they call the "glory hole" or "Black Hole of Calcutta." Stewards who work in the suites, dining rooms, and decks are painfully aware of the sharp contrast between their own cramped, unhealthy quarters and the passengers' luxurious accommodations on the decks directly above them.

Mr. Roth's company requires his stewards to work up to sixteen hours per day, seven days a week, with no overtime pay and often no time off in port. He pays a messman $6 a week. Under these conditions, Mr. Roth expects his stewards to greet passengers with a smile, carry their bags, manage the front desk, wait on passengers in the dining room and on the decks, deliver room service, organize deck games, serve the drinks, cook the meals, wash the dishes and pots and pans, feed the crew, make the beds and put away the clothes and linens, run the elevators, work the telephone switchboard, nurse the passengers who get seasick, cut and style their hair, and give massages.

The stewards do the work that's expected of them. The few who serve passengers directly can sometimes receive good tips.

But at night, when the stewards finally stumble below deck to sleep in their crowded "glory holes" hidden away like cargo in the hold, their muscles ache from having spent their day climbing up and down the steep architecture of the liner's social classes. Sitting on their hammocks and bunks, they "dish" the passengers, their supervisors, and the shipowners. Matson calls the luxury liners "floating hotels." But the stewards call their quarters "floating tenements"—nothing but slums for the crew.

"There were forty waiters in one glory hole," Jim Vieira, a former steward, tells me. "We were sleeping above the engine room. If you set your shoes on the deck when you went to bed, in the morning they'd be curled up. The toes were meeting the heels from the heat." As a teenager, Jim Vieira went to sea on the Matson liners as a scullion washing dishes in the galley. Then he quickly worked his way above deck as a first-class room steward, serving the ship's wealthiest passengers. His service is so good that the Roths choose him to be their personal room steward whenever they sail to Hawaii.

On his first trip out, young Jim Vieira notices something queer among the stewards. "In the galley," he recalls, "or in the dining room, when there weren't any passengers around, all the stewards called each other by girls' names—Miss this and Miss that." When he gets up the nerve to ask them why they did this, they say, "Why, doesn't everybody do it?" "Well," he realizes, "I guess I must be a girl, too!" So that's how Vieira discovers that there are lots of other gay teenagers and men like him on the liners. They watch over him and teach him how to survive within the strict social order of the big ships at sea.

The cooks and stewards are at the bottom of the crew's social hierarchy. On top are the masters and mates (the captain and his officers), who have the authority to give orders and discipline the crew. In the middle are the firemen in the engine department, or "black gang" (because they are covered in soot and grease), and the sailors, or "deckhands," in the deck department. Firemen and sailors do the traditional "manly" work. The stewards do what is stereotyped as the "women's work" or "colored work"—the personal service and the housekeeping. They are the ship's servants and domestic workers.

Some stewards' jobs are also stereotyped as "queer work"—activities that gay men are supposed to be especially good at. Stewards doing queer work on Matson's floating hotels are the pastry chefs, waiters, bedroom stewards, pursers, wine stewards, florists, hairdressers, and telephone operators. Although anybody can work these jobs, many of the stewards doing queer work are, in fact, gay men.

This is no secret, even in the 1930s. "It was never, never hidden," Jim Vieira tells me. "I can't say the stewards were 100 percent gay," he says, "but say 65 percent to 70 percent—and everybody knew it!" Rumor has it that the Matson Company likes to employ gay stewards on its ships. A Matson official once told Vieira that "if it wasn't for the boys, who else would we get to do that kind of women's work—to turn down the beds and lay out ladies' nightgowns?" What the Matson official also meant was "What other white men are we going to get who'll do this colored work on our all-white crews?"

So many of the stewards on the Matson liners are gay that the ships themselves earn queer nicknames among seamen. They call the *Lurline* the "Queer-line," the *Matsonia* the "Fruit-sonia," and the *Mariposa* the "Mary-posa" or "Fairy-posa." Crewmen on freighters call Matson's white liners the "fruit boats" or the "fruit ships." "I had nothing but contempt for the guys on the passenger ships," recalled Charlie Rubin, who worked the freighters. "A lot of the guys didn't act natural when passengers were around. They'd get all 'perfumed up' and worry about how they looked." This kind of contempt was known among stewards as "queer-baiting" or "queen-baiting."

Gay stewards preferred to call themselves "queens." Queens are open, daring, and know how to take care of themselves. "Queer" is not their word. It is hurled at them from the *outside* to insult them. As in "You goddam fruit queer!" But "queen" is respectful *inside* talk. "When you liked them," explains Pete Brownlee, a straight waiter who worked on the Matson liners, "you called them a queen." "A real queen," Jim Vieira explains to me, is always "stately and respected."

On some ships there are queens who reign supreme. Manuel Cabral, known as the Honolulu Queen, is an outrageous, acid-tongued, Portuguese Hawaiian waiter on the Matson liners. Straight seamen are careful never to cross him. Pete Brownlee warns that Cabral was "an out and out queen but you'd never fuck with that guy. He'd beat the shit out of you."

Many other tough queens are on the ships. There's Miss MacDonald, and Mother Shannon, and Miss Effie, and Miss Leprosy, and Grace Line Gertie, and Madame Queen, and the African Queen, and many, many more. In private, queens and other gay men call each other "waitresses" or "steward-esses" and address each other as union "sisters" as well as union "brothers." "We didn't use the word 'gay,'" Jim Vieira says. "No, it was girls' names, or 'Miss'—Miss Cook, Miss McCormick, Miss Blair. Or they'd give them theatrical names—Hedy Lamarr and names like that. The ugliest one of all was called Hedy Lamarr. The captain even called him Hedy Lamarr! It was 'Get her!' and 'Tell your sister come pick up those eggs!' and 'Tell Hedy to bring over some more of that fruit!'—that sort of thing."

New stewards learn how to live with the queens or they don't last very long. "The reason that we had to tolerate each other," Vieira explains to me, "was because we lived very closely. We *had* to get along. So we did." Generally, queens camp it up only in the crew sections of a liner—the galley, the glory hole, and the alleyways. "When they were around the passengers, they knew not to flitter and flutter," explains John Cremona, another straight steward.

Sometimes the camping turns into a drag show. Stewards on the *Mariposa* put on costume and drag during the seamen's ritual known as "crossing the line" or "Neptune's Party"—an initiation for greenhorns crossing the equator for the first time. Stewards from the *Lurline* did drag as a benefit show for orphans in Hawaii.

Occasionally the flamboyant camping in the crew areas of the liners becomes so ordinary that it spills out into the dining rooms. "The passengers would overhear us call out for Hedy," Vieira tells me, "and they'd laugh, and say, 'Why do they call that waiter Hedy?' 'Why,' we'd say, 'it's because he's Hedy *Lamarr*! There's another Hedy Lamarr who's an actress, but that's not the one we mean. This is the *real* Hedy, here.' And the passengers would laugh and laugh and laugh. But see, passengers were eager to laugh, anyway. After all, it was a holiday—at least for *them*."

But most of the time the passengers don't know about the gaiety that's going on below them. Nor do they overhear the stewards complaining about their inhumane living and working conditions. Even among themselves, stewards have to be careful about talking union, because Mr. Roth and his fellow shipowners will fire any union organizers in the crew. The cooks and stewards union, which once tried to improve wages and conditions, is now weak and can't protect them from being fired. They and other West Coast seamen's unions lost a major strike in 1921. They lost their hiring hall, too, and their wages fell; living and working conditions worsened, and union membership declined. Stewards and other seamen are now hired by agents off the dock in what waterfront workers call "shape-ups"—you bribe the agent to get and keep your job. Seamen have no minimum wage and no right to strike. They are temporary workers who don't make enough money to get married and support a family—only 7 percent of all seamen are married. Many are not U.S. citizens. They're often treated as social outcasts, as riff-raff, as trash. And they are always at the shipowners' mercy.

Not every Pacific liner has a totally white crew. The Dollar Steamship Line, which owns more ships than any other U.S. company, competes with

Matson for the Asian trade. R. Stanley Dollar, the company's president, is known for hiring seamen in China at one-third the pay that white American stewards get. This increases his profits while keeping his crews racially divided so they can't organize. When the Matson Company hires Asian stewards at all, they have to work in the laundry room and sleep in their own quarters. This divide-and-conquer strategy works. Shipowners exploit Chinese workers, while white unions attack them, sometimes with violence.

The Marine Cooks and Stewards Union—like nearly all unions on the West Coast—has built its solidarity on excluding Asian workers from its ranks. They formed their union in 1901 to protect themselves from what their constitution called "competition from alien and inferior races." Even Chinese American stewards were not allowed to become union members. On the West Coast, union meant white and male. This openly racist magazine, *The White Man*—which was "Devoted to the Movement for the Exclusion of Asiatics"—was endorsed by virtually every labor council west of the Rockies. ("The Chinese Must Go!" was the battle cry of unions as well as politicians.)

Chinese stewards are caught in the middle between white shipowners and white unions. You can search the English-language newspapers and rarely find Chinese American stewards speaking up in public to protest either union attacks or shipowner exploitation. Who would listen to them if they did raise their voices? And outside of their own communities, who would stand with them to defend them?

By 1933, Revels Cayton has been a steward on West Coast ships since he was fourteen. But neither the Matson nor the Dollar Line will hire him or other black stewards to work on their liners. Cayton is the grandson of Hiram Revels of Mississippi, who, after Reconstruction, was the first black United States senator. For years Revels Cayton had sailed on the *H. F. Alexander* and other Alexander liners. In the 1920s and '30s, these ships carried passengers up and down the West Coast. Cayton went to work at sea because the Alexander ships did hire black workers in the stewards departments. He started out as a telephone operator, then worked his way up as a bellhop and finally as a waiter.

African American stewards were allowed to work on the Alexander ships only one year before Cayton came aboard. The door opened to them in 1921, when the white seamen went out on strike. The shipping company punished the white strikers by hiring black strikebreakers to replace them. For years, strikebreaking had been a form of black protest against racist union policies that excluded them. White strikes meant more black jobs. When white seamen lost the strike, the Alexander ships kept the black stewards, at lower pay, as insurance against future strikes by white unions. These newly employed stewards formed an association, financed by the shipowners, that was in reality a company union. In return, the black stewards agreed to stay away from the real unions. Revels Cayton first got his job on the Alexander ships through this company union, which demanded payoffs in return for jobs. During the Depression, these are among the few "good" jobs that give economic stability to many families in the small African American communities of Seattle, San Francisco, and Oakland.

The white cooks and stewards working for Matson have the best working conditions on any West Coast liners. Hiring agents tell them they are lucky to be working at all. But they're still angry about their worsening conditions and scared to death of being fired for organizing. They know that all across North America, millions of less-fortunate men and women are out of work, barely able to survive. They feel powerless, and they appear to be hopelessly divided. Race against race. Normal against queer. Officers against unlicensed personnel. Radicals against those who won't rock the boat. Racial hostility, queen-baiting, and union-busting keep their divisions wide open and raw, and keep alive their fear of losing what little they have.

But below a deceptively calm surface, there's a sea change taking shape. You can see signs of it on some of the ships and in the ports. Take the Alexander ships. Black stewards are segregated, but they're building community on their ships and developing their own leaders. Some are making connections across the differences among them that offer them a way out of their difficult situations.

The stewards working on the Alexander ships spend most of their time away from friends and families. So they decide to use San Francisco's only newspaper for African Americans, the *Spokesman*, to write a weekly gossip column to let their home communities know how they're doing. Their column is called "Up and Down the Pacific Coast."

"Hello there, friends, enemies and acquaintances!" writes Till B. Toms in their first column. He's writing as if he's broadcasting a radio show. "You are listening to the *H. F. Alexander*, where nearly one hundred of our boys are beating the rap of the depression. At the close of the day all gather like one big family in their social hall. Plenty wise cracks keep us all happy even if the Depresh is on. Brotherly love still exists [among us]."

Some of the stewards on the Alexander ships are gay men. Revels Cayton tells me he worked with at least five or six gay crew members, mostly room stewards and waiters. He recalls only their nicknames: Bumblebee the janitor, Heavyhead the waiter. At times the stewards' correspondent to the *Spokesman* makes little jokes about fairies, as if they were an ordinary part of life. "Hello kind friends," he opens his column one week. "We are just entering the old home town of Seattle where men are men, women are women, and fairies carry tales."

The *Spokesman* is so popular that it becomes the unofficial newspaper for the stewards on all the Alexander ships. Its young black editor, John Pittman, has just finished graduate school in economics at the University of California at Berkeley, where he's written his dissertation on the Negro and the labor unions. His friend poet Langston Hughes, who himself worked as a steward on East Coast ships, does poetry readings to benefit the *Spokesman*. John Pittman supports a strong, left-wing union for the cooks and stewards. He also supports homosexuals. He even says so in his paper.

One day the stewards on the Alexander ships open their copies of the *Spokesman* to find an editorial by Pittman entitled "PREJUDICE AGAINST HOMOSEXUALS." This is what they read:

"In Berkeley a fortnight ago, a group of young men entertained themselves. Some wore female attire; some danced and talked as women do. All acted naturally and without restraint. They enjoyed the occasion and returned to their homes, their loved ones, or their work.

"Members of the community," Pittman warned, were making fun of "this ordinary occurrence in the lives of human beings. Both race prejudice and the prejudice against homosexuals make life in this world a living hell for men and women whose only crime is that of being DIFFERENT from the majority. . . . Both of these attitudes stink of bigotry. . . .

"This is no plea for sympathy for the homosexual," Pittman explained. "To sympathize with a person because he or she happens to be homosexual is as little appreciated and as much insulting as to sympathize with a Negro for being Black. What Negroes and homosexuals both desire is to be regarded as human beings with the rights and liberties of human beings, including the right to be let alone, to enjoy life in the way most agreeable and pleasant, to live secure from interference and insult."

John Pittman's plea for the black community to fight prejudice against homosexuals is way ahead of his time. He's making connections between union activism, racial equality, and the rights of homosexuals that few people make even today. As the stewards on the Alexander ships open their copies of the *Spokesman* and read Pittman's open defense of homosexuals, are they making the same connections? Are they talking about this with each other?

. . . . . .

When the Matson Company launches the *Lurline* in 1933, Revels Cayton is no longer working on the Alexander ships. The company union won't let him sail anymore because he's joined the Communist Party. So Cayton is hanging around the waterfront learning to organize his fellow unemployed workers. His dream is to organize the black seamen into a real union. In port cities from coast to coast, other left-wing maritime workers, many of them communists, some of them gay, are organizing, too. They're publishing anonymous newspapers with ideas that could get them thrown off the ships, too. It was "an underground movement of wonderful left-wingers," recalled Ted Rolfs, a gay left-wing steward who was nicknamed Riff-Raff Rolfs. "These guys were so inspiring in their objective," he said, "which was to create a new union of the rank and file and make it democratic." Slowly but steadily, the sea change that's been swelling in the lower depths is rising to the surface, and now it's about to make waves.

. . . . . .

It's June 1933. President Roosevelt is signing the National Industrial Recovery Act (NIRA). He's doing this after months of debate in Congress and despite the strong opposition of big business. He calls the NIRA a new "covenant" among employers, workers, and government that will bring the country out of the Depression.

Today a new era begins for American workers, a "New Deal for Labor." The law Roosevelt is signing guarantees their right to organize and bargain collectively. It protects them from being fired for joining a union. It ends employer attacks on union organizing drives and union elections. It paves the way for a minimum wage and maximum hours. And it bans company unions. Or so it reads on paper.

A few weeks later President Roosevelt goes on the air to tell the nation why he's signed this law. As cooks and stewards, along with millions of other Americans, turn on their radios, it's as if the president is talking directly to them about the troubles they've had with the shipowners.

"It is obvious," Roosevelt tells them, "that without united action a few selfish men . . . will pay starvation wages and insist on long hours of work. . . . We have seen the result of action of that kind in the continuing descent into the economic hell of the past four years. . . . [But now] the workers of this country have rights under this law which cannot be taken from them, and nobody will be permitted to whittle them away. . . . The whole country will be united to get them for you."

Merchant seamen are stunned at what they hear. The president is actually promising them that the federal government will defend their right to organize into unions so they can stop the shipowners from exploiting them. The government seems to be on their side. United Mineworkers president John L. Lewis, who helped write the law, puts it more bluntly. "The president wants you to organize!" he tells workers who aren't yet in unions. Within weeks the most dramatic wave of labor organizing in U.S. history sweeps the nation. On the ships and waterfronts, rank-and-file seamen and longshoremen begin to take over their weak and corrupt unions. They're even talking about going out on strike.

. . . . . .

Equality was in the air we breathed.
—*Mickey Blair*, steward

The *Monterey* has returned to San Francisco from a cruise in the South Pacific. The crew has heard rumors that a strike is under way on the West Coast. When Jim Vieira and other stewards walk down the *Monterey*'s gangway onto the Matson pier, they see strikers marching back and forth along the waterfront, so they too join the picket line. "It was all new to me," Jim Vieira tells me. "I [was young.] I didn't realize that the [conditions] could be improved. We *had* to win that strike."

While the *Monterey* had been out at sea, the longshoremen's union had gone out on strike for union recognition, decent wages, and their own hiring hall. The seamen's unions, including the Marine Cooks and Stewards, had decided to join them. Together they are now shutting down all shipping on the West Coast. As more ships come into port and more crews walk off, the strike spreads. Before long, a hundred vessels are tied up in San Francisco Bay, including the Matson white liners, the Dollar liners, and the Alexander ships.

Anchored in the bay is a scab ship set up by the Dollar Line to house the strikebreakers. Shipowner agents are trying to recruit unemployed black men as strikebreakers again, trying to turn race against race to break this strike. It worked in 1921, and they're sure it'll work now.

But this time the longshoremen are wise to these divide-and-conquer tactics. They take the lead and, for the first time, open their union to black workers. The Marine Cooks and Stewards Union (MCS) does the same thing. Like sister ships, the longshoremen and the stewards are becoming sister unions—both of them left-wing and both dedicated to racial equality. And now, for the first time, leaders of the black community call for black workers not to break this strike but instead to work with white unions to win it.

Revels Cayton goes down to the Alexander ships to talk to the stewards. He tells them they can't survive in a company union and their only hope is to join the MCS. Many are skeptical and torn. Cayton is a fellow steward, but the company union has kicked him off the ships as an open communist. The company union opposes the strike, but the stewards' adopted newspaper, the *Spokesman*, supports it. Many black stewards decide not to scab this time, but they stay off the picket lines. They want proof that the white union's talk about racial equality will turn into action. But other black stewards do join the white pickets. They stand together against police and get arrested together, too. Some Chinese American, Filipino, and Japanese American stewards decide to join the picket lines with them.

For these stewards of color, the idea of solidarity with white workingmen is a huge act of faith. They are staking their futures on the outside chance that if white unions win this strike, white men will treat them as equals and come to their defense when they are attacked. Nothing in their experience tells them they can trust the white unions to do this. Racism is still alive on the waterfront, even on the picket lines. But they are taking the risk anyway.

The Marine Cooks and Stewards Union sets up strike kitchens on all the waterfronts. In San Francisco, the "Maritime Palace" kitchen serves 15,000 meals a day to strikers. Among the men preparing and serving the meals are black stewards from the Alexander ships and Asian stewards from the Dollar Line ships. Gay stewards of many races are also working in the strike kitchens.

Take Jay Shannon, a 300-pound Irish American cook. The men call him "Mother Shannon," not only because he is gay but, as one straight steward puts it, "it was a sign of respect when he got over fifty." In Los Angeles, Mother Shannon sets up his own donut stand at the soup kitchen. So the guys coming off the picket line in the morning would be treated to Jay and his crew of queens making fresh donuts for them. Over the donut stand Mother Shannon hangs a sign that reads, "Famous up and down this coast, Jay Shannon and his Fluffy Duffy Donuts!"

The worst day of the 1934 strike is on July 5, when the shipowners use force to reopen the port of San Francisco. When police approach the picket line and the strikers refuse to leave, police shoot tear gas and bullets into the crowds, hitting bystanders as well as strikers. All along the waterfront, fighting breaks out between strikers and police. "Blood ran red in the streets of San Francisco yesterday," one reporter writes in the *Chronicle*. "One thousand embattled police held at bay five thousand longshoremen and their sympathizers. . . . The furies of street warfare raged for hour piled on hour. Hundreds were injured or badly gassed. Two were dead, one was dying, 32 others shot and more than three score sent to hospitals." The strikers call this day Bloody Thursday.

The two strikers whom the police shot in the back and killed were Howard Sperry, a longshoreman, and Nicholas Bordoise, a cook. The Marine Cooks and Stewards Union adopts Bordoise as one of their own. After the men's bodies are taken away, strikers chalk a memorial border around the huge blood stain and paint the words "POLICE MURDER" on the sidewalk where the men were killed. Longshoremen guard the memorial while people come by with offerings of flowers and support.

Some of the mourners that day see a short, Portuguese Hawaiian man, a member of the Marine Cooks and Stewards Union, moving back and forth on the sidewalk, keeping the flowers in order. This is Manuel Cabral, the Honolulu Queen, paying his respects to his two slain union brothers by arranging and tending the flowers along the street.

Three days later, on a Sunday afternoon, the city of San Francisco stops to honor the two men killed on Bloody Thursday. Tens of thousands of union men and women march in a silent procession from the waterfront up Market Street. At this nearly all-white event, black workingmen stay around the edges of the crowd. Harry Hay, a white gay communist who is in town with his lover to support the strikers, stands on the sidelines, too, watching in awe. "As the two flag-covered caissons passed," he remembers, accompanied by the slow beat of drums, "a posse of dockworkers knocked the bowlers off the heads of bankers who refused to show respect. . . . You couldn't have been a part of that," Harry Hay recalls, "and not have your life completely changed."

After the funeral, nearly all San Francisco unions, in solidarity with the maritime workers, go out in a general strike that shuts down the city and most of the West Coast. With this support, the longshoremen win their demands. Two years later, the seamen win their demands in a strike supported by longshoremen. Their victories are part of a wave of union organizing in which hundreds of strikes take the country by storm. Millions of women, people of color, industrial workers, and tenant farmers are organizing for the first time. General strikes, sit-down strikes, lockouts and walkouts, spontaneous wildcat strikes and job actions dominate the news. Union membership more than triples from 3 million to 9 million members in just a few years. Many in power are beginning to fear that a working-class revolution is about to take over the United States.

Finally, the stewards' lives are beginning to improve. Their wages go up, and now they are paid for overtime. And they're finally making enough money to get married and support a family. But most of all they have their own hiring hall. They, and not shape-up bosses, have the power to hire crews for each ship, and they choose them based on seniority, not on payoffs.

The hundreds of black stewards on the Alexander ships have left the company union en masse and joined the Marine Cooks and Stewards Union. "New lines were beginning to develop in our union," Revels Cayton later recalled. "The long struggle for Negro and white unity was on." The Chinese stewards on the Dollar ships are allowed to join the union, too. But these workers don't have equality yet. So now they're figuring out ways to educate their white union brothers.

At one joint meeting of the maritime unions, a Chinese American steward stands up and dares to criticize the white unions for their racist treatment of Chinese workers. He's Ben Fee, a communist who shares an apartment in San Francisco's Chinatown with his friend, Revels Cayton. Here's what Ben Fee tells the white seamen: "'The Chinese Must Go!' has long been the war-cry of many oldtime labor leaders. They blamed Chinese workers instead of the employers for their starvation wages. After the 1934 strike," he continues, "thanks to the rising strength of the militant rank and file, Chinese workers were given a chance to join the unions. But we are still forced to work for the Dollar Line, which fires us when they discover that we are union members. We call on every fair-minded union man to protest and smash such racial discrimination. Demand equal shipping rights for every union member, regardless of his color or creed!"

The Chinese American and African American stewards are making some progress, but they're still confined to their segregated ships and have second-class union status. And the Lurline still has an all-white crew.

After the strikes are over, the Lurline is back at sea. On July 5, at 4 P.M., the crew stops their work and gathers on the deck to observe this anniversary of Bloody Thursday. The flag is lowered, taps are played, and a wreath is "cast over the side to ride the waves in memory of the men who died" for the union cause. During the ceremony a member of the Marine Cooks and Stewards Union addresses the entire crew. His name is Frank McCormick. He was active on the strike committees; he is a communist; and it's no secret that he's a gay man.

The crew is silent while they hear Frank McCormick's words: "These men were shot down by police," he says to them, "while fleeing from a reign of terror let loose by certain economic forces. As workers, they made the supreme sacrifice in our behalf. Sperry and Bordoise, we shall not forget you, or the blood and red roses on the pavement, or the magnificent ideal of justice and militancy for which you died." The same day, and continuing for decades after, thousands of seamen on U.S. ships all over the Pacific Ocean, and thousands more on the West Coast waterfronts, stop their work and gather in silence to remember Bloody Thursday.

· · · · · ·

Mickey Blair first met Frank McCormick while wandering the San Francisco waterfront after the strikes. Mickey is a teenager who's been kicked out of the army and his home when it's discovered that he's gay. On the San Francisco piers he notices this handsome man twenty years his senior giving a speech to a crowd, and he finds this man very attractive. "Mainly it was his lovely speaking voice," Mickey tells me. Mickey liked the way Frank was so sure of himself as a union militant and as a gay man. "He made no bones about it. I kept thinking, 'He's honest, and I'm dishonest. He is clear, and I'm clouded.'" They start a courtship that lasts many years. When Mickey eventually joins the union, the two men start to live as a couple. "Frank was my mentor, he was my friend," Mickey tells me. "He was the family I never had."

On the day they first meet, Frank McCormick is already a member of the Communist Party. The party's policy is that homosexuals cannot become members because homosexuality is a form of bourgeois decadence. But Frank McCormick was drawn to the party's vision of a better world for working people of many races. So was his friend Tom Baker (pseudonym), a white gay man who came from a family of West Virginia coal miners. These two men manage to stay in the Communist Party without hiding their homosexuality. The party knew that if it kicked them out, it would lose some of the best activists on the ships.

Revels Cayton joined the Communist Party because he wanted to combine what he called "Negro rights" with working-class politics. In the Marine Cooks and Stewards Union he has a chance to do this. After the strikes, the stewards voted for "equal shipping to all members" and against keeping black stewards segregated on the Alexander ships. So now the time has come to begin integrating the white ships.

Revels Cayton has become the spokesman for the black stewards. His strongest ally is his friend Tom Baker, a militant unionist who doesn't care who knows he's gay. This gay white man and straight black man work as a team. Baker is the hiring hall dispatcher who sends men out to the ships. Cayton is the patrolman who goes down to the ships to troubleshoot. Their strategy is to link racial integration with better wages and conditions so that the white men can experience integration as a real benefit to them.

"[Baker] used to scare me to death," Cayton tells me. Baker would say to Cayton: "I'm ready to dispatch three black stewards onto the *Lurline* and they have to ship out, now!" It was scary, Cayton says, because "there was a very delicate balance in the hall. At one time you could start a damn riot. The white guys—you know, you're throwing in for a job and they give it to a black guy—that ain't so hot." And when the stewards actually board the ship, there's more trouble. The deckhands and firemen sometimes threaten any black steward who dares to integrate a white ship. When the union in Seattle dispatches two black messmen onto a Dollar liner, both are attacked and severely injured by white deckhands before the vessel gets to Yokohama.

To prevent this kind of violence, Cayton finds big, strong longshoremen to escort the black stewards up the gangway, and then Baker dispatches big, strong stewards to protect the black stewards from being thrown overboard once the ship goes out to sea. The union brings charges against anyone who threatens their members and ties up a ship if a white crew refuses to sail with a black steward onboard.

By the late thirties, the Matson ships are finally becoming integrated. When the Alexander ships go out of business, black stewards are reassigned to the white liners as jobs become available. They quickly demonstrate their leadership abilities, and several, like Joe Johnson and Ralph Beasley, are elected delegates by a majority of white men, many of them gay.

· · · · · ·

The Marine Cooks and Stewards Union is going way out on a limb. It's full of communists, its queens are getting bolder, and it's recruiting men of color. Other seamen begin to attack the union by "baiting" its most vulnerable and controversial members, pointing fingers and calling them names.

The newspaper of the Sailors Union of the Pacific—which is antiblack, anticommunist, and antigay—calls them the "Marine Cooks and Fruits." Sailors and firemen hurl racial insults at the stewards of color and even the white stewards. And they attack MCS leaders as "Reds." Some hostile seamen put these insults all together and call the MCS "a third red, a third black, and a third queer." Individual stewards respond by calling the sailors "deck apes" and "soupheads."

Revels Cayton, Ben Fee, Tom Baker, and Frank McCormick meet with other left-wing activists to develop a more organized strategy for the union to respond to all the name calling. They could have denied there were any homosexuals or communists in their midst or condemned them to win respectability. But instead they expose how the "baiting" itself divides union men from one another and plays into the shipowners' hands.

The union's enemies are already connecting "red, black, and queer." So these activists decide to keep the connections but turn them around instead, using them to unite rather than divide their community. Together they come up with a slogan that captures what they're searching for. One version, Cayton tells me, goes like this: *It's anti-union to red-bait, race-bait, or queen-bait.* Another version, he says, goes like this: *If you let them red-bait, they'll race-bait, and if you let them race-bait, they'll queen-bait. These are all connected. That's why we have to stick together.* With these slogans they've captured a daring new idea of solidarity that grows out of their lived experience.

Cooks and stewards quickly take up this slogan and put it into their own words. "You want to know about my union?" asks Pete Brownlee, a white heterosexual steward. "The most important thing was not that we had gays. It was that an injury to one *was* an injury to all—and we practiced it. We took care of each other. The mean guys were always the mean guys," he explains. If a "deck ape" hurled an insult at a black steward, he says, a white queen would stand there until he took it back. Or if he insulted a white queen, a black steward would stand there until he took it back. "To them," Brownlee went on about their detractors, "our union was all queers. They didn't even call us homosexuals—they called us queers. So you had to kick the shit out of a few guys once in a while. I kicked the shit out of a couple deck apes on the ship—you *had* to do it. They would torment you, do a lot of stupid shit. So 'fuck you!' we said. We didn't pay any attention to that shit. We knew that our union would back us."

The insults keep coming, but the gay stewards are getting bolder because they know their union is watching their backs. You can see the new solidarity at work below deck in the crew's messroom.

"Frank Bowers was one of the toughest queens I ever met," Mickey Blair tells me. "One time a crew member came through the food line while Miss Bowers was serving, and he says to her, 'Put some food on there, you fruit!' And Miss Bowers pulls back and says, 'Why did you call me a fruit?' And he says, 'Because you *are* a fruit *and* a cocksucker.' Well she grabs a big soup ladle and, boy, she slaps him right across the head 'Now,' she says, 'you son-of-a-bitch, I bet I'm the meanest fucking fruit you ever saw.' And I mean she drew blood. He didn't dare report her. That's the way Frank Bowers would do it, so you didn't fuck with the Marine Cooks and Stewards," Blair explains. "That was his form of militancy."

You can see the solidarity at work in the passenger dining rooms, too. One evening on the *Lurline*, Frank McCormick is working as a waiter in the first-class dining room. A passenger seated at a table calls for McCormick by clapping his hands and shouting, "Boy! Boy!" McCormick stops short, catches the attention of the other waiters, then slowly walks over to the man's table. The noisy dining room goes silent. "If you're applauding my performance," he says loud enough for everyone to hear, "I thank you for the applause. If you want my service, I am not your boy, I am a steward, and I have a name. If you do not treat me with respect, I can and will refuse to serve you." He's correct—the union's new agreements do allow stewards to refuse to serve any passenger who insults them. After some nods of recognition from the other waiters, the passenger apologizes. He and the other first-class diners begin to address the dining room staff with more respect. "Marine Cooks and Stewards," Mickey Blair remembers, "took the dignity that was in each of us and built it up, so you could get up in the morning and say to yourself 'I can make it through this day.' Equality was in the air we breathed."

After winning their strikes, the Cooks and Stewards begin to make their union more democratic. On each ship they elect a delegate to represent them. Right away the stewards start to elect gay men.

Mickey Blair was one of the gay delegates they elect. His close friend and assistant, Lonnie Gray, knew Blair was gay but, in Blair's words, "he didn't give a fuck." As delegates, they run meetings, handle beefs, and run the union's political education program. Since many delegates were gay or supportive, they could use this powerful position to defend gay stewards from attack.

This is how Mickey Blair handled antigay disputes. One day a crew member from another department comes to him and says, "You're going to have to get rid of [Frank Bowers] because he's too flamboyant." "[Now] Frank was one of my staunchest supporters," Blair tells me. "So I went over [to him], and I said, 'Miss Bowers, they want your mother to get rid of you.' He said, 'Well, I'll go if you want me to.' And I said, 'No way.'" Blair calls the accuser in to a stewards meeting and asks him, "Can you prove that this man wasn't doing his job? Did he break any rules of the contract?" "No." "Well, then you just get your ass out of here," Blair tells him. That's how Mickey Blair teaches his men that their union solidarity is big enough to defend even the most flamboyant queens. This is actually part of the delegate's responsibility, which was to build unity by fighting all forms of bigotry and prejudice. The MCS newspaper helps out by running articles on how to fight prejudice and racial discrimination, within which they include anti-Semitism. The paper publishes feature articles on Jewish history and on African American history, especially as they related to the labor movement.

A crowning glory of this new solidarity is when the membership elects Manual Cabral—the Honolulu Queen—to be janitor and sergeant-at-arms of their hall. "Oh Manual was something else!" Revels Cayton tells me. During meetings Cabral screams and dishes union officials and knits doilies for the union hall's furniture. Sometimes he does a little hula dance and shakes tambourines to make people laugh. When the union expands the hall into the top floor of the building, Cabral starts to redecorate, "fixing it up, step by step," as Revels Cayton recalls. "First it was lace curtains. They were all around. Then sofas. He had that union hall decorated like a fucking whorehouse with curtains on the windows and flowers everywhere!"

By 1940, on the eve of World War II, MCS members have a slogan attacking race-baiting, red-baiting, and queen-baiting. And they have joined other left-wing unions in the newly formed Congress of Industrial Organizations—the CIO. Mounted over their union hall's job board is this CIO motto: "Equality in hiring regardless of race, religion, nationality or political opinion." With this spirit in place, the members of the Marine Cooks and Stewards Union prepare themselves to go to war.

. . . . . .

"I was on the *Lurline* when the war was declared," Jim Vieira told me. "We had left Honolulu with 800 passengers on Friday, and Sunday [morning] we got word [at sea] that Pearl Harbor had been bombed. We had to speed up [and black out our lights.] The captain didn't want too many people congregated in one area. They were afraid of torpedoes."

In San Francisco the navy takes over the *Lurline*. Dining rooms are stripped down, refitted with bunk beds, and then filled with troops. Five days later the *Lurline* is back at sea, this time carrying over 3,000 troops along with bombs, ammunition, and supplies. The few women who had worked on the *Lurline* were taken off and replaced with male telephone operators and male nurses—the opposite of what happened on land, where "Rosie the Riveters" replaced male workers in defense plants.

The nation's shipyards are booming. War workers, including many African American men and women, are building hundreds of new ships, which in turn opens up new jobs for cooks and stewards. The Depression is finally over. The membership of the Marine Cooks and Stewards union skyrockets from 4,500 to over 15,000 as men flock into the union for wartime jobs. Who are all these new men?

Some are gay men who want to serve their country but don't want to join the military because of its antigay policies. Or they are gay men the navy has already discharged as homosexuals. When in 1943 David Barrett is kicked out of the navy for being gay, his officer tells him, "The only people who will hire you now are the Marine Cooks and Stewards Union." So Barrett goes right over to the union hall and signs up.

Some new members are black and Filipino men who want to serve at sea but won't tolerate the navy's racist, Jim Crow policies. The navy will accept only a few black and Filipino men and even then only as messmen and stewards. The navy's rationale for segregating and restricting the service of black and Filipino sailors was similar to the navy's rationale for banning homosexuals. Secretary of the Navy Frank Knox explained that "men live in such intimacy aboard ship that we simply can't enlist Negroes above the rank of messman." White sailors, the navy claimed, would refuse to work or live with black sailors or take any orders from them. The Marine Cooks and Stewards Union was more enlightened than the navy, so many black and Filipino men chose to fight the war with them instead.

Other new members of the MCS are white men who've never before had to treat men of color as equals. When some of them provoke racist incidents on the ships, union officials launch a campaign to teach these men racial tolerance.

The union's new president, Hugh Bryson, deals with this problem head-on. Bryson is a white heterosexual man, a left-winger who rose to leadership after being elected delegate on the *Matsonia*. Writing in the union's newspaper, he warns the new white men that the MCS will not tolerate any racial discrimination on the ships. "Negroes, Chinese, Filipinos, Mexicans and others helped build our Union and raise our conditions and wages," he says. "They will share in the gains they have helped to create."

During the war, the status of Chinese and Japanese American stewards also changes dramatically. The GIs on the *Lurline* and other troop ships are headed for Asia to defend China against Japanese invaders. With the U.S. and China now allies, white hostility toward the Chinese in the United States starts to fade a little as their hostility toward the Japanese increases. At its wartime convention, the Marine Cooks and Stewards Union protests after the government removes Japanese American stewards from the ships as national security risks. And the union at last officially takes the anti-Asian language out of its own constitution. It now reads, "Race is no longer pitted against race in the struggle for jobs."

Merchant seamen pay a high price during the war. Many are injured or killed when their ships are torpedoed in combat waters. Although they are civilians, they are killed at a higher rate than are servicemen in any branch of the armed services other than the Marine Corps. They make other sacrifices, too. To support the war effort, the MCS joins other U.S. unions in making a "No Strike Pledge" to President Roosevelt and the nation. They give up their right to strike for better wages and against unsafe conditions and long hours until the war is won. But the shipowners continue to profit from the war, and the government refuses to reward merchant seamen for their sacrifices. Because they are organized into unions, antiunion Pentagon officials persuade Congress to write merchant seamen out of the GI Bill of Rights, so they don't receive veterans' benefits. As the cooks and stewards return home, their government has already begun to punish them for standing together in their multiracial, left-wing union.

. . . . . .

When the war ends, the *Lurline* returns to San Francisco loaded with GIS headed for home. Most of the men who joined the Marine Cooks and Stewards Union to serve the war effort now quit and go home to their families, too. Suddenly, the union has more jobs than it has men to fill them. At the same time, the West Coast shipyards are laying off thousands of war workers. African American men were among the last hired, and now they're among the first fired. So the union goes down to the shipyards and recruits these workers. So many African American shipyard workers enter the union that by the end of 1945 these men make up more than half the union's membership. Once an all-white and openly racist union, the Marine Cooks and Stewards is now an important part of the African American community, where its name is often spoken with admiration and respect.

By the late 1940s the Marine Cooks and Stewards union makes great strides. In 1949 the union faces the fact that its leaders are still white men while the membership is now mostly men of color. So they set a goal of making their leadership reflect their membership. They achieve their goal in just one year. Several white male officials voluntarily step down or mentor men of color for leadership positions. Wally Ho, a Hawaiian Chinese steward who had been delegate on the *Matsonia* and had organized the culinary workers in Matson's Royal Hawaiian Hotel, is elected dispatcher at union headquarters. Joe Johnson, who started out on the Alexander ships, is elected secretary-treasurer.

The members also expand economic democracy within their union. From 1945 to 1949 the union triples a messman's wages. When unemployment hits the union hard, the rank and file votes to start a "swing system" for sharing jobs. By assigning four workers to every three jobs, no one is laid off, and the black shipyard workers who were recruited after the war are not once again the first fired. During strikes, union officials draw no pay. And to make sure they don't lose touch with the rank and file, officials must work on the ships for at least one trip every year.

The status of women in the union is improving, too. After the war, when Matson refused to rehire stewardesses on their liners, the MCS protested until Matson took them back. At the union's 1949 convention, stewardesses chide the men for keeping them in a second-class status. They also win a unanimous vote for their resolution "to fight for equal job rights for Negro women members of the union." Wally Ho, the hiring hall dispatcher, immediately ships Luella Lawhorn out to the *Lurline*. One of only three black women in the union, Luella Lawhorn had been a maid on the ferry between Los Angeles and Catalina Island. But the Matson Company refuses to accept her on its ships. So the entire stewards department walks off the *Lurline* in protest. Stunned passengers wait onboard to see what will happen. Within hours the company changes its mind, and the ship is allowed to sail with Sister Lawhorn on board. She's the first African American stewardess ever to work on a U.S. passenger liner sailing the Pacific Ocean.

The Marine Cooks and Stewards is earning a reputation as one of the most democratic, racially integrated, and pro-gay unions in the United States. And it's achieving real power. Working in solidarity with other unions, this little union can shut down all shipping on the West Coast to protect the rights of their members. But most threatening of all, the Korean War is heating up, and the MCS opposes using U.S. merchant vessels to send troops and supplies to Korea. This is too much power, say the leaders of government and industry, for any union that is run by commies, colored people, and queers.

. . . . . .

We were 50 years ahead of our time. We were
so democratic this country couldn't stand it!
— *Pete Brownlee*, steward

In the early 1950s, the nation turns to the right as a wave of anticommunist and antigay hysteria divides the nation. The Marine Cooks and Stewards, along with other multiracial, left-led unions, become easy targets. "Many people who see black and white together think it adds up to red," Hugh Bryson, the union's president, tells the membership at its 1949 convention. In the 1950s, red-baiting was the most effective way to bust a union, break up interracial solidarity, and isolate union militants thought to be queer.

The government uses two powerful new weapons to attack the left-wing unions: One is Coast Guard screening of maritime workers. Screening begins in the fall of 1950.

It's Monday afternoon, November 6. Stewards are gathering with other crew members at the Matson pier in Los Angeles, to board the *Lurline* on her next trip to Hawaii. Among those set to sail today are Mickey Blair, Frank McCormick, Ted Rolfs, Jim Vieira, and Bill Watkins. They walk up the gangway and over to a room where they're told to line up in front of some Coast Guard officers. The Coast Guard is here because President Truman has just signed a Port Security Act which orders them to screen tens of thousands of maritime workers, one by one and trip by trip, to determine if they should be removed from American ships as risks to national security. Back in May, a Senate report had also called for securing the nation's seaports "against sabotage through conspiracy of subversives and moral perverts." This means communists and homosexuals—or "commie queers," as they're called on the picket lines. The Coast Guard officers on the *Lurline* are checking a list of names they've gathered from undercover informants. It identifies who'll be thrown off ocean-bound vessels under the new law.

The Coast Guard officers let some crew members pass but hand others the dreaded form letter, which says, "Your passage on board this vessel would be inimical to the security of the United States. This is based on the belief that you are sympathetic to an organization, association, group, or combination of persons subversive or disloyal to the government of the United States." You don't have a right to know who named you or what they said. Crew members who are handed this letter are escorted off the *Lurline* by police. If you refuse to leave or try to go back to work, you are arrested and taken to jail.

Eighteen cooks and stewards are screened off the *Lurline* today. Ted Rolfs, Bill Watkins, and Mickey Blair are among those screened. As they're escorted down the gangway onto the docks, they glance back to see that they've been separated from Jim Vieira and Frank McCormick, Mickey's lover, who for unknown reasons the Coast Guard has allowed to sail, at least this time. "The last thing I saw," Mickey tells me, "was Frank watching us going down that plank. Frank told me later, 'I don't ever want to go through that again. Some of me died when they took you off the *Lurline* that day.'"

As the ship leaves them behind, someone with a camera asks the screened stewards, still standing on the pier, to pose for a snapshot. Later, they each sign it, then give it to Mickey Blair, who recently passed it on to me. The defense of the "*Lurline* 18" becomes a waterfront cause. "This is the worst thing that has hit our Union since the big maritime strike of 1934," an MCS leaflet declares. "The Coast Guard and shipowners are trying to take us back to the days before '34. We won then. . . . We'll win again because we're tough, and we're fighting because we know what's at stake."

By January, the Coast Guard has removed nearly every left-wing steward from West Coast ships. Three-quarters of those screened are African American men. When they testify at appeal hearings, they see more clearly what the screening is for. Appeal board members ask black stewards, "Have you ever had dinner with a mixed group? Have you ever danced with a white girl?" And they ask white stewards, "Have you ever entertained Negroes in your home? Do you have advanced thinking on racial matters?" Their answers determine whether or not they were "security risks." At Mickey Blair's appeal hearing they ask him if he's a homosexual, and they ask him if Hugh Bryson, the president of the MCS, is queer, too. "Why do you want to know about our president," Mickey snaps back. "Do you want to go out on a date with him?"

Union members rally to support the screened seamen. The "Women's Auxiliary" marches to protest the screening of their husbands, sons, and fathers. The longshoremen and the MCS set up a multiracial Seamen's Defense Committee that includes many gay men. Scotty Ballard is a gay steward who's an active leader of this committee, as is Riff-Raff Rolfs. Together, they write leaflets, sign letters, and picket Coast Guard offices.

But the screening continues. When Mickey Blair's friend Lonnie Gray is taken off his ship, police drag him away in leg irons and handcuffs and parade him through the streets. Blair helps set up Lonnie Gray's defense committee. In turn, when Mickey Blair is screened off ships in Seattle and can't find work, Lonnie Gray's family takes him in. Blair cooks meals for the family, and the children call him Uncle Mickey. "It was a camaraderie in that union," Blair recalls, "and you always went to one another's rescue."

People outside the MCS also support them, especially San Francisco's African American community. The Baptist Ministerial Alliance rallies to their defense. And the *Sun-Reporter*, the Bay Area's African American newspaper, runs a series of articles about how government screening is aimed at keeping black cooks and stewards from working on U.S. ships. Trying to boost the union's morale, Paul Robeson and W. E. B. DuBois, both honorary members of the union, come to speak at the union's 1951 convention in San Francisco to encourage them not to give up the fight.

The government's other powerful weapon against the nation's left-led, interracial unions is the Taft-Hartley Law. This antiunion law breaks the promise President Roosevelt made to American workers during the Depression that the government would protect their right to organize. The federal government uses Taft-Hartley against the MCS by declaring its hiring hall illegal, postponing its strikes, and forcing its leaders to swear they're not communists before the government will let them hold elections. Self-identified right-wing dissidents within the MCS use Taft-Hartley to set up a rival union. They're anticommunist, antigay, and attack the MCS for giving "special rights to Negroes." They're encouraged when the CIO, in its own anticommunist purge, kicks out the longshore and cooks and stewards unions along with other left-led unions. Right-wing organizers try to recruit MCS members, who now must choose whether to defend their union or "go over to the other side." Most black stewards stay with their union. But white men are split, including the gay stewards, who start to take sides and attack each other. Frank McCormick, Ted Rolfs, and Mickey Blair all stay loyal. But the Communist Party, which is now going underground, purges them and other homosexuals as security risks. Some gay stewards join the right-wing union to get back at the communists for kicking out homosexuals; other gay stewards, like Manuel Cabral, the Honolulu Queen, go right wing just to be on the winning side.

A gay leader of the right-wing union is Don Rotan. He edits their newspaper, the *Stewards News*, in which he red-baits, race-baits, and queen-baits the left-wing MCS. A cartoon in his paper portrays his right-wing union as a real man among real men, while it portrays left-wing MCS officials as tiny, effeminate men in drag ready to flee to Mexico. In the first issue of his newspaper, he reassures the right-wing members that "most of the fairies are now screened by the U.S. Coast Guard and found to be super-militant for Russia."

Right-wing stewards start to take over the *Lurline*. Tempers flare at work as the luxury liner becomes a battleground. The few remaining left-wing cooks in the kitchen refuse to help the right-wing waiters, giving them well-done steaks on orders for rare. White stewards start to intimidate black stewardesses. Luella Lawhorn is harassed. Then Sarah Ferguson is pushed down a stairway and hospitalized for back and neck injuries. A right-wing union member is arrested for carrying a gun on the *Lurline*, while another is arrested for shooting the ship's butcher. Passengers are left waiting aboard the *Lurline* as fistfights break out into riots on the ship.

The conflicts on the ships escalate into riots on the piers. In December 1953, thousands of white, right-wing stewards and sailors, armed with bottles, knives, clubs, and guns, march along the waterfront to Pier 39—which is now a tourist shopping mall. They want to take over a ship that is still controlled by the old MCS. Police try to stop the marchers, but they break through police lines and attack a multiracial group of longshoremen and stewards who are trying to defend the ship. After a violent struggle, police and MCS pickets win this battle and turn back the right-wingers. But the MCS is not winning the war.

Within a year the right-wing union, under government-supervised elections, takes over the MCS, even though nearly all of its members vote to stay independent. Then the MCS president, Hugh Bryson, is charged and convicted of perjury under the Taft-Hartley Law, for stating that he wasn't a communist. He's sentenced to five years in federal prison. J. Edgar Hoover's FBI agents—or "Mother Hoover's stoolpigeons," as the stewards call them—stalk Frank McCormick, Mickey Blair, Jimmy Vieira, Lonnie Gray, and the other screened seamen. FBI agents keep them under twenty-four-hour surveillance, "outing" stewards as homosexuals and communists to their families, landlords, and employers, getting them evicted from their homes and fired from what few jobs they can find.

The members of this tiny union could never win their David and Goliath battle against the combined forces of Congress, the Coast Guard, the FBI, the shipowners, the CIO, and the AFL. But they went down fighting. It's remarkable that they held out for so long. Their history is unknown today because, through fear and intimidation, it was first rewritten as an un-American activity, then dismissed as an insignificant failure, and, finally, erased from our nation's memory, as if what they had achieved had never even happened.

Epilogue

What happens to a dream deferred?
—*Langston Hughes*, steward

In the early 1960s, if you wandered along San Francisco's waterfront, you'd see little evidence left from the great battles that once were fought on these now empty streets and piers. The American passenger liners are gone. Their owners have registered them under foreign flags to avoid U.S. taxes, safety laws, and the unions. As shipping declined and the piers grew deserted, gay men of many races continued to occupy the old waterfront haunts, bringing them back to life as gay bars and restaurants, like the Ensign Cafe. Some former MCS members own or manage these places; others work in them as waiters, cooks, bartenders, and bouncers. You might see Bumblebee, who once sailed the Jim Crow Alexander ships, now working as a cook at the Black Cat. Or Ted Rolfs hanging out at Jack's Waterfront and the Ensign Cafe, where police come in nightly to take bribes and harass the patrons. Or you might see Ted Rolfs, along with Bill Watkins and many other screened seamen, over with the longshoremen, who have taken them in and given them jobs. You might see Don Rotan still at the right-wing union hall on Fremont Street. Believe it or not, he's persuaded his union to rent their hall to the California Motorcycle Club, a gay bikers' club, for their annual CMC carnival and orgy. Uptown you might see Revels Cayton in City Hall, where he's been appointed to the San Francisco Human Rights Commission by the mayor.

Over in the Castro district—which isn't a gay neighborhood yet—you might run into Frank McCormick and Mickey Blair, who have set up house together in an apartment upstairs from their pal Jim Vieira. Jim is still working as a steward on the ships—he's successfully appealed his screening. Frank works as a waiter in a restaurant—Chez Marguerite. Mickey works as a nursing attendant. They often get together for parties with their gay friends, all of whom are former members of the Marine Cooks and Stewards Union. But they don't join the emerging homophile movement, which came into existence just as the MCS was going down. These gay organizations are predominantly white groups seeking middle-class acceptance. They rarely address the needs of "queer" folks who are working class or people of color.

A few years later, Frank McCormick and Mickey Blair moved to Seattle to buy a house, where they lived together for years. After Frank died in the 1970s, Mickey still found ways to keep his militancy alive. A few years ago he joined ACT UP in Seattle, where he was arrested in a die-in to protest lack of AIDS funding. Now in his late seventies, he performs in a gay theater group that tours the Northwest fighting the religious right.

Although Mickey is passionate about gay politics, he knows that the gay movement is missing the commitment to working-class folks and people of color that he learned in the Marine Cooks and Stewards Union. He still dreams about militant unions with visible gay leadership that are dedicated to racial equality, economic justice, and solidarity across many lines. "We proved that it could be done so it's not just a dream," he adds. "We can do it again," he says, "only differently this time."

Mickey's union was destroyed, but their work is still unfinished. That's why Mickey calls me every few weeks from Seattle to make sure I haven't given up, to make sure I'm still uncovering and telling this forgotten story of what the Marine Cooks and Stewards accomplished so many years ago.

As we wrote in our introduction, working on this project has been both a labor of love and a labor of sorrow: love, because of the quality of work that Allan Bérubé produced and the opportunity this volume provides to have it accessible to readers, and sorrow, because we wish more than anything that Allan was still alive and could compile it himself.

We completed this book with the help of many others who valued Allan Bérubé's life and work. Waverly Lowell, our fellow trustee of Allan's literary estate, provided important guidance in making the decision about where to donate the Bérubé Papers. Rebekah Kim, the archivist of the GLBT Historical Society in San Francisco, where his papers have been deposited, provided critical aid in transferring the materials. She also helped us navigate the unprocessed collection as we looked for source materials that allowed us to write the introduction, and she graciously scanned the illustrations for us. We thank her, Paul Boneberg, Joey Plaster, and everyone else at the historical society for their commitment to preserving Allan's work and legacy. We are deeply grateful to Annette Bérubé, Allan's sister, who assisted us in multiple ways. She answered innumerable questions that we posed to her and cheered our work along, even as she was dealing with the practical demands of settling Allan's estate and the emotional toll of losing him unexpectedly.

Many people responded generously to our requests for phone interviews, email communication, and letters so that we could fill out the contours of Allan's life and locate some of his hard-to-find writings. We especially want to thank Sabrina Artel, Jim Baxter, Zachary Blair, Nan Boyd, David Gibson, Bert Hansen, Wayne Hoffman, Amber Hollibaugh, Jonathan Ned Katz, Ian Lekus, Katherine Marino, Mimi McGurl, Peter Nardi, John Nelson, Gayle Rubin, Nancy Stoller, and Allan Troxler for the assistance they provided and the information they shared with us. We received insightful and helpful readings of a draft of the introduction from Marcia Gallo, Bert Hansen, Jonathan Ned Katz, Ilene Levitt, Peter Nardi, and Nancy Stoller. We also benefited enormously from the comments on the entire collection that Elizabeth Lapovsky Kennedy and Leisa Meyer provided us.

Everyone at the University of North Carolina Press has been a joy to work with. Their enthusiasm for the project has been boundless, and their support unstinting. We especially appreciate all that Kate Torrey has done to bring this book to completion. From our first discussion of it with her when the volume was just an idea, through an initial proposal and a table of contents, through final drafts and the full manuscript, she has provided encouragement, confidence, and smart suggestions. Others at the Press, including Dino Battista, Ron Maner, Rachel Surles, and Stephanie Wenzel greatly eased the publication process.

We were fortunate to have the intellectual space in which to undertake this project during our 2009–10 sabbatical leaves. John D'Emilio acknowledges the generous support of the College of Liberal Arts and Sciences at the University of Illinois at Chicago; much of the work of this volume was done while a fellow at its Institute for the Humanities. Estelle Freedman thanks the American Council of Learned Societies and the Center for Advanced Study in the Behavioral Sciences at Stanford, which provided the ideal setting for digressing from other writing tasks in order to honor Allan's memory.

Finally, our respective life partners, Jim Oleson and Susan Krieger, have given us the emotional and intellectual support that sustained our work on this book, just as each of them has done for each of us over the past three decades. We thank them, with love, for their insights and their understanding.

MIX
Paper from
responsible sources
FSC® C013483